HORACE
ODES AND EPODES

T0381571

HORACE
ODES AND EPODES
A STUDY IN POETIC WORD-ORDER

BY

H. DARNLEY NAYLOR, M.A.

TRINITY COLLEGE, CAMBRIDGE

HUGHES PROFESSOR OF CLASSICS IN THE UNIVERSITY OF ADELAIDE

CAMBRIDGE
AT THE UNIVERSITY PRESS
1922

CAMBRIDGE
UNIVERSITY PRESS

University Printing House, Cambridge CB2 8BS, United Kingdom

Published in the United States of America by Cambridge University Press, New York

Cambridge University Press is part of the University of Cambridge.

It furthers the University's mission by disseminating knowledge in the pursuit of education, learning and research at the highest international levels of excellence.

www.cambridge.org
Information on this title: www.cambridge.org/9781107635074

First published 1922
First paperback edition 2014

A catalogue record for this publication is available from the British Library

ISBN 978-1-107-63507-4 Paperback

TO MY WIFE

PREFACE

THE text used in this edition is that of Dr Gow, with few and unimportant modifications.

I am greatly indebted to my assistant lecturer, Mr D. H. Hollidge, M.A., who read through the whole of the book in manuscript and made many valuable suggestions. My thanks also are due to my daughter, who helped me in the tiresome work of proof-reading. But for her and the reader of the University Press the number of errors would have been great.

H. D. N.

LONDON,
August, 1921.

INTRODUCTORY

THIS book is not a new commentary on part of Horace. After the work done by Gow, Page, and Wickham (to mention English commentators only) the gleanings are scarcely worth publication except in fugitive articles.

What has been written hereafter is, as the title intimates, a study in poetic order with illustrations from the *Odes*, *C. S.*, and *Epodes* of Horace. Unless the order seemed to suggest that accepted versions might be reconsidered, I have, with very rare exceptions, forborne to comment at length. Thus this book is intended to be used side by side with any edition of our poet; it is neither a *réchauffé* of previous editions nor, I hope, a collection of notes spoilt in the borrowing.

Those who hold that almost any order may pass in poetry will read my notes with impatience or something worse. I ask them to suspend judgement and to await the cumulative effect of the evidence. The rules of the game are simple enough. I make no apologies for repeating some of them. They were first clearly stated by Professor J. P. Postgate. Attention to them, or rather to the breach of them, enhances in a surprising measure the effectiveness of Latin as a vehicle for the expression of ideas. Here are the five most important rules of *normal* order: (1) Adjectives, except those of number and quantity, immediately follow the noun, or, to use a brief terminology, are postpositive; (2) Genitives are postpositive; (3) Demonstrative pronouns are prepositive; (4) Adverbs immediately precede the verb i.e. are prepositive; (5) 'Subject...object...verb' is the normal order. As everyone knows, departure from these normal positions gives interest to the word abnormally placed.

It may be asked why the Romance languages do not show survivals of this system. They do show survivals, but not many. One must remember that the introduction of Christianity caused neglect of the classical models at a very early date. During the

Dark Ages such niceties as word-order were forgotten. But, as I have said, there are a few survivals. In Spanish, for instance, an adjective may precede the noun for emphasis; thus 'a *magnificent* day!' is '*un magnifico dia!*' Then there is what may be called the emphasis of emotion. This can be seen in Spanish, French, and Italian. Contrast the cold classification of *un escritor pobre* (i.e. poor, not rich) with *un pobre escritor* (i.e. wretched, unfortunate, miserable). Parallels in French and Italian will be found quoted at §§ 34 and 36 of my Prolegomena and elsewhere in the notes. Those who know the Romance languages better than I do will, I doubt not, supply many more examples.

CONTENTS

PROLEGOMENA

§ 1. My aim is to show that word-order is no more negligible in poetry than it is in prose, and that the rules laid down by Prof. J. P. Postgate and exemplified by the author in certain Livian studies are observed by the poet no less than by the writer of prose. This is to say that when Horace, for instance, departs from the normal order, he has a purpose in so doing: he wishes to draw our attention to the abnormality and so to emphasize for us the point that he desires to make.

§ 2. It is true that there occur in his poetry orders which would not be equally common in prose; and yet such non-prose orders are surprisingly few, and, by the way, most of them are to be found in Pindar. One common type, however, with rare parallels in prose, merits special attention. It has a psychological interest which may be illustrated thus. Suppose we enter a room and see upon a table a red flower in a silver bowl, what makes more impression on the mind? Is it the antithetical colours, red and silver, and the antithetical objects, flower and bowl? Or is it the antithesis of the combinations, red flower and silver bowl? English decides for the latter; Latin poetry, more often, for the former; and, with rare exceptions, the two colours, literal or metaphorical, are put first and the two objects last. Thus while prose might write *flos purpureus stat in lance argentea*, poetry will prefer the order *purpureus argentea stat flos in lance*, or chiastic orders, such as *argentea purpureus stat flos in lance*.

§ 3. This grouping, as I have said, is, in prose, very rare. I know one case in Cicero viz. *De Off.* 2. 7. 23 *reliquorum similes exitus tyrannorum*, and two cases in Livy viz. 6. 34. 7 *parvis mobili rebus animo*, and 22. 2. 3 *omne veterani robur exercitus* (where, however, the MSS show variations); and, doubtless, other parallel instances may be found. But in poetry the device is a commonplace. The neatest type is seen in the formula adj. A, adj. B, verb, noun A, noun B. (Page on *Epod.* 16. 55 has drawn attention to this particular grouping.) Compare Lucretius 5. 1068 *suspensis teneros imitantur dentibus haustus*; Vergil *Aen.* 7. 10 *proxima Circaeae raduntur litora terrae*; Ovid *Her.* 4. 80 *exiguo flexos miror in orbe pedes*; *seu lentum valido torques hastile lacerto*; *Met.* 1. 4 *in mea perpetuum deducite tempora carmen*, and *passim*. Less common is the formula adj. A, adj. B, verb, noun B, noun A, as in Horace *Odes* 3. 27. 25 *niveum doloso credidit tauro latus*. These two types, with the verb in the centre, we will call types a^1 and a^2 respectively. The formula adj. A, adj. B, noun A, noun B, and the verb anywhere, we will call β^1; the formula adj. A, adj. B, noun B, noun A, or adj. B, adj. A, noun A, noun B, both with the verb anywhere, we will call β^2. All four types, a^1, a^2, β^1, β^2, occur in Horace's *Odes* and *Epodes*, and make a total of more than 200 instances.

§ 4. Of type a^1 the first case in the *Odes* is 1. 2. 11 *et superiecto pavidae natarunt | aequore dammae*; of type a^2 1. 3. 10 *fragilem truci | commisit pelago ratem*; of type β^1 1. 3. 23 *impiae | non tangenda rates transiliunt vada*; of type β^2 1. 1. 14 *Myrtoum pavidus nauta secet mare*, and 1. 1. 28 *rupit teretis Marsus aper plagas*.

A notorious line in Lucan (8. 343) should, I think, be regarded as a case of type β^2, viz. *quem captos ducere reges | vidit ab Hyrcanis* (A) *Indoque* (B) *a litore* (B) *silvis* (A). Had Lucan written *aque Indo*, in place of the slight chiastic variety *Indoque a*, there would have been no need to quote the line as a 'rare hyperbaton' (see Postgate *ad loc.*). Much the same defence might be raised for Manilius 1. 429 *discordes-voltu* (A) *permixtaque* (B) *corpora* (B) *partus* (A).

§ 5. But to return to Horace—the importance of bearing in mind these types is seen clearly when we face such a derangement of epitaphs as is provided by the commentators on *Epod.* 5. 19

> iubet (*Canidia*) *cupressos funebris*
> 19 *et uncta turpis ova ranae sanguine*
> *plumamque nocturnae strigis...*
> *flammis aduri Colchicis.*

Here the editors offer a bewildering variety of interpretations. The most favoured dogma appears to be that *ova* and *plumam* belong to *strigis*, and that we should translate by 'an owl's eggs and feathers smeared with blood of hideous toad.' Some commentators have their doubts, and well they may; for if the conventional interpretation *is* a Chinese puzzle, and schoolboys should not be permitted to spend valuable time on this exhilarating game. But if we follow the principles of Latin poetic order as demonstrated in §§ 3, 4 above, we shall arrive at conclusions less uncomplimentary to both Horace and Latin poetry.

The grouping *uncta turpis ova ranae* is simply that of type β^1, and *ranae* goes with both *ova* and *sanguine*, between which it lies. I submit therefore that l. 19 *must* be read by a Roman as 'and eggs anointed of foul toad by its blood.' We may, if we like, in the Horatian manner, supply *unctam sanguine* (*strigis*) with *plumam*. Dr A. S. Way in his translation (Macmillan, 1898) says rightly

> 'And the spawn a loathly toad had voided, smeared with blood,
> And the feather of a screech-owl, bird of gloom.'

§ 6. We even find three adjectives together followed by three nouns in more or less parallel order. I know but two instances, however, in the *Odes* (the *Epodes* afford no example) viz. *Odes* 1. 9. 21 and 2. 9. 13. The former runs thus:

> *latentis proditor intimo*
> *[*gratus*] *puellae risus ab angulo.*

Here *proditor* is a quasi-adjective, and a Roman would read the lines thus: 'the hider's betrayer within, the [sweet] girl laugh from the corner.' The latter passage (*Odes* 2. 9. 13) reads as follows: *at non ter aevo functus amabilem* | *ploravit omnis Antilochum senex* | *annos....* Compare too Vergil *Georgics* 4. 371 *et gemina auratus taurino cornua voltu* | *Eridanus*, and Horace *Sat.* 1. 5. 73 *nam vaga per veterem dilapso flamma culinam* | *Volcano....*

Such methods are impossible for English, but Shakespeare does with nouns and verbs something analogous in *Ant. and Cleop.* 3. 2. 17.

> 'Ho! hearts, tongues, figures, scribes, bards, poets, cannot
> Think, speak, cast, write, sing, number, ho!
> His love to Antony.'

The Variorum Edition of Shakespeare quotes a performance, even more surprising, by Sir Philip Sidney—

> 'Vertue, beautie, and speeche, did strike, wound, charme
> My heart, eyes, ears, with wonder, love, delight;
> First, second, last did binde, enforse, and arme
> His works, showes, sutes, with wit, grace, and vowes' might....'

§ 7. It is convenient at this point to insert a complete list of types a^1, a^2, β^1, and β^2 in Horace's *Odes*, *Epodes* and *C. S.*

a^1. *Odes* 1. 2. 11 *superiecto pavidae natarunt* | *aequore dammae.* Add 1. 8. 6, 7, 1. 14. 19, 20, 1. 15. 3, 4, 2. 5. 19, 20, 3. 2. 11, 12, 3. 16. 35, 36, 3. 18. 5, 3. 24. 40, 41, 4. 1. 35, 36, 4. 2. 25, 4. 8. 31, 32, 4. 9. 5, 6, 4. 10. 2, 4. 14. 47, 48 (*qui*

---

* For this second epithet to *risus* see on § 11 below.

intrusive), *Epod.* 10. 19, 20 (*cum* intrusive), 12. 5, 12. 13, 13. 11, 16. 7, 16. 33, 16. 55, 16. 63.

§ 8. a^2. *Odes* 1. 3. 10 *fragilem truci | commisit pelago ratem.* Add 1. 7. 15, 16, 1. 12. 59, 60, 1. 29. 10–12, 2. 6. 22, 23, 2. 18. 1, 2, 3. 1. 16, 3. 7. 1, 2, 3. 11. 17, 18, 3. 27. 25, 26, 3. 27. 71, 72, 4. 4. 31, 32, *Epod.* 2. 43, 10. 3, 4, 13. 13, 14, 17. 15–17.

§ 9. β^1. *Odes* 1. 3. 23, 24 *impiae | non tangenda rates transiliunt vada.* Add 1. 3. 34, 1. 5. 6, 7, 1. 5. 14–16, 1. 7. 13, 14, 1. 9. 7, 8, 1. 10. 17, 18, 1. 12. 7, 1. 12. 23, 24, 1. 15. 14, 15, 1. 15. 29, 30, 1. 16. 2, 3, 1. 17. 6, 7, 1. 18. 15, 1. 19. 11, 12, 1. 20. 1, 2, 1. 22. 3, 4, 1. 22. 17, 18, 1. 27. 21, 22 (?), 1. 28. 3 (if we read *latum*), 1. 28. 19, 20, 1. 28. 30, 31 (if *postmodo te natis = posteris*), 1. 29. 13, 14, 1. 31. 5, 6, 1. 31. 10, 11, 1. 34. 10, 11, 1. 35. 23, 24, 1. 36. 5, 6, 2. 1. 13, 2. 5. 5, 6, 2. 6. 11, 12, 2. 7. 18, 2. 7. 21, 22, 2. 9. 18, 19 (if *Augusti* may be regarded as an adjective), 2. 11. 11, 12, 2. 12. 1, 2. 14. 14, 2. 15. 14–16, 2. 16. 21, 22, 2. 17. 19, 20 (if *tyrannus* be regarded as adjectival), 2. 18. 7, 8, 3. 1. 45, 46, 3. 2. 25, 3. 3. 17, 18, 3. 3. 29, 30, 3. 4. 17, 3. 4. 29, 30 (?), 3. 4. 49, 50, 3. 4. 79, 80 (if *amatorem* be regarded as adjectival), 3. 5. 31, 32, 3. 6. 4, 3. 6. 37, 38, 3. 12. 7, 3. 12. 11, 12, 3. 16. 39, 40, 3. 19. 4, 3. 19. 5, 3. 20. 3, 4, 3. 20. 14, 3. 21. 5, 3. 21. 15, 16, 3. 26. 9, 3. 27. 33, 34, 3. 29. 4, 3. 29. 17, 18, 4. 1. 34, 4. 2. 7, 8, 4. 2. 10, 4. 2. 19, 20, 4. 3. 6, 7, 4. 4. 39, 40, 4. 4. 46, 47, 4. 4. 58, 4. 4. 66, 67, 4. 5. 1, 2, 4. 6. 23, 24, 4. 6. 25 (if *doctor* be regarded as adjectival), 4. 7. 17, 18, 4. 7. 27, 28, 4. 11. 1, 2, 4. 14. 27, 28, *C. S.* 59, 60, 61, 62, *Epod.* 2. 15, 2. 47, 2. 51, 52, 2. 55, 56, 3. 6, 7, 4. 13, 5. 19, 5. 29, 5. 39, 40, 5. 61, 62, 5. 67, 68, 9. 23, 24, 12. 19, 14. 1, 2, 16. 4, 16. 48, 17. 66.

§ 10. β^2. *Odes* 1. 1. 14 *Myrtoum pavidus nauta secet mare.* Add 1. 1. 15, 1. 1. 28, 1. 2. 39, 1. 3. 32, 1. 4. 9, 1. 5. 1, 1. 7. 15, 16, 1. 12. 22, 23, 1. 12. 43, 44, 1. 13. 4, 1. 14. 14, 1. 17. 1, 2, 1. 18. 13, 14, 1. 28. 21, 1. 32. 7, 8, 1. 32. 13, 14, 1. 35. 7, 8, 1. 35. 21, 1. 36. 10, 1. 37. 31, 32, 2. 1. 6, 2. 2. 15, 16, 2. 4. 2, 3 (if *serva* is regarded as adjectival), 2. 4. 11, 12, 2. 6. 10, 11, 2. 8. 10, 11, 2. 12. 6, 2. 12. 15, 16, 2. 16. 29, 2. 17. 3, 4, 2. 20. 2, 3, 3. 2. 2, 3. 3. 6, 3. 4. 34, 3. 4. 70, 71 (where *temptator* may be regarded as an adjective), 3. 4. 76, 3. 8. 21, 3. 12. 10, 11, 3. 13. 9, 3. 13. 14, 15, 3. 14. 5, 3. 14. 7, 8, 9, 3. 18. 11, 12, 3. 19. 22, 23, 3. 21. 4, 3. 21. 5, 3. 23. 8, 3. 24. 5, 6, 7, 3. 26. 5, 3. 27. 75, 76, 3. 29. 2, 4. 2. 42, 43, 4. 4. 54 (if *iactata* goes with *sacra*), 4. 5. 21, 4. 7. 7, 8 (if *quae rapit* is regarded as an adjective), 4. 14. 39, 40, 4. 15. 3, 4, 4. 15. 30, *C. S.* 27, 28 (if we supply *fatis* with *peractis*), *Epod.* 1. 19, 2. 17, 4. 7, 7. 5, 6, 8. 1, 8. 5, 6, 9. 29, 10. 1, 15. 11, 16. 9, 16. 34, 16. 46, 16. 53, 54, 17. 31, 32.

§ 11. In the following instances one of the nouns has a second epithet: β^1. 2. 14. 19, 20 *damnatusque longi | Sisyphus [Aeolides] laboris*; 3. 4. 49, 50 *magnum illa terrorem intulerat Iovi | [fidens] iuventus*; *Epod.* 3. 6, 7 *num viperinus his cruor | [incoctus] herbis me fefellit?* β^2. 1. 35. 21, 22 *albo rara Fides colit | [velata] panno*; *Epod.* 17. 32, 33 *Sicanā fervidā | [virens] in Aetnā flammā.*

§ 12. Sometimes a genitive takes the place of one of the adjectives e.g. β^1. 1. 2. 9 where *piscium = piscarium*; 1. 12. 3 where *cuius = quod*; β^2. 1. 23. 5 where *veris = vernus*; 3. 17. 7, 8 where *Maricae = *an adjective.

§ 13. The next type that occurs with any frequency is seen in the formula noun A, adj. B, adj. A, noun B. There are three instances with the verb in the centre. These we may call a^1: viz. *Odes* 1. 10. 18 *virgaque levem coerces | aurea turbam*; 4. 7. 13 *damna tamen celeres reparant caelestia lunae*; *Epod.* 17. 55 *Neptunus alto tundit hibernus salo.* We may, perhaps, add *Odes* 2. 1. 25–27 *quisquis...inulta cesserat impotens tellure.*

§ 14. Those classed as β^1 have the verb anywhere. The type is seen in *Odes* 1. 1. 4, 5 *metaque fervidis evitata rotis*; but most of the examples might be classed under § 24 or § 48. Add 1. 5. 13, 14, 1. 14. 5, 1. 20. 9, 10, 1. 21. 3, 4, 1. 28. 3 (if *litus* is read), 1. 28. 11, 12, 1. 31. 12, 2. 1. 4, 5, 2. 6. 5, 2. 7. 5, 2. 12. 2, 3, 2. 14. 25, 26 (?), 2. 16. 18, 19, 2. 16. 38, 2. 18. 4, 5, 2. 19. 11, 12 (with intrusive verb), 2. 19. 18, 3. 1. 21, 22, 3. 3. 5, 3. 10. 2, 3, 3. 14. 18, 3. 15. 13, 14, 3. 17. 1, 3. 19. 16, 17, 3. 19. 24, 3. 22. 7, 3. 29. 24, 3. 29. 49, 4. 6. 42, 4. 11. 6, 7, *Epod.* 2. 59, 4. 15, 4. 17, 18 (with intrusive genitive), 5. 27, 6. 13, 8. 9, 10, 9. 15, 16 (?), 11. 10, 11. 28, 14. 3 (with intrusive conjunction), 16, 37, 17. 33, 34, 17. 54. Similar is *Odes* 1. 6. 7 where *per mare=marinos.*

§ 15. The next type is seen in the formula adj. A, noun B, adj. B, noun A. I have noticed an instance in Cicero *De Off.* 3. 2. 5 *talibus aures tuas vocibus... circumsonare.* Compare *Odes* 2. 13. 34, 35 *demittit atras belua centiceps | aures.* Add 1. 7. 29, 2. 11. 10, 2. 14. 17, 18, 3. 11. 9, 3. 11. 35, 36, 3. 14. 22 (if we read *cohibente*), 3. 15. 10, 3. 16. 25, 3. 17. 4, 3. 18. 9, 3. 19. 26, 3. 22. 6, 3. 24. 36, 37, 3. 27. 59, 60 (*pendulum zona bene te secuta | laedere collum*), 4. 1. 4, 5, 4. 2. 58, 4. 4. 7 (?), 4. 4. 57, 4. 11. 11, 12 (*sordidum flammae trepidant rotantes | vertice fumum*), *Epod.* 1. 29, 2. 29, 2. 57, 58, 2. 63, 6. 7, 16. 50. Compare Vergil *Aen.* 6. 438 *tristique palus inamabilis unda.* Similar are *Odes* 1. 1. 29 *doctarum hederae praemia frontium*, and 3. 9. 14 *Thurini Calais filius Ornyti*, where the nouns *praemia* and *filius* take the place of the adjectives.

§ 16. The formula of the next type is noun A, noun B, adj. A, adj. B. I have noted a parallel in Tacitus *Ann.* 1. 1 *cuncta discordiis fessa civilibus.* Cicero *De Off.* 1. 13. 41 has *fraus odio digna maiore*, but the position of *maiore* is due to emphasis, like *solis* in his *Catiline Oration* 3. 2. 6 *ad fin. Res praetoribus erat nota solis.*

The type in parallel order (α) occurs first in *Odes* 1. 6. 13 *Martem tunica tectum adamantina.* Compare 2. 3. 15, 16, 2. 9. 21, 2. 14. 25, 26 (?), 3. 29. 20, 4. 1. 30, 4. 14. 11, 12, 4. 14. 37, *Epod.* 1. 5 *te vita si superstite | iucunda*, 17. 22. Not unlike is *Odes* 1. 2. 17, 18. But most of these cases may be classed under § 48, and many under § 24.

The chiastic type (β) is seen at *Odes* 3. 7. 13 *Proetum mulier perfida credulum.* Add 3. 24. 3, 4, and *Epod.* 8. 11, 12.

Under this section may come *Odes* 4. 8. 23, 24 where *Romuli* is equivalent to *Romulis* (adj.), and *Epod.* 13. 6 where *consule* is the equivalent of an adjective. So at *Odes* 3. 18. 1 and *Epod.* 17. 74 where the nouns are quasi-adjectival. Finally *Odes* 1. 5. 9 is of the same type as (α), the pronouns *qui* and *te* taking the place of nouns.

§ 17. Another type is adj. A, noun B, noun A, adj. B. This appears first in the *Odes* 1. 7. 20 *densa tenebit Tiburis umbra tui.* Compare 1. 31. 3 (if we read *opimas* and *feracis*), 2. 8. 11, 12, 2. 11. 9, 10, 2. 12. 11, 12 *ductaque per vias | regum colla minacium* ; 2. 17. 22, 23, 3. 5. 22 (see also § 48), 3. 14. 25, 26 *lenit albescens animos capillus | litium et rixae cupidos* ; 3. 19. 28 *me lentus Glycerae torret amor meae* ; 4. 1. 19, 20 *Albanos prope te lacus ponet marmoreum* (see note *ad loc.*) ; 4. 3. 10, 4. 4. 13, 14, 4. 4. 42 *dirus per urbes Afer ut Italas* ; 4. 8. 9, 10 *talium res est aut animus deliciarum egens* ; 4. 8. 13, 4. 14. 18 (see also § 48) ; *Epod.* 5. 5. 6 (?), 10. 15, 16. 25, 26. Most of these cases can be classed under § 48.

§ 18. Least common is the type noun A, adj. B, noun B, adj. A. The following instances occur : *Odes* 1. 1. 22 *ad aquae lene caput sacrae* ; 2. 5. 18 *Chloris albo sic umero nitens* ; 3. 4. 69, 70 *testis mearum...sententiarum notus* (see note *ad loc.*) ; 3. 16. 30 *et segetis certa fides meae* ; 3. 26. 7, 8 *arcus oppositis foribus minacis* ; 3. 27. 2, 3 *ab agro rava [decurrens] lupa Lanuvino* ; 3. 27. 10 *imbrium divina avis imminentum* ;

4. 1. 26 *numen cum teneris virginibus tuum* ; 4. 4. 61 *hydra secto corpore firmior* ; *Epod.* 5. 55, 56 *ferae dulci sapore languidae* ; 10. 9 *nec sidus atra nocte amicum*.

Even of these few instances six are, perhaps, normal, the first epithet having pre-posited stress, viz. *Odes* 2. 5. 18, 3. 26. 7, 8, 4. 1. 26, 4. 4. 61, *Epod.* 5. 55, 56, 10. 9.

§ 19. If in the example quoted above from *Odes* 1. 1. 22 *aquae lene caput sacrae* we omit *lene*, we have an order extremely common in both prose and poetry i.e. when the genitive is accompanied by an epithet, the noun upon which the genitive depends lies between that genitive and the epithet of the genitive. Thus if x=genitive noun, and y=genitive epithet, the formula is x noun y, or y noun x. The order probably arises from a desire to avoid the cacophony of similar terminations in the genitive and its epithet. A few examples may be cited from prose: Cicero *De Off.* 1. 17. 56 *morum similitudo bonorum* ; *ib.* 1. 22. 75 *clarissimae testis victoriae* ; Livy 1. 12. 10 *tanti periculo viri* ; 1. 15. 2 *iusti more belli* ; 22. 3. 3 *omnium copia rerum* etc. Then, perhaps, the order became conventional, and we find e.g. Cicero *De Off.* 1. 33. 121 *superioris filius Africani* ; Sallust *Cat.* 51. 3 *ea res magnae initium cladis fuit*.

Horace has some sixty-four examples where the termination of the genitive noun and genitive epithet is the same (type *a* in the next section), but only twenty-three where the termination of genitive noun and genitive epithet is different (type *β* in the next section). This seems to show that, with Horace, considerations of euphony led to the adoption of the order.

§ 20. (a). For type (a) compare *Odes* 1. 3. 8 *animae dimidium meae*. Add 1. 1. 7, 1. 1. 16 *oppidi* [*laudat*] *rura sui* ; 1. 2. 42, 1. 7. 11 *Larisae* [*percussit*] *campus opimae* ; 1. 10. 3, 1. 15. 17, 1. 18. 7 *modici* [*transiliat*] *munera Liberi* ; 1. 19. 15 *bimi cum patera meri* ; 1. 27. 10, 1. 28. 29, 1. 36. 11, 1. 36. 13, 2. 1. 9, 2. 1. 32, 2. 1. 38 *Ceae* [*retractes*] *munera neniae* ; 2. 4. 6 (?), 2. 6. 6 *meae sedes* [*utinam*] *senectae* ; 2. 8. 19, 2. 10. 6, 7, 2. 12. 13 (?), 2. 13. 21, 2. 17. 13, 2. 20. 5, 3. 3. 2, 3. 3. 59, 60 *avitae tecta* [*velint reparare*] *Troiae* ; 3. 4. 14, 3. 6. 8 (see note), 3. 7. 9, 3. 9. 20 *reiectaeque* [*patet*] *ianua Lydiae* ; 3. 12. 3, 3. 12. 6, 3. 14. 8 (see too § 14), 3. 16. 29, 3. 19. 18 *Berecyntiae* | [*cessant*] *flamina tibiae* ; 3. 19. 28 *Glycerae* [*torret*] *amor meae* ; 3. 20. 2, 3. 24. 49, 3. 27. 30, 3. 27. 47, 48, 3. 29. 11, 12, 3. 29. 22, 4. 1. 3, 4. 1. 15, 4. 1. 18 *largi muneribus* [*riserit*] *aemuli* ; 4. 2. 15, 4. 3. 23, 4. 4. 50, 4. 5. 27 *ferae bellum* [*curet*] *Hiberiae* ; 4. 6. 1, 4. 6. 3, 4. 6. 33, 4. 9. 12, 4. 10. 4 *puniceae flore* [*prior*] *rosae* ; 4. 11. 31, 32, 4. 12. 9, 10, 4. 12. 11, 12 *nigrae* (?) *colles Arcadiae* ; 4. 14. 50 *duraeque tellus* [*audit*] *Hiberiae* ; 4. 15. 26, *Epod.* 1. 24, 2. 44, 12. 21, 15. 3 *magnorum numen* [*laesura*] *deorum* ; 17. 16, 17. 58. Not unlike is *Odes* 3. 15. 12, although *capreae* is probably dative.

(*β*). For type (β) compare *Odes* 1. 8. 13, 14 *ut marinae* | *filium* [*dicunt*] *Thetidis sub lacrimosa Troiae* | *funera* ; 1. 1. 19 *veteris pocula Massici*. Add *Odes* 1. 4. 15 (?), 1. 17. 21, 1. 35. 11, 2. 1. 33, 34, 2. 17. 29, 30, 2. 19. 16, 2. 20. 14, 3. 2. 26, 27 *Cereris sacrum* [*vulgarit*] *arcanae* ; 3. 7. 4, 3. 9. 7, 3. 13. 8, 3. 24. 44 *virtutisque viam* [*deserit*] *arduae* ; 3. 28. 12, 3. 29. 8 (*parricidae*=adj.), 3. 29. 62, 4. 5. 36, 4. 15. 31, 32, *Epod.* 2. 42, 2. 65, 11. 23, 24 *gloriantis* [*mulierculam* | *vincere mollitia*] *amor Lycisci* ; 15. 21 *Pythagorae* [*fallant*] *arcana renati* ; 16. 45, and 17. 14. All these examples suggest that *nobilis* is genitive at *Odes* 1. 14. 12 *silvae filia nobilis*.

§ 21. A grouping, very familiar in prose, i.e. adj., verb, noun, or noun, verb, adj., is frequent in Horace. For prose compare Cicero *De Amic.* 7. 24 *maximis efferat laudibus* ; *ib.* 22. 85 *praeposteris enim utimur consiliis* ; *De Off.* 2. 16. 19 *ad exitus pervehimur optatos* etc. Livy provides instances *passim*.

Horace uses this order some 348 times; and the adjective, with only fifty-six exceptions, comes first. In the following list of examples '1' signifies that the adjective comes last. *Odes* 1. 1. 8, 1. 1. 9, 1. 1. 10, 1. 1. 20, 1. 1. 30 (l), 1. 2. 3, 1. 2. 18, 1. 3. 5, 6, 1. 3. 39, 1. 4. 4, 1. 4. 13, 1. 5. 2, 1. 5. 4, 1. 7. 32, 1. 8. 3, 4, 1. 18. 16, 1. 9. 1, 1. 9. 12, 1. 9. 20, 1. 10. 7, 1. 11. 2, 3, 1. 12. 39, 1. 13. 9, 10, 1. 13. 18, 1. 15. 5, 1. 15. 7, 1. 16. 4 (l), 1. 16. 9, 10, 1. 16. 16 (l), 1. 16. 18, 1. 17. 2, 3, 1. 17. 8, 1. 17. 12, 1. 17. 26, 1. 20. 10, 11, 1. 21. 1, 1. 21. 6, 1. 21. 9, 1. 22. 5 (l), 1. 22. 7, 1. 22. 10, 1. 22. 11 (l), 1. 22. 14, 1. 22. 18, 1. 24. 8, 1. 24. 11, 1. 25. 1 (compare 1. 25. 19, 20), 1. 25. 5 (?), 1. 25. 7, 1. 26. 7, 1. 26. 9, 1. 26. 11, 1. 26. 12, 1. 27. 4, 1. 27. 6, 1. 27. 8 (l), 1. 27. 13, 1. 27. 15, 1. 28. 5, 6, 1. 28. 13 (l), 1. 28. 17, 1. 28. 26, 1. 28. 33 (l), 1. 29. 9 (l), 1. 30. 3, 1. 31. 1, 1. 31. 2, 3, 1. 31. 7, 1. 33. 2, 3, 1. 33. 4, 1. 33. 6, 1. 34. 7, 1. 35. 2, 1. 35. 12, 1. 35. 19 (l), 1. 36. 14, 1. 36. 17 (?), 1. 36. 18, 1. 37. 25, 1. 37. 26, 2. 1. 12, 2. 1. 16, 2. 1. 19, 2. 1. 34, 2. 2. 3, 4, 2. 2. 9, 10, 2. 4. 16 (l), 2. 5. 6, 7, 2. 5. 22 (?), 2. 6. 2 (l), 2. 6. 9 (l), 2. 6. 19, 20, 2. 6. 21, 22, 2. 7. 16 (l), 2. 7. 23, 2. 8. 15, 2. 9. 12, 2. 9. 22, 2. 9. 24, 2. 10. 18, 2. 12. 8, 2. 12. 9, 2. 12. 25, 2. 13. 40, 2. 14. 8, 9, 2. 14. 12, 2. 15. 9, 10, 2. 15. 17, 2. 15. 20, 2. 16. 3, 2. 16. 9, 2. 16. 26, 27, 2. 16. 36, 37, 2. 16. 39, 2. 17. 1 (l), 2. 17. 8, 2. 17. 9, 2. 17. 11, 2. 17. 18 (l), 2. 17. 32, 2. 18. 31, 2. 19. 10, 11, 2. 19. 19 (l), 2. 20. 8, 2. 20. 10, 2. 20. 18, 2. 20. 19, 3. 1. 19, 3. 1. 26, 3. 1. 47 (l), 3. 2. 5, 3. 2. 14, 3. 2. 18, 3. 2. 23, 3. 2. 27, 3. 3. 4 (l), 3. 3. 10 (l), 3. 3. 12, 3. 3. 13, 3. 3. 25, 3. 3. 33, 3. 3. 45, 3. 3. 69, 3. 3. 72 (l), 3. 4. 6, 3. 4. 21, 22, 3. 4. 24, 3. 4. 40, 3. 4. 44 (l), 3. 4. 74, 75, 3. 5. 48, 3. 6. 10, 3. 6. 24, 3. 6. 25, 3. 6. 35, 36, 3. 7. 14, 3. 7. 28, 3. 8. 19, 20, 3. 8. 23, 3. 9. 17, 3. 9. 18 (l), 3. 9. 19, 3. 10. 12, 3. 11. 7, 8, 3. 11. 21, 22 (l), 3. 11. 27 (l), 3. 11. 31, 32, 3. 11. 39, 3. 11. 45, 3. 13. 16 (l), 3. 14. 2, 3. 14. 11, 3. 14. 13, 14, 3. 14. 18, 3. 14. 26 (l), 3. 16. 9, 3. 16. 16, 3. 16. 19, 3. 16. 27, 3. 17. 13, 3. 18. 7, 3. 18. 10 (l), 3. 19. 8, 3. 19. 11, 12, 3. 19. 13 (l), 3. 19. 27, 3. 20. 1, 3. 20. 6, 3. 20. 10 (l), 3. 20. 13, 3. 20. 15, 16, 3. 21. 9, 10, 3. 21. 21, 3. 21. 23, 3. 23. 5, 3. 23. 9, 3. 24. 16, 3. 24. 20, 3. 24. 26 (l), 3. 24. 57, 3. 24. 63, 3. 25. 5, 3. 27. 9, 3. 27. 17, 3. 27. 19, 3. 27. 21, 22, 3. 27. 41 (l), 3. 27. 43, 3. 27. 53, 3. 27. 62, 63 (l), 3. 27. 74, 3. 28. 11, 3. 28. 14, 3. 28. 15, 3. 29. 7, 3. 29. 9, 3. 29. 16, 3. 29. 20 (l), 3. 29. 40, 41, 3. 29. 53, 3. 30. 7, 3. 30. 10, 3. 30. 11, 3. 30. 13, 4. 1. 12 (l), 4. 1. 22 (?), 4. 2. 6, 4. 2. 17, 4. 2. 23, 24, 4. 2. 29, 4. 2. 45 (l), 4. 2. 54, 4. 2. 55, 4. 3. 5 (l), 4. 3. 8, 4. 4. 8, 4. 4. 33 (l), 4. 4. 41, 4. 4. 44, 4. 4. 62, 4. 4. 70 (l), 4. 5. 12, 4. 5. 19, 4. 5. 22, 4. 5. 30, 4. 5. 34, 4. 6. 18, 19, 4. 6. 35, 4. 6. 39, 4. 7. 25, 26, 4. 8. 27, 4. 9. 17, 4. 9. 22, 4. 9. 29, 4. 9. 32, 4. 9. 49, 4. 10. 5 (l), 4. 10. 8, 4. 11. 7, 8, 4. 11. 9, 4. 11. 19, 20, 4. 11. 33, 34, 4. 12. 18, 4. 12. 19 (l), 4. 13. 8, 4. 14. 5, 4. 14. 16 (l), 4. 14. 23, 24, 4. 14. 25, 4. 14. 26 (l), 4. 14. 30 (l), 4. 14. 33, 4. 14. 36, 4. 14. 38, 4. 14. 52, 4. 15. 6, 4. 15. 12, 4. 15. 13, 14, 4. 15. 20, 4. 15. 22 (l), *C. S.* 5, 7, 13, 34, 43, 49 (l), 54, 63, 71, *Epod.* 1. 14, 1. 23, 1. 26 (?), 1. 27 (?), 1. 30, 2. 3 (l), 2. 10, 2. 19, 2. 27 (l), 2. 33, 2. 36, 2. 46, 2. 49, 2. 52, 3. 14 (l), 3. 21 (l), 5. 3, 5. 24 (l), 5. 43, 5. 60, 5. 76, 5. 83, 5. 90, 5. 92, 6. 10, 6. 12, 8. 15, 8. 19, 9. 13, 14 (l), 9. 28, 10. 23, 11. 15, 11. 28, 12. 18, 13. 5, 13. 8, 15. 4 (l), 15. 5, 15. 16, 15. 23, 16. 12, 16. 28, 16. 29, 16. 35 (l), 16. 38, 16. 39, 16. 47, 16. 57, 16. 62, 17. 15, 17. 29, 17. 48, 17. 52, 17. 59 (l), 17. 61, 17. 70, 17. 72 (l), 17. 78 (l). Add with intrusive adverb *Odes* 1. 13. 8, 1. 13. 14, 15. See too §§ 30, 31, 37.

§ 22. In almost all the above passages the separated adjectives have a special significance; but most of the examples in the *C. S.* seem to serve no purpose, and are merely a metrical convenience. This is perhaps true of many cases where the adjectives come last.

§ 23. It should be observed that in the examples cited at § 21 the adjective and noun are construed with the verb. Five passages viz. *Odes* 1. 5. 2, 1. 22. 11, 1. 26. 4, 3. 14. 21, and 4. 9. 49 are somewhat different. For these see the notes *ad loc.*

§ 24. Similar to the examples in § 21 are those where the place of the verb is taken by a participle, adjective, or adverb (compare also § 14). The type is seen in *Odes*

1. 8. 12 *iaculo nobilis expedito*; 1. 18. 12 *variis obsita floribus*; *C. S.* 61 *fulgente decorus arcu*; *Odes* 1. 24. 13 *Threicio blandius Orpheo*. Other examples are *Odes* [1. 1. 1], 1. 2. 37, 1. 12. 54, 1. 13. 18, 19, 1. 35. 31, 2. 2. 1, 2, 2. 3. 3, 4, 2. 3. 21, 2. 5. 12, 2. 6. 5, 2. 8. 3, 4, 2. 11. 2, 3 (adj. last), 2. 11. 15, 2. 13. 29, 2. 15. 15 (adj. last), 2. 16. 1, 2, 2. 19. 8, 2. 20. 13, 3. 3. 23, 3. 3. 66, 67, 3. 4. 72 (see too § 37), 3. 5. 18, 3. 6. 16, 3. 6. 38, 3. 7. 7, 8, 3. 7. 12, 3. 7. 19, 20, 3. 8. 22, 3. 9. 10, 3. 9. 22, 23, 3. 10. 17, 3. 11. 3, 3. 11. 11, 12, 3. 11. 46 (adj. last), 3. 12. 8, 3. 13. 2, 3. 14. 6, 3. 17. 1 (*vetusto nobilis ab Lamo*), 3. 18. 3, 3. 23. 18, 3. 24. 1, 2, 3. 24. 53, 54, 3. 29. 49, 4. 1. 10, 4. 1. 14, 4. 2. 9 (adj. last), 4. 2. 35, 4. 5. 1 (adj. last), 4. 5. 11 (?), 4. 5. 15 (adj. last), 4. 5. 38, 39, 4. 6. 9, 4. 11. 1, 4. 13. 15, 4. 14. 7 (adj. last), *Epod.* 1. 25 (adj. last), 2. 64 (adj. last), 3. 13, 4. 3, 5. 11, 5. 15, 6. 13 (adj. last), 8. 13, 14, 9. 2, 9. 30 (adj. last), 11. 2 (adj. last), 12. 1, 15. 6, 17. 46, 17. 73.

Two points are to be noticed : first that in these examples the ablative is concerned (with nine exceptions viz. *Odes* 2. 11. 15, 3. 3. 23, 3. 7. 19, 20, 3. 9. 10, 3. 11. 11, 12, 3. 11. 46, 3. 18. 3, 4. 14. 7, *Epod.* 6. 13) ; second that the adjective comes first (with twelve exceptions). Many of these cases might be classed under § 48.

§ 25. Two examples viz. *Odes* 1. 17. 24, 25, and *Epod.* 7. 8 are abnormal, because the adjective and noun do not belong strictly or alone to the word which lies between. See the notes *ad loc.*

Perhaps *Odes* 3. 11. 1 *te docilis magistro*, and ·*Epod.* 5. 95, 15. 6 may be classed under § 24.

§ 26. When Horace puts the participle before its noun, he seems always to regard the participle as of greater importance. Usually, at least in prose, English will render the participle by a noun. It will suffice to quote from prose Cicero *De Off.* 3. 28. 102 *num iratum timemus Iovem?* (the anger of Jove) ; Sallust *Cat.* 18. 8 *post conditam urbem Romam* (the building of Rome) ; Livy 1. 1. 1 *reddendae Helenae auctores* (advocates of Helen's restoration), etc., etc.

I have noted the following examples in the *Odes, Epodes,* and *C. S.* : *Odes* 1. 1. 24 *permixtus* (the confusion of sound) ; 1. 2. 2 *rubente* (red flash of hand) ; 1. 3. 26 *vetitum* (the prohibition of sin); 1. 11. 5 *oppositis* (the opposition of the rocks) ; 1. 19. 16 *mactata* (the sacrifice of a victim) ; 1. 33. 4 *laesa* (breach of faith) ; 1. 35. 29 *iturum* (the coming journey of Caesar; 1. 37. 13 *vix una sospes* (σωθεῖσα) i.e. the safety of scarce one ship ; 1. 37. 23 *latentis* (a hiding-place) ; 1. 37. 25 *iacentem* (downfall) ; 1. 37. 29 *deliberata* (determination to die) ; 2. 1. 14 *consulenti* (the counsels of the senate) ; 2. 3. 17 *coemptis* (the purchase of estates) ; 2. 4. 10 *ademptus* (the loss of Hector) ; 2. 5. 23 *solutis* (the loosing of hair) ; 2. 7. 17 *obligatam* (your debt of a feast) ; 2. 13. 31 *exactos* (the expulsion of tyrants) ; 2. 18. 17 *secanda* (the cutting of marble) ; 3. 1. 33 *contracta* (the straitening of water space) ; 3. 2. 24 *fugiente* (by swift flight of wing) ; 3. 4. 19 *lauroque collataque myrto* (but see § 33) ; 3. 4. 26 *versa* (the turning of the line) ; 3. 5. 7 *inversi* (inversion of morals) ; 3. 5. 47 *maerentis* (the tears of friends) ; 3. 5. 51 *obstantis* (the opposition of his kindred) ; 3. 15. 10 *pulso* (the beat of drum) ; 3. 17. 11 *demissa* (the downrush of the tempest) ; 3. 23. 2 *nascente* (the birth of the moon) ; 3. 23. 19 *aversos* (displeasure of the Penates) ; 3. 26. 8 *oppositis* (opposition of doors) ; 3. 27. 22 *orientis* (rising of Auster) ; 3. 28. 4 *munitae* (the fortress of wisdom) ; 3. 28. 15 *iunctis* (team of swans) ; 4. 2. 42, 43 *impetrato* (the fulfilment of prayer for return) ; 4. 2. 47, 48 *recepto* (the coming back of Caesar) ; 4. 4. 53 *cremato fortis* (brave in spite of the burning of Troy) ; 4. 4. 61 *secto* (the cutting of its body) ; 4. 8. 18 *domita* (the conquest of Africa) ; 4. 9. 29 *sepultae* (the burial of cowardice) ; 4. 9. 30 *celata* (concealment of valour) ; 4. 9. 43 *obstantis* (obstacle formed by crowds) ; 4. 11. 3 *nectendis* (the weaving of garlands) ; 4. 11. 7, 8 *immolato* (the sacrifice of a lamb) ; 4. 11. 19 *adfluentis* (increase of years) ; 4. 11. 25 *ambustus* (the burning of Phaëthon) ; 4. 14. 52 *compositis* (laying down of arms) ; 4. 15. 2 *victas* (sacking of cities) ; *C. S.* 18, 19 *iugandis* (marriage of women); *Epod.* 2. 11 *in reducta* (in the depths of the valley) ; 2. 32 *obstantis* (the obstacle formed by the nets) ; 2. 45 *textis* (in a prison of hurdles) ; 2. 65, 66 *positosque vernas...circum...lares* (the settling of slaves round the hearth) ; 5. 33 *mutatae* (change of food) ; 9. 31 *exercitatas* (the turmoil of the Syrtes) ; 13. 5 *obducta* (frown on brow).

§ 27. What is true of participles is also true of adjectives. Striking instances are *Odes* 3. 23. 16 *fragilique myrto* (sprigs of myrtle) ; 4. 5. 23 *laudantur simili prole* (for likeness in offspring) ; *C. S.* 30 *spicea donet Cererem corona* (with wheat ears for crown). Compare Livy 9. 2. 9 *per cavam rupem* (through the cleft in the rock). That preposited adjectives are so common in Horace need cause no surprise : *a poet uses adjectives for purposes of emotion, not of classification* (see on § 36 in reference to *povera donna*).

In the following passages it may, I think, be admitted that the preposited or separated adjective is more important than the noun, and that the force of such adjective is best expressed by a noun in English prose, if not in poetry : *Odes* 1. 1. 21 *viridi*, 1. 1. 30 *gelidum*, 1. 2. 7 *altos*, 1. 2. 22 *graves*, 1. 3. 12 *praecipitem*, 1. 3. 14 *tristis*, 1. 4. 11 *umbrosis*, 1. 4. 19 *tenerum*, 1. 5. 2 *liquidis*, 1. 7. 1 *claram*, 1. 7. 2 *bimaris*, 1. 7. 10 *patiens*, 1. 7. 13 *praeceps*, 1. 7. 19 *molli* (?), 1. 9. 1 *alta* (?), 1. 9. 15 *dulcis*, 1. 12. 1 *acri*, 1. 12. 7 *vocalem*, 1. 12. 15 *variis*, 1. 12. 23 *certa*, 1. 12. 31 *minax* (?), 1. 12. 43 *saeva*, 1. 12. 58 *gravi*, 1. 13. 6 *certa*, 1. 13. 9 *candidos*, 1. 15. 16 *gravis*, 1. 15. 18 *celerem*, 1. 16. 9 *tristes*, 1. 16. 15 *insani*, 1. 16. 23 *dulci*, 1. 17. 2 *igneam*, 1. 17. 4 *pluvios*, 1. 17. 10 *dulci*, 1. 17. 24 *protervum*, 1. 18. 4 *mordaces*, 1. 18. 5 *gravem*, 1. 19. 3 *lasciva*, 1. 19. 7 *grata*, 1. 21. 6 *gelido*, 1. 21. 13 *miseram*, 1. 22. 6 *inhospitalem*, 1. 22. 14 *latis*, 1. 23. 6 *virides*, 1. 24. 15 *vanae*, 1. 24. 18 *nigro*, 1. 25. 9 *arrogantis*, 1. 25. 10 *solo*, 1. 25. 13 *flagrans*, 1. 26. 2 *protervis*, 1. 27. 4 *sanguineis*, 1. 28. 5 *aerias...rotundum*, 1. 28. 18 *avidum*, 1. 28. 28 *aequo*, 1. 29. 2 *acrem*, 1. 31. 3 *opimae*, 1. 31. 10 *aureis*, 1. 33. 2 *immitis*, 1. 33. 5 *tenui*, 1. 35. 13 *iniurioso*, 1. 36. 20 *lascivis*, 1. 37. 27 *atrum*, 1. 38. 7 *arta*, 2. 1. 33 *lugubris*, 2. 2. 2 *avaris*, 2. 2. 9 *avidum*, 2. 2. 13 *dirus*, 2. 3. 6 *remoto*, 2. 3. 11 *obliquo*, 2. 3. 27 *aeternum*, 2. 4. 3 *niveo*, 2. 4. 21 *teretis*, 2. 5. 6 *gravem*, 2. 5. 7 *udo*, 2. 5. 18 *albo*, 2. 5. 24 *ambiguo*, 2. 6. 3 *barbaras*, 2. 6. 15 *viridi*, 2. 6. 21 *beatae*, 2. 7. 9 *celerem*, 2. 7. 14 *denso*, 2. 9. 3 *inaequales*, 2. 9. 9 *flebilibus*, 2. 9. 12 *rapidum*, 2. 9. 20 *rigidum*, 2. 10. 5 *auream*, 2. 10. 7 *invidenda*, 2. 10. 14 *alteram*, 2. 10. 15 *informis*, 2. 11. 1 *bellicosus*, 2. 11. 7 *lascivos*, 2. 11. 8 *facilem*, 2. 11. 13 *alta*, 2. 11. 19 *ardentis*, 2. 12. 2 *dirum* (?), 2. 12. 5 *saevos*, 2. 12. 13 *dulcis*, 2. 12. 15 *fulgentis*, 2. 12. 21 *dives*, 2. 12. 22 *pinguis*, 2. 12. 24 *plenas*, 2. 13. 17 *celerem*, 2. 13. 38 *dulci*, 2. 14. 3 *instanti*, 2. 14. 4 *indomitae*, 2. 14. 6 *illacrimabilem*, 2. 14. 13 *cruento*, 2. 14. 21 *placens*, 2. 15. 9 *fervidos*, 2. 15. 15 *opacam*, 2. 16. 2 *atra*, 2. 16. 39 *malignum*, 2. 17. 14 *centimanus*, 2. 18. 30 *rapacis*, 2. 18. 36 *superbum*, 2. 19. 8 *gravi*, 2. 19. 9 *pervicacis*, 2. 19. 10 *uberes*, 2. 19. 13 *beatae*, 2. 20. 10 *album*, 3. 1. 1 *profanum*, 3. 1. 23 *umbrosam*, 3. 1. 26 *tumultuosum*, 3. 2. 1 *angustam*, 3. 2. 2 *acri*, 3. 3. 27 *pugnacis*, 3. 3. 30 *gravis*, 3. 3. 31 *invisum*, 3. 3. 37 *longus*, 3. 3. 46 *medius*, 3. 3. 48 *tumidus*, 3. 3. 56 *pluvii*, 3. 3. 69 *iocosae*, 3. 4. 7 *amoenae*, 3. 4. 22 *frigidum*, 3. 4. 24 *liquidae*, 3. 4. 30 *insanientem*, 3. 4. 31 *urentis*, 3. 4. 35 *pharetratos*, 3. 4. 54 *minaci*, 3. 5. 11 *aeternae*, 3. 5. 33 *perfidis*, 3. 5. 49 *barbarus*, 3. 6. 16 *missilibus* (?), 3. 6. 45 *damnosa*, 3. 8. 6 *dulcis*, 3. 9. 2 *candidae*, 3. 12. 1 *dulci*, 3. 12. 5 *operosae*, 3. 13. 2 *dulci*, 3. 13. 6 *gelidos*, 3. 13. 15 *loquaces*, 3. 14. 23 *invisum*, 3. 16. 3 *tristes*, 3. 16. 16 *saevos*, 3. 16. 17 *crescentem*, 3. 16. 26 *impiger*, 3. 16. 37 *importuna*, 3. 20. 13 *leni*, 3. 21. 3 *insanos*,

3. 23. 5 *pestilentem*, 3. 23. 6 *sterilem*, 3. 23. 7 *dulces*, 3. 23. 9 *nivali*, 3. 23. 16 *fragili*, 3. 23. 20 *saliente*, 3. 24. 20 *nitido*, 3. 24. 33 *tristes*, 3. 24. 64 *curtae*, 3. 25. 10 *nive candidam*, 3. 25. 20 *viridi*, 3. 26. 6 *lucida*, 3. 27. 2 *praegnas*, 3. 27. 4 *feta*, 3. 27. 11 *oscinem*, 3. 27. 16 *vaga*, 3. 27. 43 *longos*, 3. 27. 46 *iratae*, 3. 27. 49 *patrios*, 3. 29. 6 *udum*, 3. 29. 7 *declive*, 3. 29. 16 *sollicitam*, 3. 29. 30 *caliginosa*, 3. 29. 40 *fera...quietos*, 3. 29. 61 *avaro*, 4. 1. 8 *blandae*, 4. 2. 29 *grata*, 4. 2. 30 *uvidi*, 4. 2. 41 *laetos*, 4. 3. 2 *placidi*, 4. 3. 16 *invido*, 4. 4. 57 *duris*, 4. 4. 74 *benigno*, 4. 5. 12 *dulci*, 4. 5. 14 *curvo*, 4. 5. 22 *maculosum*, 4. 5. 23 *simili*, 4. 5. 25 *gelidum*, 4. 6. 7 *tremenda* (?), 4. 6. 9 *mordaci*, 4. 6. 33 *fugacis*, 4. 7. 5 *geminis*, 4. 7. 11 *pomifer*, 4. 8. 3 *fortium*, 4. 8. 15 *celeres*, 4. 9. 15 *regalis*, 4. 9. 23 *pudicis*, 4. 9. 33 *lividas*, 4. 9. 37 *avarae*, 4. 9. 49 *duram*, 4. 9. 51 *caris*, 4. 11. 25 *avaras*, 4. 11. 35 *atrae*, 4. 12. 11 *nigri*, 4. 12. 26 *nigrorum*, 4. 13. 6 *virentis*, 4. 13. 9 *aridas*, 4. 13. 10 *luridi*, 4. 13. 14 *clari*, 4. 13. 16 *volucris*, 4. 13. 17 *decens* (?), C. S. 30 *spicea*, 34 *supplices*, 45 *probos...docili*, *Epod.* 1. 12 *inhospitalem*, 1. 14 *forti*, 2. 6 *iratum*, 2. 16 *infirmas*, 2. 24 *tenaci*, 2. 66 *renidentis*, 3. 9 *candidum*, 3. 22 *extrema*, 4. 4 *dura*, 5. 11 *trementi*, 5. 43 *otiosa*, 5. 63 *superbam*, 6. 9 *timenda*, 6. 15 *atro*, 9. 2 *victore*, 9. 3 *alta*, 9. 32 *incerto*, 9. 35 *fluentem*, 9. 38 *dulci*, 10. 2 *olentem*, 10. 7 *altis*, 10. 9 *atra*, 10. 21 *curvo*, 12. 25 *acris*, 13. 10 *diris*, 14. 1 *mollis*, 14. 11 *cava*, 16. 16 *malis*, 16. 22 *protervus*, 16. 37 *indocili*, 16. 47 *cava*, 16. 60 *laboriosa*, 17. 1 *efficaci*, 17. 11 *feris* (?), 17. 21 *verecundus*, 17. 42 *infamis*, 17. 70 *altis*, 17. 73 *fastidiosa*.

For preposited adjectives of an unpleasant meaning see on *Odes* 2. 14. 23.

§ 28. A special case of the principle of stress with a preposited or separated epithet is that of an adjective in the comparative degree. Compare *Odes* 1. 2. 48, 1. 14. 8, 1. 27. 20, 1. 36. 6, 2. 1. 40, 2. 3. 8, 2. 9. 22, 2. 10. 10, 2. 14. 25, 2. 17. 6, 3. 6. 25, 3. 21. 8, 3. 24. 53, 4. 2. 33, *Epod.* 1. 25, 8. 13, 9. 33, 10. 11, 11. 14, 12. 4 (a separated adverb), 14. 13, 15. 2, 16. 15, 17. 61, 17. 62.

§ 29. Similar is the preposited adjective in litotes. Compare *Odes* 1. 28. 14 *non sordidus auctor*. Add 1. 18. 9, 1. 24. 17, 1. 27. 13, 1. 27. 15, 1. 36. 8, 1. 37. 32, 2. 1. 22, 2. 19. 15, 2. 20. 1, 3. 6. 10, *Epod.* 1. 10, 5. 50, 5. 73, 10. 17, 11. 21, 14. 12. I find only three cases of postposited litotes viz. *Odes* 1. 14. 18 *curaque non levis*; 2. 16. 39 *Parca non mendax*, and *Epod.* 9. 30 *ventis iturus non suis*. The *non felix* of *Epod.* 12. 25 is somewhat different; see note *ad loc.*

§ 30. Proleptic adjectives are either preposited or separated. Compare *Odes* 1. 13. 12 *impressit memorem dente labris notam*; 2. 1. 19 *fugacis | terret equos*; 2. 8. 15 *ardentis acuens sagittas* (?); 2. 9. 1 *hispidos | manant in agros*; 2. 16. 29 *abstulit clarum cita mors Achillem* (see too § 10); 3. 6. 8 *Hesperiae mala luctuosae* (see too § 20 *a*); 3. 9. 12, 3. 9. 16 *si parcent animae fata superstiti*; 3. 11. 51 *nostri memorem sepulcro | scalpe querellam*; 3. 16. 19 *late conspicuum tollere verticem*; 3. 20. 10 *dentes acuit timendos*; 3. 24. 62, 63 *improbae | crescunt divitiae*; 3. 25. 5 *aeternum meditans decus*; 3. 27. 11 *oscinem corvum prece suscitabo*; 3. 29. 51 *transmutat incertos honores*; 3. 29. 53, 54 *si celeris quatit | pinnas*; 4. 2. 17, 18 *quos Elea domum reducit | palma caelestis*; 4. 2. 22, 23 *moresque | aureos educit* (note the pause after *moresque*); 4. 3. 18 *dulcem quae strepitum, Pieri, temperas*; 4. 6. 14 *male feriatos Troas...falleret*; 4. 6. 39 *celeremque pronos | volvere menses*; 4. 6. 41 *dis amicum...reddidi carmen*; 4. 14. 36 *vacuam patefecit aulam*; 4. 14. 38 *secundos reddidit exitus*; 4. 15. 20 *miseras inimicat urbes*; C. S. 67 *meliusque semper | prorogat aevum*; *Epod.* 2. 31 *trudit acris...apros*; 3. 15, 16 *insedit vapor | siticulosae Apuliae*; 5. 95 *et inquietis adsidens praecordiis* (see too § 24); 6. 3 *inanis, si potes, vertis minas*; 11. 15, 16 *inaestuet praecordiis | libera bilis*; 15. 8 *turbaret hibernum mare*.

It should be observed that at least ten of the above passages may be classed under § 21.

§ 31. Often a preposited or separated adjective goes closely in sense with the verb, and is, to all intents and purposes, an adverb. Compare *Odes* 1. 4. 7 *alterno*, 1. 7. 28 *certus*, 1. 10. 7 *iocoso*, 1. 12. 57 *latum*, 1. 13. 8 *lentis*, 1. 13. 18 *irrupta*, 1. 15. 23 *impavidi*, 1. 16. 7 *non acuta*, 1. 17. 26 *incontinentis*, 1. 20. 6 *iocosa*, 1. 25. 5 *facilis* (?), 1. 25. 17 *laeta*, 1. 35. 26 *periura*, 2. 5. 13 *ferox*, 2. 6. 9 *iniquae*, 2. 13. 7 *nocturno*, 2. 13. 32 *densum umeris*, 2. 14. 1 *fugaces*, 2. 17. 26 *laetum*, 2. 18. 32 *aequa*, 2. 19. 5 *recenti*, 3. 1. 34 *frequens*, 3. 3. 39 *beati*, 3. 3. 42 *inultae*, 3. 3. 70 *pervicax*, 3. 4. 5 *amabilis* (?), 3. 4. 29 *libens*, 3. 5. 44 *torvus*, 3. 16. 4 *nocturnis*, 3. 18. 3 *lenis*, 3. 19. 22 *invidus*, 3. 19. 28 *lentus*, 3. 21. 10 *horridus*, 3. 21. 21 *laeta*, 3. 24. 18 *innocens*, 3. 24. 62 *improbae*, 3. 27. 41 *vana*, 3. 29. 22 *fessus*, 3. 29. 63 *tutum*, 4. 1. 21 *plurima*, 4. 1. 37 *nocturnis*, 4. 2. 14 *iusta*, 4. 3. 21 *totum*, 4. 4. 7 *verni*, 4. 4. 46 *impio*, 4. 5. 17 *tutus*, 4. 5. 19 *pacatum*, 4. 9. 42 *alto*, 4. 14. 25 *tauriformis*, *Epod*. 2. 36 *iucunda*, 2. 55 *iucundior*, 5. 25 *expedita*, 5. 47 *saeva*, 5. 92 *nocturnus*, 7. 19 *immerentis*, 8. 3 *vetus*, 10. 5 *niger*, 13. 7 *benigna*, 15. 6 *lentis*, 15. 13 *adsiduas*, 16. 1 *altera*, 16. 9 *impia*, 16. 14 *insolens*, 16. 48 *levis*, 16. 49 *iniussae*, 16. 51 *vespertinus*, 16. 52 *alta*, 17. 7 *citum*.

Some of these passages may be classed under § 21 e.g. 1. 10. 7, 1. 13. 18, 1. 17. 25, 26, 3. 24. 18, 4. 5. 19, *Epod*. 2. 36, 5. 92, 16. 51, and one instance under §§ 24, 25 viz. *Epod*. 15. 6.

§ 32. A few cases may be added where the adjective equals an adverb, though the noun is not inserted; they are *Odes* 1. 12. 39 *gratus*, 2. 10. 3 *cautus*, 2. 10. 6 *tutus*, 3. 5. 44 *torvus*, 3. 8. 27 *laetus*, 3. 9. 24 *libens*, 3. 18. 3 *lenis*, 3. 29. 33 *aequus*, *Epod*. 16. 14 *insolens*.

§ 33. If Horace wishes to show that an epithet belongs ἀπὸ κοινοῦ to two nouns, his formula, as Wickham has pointed out, is noun, conjunction + adjective, noun. Examples are *Odes* 1. 2. 1 *dirae*, 1. 5. 6 *mutatos*, 1. 12. 6 *gelido*, 1. 17. 28 *immeritam*, 1. 22. 19 *malus*, 1. 31. 16 *leves*, 1. 34. 8 *volucrem*, 2. 3. 11 *obliquo* (?), 2. 8. 3 *uno*, 2. 13. 17 *celerem*, 2. 13. 18 *Italum*, 2. 14. 21 *placens*, 2. 16. 33 *Siculae*, 2. 19. 24 *horribili*, 3. 2. 16 *timido*, 3. 3. 56 *pluvii*, 3. 4. 19 *collata*, 3. 5. 7 *inversi* (?), 3. 11. 13 *comites*, 3. 11. 39 *scelestas*, 3. 12. 9 *segni*, 3. 21. 3 *insanos*, 3. 24. 2 *divitis*, 3. 25. 13 *vacuum*, 3. 27. 27 *medias*, 3. 27. 70 *calidae*, 3. 29. 64 *geminus* (?), 4. 2. 38 *boni*, 4. 4. 5 *patrius* (?), 4. 5. 18 *alma*, 4. 14. 4 *memores*, 4. 14. 44 *dominae*, 4. 15. 12 *veteres*, *Epod*. 2. 40 *dulcis*, 5. 16 *incomptum*, 6. 5 *fulvus* (?), 15. 19 *multa*, 16. 20 *rapacibus* (?), 16. 22 *protervus*.

Compare the note on *Odes* 1. 30. 6.

§ 34. When a noun has two epithets, Horace frequently places them on either side of the noun e.g. *Odes* 1. 1. 2 *dulce decus meum*. This order is common in Italian e.g. *profondo sconforto mio*; in French e.g. Victor Hugo *Plein Ciel* l. 147 *un large et blanc hunier horizontal*, *ib.* l. 451 *l'antique universe décrépit*; and in our English poets who knew Italian e.g. Gray 'Full many a gem of purest ray serene'; Milton 'In Stygian cave forlorn,' 'that old man eloquent.' Not unlike are Milton's 'in this dark world and wide,' and Shakespeare's 'Free speech and fearless' (*Rich. II.* 1. 1. 123).

Latin prose and poetry supply numerous instances e.g. Cicero *De Off.* 1. 25. 86 *pestifera bella civilia*; *Pro Sest.* 54. 116 *in illo ardenti tribunatu suo*; *Cat.* 1. 3. 6 *tua consilia omnia*; *ib.* 1. 7. 17 *omnes cives tui*; Sallust *Iug.* 4 *utili labore meo*; *ib.* 7 *omnes fere res asperas*; *Cat.* 14. 2 *alienum aes grande*; Livy 1. 16. 7 *nullas opes humanas* and *passim*.

For poetry compare Vergil *Aen.* 9. 816 *suo cum gurgite flavo*, and Ennius *A.* 1. *fr.* 37 *tuo cum flumine sancto*; Horace *Odes* 1. 1. 2 *dulce decus meum*; 1. 4. 6 *iunctaeque Nymphis Gratiae decentes* (but see § 48); 1. 35. 21 *rara Fides* [*colit*] | *velata panno*;

2. 1. 21 *magnos...duces...sordidos*; 3. 3. 9, 10 *vagus Hercules | enisus*; 3. 4. 50 *fidens iuventus horrida*; 3. 13. 15, 16 *loquaces | lymphae [desiliunt] tuae*; 3. 19. 11, 12 *novem | [miscentur] cyathis [pocula] commodis*; 4. 4. 23, 24 *lateque victrices catervae | consiliis iuvenis revictae*; *C. S.* 19, 20 *feraci | lege marita*; *Epod.* 5. 75 *vocata mens tua*; 11. 28 *teretis pueri...renodantis.*

In the following passages we have (1) the genitive, (2) an adjectival phrase in place of one adjective, or (3) two genitives in place of two adjectives: *Odes* 1. 37. 9 *contaminato cum grege turpium* (but see § 35); 3. 22. 1 *montium custos nemorumque*; 3. 25. 14, 15 *Naiadum potens | Baccharumque*; 3. 29. 14, 15 *mundaeque [parvo sub lare pauperum] | cenae sine aulaeis et ostro*; 3. 29. 38, 39 *non sine montium | clamore vicinaeque silvae*; 3. 29. 55, 56 *probamque | pauperiem sine dote quaero*; *Epod.* 9. 19, 20 *hostiliumque navium portu latent | puppes sinistrorsum citae.*

Perhaps under this section may be set the two adverbs or adverbial equivalents of *Odes* 2. 7. 1, 2 *O saepe mecum tempus in ultimum | deducte Bruto militiae duce*, and of 2. 13. 24, 25 *Aeoliis fidibus querentem | Sappho puellis de popularibus.* Compare 3. 25. 7, 8 *adhuc | indictum ore alio.* Not unlike are 3. 17. 11 *demissa tempestas ab Euro*, and 4. 6. 10 *impulsa cupressus Euro.*

§ 35. The prose order of adjective, complement, noun (or noun, complement, adjective), e.g. Livy 1. 3. 8 *celebre apud posteros nomen* and *passim*, is frequent in poetry. If however the complement is a genitive, Horace often leaves it outside; or, in other words, he puts the epithets on either side of the noun. This order is common in prose. Compare Cicero *De Off.* 1. 19. 64 *omnem morem Lacedaemoniorum*; *ib.* 1. 33. 120 *in deligendo genere vitae* (with *genus* this order is frequent in Cicero*); *ib.* 1. 18. 61 *rhetorum campus de Marathone*; Livy 1. 16. 8 *facta fide immortalitatis*; 34. 7. 4 *aliquam tamen causam tenacitatis*; Sallust *Cat.* 17. 1 *magna praemia coniurationis*, etc.

In Horace the type is seen at *Odes* 1. 4. 1 *grata vice veris.* Compare 1. 4. 15, 1. 10. 1, 1. 10. 2, 1. 13. 1, 2, 1. 13. 16, 1. 18. 2, 1. 18. 10, 1. 18. 14 (but see § 45), 1. 21. 10, 1. 28. 14, 15, 1. 36. 2, 1. 37. 9, 2. 1. 17, 2. 1. 24, 2. 3. 8, 2. 3. 13, 14, 2. 6. 24, 2. 8. 9, 2. 13. 7, 8, 2. 13. 17, 18, 2. 15. 6, 2. 16. 10, 11, 3. 3. 26, 3. 3. 35, 36, 3. 12. 4, 3. 23. 14, 3. 24. 2, 3. 27. 21, 22, 3. 28. 1, 2, 3. 30. 2, 3. 30. 6, 4. 11. 4, 4. 12. 11, 12, 4. 14. 21, 22, 4. 14. 29, *C. S.* 35, *Epod.* 2. 2, 16. 5, 16. 60.

As a rule there is a special reason for the order. Compare also on § 43.

§ 36. With the vocative Horace almost always places the adjective in front e.g. *Odes* 1. 4. 14 *o beate Sesti.* The order is natural: the emotion is contained in the epithet, and the epithet therefore springs first to the lips. Compare Italian *povera donna* (unhappy woman!) and *donna povera* (a woman poorly off). So French *pauvre femme!* and *une femme pauvre.* In English the stress and intonation when we say 'Lucky dog!' is parallel. Perhaps a similar principle explains Shakespeare's 'Good my lord!,' 'Sweet my coz!' etc.

Other examples in Horace are *Odes* 1. 10. 1 *facunde nepos*; 1. 18. 6 *decens Venus*; 1. 18. 11 *candide Bassareu*; 1. 20. 5 *care Maecenas*; 1. 27. 20 *digne puer*; 2. 3. 4 *moriture Delli*; 2. 13. 11 *triste lignum*; 2. 20. 7 *dilecte Maecenas*; 3. 21. 4 *pia testa*; 3. 23. 2 *rustica Phidyle*; 3. 27. 57 *vilis Europe*; 4. 6. 28 *levis Agyieu*; *C. S.* 9 *alme sol*; *Epod.* 3. 20 *iocose Maecenas*; 5. 50 *non infideles arbitrae*; 5. 74 *o multa fleturum caput*; 9. 4 *beate Maecenas*; 13. 12 *invicte mortalis...dea nate puer*; 14. 5 *candide Maecenas*; 17. 47 *prudens anus.* [Add *Sat.* 1. 10. 86, and *Epist.* 1. 4. 1.]

---

* The genitive outside is a frequent order in Livy when a preposition precedes the epithet. See my 'More Latin and English Idiom' pp. 31, 32. Compare § 42.

In the *Odes, Epodes,* and *C. S.* I find only five clear exceptions viz. *Odes* 1. 2. 33 *Erycina ridens*; 1. 26. 9 *Pimplei dulcis*; 2. 1. 37 *Musa procax* (?); 2. 4. 2 *Xanthia Phoceu*; and 4. 5. 5, 4. 5. 37 *dux bone.* The instances at *Odes* 1. 19. 1, 4. 1. 4, 5, 4. 2. 46, 47 are somewhat different; see notes *ad loc.* Add too the abnormal case at *Odes* 4. 14. 44 (see § 44).

§ 37. Generic adjectives tend to be preposited or separated in both prose and poetry. Compare Livy *Pref.* § 6 *poeticis magis decora fabulis*; 1. 47. 10 *muliebri dono*; 44. 5. 2 *hostilem tumultum*, etc.

The following examples occur in the *Odes* and *Epodes* viz. *Odes* 1. 1. 12 *Attalicis condicionibus* (see end of this section); 1. 8. 15, 16 *virilis | cultus*; 1. 16. 21 *hostile aratrum* (Horace always puts *hostilis* in front of the noun); 1. 37. 2 *Saliaribus | ornare pulvinar deorum | tempus erat dapibus*; 2. 12. 6 *Herculea manu*; 2. 12. 22 *Mygdonias opes*; 3. 1. 7 *Giganteo triumpho*; 3. 1. 18 *Siculae dapes*; 3. 2. 20 *popularis aurae*; 3. 3. 28 *Hectoreis opibus* (?); 3. 4. 34 *equino sanguine*; 3. 4. 72 *virginea domitus sagitta* (see too § 24); 3. 5. 43 *virilem...vultum*; 3. 12. 3 *patruae verbera linguae* (see too § 20 a); 3. 16. 41 *si Mygdoniis regnum Alyattei | campis continuem*; 3. 19. 8 *Paelignis caream frigoribus* (see too § 21); 3. 21. 9, 10 *Socraticis madet | sermonibus* (see too § 21); 4. 12. 18 *Sulpiciis accubat horreis* (see too § 21); *Epod.* 5. 53 *hostilis domos*; 5. 86 *Thyesteas preces*; 5. 100 *Esquilinae alites* (?); 8. 8 *equina...ubera*; 9. 19 *hostiliumque navium*; 16. 39 *muliebrem tollite luctum* (see too § 21).

Sometimes a genitive which stands outside adjective and noun (see § 35 *ad init.*) is generic in meaning. Compare *Odes* 1. 12. 35 *Catonis | nobile letum* (see too § 43); 2. 1. 24 *atrocem animum Catonis* (see too § 35); 2. 18. 5, 6 *neque Attali | ignotus heres regiam occupavi.* At 3. 14. 1 *Herculis ritu* the name may be generic; but Horace always has a preposited genitive with *ritu* (see note *ad loc.*). Under this section may be classed 2. 14. 28 *pontificum potiore cenis.*

§ 38. A genitive may also be either (*a*) preposited or (*b*) separated and preposited because it is more important than the word upon which it depends. It thus may represent the subject, object, indirect object and so on. Such genitives are found often enough in prose e.g. Livy *Pref.* § 4 *legentium plerisque=legentibus plerisque* (dat.); *ib.* § 5 (*cura*) *quae scribentis animum...flectere...posset=scribentem animo.* (In the same way a preposited adjective may equal such a genitive; compare on *Odes* 1. 3. 36, and 2. 12. 6.)

In Horace's *Odes* and *Epodes* all the cases are represented, e.g. *Odes* 1. 7. 11 *nec tam Larisae percussit campus*, where *Larisae* is logical subject; 1. 3. 17 *quem mortis timuit gradum*, where *mortis* is logical object; 1. 12. 55 *subiectos Orientis orae | Seras*, where *Orientis* is logical indirect object; 1. 21. 5 *laetam fluviis et nemorum coma*, where *nemorum* is logical ablative.

In the following instances 'n' signifies that the genitive equals a nominative; 'a' that it equals an accusative; 'd' that it equals a dative; and 'abl.' that it equals an ablative. *Odes* 1. 1. 16 *oppidi* (a); 1. 2. 9 *piscium* (n); 1. 2. 26 *imperi* (d); 1. 3. 17 *mortis* (a); 1. 4. 15 *vitae* (n); 1. 7. 2 *Corinthi* (a); 1. 7. 5 *Palladis* (a); 1. 7. 11 *Larisae* (n); 1. 7. 13 *Tiburni* (n); 1. 12. 35 *Catonis* (a); 1. 12. 55 *Orientis* (d); 1. 17. 17 *Caniculae* (a); 1. 19. 5 *Glycerae* (n); 1. 20. 6 *fluminis* (n); 1. 20. 8 *montis* (n); 1. 21. 5 *nemorum* (abl.); 1. 28. 3 *pulveris* (n); 1. 31. 4 *Sardiniae* (a); 1. 33. 6 *Cyri* (n); 1. 35. 30 *iuvenum* (a); 1. 36. 2 *vituli* (abl.); 2. 1. 2 *belli* (a); 2. 1. 20 *equitum* (a); 2. 1. 25 *deorum* (n); 2. 3. 15 *sororum* (n); 2. 3. 25 *omnium* (d); 2. 5. 3 *tauri* (a); 2. 5. 21 *puellarum* (d); 2. 11. 19 *Falerni* (a); 2. 12. 22 *Phrygiae* (a); 2. 14. 10 *terrae* (abl.); 2. 14. 22 *arborum* (n); 2. 15. 10–12 *Romuli...Catonis... veterum* (n); 2. 17. 13 *Chimaerae* (n); 2. 17. 22 *Iovis* (n); 2. 18. 9 *ingeni* (n); 2. 18. 20

maris (a) ; 2. 19. 13 *coniugis* (a) ; 2. 19. 20 *Bistonidum* (a) ; 2. 19. 31 *recedentis* (a) ; 3. 1. 20 *avium citharaeque* (n) ; 3. 1. 42 *purpurarum* (n) ; 3. 2. 15 *iuventae* (d) ; 3. 3. 2 *civium* (n) ; 3. 3. 34 *nectaris* (a) ; 3. 3. 40 *Priami Paridisque* (d?) ; 3. 3. 61 *Troiae* (n) ; 3. 4. 77 *Tityi* (a) ; 3. 5. 21 *civium* (a) ; 3. 5. 41 *coniugis* (a) ; 3. 5. 53 *clientum* (a) ; 3. 6. 9 *Pacori* (n) ; 3. 6. 41 *montium* (a) ; 3. 8. 8 *arboris* (abl.) ; 3. 8. 18 *Cotisonis* (n) ; 3. 11. 6 *divitum* (d) ; 3. 16. 2 *canum* (n) ; 3. 16. 11 *auguris* (n) ; 3. 16. 13 *urbium* (a) ; 3. 17. 3 *nepotum* (a) ; 3. 17. 6 *Formiarum* (a) ; 3. 17. 7 *Maricae* (d) ; 3. 21. 11 *Catonis* (n) ; 3. 22. 7 *verris* (abl.) ; 3. 24. 8 *mortis* (abl.) ; 3. 24. 44 *virtutis* (a) ; 3. 27. 1 *parrae* (n) ; 3. 29. 6 *Aefulae* (a) ; 4. 2. 46 *vocis* (n) ; 4. 3. 8 *regum* (a) ; 4. 3. 13 *Romae* (n) ; 4. 4. 27 *Augusti* (n) ; 4. 4. 30 *patrum* (n) ; 4. 5. 3 *patrum* (d) ; 4. 6. 36 *pollicis* (a) ; 4. 11. 4 *hederae* (n) ; 4. 13. 7 *Chiae* (a) ; 4. 13. 25 *cornicis* (d) ; 4. 14. 21 *Pleiadum* (abl.) ; 4. 14. 22 *hostium* (a) ; 4. 14. 29 *barbarorum* (a) ; 4. 14. 45 *fontium* (a) ; 4. 14. 49 *Galliae* (n) ; 4. 15. 7 *Parthorum* (d) ; *Epod.* 1. 20 *serpentium* (a) ; 1. 21 *auxili* (a) ; 2. 11 *mugientium* (a) ; 5. 1 *deorum* (n) ; 5. 41 *masculae libidinis* (a) ; 5. 71 *veneficae* (abl.) ; 9. 19 *navium* (n) ; 11. 25 *amicorum* (n) ; 13. 13 *Assaraci* (n) ; 15. 21 *Pythagorae* (n) ; 16. 17 *Phocaeorum* (n) ; 16. 61 *astri* (n) ; 17. 3 *per et Dianae* (a) ; 17. 81 *artis* (a).

§ 39. The genitive, when objective, tends to be preposite or separated e.g. *Odes* 1. 1. 26 *coniugis immemor* ; 1. 6. 1 *scriberis...hostium victor.* Add 1. 6. 10 *lyrae Musa potens* (see note *ad loc.*) ; 1. 12. 37 *animaeque magnae | prodigum Paulum* (see also on § 43) ; 1. 15. 30 *graminis immemor* ; 1. 18. 16 *arcanique fides prodiga* (see also § 43) ; 1. 34. 2 *sapientiae consultus* ; 2. 18. 18 *sepulcri | immemor* ; 3. 9. 10 *citharae sciens* ; 3. 10. 19 *liminis aut aquae | caelestis patiens latus* ; 3. 11. 11 *nuptiarum expers* (=*inscia*) ; 3. 11. 51 *nostri memorem* ; 3. 14. 26 *rixae cupidos* ; 3. 19. 16 *rixarum metuens* ; 4. 4. 6 *laborum propulit inscium* ; 4. 9. 35 *rerumque prudens* ; 4. 14. 7 *legis expertes Latinae* (see also § 24) ; *C. S.* 1 *Phoebe silvarumque potens Diana* (see also § 43) ; 19 *prolisque novae feraci | lege marita* ; *Epod.* 5. 22 *venenorum ferax.*

Exceptions are *Odes* 1. 3. 1, 1. 8. 4, 1. 15. 25, 3. 24. 22, 3. 27. 14, 3. 27. 29, 3. 29. 41, 4. 6. 43.

§ 40. Horace, perhaps imitating Greek, sometimes appears to place the genitive early in the loose sense of 'with reference to,' 'in respect of,' 'as for,' e.g. *Odes* 1. 3. 3 *ventorumque regat pater*='and, as for the winds, may the father thereof guide thy bark...'; 2. 8. 7 *iuvenumque prodis | publica cura*='and, as for our youth,...'; 2. 20. 23 *compesce clamorem ac sepulcri | mitte supervacuos honores*='restrain lamentations and, as for the tomb,....'; 3. 4. 77 *incontinentis...Tityi* (?) ; 3. 25. 4 *egregii Caesaris au- diar | aeternum meditans decus*='with reference to glorious Caesar I shall be heard...'; *Epod.* 1. 13 *vel Occidentis usque ad ultimum sinum*=' or, as for the West....' Add *Epod.* 11. 13, and *Odes* 4. 1. 22.

§ 41. In naming the descent of a person Horace puts the name of the ancestor first in the genitive, since the ancestor is the person to whom our attention is especially directed. Compare *Odes* 1. 3. 27 *Iapeti genus* (=*Iapetionides*) ; 1. 19. 2 *Semelae puer*; 2. 14. 18 *Danai genus* (=*Danaides*) ; 2. 18. 37 *Tantali | genus* (*Tantalides*) ; 3. 11. 23 *Danai puellas* (=*Danaides*) ; 3. 12. 4 *Cythereae puer ales* (see also § 35) ; 4. 2. 13 *deorum | sanguinem* ; 4. 6. 37 *Latonae puerum* ; 4. 8. 22 *Iliae | Mavortisque puer*; *Epod.* 5. 64 *Creontis filiam.* For an apparent exception viz. *Odes* 1. 10. 1 *facunde nepos Atlantis* see on § 35.

Perhaps on the analogy of the above examples Horace writes *Iustitiae soror* at *Odes* 1. 24. 6 ; *Pelopis genitor* at *Odes* 1. 28. 7, 2. 13. 37, *Epod.* 17. 65 ; *Andromedae pater* at *Odes* 3. 29. 17. See too on *Odes* 1. 10. 6, 1. 12. 49, and 2. 18. 34.

§ 42. When a preposition occurs, the genitive, as in prose, is often prepositer (compare the footnote at § 35). Thus Cicero *De Off.* 1. 1. 1 has *in dicendi exercita-*

tione...in utriusque orationis facultate and *passim*. For Horace compare *Odes* 1. 7. 8 *in Iunonis honorem*; 2. 13. 12 *in domini caput*; 3. 6. 26 *inter mariti vina*; 4. 5. 10 *trans maris aequora*; *Epod.* 1. 11 *per Alpium iuga*; 4. 8 *cum bis trium ulnarum toga*. Perhaps *solis* in *Odes* 3. 27. 12 may be excused on this principle.

§ 43. In § 35 we have shown how the normal prose order viz. adj., complement, noun, or noun, complement, adj. may be varied (if the complement is genitive) in the form adj., noun, complement, or complement, noun, adj. But in the following instances we have the order genitive, adj., noun: *Odes* 1. 12. 35 *Catonis | nobile letum* (compare § 37); 1. 12. 37 *animaeque magnae | prodigum Paulum* (compare § 39); 1. 18. 16 *arcanique fides prodiga* (compare § 39); 1. 22. 15 *leonum | arida nutrix* (see note *ad loc.*); 1. 25. 19 *hiemis sodali | dedicet Hebro* (see note *ad loc.*); 1. 32. 14 *o laborum | dulce lenimen* (see note *ad loc.* and compare *Odes* 4. 3. 17); 1. 35. 30 *iuvenum recens | examen* (compare § 38) : 2. 8. 7 *iuvenumque prodis | publica cura* (see note *ad loc.* and compare *Odes* 2. 20. 23, 3. 25. 4, 4. 3. 17, *Epod.* 1. 13); 2. 12. 22 *pinguis Phrygiae Mygdonias opes* (compare § 38); 2. 18. 5, 6 *Attali ignotus heres*; 2. 18. 9 *At fides et ingeni | benigna vena* (compare § 38); 2. 19. 10 *lactis et uberes...rivos*; 2. 20. 23 *sepulcri | mitte supervacuos honores* (see note *ad loc.* and compare 2. 8. 7 above); 3. 6. 32 *dedecorum pretiosus emptor* (see note *ad loc.*); 3. 16. 15 *navium | saevos illaqueant duces* (see note *ad loc.*); 3. 25. 4 *egregii Caesaris audiar | aeternum meditans decus* (see note *ad loc.* and compare 2. 8. 7 above, where the preposited genitive bears the sense 'in respect of'); 3. 29. 6 *ne semper udum Tibur et Aefulae | declive contempleris arvum* (compare § 38); 4. 1. 22 *lyraeque et Berecyntiae | delectabere tibiae | mixtis carminibus* (compare *Odes* 1. 1. 23); 4. 2. 41 *urbis | publicum ludum* (see note *ad loc.*); 4. 2. 46 *tum meae, si quid loquor audiendum, | vocis accedet bona pars* (compare § 38); 4. 3. 8 *quod regum tumidas contuderit minas* (compare § 38); 4. 3. 17 *o testudinis aureae | dulcem quae strepitum, Pieri, temperas* (see note *ad loc.* and compare 2. 8. 7 above); 4. 5. 3, 4 *patrum | sancto concilio* (see note *ad loc.*); 4. 8. 29 *sic Iovis interest | optatis epulis impiger Hercules* (see note *ad loc.*); 4. 9. 7 *Alcaei minacis | Stesichorique graves Camenae* (see note *ad loc.*, and compare 4. 8. 29); 4. 12. 6 *Cecropiae domus aeternum opprobrium*; 4. 12. 17 *nardi parvus onyx eliciet cadum* (see note *ad loc.*); 4. 14. 29 *ut barbarorum Claudius agmina | ferrata vasto diruit impetu* (compare § 38); 4. 14. 38 *belli secundos reddidit exitus* (see note *ad loc.*); 4. 15. 7 (*signa) derepta Parthorum superbis | postibus* (compare § 38); 4. 15. 14, 15 *famaque et imperi | porrecta maiestas* (see note *ad loc.*); *C. S.* 1 *silvarumque potens Diana* (compare § 39); *Epod.* 1. 13 *vel Occidentis usque ad ultimum sinum* (see note *ad loc.* and compare 2. 8. 7 above); 2. 11 *mugientium | prospectat errantis greges* (compare § 38); 3. 1 *parentis olim si quis impia manu | senile guttur fregerit* (see note *ad loc.*); 4. 9 *ut ora vertat huc et huc euntium liberrima indignatio* (see note *ad loc.*); 5. 41 *non defuisse masculae libidinis | Ariminensem Foliam* (compare § 38); 13. 17, 18 *omne malum vino cantuque levato | deformis aegrimoniae dulcibus alloquiis* (see note *ad loc.*); 17. 3 *per et Dianae non movenda numina* (see note *ad loc.* and compare § 38).

For complements other than genitives in abnormal positions see § 49.

§ 44. In the following instances we find the rare order noun, adj., genitive : *Odes* 1. 19. 1 *mater saeva cupidinum* (see note *ad loc.*); 2. 13. 23 *sedesque discriptas piorum* (see note *ad loc.*); 2. 17. 18, 19 *pars violentior | natalis horae* (see note *ad loc.*); 3. 4. 61 *qui rore puro Castaliae lavit | crinis solutos* (see note *ad loc.*); 3. 5. 13 *hoc caverat mens provida Reguli* (see note *ad loc.*); 3. 15. 15 *flos purpureus rosae* (see note *ad loc.*); 4. 7. 19 *cuncta manus avidas fugient heredis* (see note *ad loc.*); 4. 14. 43 *o tutela praesens | Italiae*. Add, perhaps, *Odes* 1. 3. 1. See too § 52 *ad fin.*

§ 45. A few cases occur in which the noun and adjective form together a quasi-compound noun, and the genitive therefore only appears to stand outside. For prose compare Livy 34. 9. 6 *pars-tertia civium*, and Cicero *Verr. II.* 4. 48. 107 *omni tempore-anni* (though this might be included under § 35). In the *Odes* we find the following parallels : 1. 13. 16 *quinta-parte sui nectaris* (but see also § 35); 1. 18. 14 *caecus amor-sui*; 2. 15. 6 *omnis copia-narium* (see also § 35); 2. 17. 18 *pars-violentior | natalis horae* (but this instance should rather be included under § 44 above); 3. 30. 6 *multaque-pars mei* (see also § 35).

§ 46. The normal order adj., complement, noun, or noun, complement, adj. is frequently varied by the intrusion of a verb. Compare Cicero *De Off.* 1. 32. 118 *rectam vitae secuti sunt viam* ; Livy 1. 34. 8 (*aquila*) *suspensis demissa leniter alis*. In the *Odes* and *Epodes* are the following examples : (*a*) with a single verb intrusive, 1. 8. 10 *livida gestat armis bracchia*; 1. 12. 9, 10, 1. 12. 11, 12, 1. 13. 2, 3, 1. 18. 8, 1. 24. 14, 1. 28. 19, 2. 9. 18, 19, 2. 12. 3, 4, 2. 13. 16, 2. 13. 35, 36, 2. 14. 15, 16, 2. 16. 23, 2. 17. 24, 25, 2. 18. 23, 24, 2. 19. 22, 3. 5. 39, 40, 3. 6. 13, 14, 3. 10. 9, 3. 17. 7, 8 3. 21. 19, 20, 3. 27. 18, 19, 3. 27. 59, 60, 4. 2. 2, 3, 4. 4. 46, 47, 4. 6. 15, 16, 4. 9. 13, 14, 4. 11. 15, 16, 4. 12. 7, 8, 4. 12. 14, *Epod.* 3. 11, 3. 15, 5. 13, 14, 16. 66, 17. 44; (*b*) with two or more intrusive words, 1. 3. 30 *nova febrium | terris incubuit cohors* ; 1. 4. 7 *gravis Cyclopum | Volcanus ardens visit officinas* ; 1. 17. 15 *benigno | ruris honorum opulenta cornu* ; 1. 29. 1, 2 *beatis nunc Arabum invides gazis* ; 3. 10. 10 *ne currente retro funis eat rota* (see note *ad loc.*); 4. 1. 1 *intermissa, Venus, diu rursus bella moves ?* ; . 4. 1. 8 *quo blandae iuvenum te revocant preces* ; 4. 3. 14 *inter amabilis | vatum ponere me choros* ; 4. 12. 7 *barbaras | regum est ulta libidines* ; *Epod.* 15. 9 *intonsosque agitaret Apollinis aura capillos*; 17. 31 *atro delibutus Hercules | Nessi cruore* (see note *ad loc.*).

§ 47. A complement may stand outside the noun and epithet if the latter be of such a kind as to make us expect the occurrence of a complement. This is common in prose e.g. Livy 36. 10. 7 *urbis sitae in plano*, and *passim*. In the *Odes* and *Epodes* the following cases occur : 1. 3. 1 *diva potens Cypri* (see too § 44); 1. 9. 23 *pignusque dereptum lacertis*; 1. 17. 27 *haerentem coronam | crinibus*; 1. 27. 20 *digne puer meliore flamma*; 1. 28. 8 *Tithonusque remotus in auras*; 1. 35. 29 *iturum Caesarem in ultimos Britannos*; 2. 1. 7 *per ignis suppositos cineri*; 2. 2. 7 *pinna metuente solvi*; 2. 5. 3 *tauri ruentis | in venerem*; 2. 5. 23 *discrimen obscurum solutis | crinibus*; 2. 11. 5 *poscentis aevi pauca*; 2. 13. 11 *te caducum | in domini caput*; 2. 17. 27 *truncus illapsus cerebro*; 3. 5. 3 *adiectis Britannis | imperio*; 3. 5. 14 *Reguli | dissentientis condicionibus* ; 3. 5. 15 *exemplo trahenti* (?) *| perniciem* ; 3. 7. 17 *paene datum Pelea Tartaro* ; 3. 8. 3 *positusquę carbo in | caespite vivo* ; 3. 8. 10 *corticem adstrictum pice dimovebit* ; 3. 10. 11 *Penelopen difficilem procis* ; 3. 14. 15 *tenente | Caesare terras* ; 3. 26. 10 *Memphin carentem Sithonia nive*; 3. 29. 10 *molem propinquam nubibus* ; 3. 29. 35 *fluminis... | delabentis Etruscum | in mare*; 4. 5. 33 *mero | defuso pateris* ; 4. 9. 11 *commissi calores | Aeoliae fidibus puellae* ; 4. 14. 22 *choro scindente nubes* ; *Epod.* 2. 20 *certantem et uvam purpurae* ; 2. 60 *haedus ereptus lupo* ; 6. 6. *amica vis pastoribus* ; 6. 14 *acer hostis Bupalo* ; 9. 1 *repostum Caecubum ad festas dapes* ; 17. 67 *Prometheus obligatus aliti*.

§ 48. Again, in prose, if one complement is already placed between the noun and epithet, a second or third complement may lie outside, e.g. Livy 21. 52. 6 *nimium cultorum fidem in Romanos* ; 3. 40. 3 *foederis nefarie icti cum collegis*, and *passim*. This order is a commonplace in Greek e.g. αἱ ἐν τῷ λιμένι νῆες ὁρμοῦσαι. In the *Odes* and *Epodes* I find the following examples : 1. 1. 31 *Nympharumque leves cum Satyris chori*; 1. 4. 6 *iunctaeque Nymphis Gratiae decentes* (see also § 34); 1. 6. 5 *gravem | Pelidae stomachum cedere nescii* ; 1. 6. 15 *aut ope Palladis | Tydiden superis parem* ; 1. 21. 11 *insignemque pharetra | fraternaque umerum lyra* ; 1. 25. 11 *Thracio bacchante magis sub inter-lunia vento* ; 1. 28. 16 *et calcanda semel via leti* ; 2. 19. 13

beatae coniugis additum | stellis honorem; 2. 19. 14 *tectaque Penthei | disiecta non leni ruina*; 3. 5. 22 *retorta tergo bracchia libero* (see too § 17); 3. 8. 11 *amphorae fumum bibere institutae | consule Tullo*; 3. 10. 14 *nec tinctus viola pallor amantium*; 3. 12. 10 *per apertum fugientis agitato | grege cervos*; 3. 16. 6 *Acrisium virginis abditae custodem pavidum*; 3. 29. 20 *sole dies referente siccos*; 3. 29. 33 *fluminis... | cum pace delabentis Etruscum | in mare* (see also § 47); 4. 4. 27 *Augusti paternus | in pueros animus Nerones*; 4. 14. 11 *arces | Alpibus impositas tremendis*; 4. 14. 18 *devota morti pectora liberae* (see also § 17); 4. 15. 8 *vacuum duellis | Ianum Quirini*; 4. 15. 29 *virtute functos more patrum duces*; *Epod.* 4. 17 *tot ora navium gravi | rostrata duci pondere* (see note *ad loc.*); 5. 23 *et ossa ab ore rapta ieiunae canis*; 5. 69 *indormit unctis omnium cubilibus | oblivione paelicum*; 7. 19 *Remi | sacer nepotibus cruor*; 12. 10 *colorque | stercore fucatus crocodili.* But see also §§ 14, 16, 17, and 24.

§ 49. In the following instances the complement stands abnormally outside. Almost always there is a special reason for divergence from the regular order. See *Odes* 1. 1. 23 *lituo tubae | permixtus sonitus* (compare *Odes* 4. 1. 22 quoted in § 43); 1. 2. 23 *audiet pugnas vitio parentum | rara iuventus* (perhaps a case of *coniunctio* as at 1. 12. 29, 2. 2. 6, 2. 18. 38, 3. 2. 4, *Epod.* 4. 9, 5. 45, 13. 18, 15. 7, 16. 19); 1. 6. 14 *aut pulvere Troico | nigrum Merionen*; 1. 7. 3 *vel Baccho Thebas vel Apolline Delphos | insignis*; 1. 7. 25 *melior fortuna parente*; 1. 28. 9 *et Iovis arcanis Minos admissus*; 1. 37. 13 *una sospes navis ab ignibus*; 1. 37. 14 *mentemque lymphatam Mareotico*; 2. 2. 6 *notus in fratres animi paterni* (see on 1. 2. 23 quoted above); 2. 5. 23 *discrimen obscurum solutis | crinibus ambiguoque vultu*; 2. 18. 38 *hic levare functum | pauperem laboribus | vocatus* (see on 1. 2. 23 quoted above); 3. 3. 52 *omne sacrum rapiente dextra*; 3. 4. 26 *versa acies retro* (compare 4. 1. 1 and *Epod.* 5. 80, both cited below); 3. 6. 19 *hoc fonte derivata clades*; 3. 17. 11 *demissa tempestas ab Euro* (see § 34 *ad fin.*); 3. 24. 1 *intactis opulentior | thesauris Arabum* (see also § 24); 3. 24. 38 *nec Boreae finitimum latus*; 3. 25. 11, 12 *pede barbaro | lustratam Rhodopen*; 3. 30. 14 *sume superbiam | quaesitam meritis*; 4. 1. 1 *intermissa Venus diu* (?); 4. 6. 10 *pinus aut impulsa cupressus Euro* (compare 3. 17. 11 quoted above, and see § 34 *ad fin.*); *Epod.* 2. 20 *certantem et uvam purpurae* (but see rather § 47); 3. 3 *edit cicutis alium nocentius*; 5. 17 *sepulcris caprificos erutas*; 5. 49 *o rebus meis | non infideles arbitrae*; 5. 65 *cum palla, tabo munus imbutum, novam | incendio nuptam abstulit*; 5. 80 *tellure porrecta super* (compare 3. 4. 26 quoted above); 9. 1 *repostum Caecubum ad festas dapes* (but see rather § 47); 14. 7 *inceptos, olim promissum carmen, iambos*; 16. 6 *novisque rebus infidelis Allobrox*; 16. 8 *parentibusque abominatus Hannibal*; 16. 19 *habitandaque fana | apris reliquit*; 17. 62 *sed tardiora fata te votis manent* (?). See also § 43, and § 47, and the note on *Odes* 3. 1. 24.

§ 50. (*a*) Words may lie between epithet and noun while they belong ἀπὸ κοινοῦ to the verb. Such an order is common in prose and poetry. Compare Pliny 4. 13 *quia nullos hic praeceptores habemus* i.e. 'because we have here (*hic habemus*) no local (*nullos hic*) teachers'; Catullus 3. 17 *tua nunc opera meae puellae | flendo turgiduli rubent ocelli*; Ovid *Fast.* 2. 406 *Hi redeunt udis in sua tecta genis*; Vergil *Aen.* 2. 58 *iuvenem...pastores magno ad regem clamore trahebant*; *ib.* 9. 214 *aterque ad sidera fumus | erigitur*; Livy 22. 1. 11 *nuntiant...cruentas in corbem spicas cecidisse* (?).

Similar examples in Horace are *Odes* 2. 7. 6 *morantem saepe diem mero | fregi*; 3. 17. 2 *priores hinc Lamias ferunt | denominatos*; 3. 29. 48 *quod fugiens semel hora vexit*; *Epod.* 12. 20 *nova collibus arbor inhaeret*; 17. 37 *iussas cum fide poenas luam*; 17. 63 *ingrata misero vita ducenda est.*

(*b*) In the following cases the pause at the end of the line prevents us from feeling that an apparent complement belongs to the words between which it lies: *Odes* 1. 4. 19 *iuventus | nunc omnis*; 1. 12. 27 *alba nautis | stella refulsit*; 1. 12. 31

minax...ponto | *unda recumbit*; 1. 17. 3 *defendit aestatem capellis* | *usque meis*; 1. 27. 16 *ingenuoque semper* | *amore peccas*; 2. 9. 17 *desine mollium* | *tandem querellarum* (see, however, *Epod.* 17. 6 quoted in subdivision (*c*) below); 3. 8. 7 *album* | *Libero caprum*; 4. 3. 1 *quem tu, Melpomene, semel* | *nascentem placido lumine videris*; 4. 7. 3 *decrescentia ripas* | *flumina praetereunt*; 4. 8. 14 *per quae spiritus et vita redit bonis* | *post mortem ducibus*; 4. 11. 35 *minuentur atrae* | *carmine curae*; *Epod.* 5. 65 *cum palla... novam* (v.l. *nova*) | *incendio nuptam abstulit.*

(*c*) Where the noun comes first, it is obvious that the complement is less hemmed in. This fact may justify the following: *Odes* 1. 10. 13 *quin et Atridas duce te superbos* | *Ilio dives Priamus relicto...fefellit*; 1. 24. 16 (*imagini*) *quam virga semel horrida* | *nigro compulerit Mercurius gregi*; 3. 19. 9 *da lunae propere novae*; 3. 26. 11 *sublimi flagello* | *tange Chloen semel arrogantem*; 4. 1. 26 *numen cum teneris virginibus tuum*; 4. 12. 27 *misce stultitiam consiliis brevem*; *Epod.* 17. 6 *Canidia parce vocibus tandem sacris* (contrast *Odes* 2. 9. 17 quoted in subdivision (*b*) above).

(*d*) A few cases are the accidental result of other forms of grouping e.g. *Odes* 1. 17. 1 *Velox amoenum saepe Lucretilem* | *mutat Lycaeo Faunus* (see § 10); 2. 5. 18 *Chloris albo sic umero nitens* (see note *ad loc.*); 4. 1. 19 *Albanos prope te lacus* | *ponet marmoream* (see note *ad loc.*, and § 17); *Epod.* 2. 13 *inutilisve falce ramos amputans* (see note *ad loc.*); 6. 7 *agam per altas aure sublata nives* (see note *ad loc.*, and § 15).

(*e*) Three cases are doubtful viz. *Odes* 1. 30. 5 *fervidus tecum puer*; 4. 1. 1 *intermissa Venus diu* | *rursus bella moves* (see also § 49); *Epod.* 2. 25 *altis interim ripis.*

(*f*) One instance *Odes* 1. 2. 49 *hic magnos potius triumphos* is paralleled by Livy *Pref.* § 13 *cum bonis potius ominibus.* In the Livian passage there is undoubted stress on *bonis*; perhaps too there is stress on Horace's *magnos.*

(*g*) Although the *Odes* and *Epodes* provide no parallel*, I may be allowed to refer to two examples in Vergil viz. *Aen.* 2. 153 *sustulit exutas vinclis ad sidera palmas*, and 6. 847 *excudent alii spirantia mollius aera.* In such cases the previous occurrence of the verb makes the order of the adverb or adverb-phrase much less harsh.

§ 51. In Latin prose, if a transitive verb has a personal object and an abstract or non-personal subject, the personal object is frequently put first. Compare Livy *Pref.* § 11 *nisi me amor negotii suscepti fallit*, and *passim* (see my 'More Latin and English Idiom,' Appendix A). Examples are numerous in Horace e.g. *Odes* 1. 1. 23 *multos castra iuvant*; 1. 1. 29 *me...hederae...dis miscent*; 1. 2. 47 *neve te...aura tollat*; 1. 4. 16 *iam te premet nox*; 1. 5. 13 *me...paries indicat*; 1. 7. 10 *me...percussit campus*; 1. 7. 19 *seu te...castra tenent*; 1. 7. 25 *nos...feret...fortuna*; 1. 12. 41 *hunc...tulit... paupertas*; 1. 16. 22 *me...temptavit...fervor*; 1. 24. 5 *Quintilium...sopor urget*; 1. 28. 1 *te...cohibent...munera*; 1. 28. 15 *omnis una manet nox*; 1. 28. 21 *me...Notus obruit*; 1. 28. 34 *teque piacula nulla resolvent*; 1. 31. 15 *me pascunt olivae*; 2. 2. 7 *illum aget pinna*; 2. 5. 22 *sagacis falleret...discrimen*; 2. 7. 15 *te...unda tulit*; 2. 17. 13 *me...spiritus...divellet*; 2. 17. 22 *te Iovis...tutela...eripuit*; 3. 1. 25 *desiderantem... sollicitat mare*; 3. 1. 41 *dolentem...delenit usus*; 3. 3. 1 *virum...ardor...quatit*; 3. 4. 5 *me ludit...insania*; 3. 4. 26 *non me...exstinxit arbor*; 3. 10. 13 *te...pallor...curvat*; 3. 13. 9 *te...hora...nescit tangere*; 3. 15. 11 *illam cogit amor*; 3. 15. 13 *te lanae... decent*; 3. 16. 1 *Danaën turris...munierat*; 3. 19. 28 *me...torret amor*; 3. 27. 1 *impios... omen ducat*; 3. 27. 61 *te rupes...delectant*; 3. 29. 62 *me...aura feret*; 4. 7. 23 *te facundia ...restituet*; 4. 8. 25 *Aeacum virtus...consecrat*; 4. 13. 11 *te quia rugae turpant*; *Epod.* 1. 31 *me benignitas tua ditavit*; 11. 9 *amantem languor...arguit*; 13. 13 *te manet tellus*; 15. 21 *te Pythagorae fallant arcana.*

In many of these instances there is special reason for bringing forward the pronoun. See the notes in each case.

* See, however, *Epist.* 2. 1. 33 and *A.P.* 209.

§ 52. Often, at least in poetry*, we find an adjective set next to a noun with which it is not in grammatical agreement, and yet, obviously, qualifying this noun as well as the other noun with which it agrees grammatically. Vergil provides many instances e.g. *Georg.* 4. 438 *vix defessa senem passus componere membra*, where *defessa* belongs equally to *senem* and *membra*; *Aen.* 4. 154 *agmina cervi | pulverulenta fuga glomerant*, and *Aen.* 12. 742 *ergo amens diversa fuga petit aequora Turnus*.

There are not a few examples of this quasi-hypallage in Horace's *Odes* and *Epodes*. The first case is *Odes* 1. 3. 40 (*neque...patimur*)...*iracunda Iovem ponere fulmina*, where *iracunda* belongs in sense to *Iovem* and in grammar to *fulmina*.

Other examples are *Odes* 1. 4. 4 *nec prata canis albicant pruinis* (i.e. *canis* also with *prata*; but see too § 21); 1. 4. 7 *gravis* also with *Cyclopum*; 1. 7. 11 *opimae* also with *campus*; 1. 16. 11 *tremendo* also with *Iuppiter*; 1. 22. 7 *fabulosus* also with *loca*; 1. 28. 11 *Troiana* also with *clipeo*; 1. 35. 1 *gratum* also with *diva* (?); 1. 35. 34 *dura* also with *nos*; 1. 37. 7 *dementis* also with *regina* (?); 1. 37. 18 *citus* also with *leporem*; 1. 37. 19 *nivalis* also with *campis*; 2. 3. 14 *amoenae* also with *flores*; 2. 6. 5 *Argeo* also with *Tibur*; 3. 1. 42 *clarior* also with *purpurarum*; 3. 3. 59 *avitae* also with *tecta*; 3. 6. 38 *Sabellis* also with *proles*; 3. 7. 30 *querulae* also with *cantu*; 3. 19. 20 *tacita* also with *fistula*; 3. 21. 19, 20 *iratos* also with *regum*; 3. 24. 10 *vagas* also with *plaustra*; 3. 24. 44 *arduae* also with *viam*; 3. 29. 1 *Tyrrhena* also with *regum*; 4. 1. 1 *intermissa* with *Venus* and *bella*; 4. 1. 39 *Martii* also with *gramina* (?); 4. 5. 9 *invido* also with *Notus*; 4. 5. 27 *ferae* also with *bellum*; 4. 7. 21 *splendida* also with *Minos*; *Epod.* 2. 5 *truci* also with *miles*; 4. 17, 18 *gravi* also with *navium*; 13. 16 *caerula* also with *domum* (?); 16. 30 *nova* with *monstra* as well as with *libidine* (?). Perhaps *Odes* 1. 19. 1, 2. 13. 23, 3. 15. 15, and *Epod.* 10. 5 may come under this section.

§ 53. At *Odes* 1. 2. 51 *neu sinas Medos equitare inultos | te duce, Caesar* the sentence is constructionally complete at *equitare*. All that follows is of added interest, i.e. '—unpunished—with you to lead—a Caesar!' For this crescendo effect compare Livy 34. 4. 5 *ego hos malo propitios deos* i.e. 'I prefer these, because they bring blessing (and not harm) and because they are gods (and not mere works of art)'; *ib.* 5. 2 *vir gravissimus, consul, M. Porcius*. See too Cicero *Pro Caec.* 9. 28.

For examples in the *Odes*, C. S., and *Epodes* compare *Odes* 1. 1. 16, 17, 1. 2. 19, 1. 3. 13, 1. 4. 5, 1. 5. 5, 1. 5. 9, 1. 5. 11, 1. 6. 2, 1. 6. 19, 1. 7. 27, 1. 7. 31, 1. 8. 4, 1. 8. 11, 12, 1. 8. 14, 1. 9. 18, 1. 12. 38, 1. 12. 48, 1. 12. 54, 1. 15. 2, 1. 15. 28, 1. 15. 32, 1. 17. 4, 1. 17. 6, 1. 17. 22, 1. 18. 16, 1. 19. 6, 1. 22. 12, 1. 25. 15, 1. 25. 16, 1. 28. 27, 1. 29. 3, 1. 29. 10, 1. 31. 8, 1. 31. 15, 1. 32. 16, 1. 33. 15, 1. 34. 14, 1. 35. 4, 1. 35. 28, 1. 37. 6, 1. 37. 9–11, 1. 37. 26, 1. 38. 6 (?), 2. 1. 8, 2. 1. 24, 2. 1. 28, 2. 1. 40, 2. 2. 2, 2. 3. 5, 2. 3. 8, 2. 3. 24, 2. 3. 27, 2. 4. 7, 2. 7. 7, 2. 7. 28, 2. 8. 7, 2. 8. 16, 2. 8. 20, 2. 11. 2, 3, 2. 11. 20, 2. 11. 23, 24, 2. 14. 12, 2. 14. 26, 2. 15. 8, 2. 16. 23, 2. 18. 36, 2. 19. 29, 3. 1. 7, 3. 2. 17, 3. 2. 20, 3. 2. 24, 3. 4. 20, 3. 5. 9, 3. 5. 10–12, 3. 5. 28, 3. 6. 27, 28, 3. 6. 44, 3. 6. 47, 3. 7. 3–5, 3. 7. 26, 3. 8. 7, 8, 3. 8. 12, 3. 9. 3, 3. 11. 2 (contrast 3. 11. 20), 3. 13. 14, 3. 14. 28, 3. 16. 8, 3. 16. 10, 11, 3. 16. 12, 3. 16. 15, 3. 17. 9, 3. 19. 9, 3. 21. 6, 3. 21. 14, 3. 23. 20, 3. 24. 14, 3. 24. 30, 3. 25. 1, 3. 25. 3, 3. 25. 20, 3. 27. 12, 3. 27. 36, 3. 27. 66, 3. 30. 8, 4. 1. 20, 4. 1. 39, 4. 3. 23, 4. 4. 3, 4, 4. 4. 28, 4. 4. 72, 4. 5. 24, 4. 5. 27, 4. 6. 34 (?), 4. 6. 43, 44, 4. 8. 23, 24, 4. 9. 4, 4. 9. 23, 4. 9. 26, 4. 12. 4, 4. 12. 28, 4. 14. 13, 4. 14. 32, C. S. 43, 44, *Epod.* 1. 21, 2. 4, 4. 12, 4. 20, 5. 58, 59, 5. 87, 88, 5. 93, 5. 98, 7. 12, 9. 8, 9. 9, 9. 10, 11. 2, 11. 16, 17, 12. 3.

* For Livy's use of hypallage see Weissenborn-Müller on 1. 1. 4 *maiora rerum initia*.

HORACE

ODES
CARMEN SECULARE
EPODES

ODES

BOOK I

I.

Maecenas atavis edite regibus,
o et praesidium et dulce decus meum :
sunt quos curriculo pulverem Olympicum
collegisse iuvat metaque fervidis
evitata rotis palmaque nobilis   5
terrarum dominos evehit ad deos :
hunc, si mobilium turba Quiritium

In these notes (*p*) = preposited, (*s*) = separated, (*ps*) = preposited and separated, (*pp*) = postposited, (*pps*) = postposited and separated, (P.) = Prolegomena.

I. 1. regibus equals *regiis* (*s*); it is emphatic and predicative i.e. 'sprung from forbears *that were royal.*' Compare *Odes* 4. 5. 1 *Divis orte bonis* and Cic. *De Off.* 1. 32. 116 (*ad fin.*) *obscuris orti maioribus.* It should be observed that *regibus edite* would scan equally well. Horace, of course, may have desired to avoid three final s's in succession. See too P. 24.

For the intervening vocative see on *Odes* 1. 5. 3.

2. dulce decus meum : *decus* stands between the two epithets. See P. 34.

4, 5. metaque fervidis | evitata rotis : for the grouping see P. 14.

6. terrarum (*p*): lords of *this* world, they feel that they are equals of the *heavenly* beings (*ad deos* last). The order seems to support the view that *terrarum dominos* belongs to *quos* and not to *deos*. The stress on *terrarum* is not appropriate to the gods; they are rather 'lords of heaven' as Catullus calls them 68. 36. (76) *caelestes pacificasset eros*, or 'lords of the universe' as in Ovid *Ex Ponto* 2. 2. 12 *in rerum dominos movimus arma deos* (for the frequent position of *rerum* see P. 42). In *Ex Ponto* 2. 8. 26 *terrarum dominum quem sua cura facit* Augustus is fittingly called 'lord of this world, while *ib.* 1. 9. 35, 36 *nam tua non alio coluit penetralia ritu | terrarum dominos quam colis ipse deos* does not prove that *terrarum dominos* refers to *deos*, since the lines may mean 'Celsus honoured you no less than you honour these *earthly* lords (especially the emperor) as if they were gods' (note particularly l. 49 *quem tu pro numine vivus habebas*).

For *evehit ad deos* compare *Odes* 4. 2. 17, and Juvenal 1. 38.

7. hunc : note the contrasted persons placed early—*illum* l. 9, *gaudentem* l. 11, *multos* l. 23.

certat tergeminis tollere honoribus ;
illum, si proprio condidit horreo
quicquid de Libycis verritur areis.   10
gaudentem patrios findere sarculo
agros Attalicis condicionibus
numquam demoveas, ut trabe Cypria
Myrtoum pavidus nauta secet mare;
luctantem Icariis fluctibus Africum   15
mercator metuens otium et oppidi
laudat rura sui: mox reficit rates
quassas, indocilis pauperiem pati.

7, 8. **mobilium** (*ps*) equals '*though* fickle, they yet give him *all three* offices,' *tergeminis* (*ps*). But the order *mobilium turba Quiritium* is frequent (see P. 19 and 20a); and so is the grouping *tergeminis tollere honoribus* (see P. 21).

9. **proprio** (*ps*) i.e. all his own, not shared in partnership nor owned by the government. Compare *privatis Odes* 2. 15. 15, *meis Odes* 3. 16. 27, *Epod.* I. 26, and *suis Epod.* 2. 3. But see too P. 21.

10. **Libycis** (*ps*): the corn comes, not from his own estate, but from *Africa*; also see P. 21.

11. **patrios** (*ps*): this man delights in his *ancestral* farm, however small. Contrast *Libycis...areis* of l. 10, and see on *proprio* l. 9 above.

12. **Attalicis** (*p*): the generic adjective is often, as one would expect, prepositive. See P. 37.

14. **Myrtoum**: perhaps the worst sea in the Mediterranean (cp. *Odes* 4. 5. 9, 10), off Cape Malia, enough to frighten an experienced sailor, much more a novice. One need not be a confirmed believer in Porphyrion's *speciem pro genere ponit*. See on *Odes* I. 35. 7.

For the two adjectives *Myrtoum pavidus* followed by the two nouns in chiastic order see P. 10, and for the collocation of the adjectives see *Odes* I. 5. 9.

mare: single word after the verb, as so often in Livy.

15. **Icariis** (*p*): again the sea is the dangerous Aegean. See too P. 10.

16, 17. **otium et oppidi**: a Roman reads this as 'retirement and town'; for though *oppidi* is genitive, he feels it to be object of *laudat* until *rura* is reached; see P. 38, and P. 20 a.

sui (*s*): the word probably has emphasis; it is an emphatic afterthought (see P. 53)—'this is his own, his native land.' So he thinks on the stormy waters, but soon....

18. **quassas** standing alone at the commencement of the line has stress (see on *Odes* 4. 9. 26). The participle is concessive—'although the storm, now forgotten, had shattered them.'

est qui nec veteris pocula Massici
nec partem solido demere de die   20
spernit, nunc viridi membra sub arbuto
stratus, nunc ad aquae lene caput sacrae.
multos castra iuvant et lituo tubae
permixtus sonitus bellaque matribus
detestata. manet sub Iove frigido   25
venator tenerae coniugis immemor,
seu visa est catulis cerva fidelibus,
seu rupit teretis Marsus aper plagas.
me doctarum hederae praemia frontium

19. **veteris** (*ps*): Massic wine is good, but *old* Massic better. See also
P. 20 β.

20. **partem solido** i.e. 'part from whole' (*solidus* ὅλος); hence the order
of artificial antithesis e.g. *unus omnia* etc. For *solido demere de die* see P. 21.

21. **spernit:** the verb should have stress; see on *Odes* 4. 9. 26.

viridi (*ps*) i.e. 'under the greenery (of the arbutus)'; see P. 27, and on
Odes 4. 8. 33.

22. **stratus:** stretched idly; an important part of the picture; hence the
stress. See on *Odes* 4. 9. 26.

ad aquae lene caput sacrae: for the order see P. 18. It is only a slight
extension of the frequent type *aquae caput sacrae* (see on P. 20 *a*); but
a Roman would read the words as they come—'near water gently springing
(*caput*) at the shrine,' for springs were sacred and had their shrine and altar.

23. **multos castra:** see P. 51 and on l. 7 above.

23, 24. **lituo tubae | permixtus sonitus:** the normal prose order would be
permixtus lituo sonitus tubae (see P. 48), or *permixtus lituo tubae sonitus*.
Horace wishes us to hear both instruments early, as if we had *lituus tubaque*,
with *permixtus sonitus* in apposition. Compare *Odes* 4. 1. 22. For *permixtus*
(*p*), the confusion (of sound) see P. 26, and for *tubae permixtus sonitus*
see P. 49.

25. **manet:** comes first with stress—he stays on and on.

26. **tenerae** (*p*): because she is delicate he ought to have remembered
her. Compare *Odes* I. 21. 1.

coniugis: the word lies between *venator* and *immemor* according to rule
(see on *Odes* I. 7. 29); but, in any case, objective genitives tend to be prepositive (see P. 39).

27. **fidelibus** (*s*): because they have faithfully remained, they have seen
the quarry.

28. **teretis Marsus aper plagas:** for the grouping see on P. 10. The
adjective *teretis* goes closely with *rupit* and may mean either 'because slender,'
or 'though strong.'

29. **me:** for its position see P. 51, and compare l. 30 *me...nemus* (*secernit*).

dis miscent superis, me gelidum nemus 30
Nympharumque leves cum Satyris chori
secernunt populo, si neque tibias
Euterpe cohibet nec Polyhymnia
Lesboum refugit tendere barbiton.
quodsi me lyricis vatibus inseres, 35
sublimi feriam sidera vertice.

II.

Iam satis terris nivis atque dirae
grandinis misit pater et rubente
dextera sacras iaculatus arces
    terruit urbem,

me doctarum: the collocation makes a Roman read thus—'I am among the poets, I, as poet, have the ivy, a poet's reward.'

doctarum hederae praemia frontium: a pretty chiastic grouping; compare *Odes* 3. 9. 14 *Thurini Calais filius Ornyti*. If we look upon the appositional *praemia* as equivalent to an adjective we have the grouping of P. 15.

30. **superis** (*s*): perhaps = the gods of heaven above, i.e. the realm of poetic fancy; not the materialistic *deos* of l. 6, anthropomorphic, endowed with human passions—pride and love of power. But see P. 21.

gelidum (*p*): the coolness (of the glade); see P. 27. The characteristic feature of the *nemus* is coolness, for *nemus* properly means the small open space in which the altar stood, surrounded by trees (*lucus*).

31. **Nympharum**: the word is logical subject and prepares us by its position for the antithesis Satyrs. A Roman reads the line thus: 'Nymphs lightly with Satyrs dancing.' The Nymphs dance lightly though they have awkward Satyrs for partners. Here there are two complements to *leves... chori*, and one complement (*Nympharum*) is placed outside; see P. 48.

32. **populo**: last, with some stress. Horace *odit profanum volgus*.

tibias, preceding the subject, prepares us for the chiastic *barbiton*. The *tibiae* accompany choral odes; the *barbitos* accompanies songs for a private circle.

34. **Lesboum** (*ps*): the order recalls to mind the names of great lyrists such as Alcaeus and Sappho. The stress is echoed in *lyricis* (*p*) of l. 35.

35. **lyricis** (*p*): if you rank me as a mere writer of lyrics (contrast an epic), I shall be more than satisfied.

36. **sublimi** (*ps*): contrast *demisso*. Horace means that instead of being bowed down with shame because he cannot emulate the massive power of a Vergil or a Homer, he lifts up his head aloft in pride at being classed among lyrists.

II. 1. **satis...nivis**: for the separation of the partitive genitive compare

terruit gentis, grave ne rediret   5
saeculum Pyrrhae nova monstra questae,
omne cum Proteus pecus egit altos
    visere montis,

piscium et summa genus haesit ulmo,
nota quae sedes fuerat columbis,   10
et superiecto pavidae natarunt
    aequore dammae.

Odes I. 3. 37, I. 35. 35, *Epod.* 7. 3, 4, 15. 12, and see note on *Epod.* I. 21.
This separation is almost the rule in Livy e.g. I. 12. 1, 3. 49. 8, 3. 58. 8,
4. 53. 13, 21. 8. 5, etc. and 34. 2. 1, 6. 3, 12. 3, 14. 5, 29. 6, etc.

    1, 2. **dirae** (*p*): the terror (of hail); see P. 27 and note on *Odes* 2. 14. 23.
But the adjective may be ἀπὸ κοινοῦ, with both *nivis* and *grandinis*; see
P. 33.

    2. **pater** goes, by *coniunctio*, with *misit* and *terruit*; hence its position.
rubente (*p*): i.e. red flash (of hand); see P. 26.

    3. **sacras** (*ps*) equals 'though sacred to himself.' Compare *Odes* I. 12. 60
fulmina lucis. But see also P. 21.

    4. **urbem** placed after the verb, with stress, in contrast to *gentis*, itself
after its verb. The antithesis is Rome and the empire.

    5. **grave** (*ps*): the position of *grave* makes it quasi-internal with *rediret*,
i.e. 'lest a noxious return should be of Pyrrha's age.' The adjective *gravis* is
frequently used of recurring (note *rediret*) seasons of unhealthy or noxious
kind. The regular phrase for the unwholesome part of the year is *grave
tempus*, with *grave* prepositive; compare Livy 3. 6. 2 *grave tempus*, 3. 8. 1
graviore tempore anni iam circumacto and *passim*. See also note on *Odes*
2. 14. 23.

    6. **nova** i.e. unheard of, horrible; see on *Epod.* 16. 30. This adjective is
almost always prepositive as in *novus homo*. Compare *Odes* I. 14. 1, etc., but
contrast *Odes* I. 7. 29, I. 26. 10, 3. 4. 12, 3. 25. 3, 4. 4. 16, 4. 12. 19.

    7. **omne** (*s*): Proteus could not leave even part of his flock below.
altos (*ps*): not merely 'high mountains,' but, predicative, 'to the top of
the mountains'—ἐς ἄκρα τὰ ὄρη—or 'to the heights (of the mountains)'; see
P. 27 and also P. 21.

    9. **piscium** (*ps*): the order prepares us for the antithesis *columbis*; but
piscium also equals *piscarium*, and the grouping is then that of ll. 11, 12
below; see P. 7 and 12. Moreover *piscium* is logical subject; see on
P. 38.
ulmo: see on *Odes* I. 1. 14 *ad fin.*

    10. **nota** (*ps*): the tree was so high that it had been a *well-known* land-
mark, white with doves.
columbis: last, in antithesis to *piscium* l. 9 above.

    11, 12. **superiecto pavidae natarunt | aequore dammae:** for this important
grouping see P. 7.

vidimus flavum Tiberim retortis
litore Etrusco violenter undis
ire deiectum monumenta regis   15
    templaque Vestae,
Iliae dum se nimium querenti
iactat ultorem, vagus et sinistra
labitur ripa Iove non probante u-
xorius amnis.   20

13. **vidimus:** the verb in this emphatic position equals ἐφορᾶν i.e. 'we have lived to see.' Compare Livy *Pref.* § 5, 1. 46. 8, 6. 34. 10, 21. 53. 5, 34. 7. 5.

flavum (*p*): yellow and therefore flooded. So *Odes* 1. 8. 8 *cur timet flavum (p) Tiberim tangere*, and 2. 3. 18 *villaque flavus quam Tiberis lavit* (see note *ad loc.*). In Vergil *Aen.* 7. 31, as in Ovid *Met.* 14. 447, *flava* seems to refer to the yellow sand stirred up by the swirl and deposited at the mouth of the river. At *Aen.* 9. 816 *flavo* is postposited and *may be* a mere standing epithet : but there is a variant *vasto*, and Vergil would hardly call Tiber *caeruleus* (*Aen.* 8. 64) if *flavus* were the conventional epithet. At *Catal.* 13 (5), 23 the reading is uncertain, but, if *flavum* be read, the context suggests muddy water. The colour of the Tiber is said to vary largely with the colour of the sky. In *Il Piacere*, d'Annunzio, describing a fine May morning in Rome, writes *sul ponte apparve il Tevere lucido*.

14. **violenter** is separated from *retortis* to emphasize the strength and violence of the flood ; perhaps, also, it may be felt adjectively with *undis* cp. Livy's *deinceps reges*, etc.

17. **Iliae dum se:** characteristic early grouping of case relations. Compare Cicero *T. D.* 5. 39. 115 *Polyphemum! Homerus...cum ariete colloquentem facit;* Livy *Pref.* § 9 *ad illa mihi pro se quisque intendat animum.* Note especially *Odes* 1. 22. 9 *me silva lupus*, and add 1. 2. 47, 1. 3. 1, 1. 4. 7, 8, 1. 5. 1, 1. 6. 17, 1. 7. 21 (cp. on 1. 8. 2), 1. 10. 9, 1. 10. 13, 1. 13. 1, 1. 15. 11, 1. 15. 29, 1. 17. 14, 1. 17. 22, 23, 1. 23. 1, 1. 23. 9, 1. 25. 7, 1. 25. 9, 1. 26. 9, 1. 27. 14, 1. 28. 9, 1. 29. 5, 1. 33. 3, 4, 1. 35. 5, 1. 35. 9, 1. 35. 21, 1. 35. 36, 1. 37. 6, 7, 2. 3. 6, 2. 4. 17, 2. 6. 21, 2. 7. 13, 2. 16. 33, 2. 17. 13, 2. 17. 22, 2. 19. 21, 2. 20. 17, 3. 2. 6, 3. 3. 13, 3. 3. 33, 3. 3. 41, 3. 4. 9, 3. 5. 18, 3. 5. 21, 3. 6. 5, 3. 6. 41, 3. 7. 18, 3. 9. 9, 3. 11. 42, 3. 21. 14, 3. 21. 21, 3. 29. 25, 4. 2. 27, 4. 4. 4, 4. 5. 9, 4. 9. 30, 4. 12. 22, 4. 15. 1, *Epod.* 10. 5, 12. 16, 17, 17. 42. For noun (*Iliae*), pronoun (*se*), epithet (*querenti*), epithet (*ultorem*) see P. 16. **nimium** seems to go with both *querenti* and *iactat*.

18. **ultorem, vagus:** why may we not omit the comma at *ultorem* and take *vagus*, as if *vagando*, with *iactat ultorem* i.e. he avenges Ilia by wandering beyond his limits?

sinistra (*ps*): flooding on the *left* bank would affect the forum and interrupt business. But see P. 21.

19. The sentence is grammatically complete at *ripa* ; what follows is an emphatic addendum (see on P. 53) i.e. 'though Jove forbade, because his *wife*

audiet civis acuisse ferrum,
quo graves Persae melius perirent,
audiet pugnas vitio parentum
    rara iuventus.

quem vocet divum populus ruentis   25
imperi rebus? prece qua fatigent
virgines sanctae minus audientem
    carmina Vestam?

cui dabit partis scelus expiandi
Iuppiter? tandem venias precamur   30
nube candentis umeros amictus,
    augur Apollo;

ordered.' Hence *uxorius* is preposited, as if we had *Iove non probante, uxore
iubente.*

21–24. **audiet...audiet pugnas...iuventus:** the inverted sentence and the
repetition of *audiet* make the verb emphatic—they will hear of these things,
but not imitate them.

21. **civis...ferrum:** the separation of *civis* from *ferrum* brings out the
point; citizens (i.e. fellow-citizens) should not arm *contra civis*, but *contra
Persas.*

22. **graves** (*p*): the interest lies in the adjective—the pest consisting of
Persae; see P. 27, and on *Odes* 2. 14. 23.

If *melius* had been placed next to *quo*, the meaning would have been 'in
order that the Persae might more easily perish.' In its present position the
construction is *quo* (with which) *melius esset* (it would have been better) *si
Persae perirent* (if the Persae had been perishing).

23. **vitio parentum:** the phrase, perhaps, goes with both *pugnas* and *rara.*
The civil wars were due to the crimes of their fathers, and so was the reduced
population. If Horace had not wished the words *vitio parentum* to be heard
with both *pugnas* and *rara,* he would not have abandoned the normal order
rara vitio parentum iuventus. See P. 49.

24. **rara** (*p*): the *iuventus* of Rome should have been *frequens.*

25. **quem...divum:** if *divum* be genitive plural, compare l. 1 above for
the separation; if accusative, there is slight stress, contrast *hominem*; but
see on *prece qua* l. 26.

ruentis (*p*): the *imperium* should *stare.*

26. **imperi** (*p*): see P. 38.

prece qua: emphatic for *qua prece*—the people 'call,' the holy Virgins
'pray,' and are instant in prayer; hence *fatigent* comes early. Perhaps *vocet*
is brought forward to prepare us for the antithesis. Compare *Odes* I. 29. 7.

30. **Iuppiter** has stress (see on *Odes* 4. 9. 26) i.e. Great Juppiter.

31. **candentis** (*p*): the word is preposited to bring it next to the antithetical *nube.*

sive tu mavis, Erycina ridens,
quam Iocus circum volat et Cupido;
sive neglectum genus et nepotes   35
    respicis auctor,

heu nimis longo satiate ludo,
quem iuvat clamor galeaeque leves,
acer et Mauri peditis cruentum
    vultus in hostem;   40

sive mutata iuvenem figura
ales in terris imitaris, almae
filius Maiae, patiens vocari
    Caesaris ultor:

serus in caelum redeas diuque   45
laetus intersis populo Quirini,
neve te nostris vitiis iniquum
    ocior aura

33. **Erycina ridens:** see on P. 36.

34. **volat:** note the position by *coniunctio*; *circum volat* is practically one word.

35. **neglectum** (*p*): Mars had abandoned his offspring, Romulus and Remus, at the outset of Rome's history, and he abandons them again, although responsible for their existence (*auctor*); hence *auctor* comes last in l. 36.

37. **longo** (*s*): the position gives additional point to *ludo* when we hear it. Mars is watching 'games' and these—*mirabile dictu*—are 'too long.' But see P. 24.

39. **acer et Mauri peditis...vultus:** for the grouping see P. 10.

cruentum (*ps*) has stress. As Bentley says, the *Mauri* were not *fortes*; but they can scowl at a bleeding (fallen) foeman. This position of *cruentum* perhaps makes *Marsi* a less probable emendation. The word *peditis* might mean that the Maurian has dismounted.

41. **mutata iuvenem figura:** for the order see on *Odes* I. 10. 14. Compare too on *Odes* 3. 2. 32.

42. **ales in terris:** an angel, as it were, on earth.

almae (*ps*): nurturing like a kindly mother, not destroying like Mars. See also P. 20 a.

44. **Caesaris** (*p*): perhaps equals 'Great Caesar'; compare *Odes* I. 37. 16.

45. **serus** is predicative.

redeas: for the *re-* compare ἀπό in ἀποθέωσις.

diu goes with both *laetus* and *intersis*.

47. **te:** for its position see P. 51.

nostris (*p*): the order brings out the antithesis, and case relations come early; see *Odes* I. 2. 17.

tollat; hic magnos potius triumphos,
hic ames dici pater atque princeps,   50
neu sinas Medos equitare inultos,
    te duce, Caesar.

III.

Sic te diva potens Cypri,
    sic fratres Helenae, lucida sidera,
ventorumque regat pater
    obstrictis aliis praeter Iapyga,
navis, quae tibi creditum   5
    debes Vergilium, finibus Atticis
reddas incolumem precor
    et serves animae dimidium meae.

48. **ocior** (*p*) i.e. 'all too swift': comparatives are naturally prepositive; see P. 28.

49. **tollat** has stress; contrast *hic*. See on *Odes* 4. 9. 26.

potius is emphasized by separation from *hic*. See P. 50 *f*.

51, 52. **inultos** | …**Caesar:** for these emphatic addenda see P. 53.

52. **te duce:** Horace writes an ablative absolute as if *ne Medi equitent* had preceded.

III. 1. **te diva:** see on *Odes* I. 2. 17.

potens Cypri: *Cypri* may stand outside *diva potens* because we still wait for an object; see P. 47. On the other hand objective genitives more often precede (see P. 39), and it is hard to see why Horace should not have written *diva Cypri potens*. See too P. 44.

2. **lucida** (*p*): perhaps equals 'not obscured by storm.' Wickham, Gow, and others, in view of Pliny *N.H.* 2. 101 (ch. XXXVII) and Statius *Silv.* 3. 2. 8, see a reference to St Elmo's fire; but the stars Castor and Pollux may be meant. These rise in front of the Lion, and are brilliant objects in the evening sky from January to April i.e. during most of the stormy months. To pray that they may be bright is to pray for fine weather at such a time. See on *Odes* I. 12. 27, 3. 29. 64, and 4. 8. 31. Had Vergil been travelling in the summer, Horace would scarcely have been so anxious. Compare too *Odes* 4. 14. 21.

3. **ventorum** (*ps*) equals 'and as for winds may their father...'; see P. 40. The word *ventorum* is brought close to *sidera* in artificial antithesis.

5, 6. **quae tibi creditum** | **debes:** the sentence may be felt as complete at *debes*, for *creditum* can be quasi-substantival (τὴν παρακαταθήκην); this gives *Vergilium* some emphasis—'even Vergil.' But see also P. 21.

7. **incolumem:** predicative.

8. **animae dimidium meae:** for the grouping see P. 19 and 20 *a*.

illi robur et aes triplex
    circa pectus erat, qui fragilem truci   10
commisit pelago ratem
    primus, nec timuit praecipitem Africum
decertantem Aquilonibus,
    nec tristis Hyadas, nec rabiem Noti,
quo non arbiter Hadriae   15
    maior, tollere seu ponere vult freta.
quem mortis timuit gradum,
    qui siccis oculis monstra natantia,
qui vidit mare turbidum et
    infamis scopulos Acroceraunia?   20
nequicquam deus abscidit
    prudens Oceano dissociabili
terras, si tamen impiae
    non tangenda rates transiliunt vada.

10, 11. **fragilem truci | commisit pelago ratem:** for the grouping see P. 8. Note the happy juxtaposition of weakness (*fragilem*) and violence (*truci*), of open sea (*pelago*) and a tiny boat (*ratem*).

12. **primus:** emphatic because it comes late ; its normal position would be immediately after *qui*. See too on *Odes* 4. 9. 26.

praecipitem (*p*): as if we had *praecipitationem Africi*, like *rabiem Noti* of l. 14 below. So in l. 14 *tristis Hyadas* equals *tristitiam Hyadum*. See on P. 27.

13. **decertantem Aquilonibus:** these words are emphatic addenda— 'engaged in a death struggle with the North wind.' See on P. 53.

14. **tristis** (*p*): see l. 12 above, and also on *Odes* 2. 14. 23.

16. **maior:** for stress see on *Odes* 4. 9. 26.

freta: see on *Odes* 1. 1. 14 *ad fin.* Especially common is an iambus or pyrrhic in this position.

17. **mortis** (*ps*): see on P. 38. But there is great stress on *mortis*—even Death had no terrors for him.

gradum: see on *freta* l. 16 above.

18. **siccis** (*p*): Greek would express the emphasis by ξηροῖς καὶ οὐ νοτεροῖς ὄμμασιν.

19. **turbidum et:** for the position of *et* compare on *Odes* 1. 35. 39.

20. **infamis** (*p*): see on *Odes* 2. 14. 23.

21. **nequicquam** is emphatic by separation from the verb.

22. **prudens** is predicative sc. ὤν—'in his providence.'

23. **terras** has stress; see on *Odes* 4. 9. 26. Contrast *Oceano* l. 22 and *vada* l. 24.

23, 24. **impiae | non tangenda rates transiliunt vada:** for the grouping

audax omnia perpeti   25
     gens humana ruit per vetitum nefas:
audax Iapeti genus
     ignem fraude mala gentibus intulit;
post ignem aetheria domo
     subductum macies et nova febrium   30
terris incubuit cohors,
     semotique prius tarda necessitas
leti corripuit gradum.
     expertus vacuum Daedalus aera
pennis non homini datis;   35
     perrupit Acheronta Herculeus labor.
nil mortalibus ardui est:
     caelum ipsum petimus stultitia, neque

see P. 9. As in ll. 10, 11 there is happy juxtaposition—the impious invade the inviolable, the tiny boats the dangerous shoals.

     25. **audax** sc. οὖσα.

     26. **per vetitum** (*p*): (breaks) through the barrier (to sin); see P. 26.

     27. **Iapeti** (*p*) **genus**: see P. 41.

     29. **ignem aetheria**: the adjective is placed in front of *domo* to bring *ignem* and *aetheria* together, as if 'fire from heaven.' The *aether* is the home of celestial fires.

     30, 31. **nova febrium | ...cohors**: for the order with intrusive words see on P. 46 *b*.

     32, 33. **semotique prius tarda necessitas | leti**: for the grouping see on P. 10. A Roman reads it thus: 'far-removed before and slow, the doom of death now hastened its steps.' The adjectives are predicative i.e. 'though far-removed' and 'though slow before.'

     prius: in *coniunctio* order with *semoti* and *tarda*; so *leti* with *necessitas* and *gradum*. For the position of the last word see on *freta* l. 16 above.

     34. **expertus vacuum Daedalus aera**: for the grouping see P. 9. The position of *vacuum* has point; the air was an empty ocean on which no man was nor had been since the making of the world. The separation of *aera* gives the effect of 'and that void is air, not water.'

     35. **pennis...datis**: an afterthought, as the order shows—'and with wings not to man given'; see P. 53. The *non* qualifies *homini* as it should do; English carelessly says 'to man not given.'

     36. **Herculeus** (*p*): compare *Odes* 2. 12. 6 *Herculea manu*. The adjective *Herculeus* is preposited because it contains the real subject (see on *Odes* I. 15. 33), as if we had *Hercules labore*; or we may regard *Herculeus* as equal to *Herculis*—a preposited genitive with the force of a nominative (see P. 38).

     37. **ardui**: for the separation of the partitive genitive see on *Odes* I. 2 I

per nostrum patimur scelus
iracunda Iovem ponere fulmina.   40

IV.

Solvitur acris hiems grata vice veris et Favoni,
    trahuntque siccas machinae carinas,
ac neque iam stabulis gaudet pecus aut arator igni,
    nec prata canis albicant pruinis.
iam Cytherea choros ducit Venus imminente luna,   5
    iunctaeque Nymphis Gratiae decentes
alterno terram quatiunt pede, dum gravis Cyclopum
    Volcanus ardens visit officinas.
nunc decet aut viridi nitidum caput impedire myrto,
    aut flore, terrae quem ferunt solutae;   10

satis...nivis. In any case *mortalibus* is the word of interest and is therefore brought forward = καὶ τοῖς θνητοῖς.

38. **stultitia**: a postposited adverb—'in our utter folly.'

39. **nostrum** (*ps*): we have only *ourselves* to blame. See also P. 21.

40. **iracunda**: a Roman reads *iracunda* as if *iracundum* with *Iovem*; see P. 52.

IV. 1. **acris** (*p*)...**grata** (*p*): both are preposited because contrasted—harsh winter but kindly spring. For the position of *veris et Favoni* see P. 35.

2. **siccas** (*ps*): i.e. dry, not wet; they have been out of the water so long, and fine weather has begun.

3. **stabulis...pecus...arator igni**: note the chiasmus.

4. **canis** (*ps*): a Roman, perhaps, first feels the adjective with *prata* (see on P. 52), but compare on P. 21.

5. **Cytherea**: may be regarded as a noun, but Gow thinks it means 'in Cythera'; if so compare *Odes* I. 31. 9. If *Cytherea* be a noun, the sentence is complete at *ducit*; the words following then form a picturesque after-thought—'Yes, Venus in the moonlight'; see on P. 53.

6. **iunctaeque Nymphis Gratiae decentes**: for the second epithet (*decentes*) outside, see P. 48, and compare P. 34.

7. **alterno** equals an adverb; see on P. 31. For *pede* see on *Odes* I. 3. 16. Compare l. 13 below *aequo pulsat pede.*

7, 8. **gravis Cyclopum | ...officinas**: see P. 46 *b*. Here *Volcanus* comes near *Cyclopum* in order to group together the persons concerned (see on *Odes* I. 2. 17): *ardens* comes next, i.e. hot and eager, in artificial contrast to *gravis*, which suggests heavily burdened and toilsome, going in sense with both *Cyclopum* and *officinas* (see P. 52).

9. **viridi nitidum caput...myrto**: for the grouping see P. 10. The green on the glossy hair is a pretty picture suggested by the collocation *viridi nitidum.*

nunc et in umbrosis Fauno decet immolare lucis,
    seu poscat agna sive malit haedo.
pallida mors aequo pulsat pede pauperum tabernas
    regumque turris. o beate Sesti,
vitae summa brevis spem nos vetat incohare longam.   15
    iam te premet nox fabulaeque manes
et domus exilis Plutonia: quo simul mearis,
    nec regna vini sortiere talis
nec tenerum Lycidan mirabere, quo calet iuventus
    nunc omnis et mox virgines tepebunt.   20

10. **terrae quem ferunt:** the position of *terrae* may be due to careless imitation of such idioms as are found at *Odes* 1. 8. 2, and 1. 38. 3. In Vergil *Aen.* 6. 792 *Augustus Caesar, Divi genus, aurea condet | saecula qui rursus Latio* the stress on *aurea...saecula* is clearly marked by the order. But such familiar grouping as *flore terris lato solutis* (see P. 9) may have been in Horace's mind.

    solutae is emphatic, i.e. only when earth has been freed from the chains of the frost.

11. **in umbrosis** (*ps*): see P. 27. By this time the trees of the *lucus* would have grown sufficiently to provide shade.

12. **agna** is put after the verb to prepare us for the alternative *haedo*.

13. **pallida** (*p*): perhaps on the analogy of *atra Cura*; see on *Odes* 2. 14. 23.

    aequo i.e. impartially; see note on l. 7 above. See also P. 21.

    pauperum (*p*) to prepare us for the preposited antithesis *regum*.

14. **beate** (*p*): see on P. 36.

15. **vitae** (*p*): the position may be explained in several ways; *vitae* is the important word and is practically subject (see P. 38); *summa* may have an attribute on either side (see P. 35); it is possible that *brevis* is genitive with *vitae* (see P. 20 β).

    longam (*s*) is predicative and quasi-proleptic: we rough hew hopes of a life that is to be long—τὴν ἐλπίδα τείνειν μακράν.

16. **te premet nox:** for order see P. 51. But there is also stress on *te*: Horace makes the application personal.

    fabulae is a noun becoming an adjective and, as Page says, equals *fabulosi* (compare *virgo charta*, γέρων λόγος, virgin effort). Horace says 'all that is left for you is night, and the storied life of the dead, and the ghostly world'; he intentionally throws doubt on it all by making *fabulae* prepositive. Even such a world is doubtful (he cries); therefore eat, drink, and be merry.

18. **talis:** for its position see on *Odes* 1. 3. 16.

19. **tenerum** (*p*): the delicate charm (of Lycidas); see on P. 27. The epithet is proper to a woman; cp. *Odes* 1. 1. 26, and see *Epod.* 11. 4.

20. **nunc** (*pps*): the position prepares us for the antithesis *mox*, which itself is separated from *tepebunt*. See also on P. 50 *b*.

    omnis (*pps*) is emphatic.

V.

Quis multa gracilis te puer in rosa
perfusus liquidis urget odoribus
　　grato, Pyrrha, sub antro?
　　　　cui flavam religas comam,

simplex munditiis? heu quotiens fidem　　　　　5
mutatosque deos flebit et aspera
　　nigris aequora ventis
　　　　emirabitur insolens,

qui nunc te fruitur credulus aurea,
qui semper vacuam, semper amabilem　　　　10
　　sperat, nescius aurae
　　　　fallacis. miseri, quibus

V. The order of this Ode is often strained. Is it a translation?

1. **multa gracilis...puer in rosa:** for the grouping see P. 10.
te puer: see on *Odes* I. 2. 17.

2. **liquidis** (*ps*): i.e. (drenched) with the liquid of scents (see P. 27); but *liquidis...odoribus* may be grouped with *urget* also i.e. courts thee with scents (see P. 21 and 23).

3. **grato** (*ps*): the order is, perhaps, on the analogy of *grato Pyrrhae* (dat.) *sub antro*. For the intervening vocative compare *Odes* I. I. I, I. 7. 19, I. 9. 8, I. 17. 10, I. 32. 4, 2. I. 14, 2. 13. 27, 3. 2. I, 3. 4. 2, 3. 13. 2, 4. I. I (?), 4. I. 40, 4. 5. I, 4. 5. 5, 4. 14. 3, 4. 15. 4, *Epod.* 5. 73.

4. **flavam** (*ps*): golden hair would be the special beauty of a lady named Pyrrha. See also P. 21, and compare *Odes* 3. 9. 19.

5. **simplex munditiis:** an addendum; see on P. 53.

5, 6. **fidem | mutatosque deos:** for the position of *mutatos* see on P. 33.

6, 7. **aspera | nigris aequora ventis:** for the grouping see P. 9.

8. **insolens** i.e. ἄτε ἀήθης ὤν—because he is unused to them.

9. **credulus aurea:** an emphatic addendum; see P. 53. A Roman reads the words thus: 'Fool to trust her flash of gold!' Compare *Odes* I. 6. 9, I. 13. 14.

For the grouping *qui...te...credulus aurea* see P. 16 *ad fin.*

nunc has stress by separation from *fruitur*: Horace could have made the line scan with *te nunc*.

11. **sperat** has stress; see *Odes* 4. 9. 26.

nescius sc. ὤν i.e. 'because he knows not'—an addendum; see P. 53.

12. **fallacis** has stress; see *Odes* 4. 9. 26. He knows the breeze but not its shiftiness.

intemptata nites: me tabula sacer
votiva paries indicat uvida
    suspendisse potenti   15
       vestimenta maris deo.

VI.

Scriberis Vario fortis et hostium
victor Maeonii carminis aliti,
quam rem cumque ferox navibus aut equis
    miles te duce gesserit.

nos, Agrippa, neque haec dicere, nec gravem   5
Pelidae stomachum cedere nescii,
nec cursus duplicis per mare Ulixei,
    nec saevam Pelopis domum

conamur, tenues grandia, dum pudor
imbellisque lyrae Musa potens vetat   10
laudes egregii Caesaris et tuas
    culpa deterere ingeni.

13, 14. **me...paries:** the accusative *me* put early equals 'as for me.'

tabula sacer | votiva paries: for the grouping see on P. 14. A Roman would read thus: 'me the tablet in the temple (*sacer*), the vow upon the wall....'

14, 15. **uvida** is predicative with *suspendisse* i.e. 'have hung all dripping.'

uvida | ...potenti | vestimenta...deo: for the grouping see P. 9.

16. **maris** although governed by *potenti* is also preposited genitive with *deo* i.e. wet things (*uvida*) to the water-god. Compare *lyrae Odes* 1. 6. 10.

VI. 1. **Vario:** a Roman must surely read this as equivalent to *a Vario*, whether we write *alite* or *aliti*.

hostium (*p*): the objective genitive is often prepositive; see P. 39.

2. **victor** perhaps has stress; see on *Odes* 4. 9. 26.

Maeonii (*p*): i.e. you want a Homer, not a lyrist. From *Maeonii* to *aliti* is an emphatic addendum—'because he is an Homeric bard'; see on P. 53.

3. **quam rem cumque:** so English 'what thing soever,' cp. *Odes* 1. 7. 25, 1. 9. 14, 1. 16. 2, 1. 27. 14, 1. 32. 15 (?). Note that this tmesis occurs only in Book I. of the Odes.

5, 6. **gravem...nescii:** for the second complement (*cedere nescii*) placed outside see on P. 48.

7. **cursus...Ulixei:** for the grouping see on P. 14 *ad fin.*

9. **tenues grandia:** compare *Odes* 1. 5. 9 *credulus aurea*, 1. 13. 14 *dulcia barbare*, 1. 15. 2 *perfidus hospitam*.

10. **imbellis** (*p*): contrast *Maeonii* (*p*) of l. 2 above.

quis Martem tunica tectum adamantina
digne scripserit aut pulvere Troico
nigrum Merionem aut ope Palladis   15
    Tydiden superis parem?

nos convivia, nos proelia virginum
sectis in iuvenes unguibus acrium
cantamus vacui, sive quid urimur,
    non praeter solitum leves.   20

VII.

Laudabunt alii claram Rhodon aut Mytilenen
    aut Epheson bimarisve Corinthi
moenia vel Baccho Thebas vel Apolline Delphos
    insignis aut Thessala Tempe;

lyrae (*p*): the lyric is contrasted with the epic of l. 2 above. The genitive *lyrae* depends partly on *Musa*, partly on *potens*. Compare *maris Odes* I. 5. 16 and see on P. 39.

11. **egregii** (*p*): peerless. The adjective is naturally emphasised to flatter Caesar (cp. *Odes* 3. 25. 4, and see on *Odes* 3. 27. 73).

12. **ingeni** (*s*): ability is the point; I should fail not from lack of effort or of desire, but of power and aptitude.

13. **Martem...adamantina**: for the grouping see P. 16.

14, 15. **pulvere...Merionem**: normally *pulvere Troico* would lie between *nigrum* and *Merionem*, but Horace, perhaps, wishes to mention the Trojan war early. See P. 49.

15, 16. **ope Palladis...parem**: for the second complement outside see P. 48.

17. **nos convivia, nos proelia**: for early grouping of case relations see on *Odes* I. 2. 17. There is, of course, emphasis on *nos* because the pronoun is inserted.

19. **vacui** is an afterthought (see P. 53) = 'that is when we are heart-whole.' It is usual to supply *cantamus* with *leves* and to translate *non praeter* as if *secundum*; but it is just possible that *leves* may be a verb i.e. 'one would not raise me above my wont.' In any case the sense must be 'my forte is to sing of dinners and flirting when my heart is free, and, if I *am* in love, you will still find me playful and frivolous'; i.e. I have not the *gravitas* needful for the epic style. For *seu* = or if, and if, see *Odes* 3. 4. 22.

VII. 1, 2. **alii**: the position gives the effect of οἱ μὲν ἄλλοι i.e. 'others may...but I (ἐγὼ δέ—the *me* of l. 10 below) will praise Tibur.'

claram (*p*) i.e. 'the fame or, possibly, sunshine (of Rhodes)'; *bimaris* (*p*) i.e. 'the twin seas (of Corinth)'; see P. 27. We may, however, consider the adjectives as predicative i.e. 'will praise as famous, as *bimarem*.'

2, 3. **Corinthi** (*p*) | **moenia** i.e. 'Corinth with its walls'; see on P. 38.

moenia should have stress; see on *Odes* 4. 9. 26.

sunt quibus unum opus est intactae Palladis urbem   5
   carmine perpetuo celebrare et
undique decerptam fronti praeponere olivam;
   plurimus in Iunonis honorem
aptum dicet equis Argos ditisque Mycenas:
   me nec tam patiens Lacedaemon   10
nec tam Larisae percussit campus opimae
   quam domus Albuneae resonantis
et praeceps Anio ac Tiburni lucus et uda
   mobilibus pomaria rivis.

3, 4. vel Baccho Thebas... | **insignis:** for *Baccho* standing outside *Thebas* and *insignis*, as *Apolline* outside *Delphos* and *insignis*, see on P. 49. Horace desires to bring out the artificial antithesis of Bacchus and Apollo.

insignis may have stress; see on *Odes* 4. 9. 26.

Thessala (*p*): there were many Tempe; but the Thessalian vale was the original and most famous.

5. **intactae** (*p*): the ritual and titular epithet is naturally stressed. Compare *Odes* I. 19. 3, 3. 4. 64, 3. 5. 11, 3. 6. 35, 3. 7. 18, 3. 29. 64(?), 4. 4. 49, 4. 6. 28, *Epod.* 3. 17.

Palladis (*p*) **urbem** i.e. 'Pallas and her city'; see P. 38. There is also implied the contrast of Bacchus and Apollo.

6. **celebrare et:** for the position of *et* compare on *Odes* I. 35. 39.

7. **undique decerptam** (*ps*): there seems to be some chiastic echo of *perpetuo*, and the words may suggest monotonous and prolix treatment. See the commentators, who compare *Odes* I. 29. 13.

8. **Iunonis**(*p*): contrast Bacchus, Apollo, and Pallas; but see also on P. 42.

9. **aptum** (*ps*) is predicative i.e. 'will sing of as *aptum equis*'; so *ditis* (*p*)='(will sing of) as wealthy,' or 'the wealth (of Mycenae).' Compare *claram* in l. 1 above. Moreover Horace is quoting the stock epithets of Homer (see Wickham) and wishes to draw our special attention to the wording of Grecian praise.

10. **me** comes early in contrast to *alii* of l. 1 above. See also P. 51.

tam belongs to *percussit* and is emphatic by separation; the stress would, in prose, be expressed by 'not half so much.' Compare *tam* in the next line.

patiens (*p*) i.e. 'the hardiness (of Sparta)'; see on P. 27.

11. **Larisae** (*ps*) equals 'nor Larissa...,' as if it were subject, parallel to Lacedaemon. See P. 38.

Larisae...campus opimae: this grouping may be classed under P. 19 and 20 *a* (q.v.); and moreover *opimae* may be felt with *campus*; see P. 52. The adjective is again a translation (ἐριβῶλαξ).

12, 13. **Albuneae resonantis** | **et praeceps Anio:** observe the chiasmus. Further, *praeceps* (*p*) equals 'the falls of the Anio' at Tibur. See on P. 27 and the note at *Odes* 3. 29. 6.

13, 14. **Tiburni** (*p*) equals 'Tiburnus and his grove'; see P. 38.

N. H.   2

albus ut obscuro deterget nubila caelo   15
   saepe Notus neque parturit imbris
perpetuos, sic tu sapiens finire memento
   tristitiam vitaeque labores
molli, Plance, mero, seu te fulgentia signis
   castra tenent seu densa tenebit   20
Tiburis umbra tui. Teucer Salamina patremque
   cum fugeret, tamen uda Lyaeo
tempora populea fertur vinxisse corona,
   sic tristis affatus amicos:
'quo nos cumque feret melior fortuna parente,   25
   ibimus, o socii comitesque!

uda | ...rivis: for the grouping see on P. 9. Note the happy juxtaposition *uda mobilibus*—waters rushing. Wickham sees a reference to water-mills.

15, 16. **albus ut obscuro deterget...caelo | ...Notus:** for the grouping see on P. 8. Romans love such antitheses as *albus obscuro* (compare on *Odes* I. 6. 9). See too Page on the emphasis of *albus*.

16. **saepe** (*pps*) equals πολλάκις μὲν οὐκ ἀεὶ δέ, and prepares us for the emphatic *perpetuos* of l. 17.

Notus comes late in contrast to *tu* of l. 17.

17. **perpetuos** (*pps*) is emphatic by position: it stands alone at the commencement of the line (see on *Odes* 4. 9. 26).

18. **tristitiam vitaeque labores:** if we put no stop at *tristitiam*, then *vitae* may be in *coniunctio* position with the nouns. Others put a stop at *tristitiam* (which then has emphasis; see *Odes* 4. 9. 26) and take *molli* as the imperative of *mollire*; in that case *vitae labores* will equal 'life and its toils' (see P. 38).

19. **molli**, if an adjective, is preposited and separated, and equals 'mellow, not harsh'; but also see P. 27. For the separation by the vocative compare on *Odes* I. 5. 3.

te: for its position see P. 51.

20, 21. **densa... | Tiburis umbra tui:** for the grouping see P. 17.

Teucer Salamina patremque: see on *Odes* I. 2. 17.

23. **populea** (*ps*): although he had been engaged in conviviality (the worship of Bacchus), he put on not the vine leaf or ivy, but the poplar leaf of Hercules the wanderer.

24. **tristis** (*ps*) is predicative and means 'because sad'; he wishes to encourage them.

25. **nos:** for position see on P. 51.

cumque: compare on *Odes* I. 6. 3.

melior fortuna parente: the position of *parente* (outside *melior* and *fortuna*) is a bitter afterthought (see on P. 53) i.e. 'fortune kinder—than my sire.' Compare *Odes* I. 15. 28, and see P. 49.

nil desperandum Teucro duce et auspice Teucro:
 certus enim promisit Apollo
ambiguam tellure nova Salamina futuram.
 o fortes peioraque passi   30
mecum saepe viri, nunc vino pellite curas:
 cras ingens iterabimus aequor.'

VIII.

Lydia, dic, per omnis
 te deos oro, Sybarin cur properes amando
perdere, cur apricum
 oderit campum, patiens pulveris atque solis,
cur neque militaris   5
 inter aequalis equitet, Gallica nec lupatis

27. **Teucro duce...Teucro**: these words form an emphatic addendum ; see P. 53. Note the chiastic order *Teucro duce...auspice Teucro*.

28. **certus** (*ps*) equals an adverb 'without oracular evasion'; see on P. 31.

29. **ambiguam tellure nova Salamina**: the order is normal (adjective, complement—*tellure nova*—, noun) cp. *Odes* I. I. 26, I. 8. 14, etc., 2. 7. 7, 8, 2. 8. 6, etc., *Epod.* 9. 5, 17. 33. But the grouping may be regarded as that of P. 15.

nova (*pp*) probably has stress; see on *Odes* I. 2. 6.

31. **mecum saepe viri**: emphatic addenda i.e. 'with me—often—like heroes.' See on P. 53.

curas: for its position see *Odes* I. 3. 16.

32. **cras** (*s*): i.e. without a day's delay.

ingens (*s*): i.e. for all its monstrous and mysterious size. Professor Conway has shown the air of mystery which so often attaches to *ingens* in Vergil (cp. *Odes* 4. 9. 19). See also P. 21.

VIII. 1, 2. **per omnis | te deos oro**: the position of *te* in such petitions is common in both Latin and Greek. Compare Terence *Andr.* 834 *per ego te deos oro*, and see Livy 23. 9. 2 *per ego te...precor.* So Ovid *Heroid.* 10. 73, and Horace *Epod.* 5. 5, 17. 3. Here however the presence of *omnis* (separated and therefore emphatic) conceals the hyperbaton.

Sybarin is brought forward out of its clause so as to make clear, and that early, the persons concerned in the Ode. The subject is the loves of Lydia and Sybaris (see on *Odes* I. 2. 17). Perhaps too the order is on the analogy of Greek οἶδά σε τίς εἶ. Compare too note on *Odes* I. 4. 10.

3. **apricum** (*ps*): the heat (of the Campus); see on P. 27, and also P. 21.

4. **patiens...solis**: a concessive addendum (see on P. 53) i.e. though accustomed to endure.

5. **militaris**: concessive i.e. 'though a soldier.'

temperet ora frenis?

    cur timet flavum Tiberim tangere? cur olivum
sanguine viperino

    cautius vitat neque iam livida gestat armis   10
bracchia, saepe disco,

    saepe trans finem iaculo nobilis expedito?
quid latet, ut marinae

    filium dicunt Thetidis sub lacrimosa Troiae
funera, ne virilis   15

    cultus in caedem et Lycias proriperet catervas?

IX.

Vides ut alta stet nive candidum
Soracte nec iam sustineant onus
   silvae laborantes geluque
      flumina constiterint acuto.

6, 7. **Gallica...frenis:** for the grouping see P. 7.

8. **flavum** (*p*): i.e. when it is yellow and therefore in flood. See on *Odes* I. 2. 13.

10, 11. **livida** may go with *gestat*, as if 'wears black and blue'; but see on P. 46 *a*. For *bracchia* see on *Odes* 4. 9. 26.

11, 12. **saepe...expedito:** these words are a concessive addendum (see P. 53) i.e. though often before renowned.

trans finem iaculo: the words may be read together because *iaculum* means 'something thrown'; so Latin prose can say *reditus in urbem, iter ad oppidum* etc. Ultimately *trans finem* goes with *expedito*.

expedito (*s*) is emphatic and equals 'a *clear* throw, *right* beyond the limit.' But see P. 24.

13, 14. **marinae | filium...Thetidis:** see on P. 20 β. For the phrase compare *Odes* 4. 6. 6.

14, 15. **sub lacrimosa Troiae | funera:** an emphatic addendum—'and that upon the eve of Troy's fall' (see on P. 53). For the order of the words see on *Odes* I. 7. 29.

funera probably has stress; see on *Odes* 4. 9. 26.

virilis (*p*): contrast *muliebris cultus* which he was wearing. See also on P. 37.

16. **Lycias** (*ps*): the words *in caedem et Lycias* sound like a hendiadys *in caedem et Lycios* i.e. amid the murderous Lycians; then *catervas=crebros*. But see P. 21.

IX. 1, 2. **alta** (*ps*): with depth (of snow); see P. 27, but compare also P. 21. A heavy fall of snow would make Soracte stand out clear and white *candidum* is predicative).

dissolve frigus ligna super foco   5
large reponens atque benignius
   deprome quadrimum Sabina,
     o Thaliarche, merum diota.

permitte divis cetera; qui simul
stravere ventos aequore fervido   10
   deproeliantis, nec cupressi
     nec veteres agitantur orni.

quid sit futurum cras, fuge quaerere, et
quem fors dierum cumque dabit, lucro
   appone, nec dulcis amores   15
     sperne puer neque tu choreas,

donec virenti canities abest
morosa. nunc et campus et areae
   lenesque sub noctem susurri
     composita repetantur hora,   20

Soracte has stress (see on *Odes* 4. 9. 26) i.e. much more are the higher and less precipitous mountains covered with snow. Soracte is only 2265 ft. in height (according to Baedeker) and is some 26 miles from Rome.

4. **acuto** (*s*): the adjective is causal and explains why the rivers have ceased to flow; the frost is abnormally hard.

7, 8. **quadrimum Sabina…merum diota**: for the grouping see P. 9. For the intrusive vocative—*o Thaliarche*—see on *Odes* 1. 5. 3.

10, 11. **aequore fervido | deproeliantis**: a concessive addendum (see P. 53) i.e. though in a death-struggle with the sea. For the stress on *deproeliantis* see *Odes* 4. 9. 26.

12. **veteres** (*ps*): even the gnarled old ash-trees have been shaken; but see P. 21.

13. **cras** (*pp*): do not ask about the future, not even about the nearest future—tomorrow.

et: for its position compare on *Odes* 1. 35. 39.

14. **dierum** should belong to both *fors* and *quemcumque* i.e. 'whatever of days the fortune of days shall give.' For *cumque* see on *Odes* 1. 6. 3.

15. **appone** has stress (see on *Odes* 4. 9. 26): do not subtract days by anticipating them; only add them, when past, to the credit account.

dulcis (*p*): the sweets (of love); see on P. 27.

16. **puer** sc. ὤν i.e. 'while young.' Compare Persius *Sat.* 6. 21 *hic bona dente | grandia magnanimus peragit puer*; Horace *Epist.* 1. 2. 68 *nunc adbibe puro | pectore verba puer*.

17. **donec virenti**: the order is as if Horace had written *donec vires et*….

18. **morosa** perhaps an emphatic addendum—'with its crabbed ways'; see on P. 53, and *Odes* 4. 9. 26.

nunc et latentis proditor intimo
gratus puellae risus ab angulo
pignusque dereptum lacertis
aut digito male pertinaci.

X.

Mercuri, facunde nepos Atlantis,
qui feros cultus hominum recentum
voce formasti catus et decorae
more palaestrae,

te canam, magni Iovis et deorum   5
nuntium curvaeque lyrae parentem,
callidum quicquid placuit iocoso
condere furto.

te, boves olim nisi reddidisses
per dolum amotas, puerum minaci   10
voce dum terret, viduus pharetra
risit Apollo.

20. **composita** (*s*): prearrangement is the point; hence the order. But see P. 21.

21, 22. **latentis...angulo**: for the grouping see on P. 6. For the normal group *gratus puellae risus* see *Odes* 1. 7. 29.

23. **lacertis**: for its position see P. 47.

X. 1. **facunde** (*p*): see on P. 36; but for the group *facunde nepos Atlantis* see on P. 35.

2. **feros cultus hominum**: for grouping see on P. 35.

3, 4. **catus** sc. ὤν. Compare *puer* at *Odes* 1. 9. 16.

decorae (*p*): grace, in place of uncouthness, is the point.

decorae | more palaestrae: for the grouping see on P. 20a.

5. **magni...deorum**: the genitives are preposited because Mercury is no mere lackey of nonentities, but envoy of great Jove and the gods.

6. **curvae** (*p*): the epithet refers to the bellied shape of the real or imitation tortoise-shell which formed a sounding-board, contrasted with the square box of the cithara. In any case *curvus* is always prepositive in Horace. See too *Odes* 3. 28. 11.

lyrae (*p*): the order, perhaps, suggests the antithesis of orator (*facunde* l. 1), and envoy (*nuntium* l. 6), to musician (*lyrae*); but it is possible to compare the order of *Andromedae pater* at *Odes* 3. 29. 17. See P. 41 *ad fin.*

7. **iocoso** (*ps*) i.e. in jest, as if *per iocum*; see P. 31, and also P. 21.

9. **te, boves olim**: for case relations grouped early i.e. 'the old story (*olim*) of you and the oxen,' see on *Odes* 1. 2. 17. There is no need to place a comma after *te* or after *amotas*.

quin et Atridas duce te superbos
Ilio dives Priamus relicto
Thessalosque ignis et iniqua Troiae   15
    castra fefellit.

tu pias laetis animas reponis
sedibus virgaque levem coerces
aurea turbam, superis deorum
    gratus et imis.   20

10. **per dolum amotas, puerum**: a Roman may read *amotas* as if a deponent agreeing with *puerum*—δόλῳ κλέψαντα παῖδα. See note on l. 14 below and especially the citation from Livy 1. 4. 6.

minaci (*p*): threats might frighten a *boy*; hence the juxtaposition of *puerum minaci*.

11. **viduus** sc. ὤν.

12. **Apollo** comes last in antithesis to *te* of l. 9. Compare Livy 1. 5. 7 where a long sentence begins with *Romulus* and ends with *Remus*.

13. **Atridas duce te**: for the grouping see note on l. 9. The order gives the sense 'and now for the Atridae and your leading past them (cruel pair!) Priam....' But the position of *superbos* is very awkward; see however P. 50*c*. If we had *superbos duce te Atridas*, the words ,could hardly mean anything save 'the Atridae proud of your leadership,' and it may be that even with the adjective last there would be ambiguity for anyone ignorant of the facts.

14. **Ilio dives Priamus relicto**: the position of *Priamus* between *Ilio* and *relicto*, as if *relicto* were a deponent governing *Ilio* ("Ιλιον ὁ Π. καταλιπών), is common in Livy and Caesar. Compare Livy 1. 7. 11 *dextra Hercules data*; 1. 4. 6 *tenet fama...eam (lupam) summissas* (as if καθεῖσαν) *infantibus adeo mitem praebuisse mammas*; 4. 44. 10 *causa ipse pro se dicta damnatur*; and see *C.R.* Vol. xv. p. 315. So Vergil *Aen.* 8. 707 *ventis regina vocatis* and *passim*; Ovid *Ex Ponto* 1. 3. 73 *caede puer facta*; *Fast.* iv. 297 *fune viri contento bracchia lassant*. Horace has many examples e.g. *Odes* 1. 2. 41, 1. 12. 45, 1. 30. 5, 1. 35. 23, 2. 1. 37, 2. 2. 5, 3. 3. 43, 44, 3. 22. 6, 3. 27. 67, 68, 3. 28. 16, *C.S.* 33. Add *Odes* 1. 16. 27, and 1. 22. 11.

dives (*p*) i.e. with all his treasures to bribe Achilles.

15. **Thessalos** (*p*): i.e. of the *enemy* and that enemy the most bitter.

17, 18. **pias laetis animas reponis | sedibus**: for the grouping see on P. 9. The order is picturesque: the pious to happiness, their souls to a fixed dwelling; they do not wander homeless and unlaid. Hence, perhaps, there is some stress on *sedibus*; see *Odes* 4. 9. 26.

18, 19. **virgaque...turbam**: for the grouping see P. 13.

20. **gratus** sc. ὤν. The word lies, by *coniunctio*, between *superis* and *imis*.

This Ode would seem to be an early experiment in translation, if one may judge by the frequency of strained order and the absence of caesura in ll. 1, 6, 10, and 18; contrast such Odes as 1. 2, and 1. 22.

XI.

Tu ne quaesieris (scire nefas) quem mihi, quem tibi
finem di dederint, Leuconoe, nec Babylonios
temptaris numeros. ut melius, quicquid erit, pati,
seu pluris hiemes seu tribuit Iuppiter ultimam,
quae nunc oppositis debilitat pumicibus mare   5
Tyrrhenum. sapias, vina liques et spatio brevi
spem longam reseces. dum loquimur, fugerit invida
aetas: carpe diem, quam minimum credula postero.

XII.

Quem virum aut heroa lyra vel acri
tibia sumis celebrare, Clio,
quem deum? cuius recinet iocosa
    nomen imago

aut in umbrosis Heliconis oris   5
aut super Pindo gelidove in Haemo?
unde vocalem temere insecutae
    Orphea silvae

XI. 1, 2. **quem mihi...** | **finem:** *mihi* is brought forward in antithesis to *tibi*.

finem comes early because 'end' is the point, and the text is *carpe diem*, not *respice finem*.

Babylonios (*ps*): see on P. 21.

4. **ultimam** is last in contrast to *pluris*.

5. **oppositis** (*s*) i.e. 'before the opposition (of the rocks)'; compare *Odes* 3. 26. 8, and see on P. 26.

6. **Tyrrhenum** should have stress (see on *Odes* 4. 9. 26); winter is causing storms that disturb not merely the notorious Adriatic, but the more peaceful Tyrrhenian sea. But see *Epist.* 2. 1. 202, and *Odes* 4. 4. 54.

6, 7. **brevi** | **...longam:** the antithesis is expressed by parallel order, and by making adjectives of quantity postpositive.

invida (*p*): see on *Odes* 2. 14. 23.

8. **aetas** has stress (see on *Odes* 4. 9. 26); Horace harps upon time and its flight.

postero comes last in contrast to *diem* sc. *praesentem*.

XII. 1. **acri** (*p*) i.e. 'shrillness (of the pipe)'; see on P. 27 and the note at *Odes* 3. 4. 3, 4.

3, 4. **cuius...iocosa** | **nomen imago:** for the grouping see on P. 12.

6. **gelido** probably goes with both *Pindo* and *Haemo*; see on P. 33.

7, 8. **vocalem** (*ps*) i.e. 'the voice (of Orpheus)'; see on P. 27; but *vocalem...silvae* might be classified under P. 9.

arte materna rapidos morantem
fluminum lapsus celerisque ventos,   10
blandum et auritas fidibus canoris
    ducere quercus.

quid prius dicam solitis parentis
laudibus, qui res hominum ac deorum,
qui mare et terras variisque mundum   15
    temperat horis?

unde nil maius generatur ipso
nec viget quicquam simile aut secundum;
proximos illi tamen occupavit
    Pallas honores,   20

proeliis audax; neque te silebo,
Liber, et saevis inimica virgo
beluis, nec te, metuende certa
    Phoebe sagitta.

9, 10. **rapidos** (*ps*)...**celeris** (*p*): both adjectives are emphatic i.e. 'for all their speed'; for the intrusive *morantem* see on P. 46 *a*.

11, 12. **auritas...quercus**: for the grouping see on P. 46 *a*.

fidibus canoris: these words go with both *auritas* and *ducere* i.e. oaks with ears pricked up by reason of his tuneful strings he led by means of these strings.

14. **laudibus** should have stress; see on *Odes* 4. 9. 26.

15. **variis** (*ps*) is set purposely before *mundum* (κόσμος); the antithesis is change and variety amidst law and order. See also on P. 27.

17. **ipso** is last with emphasis i.e. than the mighty master (*ipse*, αὐτός) of it all.

19. **proximos** (*ps*) is put first to emphasize the antithesis *secundum* i.e. there is no one in the race to be called *secundus* (following on the heels of), though there is somebody *proximus* (next), but only a very poor second. See on l. 51 below.

21. **proeliis audax**: it is possible, with Bentley and others, to take these words with *Pallas*, putting a comma, not full stop, after *honores*; they may however go with both *Pallas* and *Liber*.

22. **Liber** should have stress; contrast *Pallas*. See on *Odes* 4. 9. 26.

22, 23. **saevis...beluis**: for the grouping see on P. 10. The antithetical words are neatly grouped together: to the savage inimical, a maiden against *beasts*. The stress on *beluis* is due to its position; see on *Odes* 4. 9. 26.

23, 24. **metuende...sagitta**: for the grouping see on P. 9.

certa (*ps*) i.e. 'the sure aim (of his arrows)'; see on P. 27. In the *Odes*, *Epodes*, and *C.S. certus* is never postposited.

dicam et Alciden puerosque Ledae,   25
hunc equis, illum superare pugnis
nobilem; quorum simul alba nautis
    stella refulsit,

defluit saxis agitatus umor,
concidunt venti fugiuntque nubes,   30
et minax, quod sic voluere, ponto
    unda recumbit.

Romulum post hos prius, an quietum
Pompili regnum memorem, an superbos
Tarquini fasces, dubito, an Catonis   35
    nobile letum.

Regulum et Scauros animaeque magnae
prodigum Paulum superante Poeno
gratus insigni referam camena
    Fabriciumque.   40

27. **nobilem** should have stress; see on *Odes* 4. 9. 26.

alba: the adjective seems to be predicative with *refulsit*. See also on
P. 50 *b*. For the *stella* see on *Odes* 1. 3. 2, 3. 29. 64, and 4. 8. 31.

29. **saxis** is ablative partly with *defluit*, partly with *agitatus*; the water
flows down from the rocks after being broken into spray (*agitatus*) by the
rocks; hence *saxis* stands outside *agitatus* and *umor*. See P. 49, and the
note there on *Odes* 1. 2. 23.

31, 32. **minax...unda recumbit:** the words *quod sic voluere* are parenthetic; therefore *ponto* may be felt not only with *recumbit* but also with
minax. The separation of *minax* gives it the force of a noun, as if we had
minae undarum sedantur; see on P. 27.

35. **Catonis** stands outside *nobile* and *letum* in order, perhaps, to keep
the list clear—Romulus, Numa, Tarquin, Cato. The effect of the order is
'Cato and his noble death.' See on P. 37 *ad fin.*, 38, and 43. Contrast *Odes*
2. 1. 24 *atrocem animum Catonis*.

37, 38. **animaeque magnae | prodigum:** a Roman would read thus:
'and the great (emphatic because postposited) soul's unstinted sacrifice of
Paulus.' The quasi-objective genitive is often preposited; see on P. 39.
This is, perhaps, why *animae magnae* stands outside *prodigum* and *Paulum*;
see P. 43.

38. **superante Poeno:** a causal addendum; see on P. 53. See too on *Odes*
3. 1. 34.

39. **gratus** sc. ὤν. The adjective equals an adverb; see on P. 32.

insigni (*ps*): we may contrast *imbellis...lyrae* of *Odes* 1. 6. 10. See too
P. 21.

hunc et incomptis Curium capillis
utilem bello tulit et Camillum
saeva paupertas et avitus apto
    cum lare fundus.

crescit occulto velut arbor aevo   45
fama Marcelli; micat inter omnis
Iulium sidus velut inter ignis
    luna minores.

gentis humanae pater atque custos,
orte Saturno, tibi cura magni   50
Caesaris fatis data: tu secundo
    Caesare regnes.

ille seu Parthos Latio imminentis
egerit iusto domitos triumpho
sive subiectos Orientis orae   55
    Seras et Indos,

41–43. **hunc...tulit...paupertas**: for the order of *hunc* see on P. 51.

incomptis (*ps*): with hair and beard unshorn; not *comptis capillis* like the young buck of Horace's time; but see *Odes* 3. 2. 32.

saeva (*p*) i.e. the harshness (of *paupertas*); see on P. 27, and note at *Odes* 2. 14. 23.

43, 44. **avitus...fundus**: for the grouping see on P. 10.

45. **occulto velut arbor aevo** i.e. τὸ δένδρον λανθάνει γηράσκον. For the construction and order see on *Odes* 1. 10. 14.

46, 47. **inter omnis | Iulium** (*p*): the adjective *Iulium* is preposited for emphasis and reminds us of such combinations as *inter omnis unus*.

48. **minores** (*pps*): i.e. ἅτε μείους ὄντας—a causal addendum; see on P. 53. Compare too *Odes* 3. 2. 32.

49. **gentis** (*p*) **humanae**: the order perhaps suggests a contrast to *magni Caesaris*, who is something above the ordinary *gens humana*; but see P. 41 *ad fin*.

51. **secundo** (*p*) i.e. not merely a bad second (*proximo*); see on l. 19 above.

54. **iusto domitos triumpho**: perhaps an emphatic addendum (see on P. 53); but *iusto triumpho* may also be heard with *egerit*.

iusto (*ps*): the triumph was 'well earned' by the prowess of Augustus' soldiers, and 'deserved' by the Parthians after the disaster of Carrhae. But see P. 24.

55. **Orientis** (*p*): the genitive comes first because it contains the point; see on P. 38.

te minor latum reget aequus orbem;
tu gravi curru quaties Olympum,
tu parum castis inimica mittes
    fulmina lucis.   60

XIII.

Cum tu, Lydia, Telephi
    cervicem roseam, cerea Telephi
laudas bracchia, vae meum
    fervens difficili bile tumet iecur.

tunc nec mens mihi nec color   5
    certa sede manent, umor et in genas
furtim labitur, arguens
    quam lentis penitus macerer ignibus.

uror, seu tibi candidos
    turparunt umeros immodicae mero   10
rixae, sive puer furens
    impressit memorem dente labris notam.

57. **te minor**: compare *Odes* 3. 6. 5 *dis te minorem quod geris imperas.*
latum (*ps*) equals *late*; see on P. 31.
58. **gravi** (*p*) i.e. with the weight (of the chariot); see on P. 27.
59, 60. **parum castis...lucis**: for the grouping see on P. 8. A Roman
would read the lines thus: 'to the unchaste inimical thou wilt send thunder-
bolts on their groves.' For the juxtaposition of *fulmina* and *lucis* compare
Odes I. 2. 3 *sacras iaculatas arces.*
XIII. 1, 2. **Lydia, Telephi**: the case relations are grouped early; see on
Odes I. 2. 17.
1, 2. **Telephi | cervicem roseam**: for the order see on P. 35.
2, 3. **cerea Telephi | laudas bracchia**: for the order see on P. 46 *a*. Note
the artificial antithesis (due to chiasmus) of *roseam* and *cerea*.
3. **vae meum**: the words would be read as if *vae mihi*; compare on *Odes*
I. 20. 10, I. 26. 8, 2. 6. 6, 3. 4. 69, and *Epod.* 11. 15, and see note at *Odes* I. 15. 33.
meum (*ps*): there is the contrast to *Telephi.*
4. **fervens...iecur**: for the grouping see on P. 10.
6. **certa** (*p*) i.e. fixity (of place); see on P. 27, and *Odes* I. 12. 23.
8. **lentis** (*ps*) equals *lente*; see on P. 31.
ignibus: for position see on *Odes* I. 3. 16, but compare P. 21 *ad fin.*
9. **candidos** (*ps*) i.e. the whiteness (of thy shoulders); see on P. 27. Compare also on P. 21, and see note on *Odes* 2. 4. 3.
11. **rixae**: see on *Odes* 4. 9. 26.
12. **memorem** is proleptic and goes closely with *impressit* i.e. imprinted
so as to be remembered; see on P. 30.

non, si me satis audias,
  speres perpetuum dulcia barbare
laedentem oscula, quae Venus   15
  quinta parte sui nectaris imbuit.
felices ter et amplius,
  quos irrupta tenet copula nec malis
divulsus querimoniis
  suprema citius solvet amor die.   20

XIV.

O navis, referent in mare te novi
fluctus! o quid agis? fortiter occupa
  portum! nonne vides ut
   nudum remigio latus

et malus celeri saucius Africo   5
antennaeque gemant ac sine funibus
  vix durare carinae
   possint imperiosius

14, 15. **dulcia barbare:** for the antithetical grouping—sweetness and barbarity—compare *Odes* I. 5. 9. For the grouping *dulcia...oscula* compare P. 21 *ad fin.*

16. **quinta...nectaris:** the position of *sui nectaris* may be justified under P. 35 or 45.

sui (*p*): her own, her special nectar.

17. **ter et amplius** (*pp*): there is emphasis—'yea thrice happy.'

18, 19. **irrupta** (*ps*): for the position see P. 21. But *irrupta* may also be felt as an adverb 'unbreakably' (see P. 31); compare *contemptus* in the sense of 'contemptible.'

nec malis: note that the negative of *nec* qualifies both *divulsus* and *citius solvet*. For the position of *malis* see on P. 24.

20. **suprema** (*ps*) is most emphatic i.e. 'the very very last day.'

XIV. 1. **novi** (*p*): see on *Odes* I. 2. 6.

2. **fluctus** perhaps has stress (see on *Odes* 4. 9. 26); currents are as dangerous as *undae*; but the jerky effect of *fluctus, portum* (l. 3), *aequor* (l. 9), and *fidit* (l. 15) may be intentional, representing the agitation of the poet.

fortiter: see the note of C. A. Vince in the *C.R.* Vol. XXXIV, p. 101.

3. **portum:** see preceding note; it is a cry of agony—'to the harbour, the harbour!'

5. **malus...Africo:** for the grouping see on P. 14. The preposited *celeri* has point: it is the swiftness and force that breaks the mast; see on P. 27.

8. **imperiosius** (*p*) i.e. 'the tyranny (of the sea)'; see on P. 27. In any case comparatives tend to come early; see on P. 28.

aequor? non tibi sunt integra lintea,
non di, quos iterum pressa voces malo.   10
   quamvis Pontica pinus,
     silvae filia nobilis,

iactes et genus et nomen inutile,
nil pictis timidus navita puppibus
   fidit. tu nisi ventis   15
     debes ludibrium, cave.

nuper sollicitum quae mihi taedium,
nunc desiderium curaque non levis,
   interfusa nitentis
     vites aequora Cycladas.   20

XV.

Pastor cum traheret per freta navibus
Idaeis Helenen perfidus hospitam,
   ingrato celeris obruit otio
     ventos ut caneret fera

9. **aequor** should have stress (see on *Odes* 4. 9. 26)—even though the waters might be comparatively calm. See however Verg. *Aen.* 3. 157, and *Odes* 3. 27. 23, and 4. 4. 54, where *aequor* is used of stormy seas.

integra is predicative.

10. **pressa voces malo**: it would seem that *malo* belongs to both *pressa* and *voces*. With the latter it equals 'in thy bitter hour' (lit. by reason of *malum*); but it cannot go with *pressa* alone, for then Horace could and would have written *pressa malo voces*. Compare *Odes* 1. 23. 12 and *Epod.* 9. 31. It is just possible that *malo* is dative; cp. *Odes* 1. 2. 25.

11. **Pontica** (*p*): because it affords the best wood. Compare *Noricus* at *Odes* 1. 16. 9.

12. **silvae filia nobilis**: for the grouping see on P. 20 β *ad fin.*

14, 15. **pictis...puppibus**: for the grouping see on P. 10. The word *pictis* is emphatic; the sailor feels that the figure-heads on the stern are merely painted idols; he is therefore frightened and puts no trust in them.

nil...fidit: there is stress on *nil* by separation, and on *fidit* by position (see on *Odes* 4. 9. 26); *confidence* is impossible.

17. **sollicitum** (*ps*) has emphasis: a *taedium* may be merely *leve*, like *levi exilio* of Suetonius, *Aug.* 51. Compare the chiastic *non levis* of l. 18 (see on P. 29).

19, 20. **interfusa...Cycladas**: for the grouping see on P. 7.

XV. 1. Pastor: by all rules of normal order *pastor* should be subject to both *traheret* and *obruit*. It is true that plenty of cases may be quoted in which the subject of the subordinate clause precedes the conjunction without

Nereus fata: 'mala ducis avi domum,   5
quam multo repetet Graecia milite,
coniurata tuas rumpere nuptias
    et regnum Priami vetus.

heu heu, quantus equis, quantus adest viris
sudor! quanta moves funera Dardanae   10
genti! iam galeam Pallas et aegida
    currusque et rabiem parat.

nequicquam Veneris praesidio ferox
pectes caesariem grataque feminis
inbelli cithara carmina divides;   15
    nequicquam thalamo gravis

being subject of the principal clause; but in such cases the new subject is
inserted with the principal verb. Here there is no hint of a new subject until
we reach the subordinate clause *ut caneret*. Nauck quotes *Odes* 1. 16. 5 where
there is scarcely any difficulty, and Vergil *Aen*. 12. 641 *occidit infelix ne nos-
trum dedecus Ufens | aspiceret*; but this latter example is comparatively simple
because no other subject to *occidit* is possible (see too P. 10). May not *obruit*
be a kind of middle? i.e. 'Because Paris was carrying off another man's wife,
he brought on himself a calm so that Nereus was enabled to tell his fate.'

2. **Idaeis Helenen**: the antithesis of Trojan (ship) and Greek woman is
well brought out.

perfidus hospitam: see on *Odes* 1. 6. 9 and P. 53.

3, 4. **ingrato...ventos**: for the grouping see on P. 7. The antithesis of
ingrato and *celeris* has point: the swift winds do not love inaction.

fera (*ps*) i.e. *mala, non bona*.

5. **mala** (*ps*) has emphasis; compare Livy *Pref*. § 13 *cum bonis potius
ominibus*. But see also P. 21.

6. **multo** (*s*) is emphatic i.e. 'with myriads of soldiers.' In English prose
we prefer definite figures; Latin is satisfied with obscurer and, to our ears,
weaker expressions. Thus Livy 1. 12. 10 *favore multorum addito animo* may
be translated 'the cheers of thousands gave him fresh courage.' Compare too
Plato's famous epigram ὡς πολλοῖς ὄμμασιν εἴς σε βλέπω.

7. **tuas** (*ps*): perhaps in antithesis to *Priami*; but see P. 21.

9, 10. **quantus...sudor! quanta...funera**: for the separation of *quantus*
and *quanta* from their respective nouns see on *Odes* 1. 27. 11.

sudor perhaps has stress; see on *Odes* 4. 9. 26.

Dardanae (*p*) i.e. you are destroying *your own* people; see on *tuae* l.21 below.

11. **genti** has stress (see on *Odes* 4. 9. 26) i.e. you are destroying a whole
nation. See l. 22 below.

Pallas lies by *coniunctio* between *galeam* and *aegida*. For *galeam Pallas*
see on *Odes* 1. 2. 17.

13. **Veneris** (*p*): Venus should protect a lover and an adulterer; the order
too makes *ferox* all the more effective: it is Mars who renders a man *ferocem*.

hastas et calami spicula Cnosii
vitabis strepitumque et celerem sequi
Aiacem: tamen, heu, serus adulteros
    crines pulvere collines.   20

non Laertiaden, exitium tuae
gentis, non Pylium Nestora respicis?
urgent impavidi te Salaminius
    Teucer, te Sthenelus sciens

pugnae, sive opus est imperitare equis,   25
non auriga piger. Merionen quoque
nosces. ecce furit te reperire atrox
    Tydides, melior patre:

14, 15. **grataque...inbelli cithara carmina:** for the grouping see on P. 9.
inbelli: compare *Odes* 1. 6. 10.

16. **thalamo** is locative: in thy bridal bower.

gravis (*p*) i.e. 'the dangers (of the spear)'; see P. 27 and on *Odes* 2.
14. 23.

17. **calami spicula Cnosii:** for the grouping see on P. 20 *a.*

18. **vitabis** may = 'you will seek to avoid'—a conative future; see on
Odes 1. 20. 10.

celerem (*p*): see on P. 27.

19. **Aiacem:** the stress (see *Odes* 4. 9. 26) on this name of woe is most
effective.

adulteros (*p*) i.e. your lover's locks (all neat and glossy) shall be dragged
in the dust; the implied antithesis is neatness and dirt.

21, 22. **tuae** (*p*): see on *Dardanae* (*p*) l. 10 above.

gentis has stress (see on *Odes* 4. 9. 26); compare on l. 11 above.

22, 23. **Pylium** (*p*)...**Salaminius** (*p*): such adjectives describing the
locality of the chieftain's 'seat' are naturally, and among all nations, of
interest and importance. Compare *Odes* 4. 4. 64, and 4. 6. 4. Here there is
further point in emphasizing the adjectives, which give the effect of '*Pylos
to Salamis*' (China to Peru) i.e. Greece from west to east is against you.

impavidi equals an adverb 'valiantly'; see on P. 31.

24. **Teucer:** see *Odes* 4. 9. 26 ; but the reading is uncertain.

25. **pugnae** has stress (see on *Odes* 4. 9. 26) in antithesis to *auriga*. See
too P. 39 *ad fin.*

26. **non auriga piger:** this is literally 'not, as a driver, slack.' The contrast is *pedes* implied in *sciens pugnae.*

27. **nosces** has stress (see on *Odes* 4. 9. 26) and equals 'thou shalt have
reason to know.'

atrox sc. ὤν i.e. when his blood is up, when he sees red.

28. **melior patre** is an emphatic addendum; the sense is 'very brave
because braver than his sire'; see on P. 53, and compare *Odes* 1. 7. 25.

quem tu, cervus uti vallis in altera
visum parte lupum graminis immemor,　　　30
sublimi fugies mollis anhelitu,
　　non hoc pollicitus tuae.

iracunda diem proferet Ilio
matronisque Phrygum classis Achillei:
post certas hiemes uret Achaicus　　　35
　　ignis Iliacas domos.'

XVI.

O matre pulchra filia pulchrior,
quem criminosis cumque voles modum
　　pones iambis, sive flamma
　　sive mari libet Hadriano.

29, 30. **tu, cervus uti**: the subjects likened are brought together (compare *Odes* 4. 2. 27). For the position of *uti* compare *Odes* I. 23. 9, 1. 37. 17, 3. 15. 10, 4. 4. 57, 4. 12. 24, *Epod.* 6. 16, and *Sat.* I. 2. 105, 1. 3. 89. See too *Epod.* 8. 8.

cervus...vallis in altera: a Roman would read these words thus: 'like a stag in the valley on the other side'; he can wait for *parte* with *a dextra, a sinistra* in daily use. The words *vallis in altera* are felt with both *cervus* and *visum...lupum*; each animal is *in altera parte* to the other (compare *Odes* 2. 2. 10). The genitive *vallis* is preposited in order to give the elements of the scene early—a stag and a valley; see on *Odes* I. 2. 17.

in altera | visum parte lupum: for the grouping see on P. 9.

graminis: for the objective genitive placed in front see on P. 39.

31. **sublimi** (*ps*): his *anhelitus* is not *modicus* but *sublimis*; see Page *ad loc.*

mollis sc. ὤν i.e. because you are 'soft.' Paris, being *mollis*, is scant of breath.

32. **non hoc pollicitus tuae**: an emphatic addendum; see on P. 53.

33. **iracunda**: the subject lies in the adjective i.e. 'wrath shall put off the evil day—the wrath of Achilles' fleet.' Compare Livy *Pref.* § 5 (*mala*) *quae nostra* (=we) *tot per annos vidit aetas* (=in our lifetime). See on *Odes* I. 3. 36, I. 18. 8, 1. 21. 16, 1. 26. 9, 1. 31. 9, 2. 8. 23, 3. 4. 69, 4. 2. 45, 4. 4. 7, 4. 4. 17, 4. 4. 73, 4. 6. 21. For a somewhat similar use of a possessive adjective with the sense of an ethical dative see on *Odes* I. 13. 3, and compare the use of the preposited genitive noted at P. 38.

35. **certas** (*p*) i.e. fixed, limited in number, not unlimited. Compare *Epod.* 13. 15 *certo subtemine*.

Achaicus (*p*): because contrasted with *Iliacas* (*p*) or *Pergameas* (*p*) in l. 36.

Throughout this Ode the order seems strained and suggests a translation.

XVI. 2, 3. **quem...cumque**: see on *Odes* I. 6. 3.

non Dindymene, non adytis quatit 5
mentem sacerdotum incola Pythius,
 non Liber aeque, non acuta
  si geminant Corybantes aera,

tristes ut irae, quas neque Noricus
deterret ensis nec mare naufragum 10
 nec saevus ignis nec tremendo
  Iuppiter ipse ruens tumultu.

fertur Prometheus addere principi
limo coactus particulam undique
 desectam et insani leonis 15
  vim stomacho apposuisse nostro.

irae Thyesten exitio gravi
stravere et altis urbibus ultimae
 stetere causae, cur perirent
  funditus imprimeretque muris 20

quem criminosis...modum | pones iambis: for the grouping see on P. 9.

4. Hadriano (*s*): see on P. 21. The lady addressed may have been some old Apulian acquaintance living on the east coast of Italy.

5. adytis is placed early for emphasis; it is 'opposed to the more widely diffused *afflatus*, ἐνθουσιασμός, of Cybele or Bacchus' (Wickham).

7. acuta (*ps*): the adjective equals an adverb (*acute*) and goes with *geminant*; see on P. 31.

9. tristes (*p*) i.e. 'the odiousness, balefulness (of passion)'; see on P. 27, and *Odes* 2. 14. 23.

ut: for its position see on *Odes* I. 15. 29, 30.

Noricus (*ps*) i.e. the best steel sword from the Tyrol; compare *Epod.* 17. 71, and see *Odes* I. 14. 11, 4. 9. 17. But see also P. 21.

11. saevus (*p*): see on *Odes* 2. 14. 23.

tremendo (*ps*): the word may be felt first with *Iuppiter*; see on P. 52, and *Epod.* 6. 9. As Latin still waits for a noun to go with *tremendo*, there is no real pause at *ruens* and the rhythm is thus less exceptional. See Page *ad loc.* Compare also note at *Odes* 4. 8. 33.

13. principi (*p*) i.e. from the very beginning this *ira* has been planted in us.

15. desectam may be felt again with *vim*.

insani (*p*) i.e. 'the madness (of a lion)'; see on P. 27.

leonis (*p*): contrast the qualities of the hare, fox etc.; the position also prepares us for the antithesis *nostro*.

16. nostro (*s*): contrast *leonis*; but see also P. 21.

18. stravere perhaps has stress; see on *Odes* 4. 9. 26.

hostile aratrum exercitus insolens.
compesce mentem! me quoque pectoris
   temptavit in dulci iuventa
     fervor et in celeris iambos

misit furentem: nunc ego mitibus   25
mutare quaero tristia, dum mihi
   fias recantatis amica
     opprobriis animumque reddas.

XVII.

Velox amoenum saepe Lucretilem
mutat Lycaeo Faunus et igneam
   defendit aestatem capellis
     usque meis pluviosque ventos.

altis (*p*) i.e. with high citadel and therefore better protected.

ultimae (*ps*) has emphasis, like *principi* in l. 13 above; see also P. 21.

20. **funditus** (*pp*) is emphatic; see also on *Odes* 4. 9. 26.

21. **hostile** is preposited because *aratrum* is the emblem of peace; moreover Horace always places *hostilis* in front (see on *Odes* 2. 12. 22) and usually makes generic adjectives preposited (see on P. 37).

22. **me**: for its order see on P. 51.

pectoris: a Roman might read this genitive as if 'in my heart' (compare *animi*); ultimately it goes with *fervor*.

23. **dulci** (*p*) i.e. 'the sweetness, gladness (of youth)'; see on P. 27.

24. **celeris** (*p*) i.e. too quick for me; they ran away with me.

25. **mitibus** is put early to prepare us for the antithesis *tristia*, which is placed last.

26, 27. **mihi...recantatis**: *mihi* is felt with *recantatis* as though the latter were a deponent in agreement with it. The construction is an extension of the idiom noted at *Odes* I. 10. 14. Moreover she is *amica* in the atmosphere of recanted libels; see on *Odes* 4. 8. 33.

XVII. 1, 2. **Velox amoenum...Lucretilem | mutat...Faunus**: for the grouping see on P. 10. The two adjectives (*velox amoenum*) make it unnecessary to take *saepe* with *amoenum Lucretilem* only; see on P. 50 *d*. The adverb goes with the whole sentence; see on *Odes* 2. 9. 13.

igneam (*ps*) i.e. 'the fires (of summer)'; see on P. 27 and P. 21.

4. **usque meis** may be regarded as an emphatic addendum i.e. 'and that without ceasing and those goats mine'; see on P. 53. The pause at the end of l. 3 obviates the necessity of grouping *capellis | usque meis* together; see on P. 50 *b*.

pluvios (*p*) i.e. 'the rain (of, brought by, the winds)'; see on P. 27.

impune tutum per nemus arbutos   5
quaerunt latentis et thyma deviae
 olentis uxores mariti,
  nec viridis metuunt colubras

nec Martialis haediliae lupos,
utcumque dulci, Tyndari, fistula   10
 valles et Usticae cubantis
  levia personuere saxa.

di me tuentur, dis pietas mea
et Musa cordi est. hinc tibi copia
 manabit ad plenum benigno   15
  ruris honorum opulenta cornu.

5. **tutum** (*ps*) i.e. 'because it is safe'; the epithet is naturally brought close to *impune*.

6, 7. **latentis** is a concessive addendum—'though lying out of sight' (see P. 53); the search would thus be a long one and involve much distance.

deviae | ...mariti: for the grouping see on P. 9. The collocation *deviae olentis* suggests playfully that they were not unwilling to avoid his smell.

8. **viridis** (*ps*): the colour would help to conceal the vipers and so make them the more dangerous; hence the emphasis. But see also on P. 21.

9. **haediliae**: if we read *Haediliae* (gen.), the order is normal. The reading *haediliae* (nom.) gives to the stock epithet *Martialis* an inexplicable emphasis.

10. **dulci** (*ps*) i.e. 'the sweetness, sweet music (of the flute)'; see on P. 27. For the intervening vocative see on *Odes* 1. 5. 3.

11. **Usticae** goes with both *valles* and *levia saxa* by *coniunctio*.

12. **levia** (*ps*): see on P. 21.

13. **mea**: see on *Odes* 2. 12. 13, 14.

14. **tibi copia**: see on *Odes* 1. 2. 17. The dative *tibi* is quasi-ethical i.e. 'you will find that....'

15, 16. **ad plenum** (*pp*): the adverb phrase is emphatic i.e. 'into thy lap till it is full' (Wickham).

benigno | ...cornu may well be ablative (=from) depending on *manabit*. The adjective *benigno* echoes and amplifies *ad plenum*; it equals ἀφθόνως and is the opposite of *maligne*. If there were no *opulenta*, everything would be normal (see on *Odes* 1. 7. 29) i.e. 'from the horn rich in the glories of the country.' Horace throws in *opulenta* (see P. 46 *b*), with which, as well as with *benigno*, the words *ruris honorum* may be taken. He thus emphasizes the rich productiveness of his home in a crescendo—*ad plenum, benigno, opulenta*.

ruris (*p*) **honorum**: to the jaded poet of the *Town* the emotional interest (*o tunicata quies!*) lies in *ruris*.

hic in reducta valle Caniculae
vitabis aestus et fide Teia
   dices laborantis in uno
      Penelopen vitreamque Circen.   20

hic innocentis pocula Lesbii
duces sub umbra, nec Semeleius
   cum Marte confundet Thyoneus
      proelia, nec metues protervum

suspecta Cyrum, ne male dispari   25
incontinentis iniciat manus
   et scindat haerentem coronam
      crinibus immeritamque vestem.

17. **reducta** (p) i.e. because it is retired, sequestered, and therefore cool.
Caniculae (ps) i.e. the dog (and its heat); see on P. 38.
19. **laborantis in uno**: these words go closely with *dices* i.e. 'will speak of as lovesick for one.'
20. **vitream** (p): the epithet suggests the immortal; thus Penelope, the mortal, and Circe the goddess, are in love with the same man (*in uno*).
21. **innocentis** (ps): even a lady may drink Lesbian without impropriety and without headache; but see P. 20 β.
22, 23. **sub umbra** is an emphatic addendum i.e. 'and in the cool shade'; see on P. 53.
Semeleius | cum Marte: for case relations grouped early see *Odes* I. 2. 17. A Roman would read the words thus: 'nor Semele's son with Mars shall join....'
Thyoneus goes closely with *confundet* i.e. 'like the Son of Thunder he is.'
24. **proelia** has stress; see on *Odes* 4. 9. 26.
24, 25. **protervum** (ps) equals *protervitatem* (*Cyri*); see on P. 27. But see also P. 24 and P. 25. Observe that in the group *protervum suspecta Cyrum* we may feel *protervum...Cyrum* as equal to *a protervo Cyro*, and thus the order is less startling (see on *Epod.* 7. 8).
suspecta i.e. 'because suspected.'
26. **incontinentis** (ps) equals *incontinenter*; see on P. 31 and P. 21.
27. **haerentem** (p): he has to tear '*because* the garland cleaves.'
28. **crinibus** would normally lie between *haerentem* and *coronam*, but *haerentem* is a word which can hardly be absolute and we wait, without difficulty, for the dative; see on P. 47. The effect too of the order is 'he tears garland, hair, and clothes.'
immeritam is felt with both *crinibus* and *vestem*; see on P. 33.

XVIII.

Nullam, Vare, sacra vite prius severis arborem
circa mite solum Tiburis et moenia Catili:
siccis omnia nam dura deus proposuit, neque
mordaces aliter diffugiunt sollicitudines.
quis post vina gravem militiam aut pauperiem crepat?   5
quis non te potius, Bacche pater, teque, decens Venus?
ac nequis modici transiliat munera Liberi,
Centaurea monet cum Lapithis rixa super mero
debellata, monet Sithoniis non levis Euhius,

XVIII. 1. **Nullam** (*ps*): this adjective by position, as so often in Cicero, becomes an emphatic negative i.e. 'Do not sow *any*....'

sacra (*p*) i.e. because god-given. The words *sacra vite* precede *prius* for emphasis; 'nothing,' says Horace, 'before the *vine*.'

2. **mite solum Tiburis**: for the grouping see P. 35.

3. **siccis omnia nam dura**: these words sound like 'to the dry all things are hard'; then *deus proposuit* reads as a parenthesis i.e. 'so has Heaven ordained.' Both *siccis* and *omnia* have stress because they come early and precede *nam*. For *nam* late see on *Epod.* 14. 6.

4. **mordaces** (*ps*): i.e. the canker (of anxiety); see on P. 27, and on *Odes* 2. 14. 23. Compare *curas edacis* (*Odes* 2. 11. 18), and *vitiosa...cura* (*Odes* 2. 16. 21).

sollicitudines: for position see on *Odes* 1. 3. 16.

5. **gravem** (*p*): i.e. 'the hardship (of campaigns)'; see on P. 27, and on *Odes* 2. 14. 23. Compare also *Odes* 1. 29. 2 *acrem* (*p*) *militiam*.

6. **decens** (*p*): for its position see on P. 36.

7. **modici** (*ps*): as if Horace had written *ne quis modum transiliat*; the stress, of course, is all on 'moderation.' For the grouping *modici...munera Liberi* see on P. 20 a. It is tempting to believe that *modici Liberi* is a kind of oxymoron—'limited freedom.'

8. **Centaurea monet cum Lapithis rixa**: for case relations early see on *Odes* 1. 2. 17, and for the intrusive *monet* see on P. 46 a. The adjective *Centaurea* contains the subject *Centauri* (see on *Odes* 1. 15. 33), and the Latin reads thus: 'the Centaurs are a warning and the Lapithae with their quarrel fought out over the wine.'

9. **debellata** has stress; see on *Odes* 4. 9. 26.

Observe the pretty combination of epithet, complement, noun (*Centaurea... cum Lapithis rixa*) with noun, complement, epithet (*rixa super mero debellata*).

monet...Euhius i.e. there is a warning in the Sithonians and the heavy hand (*non levis*) of Evius. The normal order (*non levis Sithoniis Euhius*) is abandoned in order to bring *Sithoniis* early, parallel to *Centaurea*. The antitheses are 'Centaurs versus Lapithae' and 'Sithonians versus Evius.'

non levis (*p*): see on P. 29.

cum fas atque nefas exiguo fine libidinum   10
discernunt avidi. non ego te, candide Bassareu,
invitum quatiam nec variis obsita frondibus
sub divum rapiam. saeva tene cum Berecyntio
cornu tympana, quae subsequitur caecus amor sui
et tollens vacuum plus nimio gloria verticem   15
arcanique fides prodiga, perlucidior vitro.

XIX.

Mater saeva Cupidinum
    Thebanaeque iubet me Semelae puer

10. **exiguo fine libidinum:** for the grouping see on P. 35.

11. **avidi** coming last has emphasis and is causal i.e. 'because they are greedy and full of passion.'

candide (*p*): for its position see on P. 36.

12. **variis obsita frondibus:** for the grouping see on P. 24.

13, 14. **saeva...cum Berecyntio | cornu tympana:** for the grouping see on P. 10.

Berecyntio is always preposited in Horace; the sound of a horn is not dangerous, but the sound of Cybele's is. Compare on *Odes* 3. 19. 18 and 4. I. 22.

quae subsequitur: the picture seems to be that of a pageant; first come horn and drums, then comes blind Self-love, then vain Pride, then Faith unfaithful. Compare Lucretius 5. 737–747.

caecus (*p*): Love is blind, but especially blind is Self-love; *amor sui* may be regarded as one word φιλαυτία (see on P. 45). But *caecus amor sui* may be classified under P. 35.

15. **tollens vacuum...gloria verticem:** for the grouping see on P. 9.

plus nimio has emphasis because it follows and is separated from its verb *tollens*.

16. **arcani** has emphasis, for it should lie between *fides* and *prodiga* (see on P. 43); Faith should be prodigal of Faith only, not of secrets. It may, however, be remembered that an objective genitive usually precedes the word upon which it depends (see on P. 39).

perlucidior vitro is an emphatic addendum; see on P. 53. The statue of Fides is said to have worn, perhaps on the right hand, a white veil, symbolizing that Fides was frank and open (white), yet kept her secrets (veil); but to be *perlucidior vitro* is going too far altogether. Compare on *Odes* I. 35. 21, and for the white veil see Livy I. 21. 4, and Servius on Vergil *Aen.* I. 292 and 8. 636. Ovid speaks of *fides* as *liquida* (*Ex Ponto* I. 9. 10).

XIX. I. **Mater saeva Cupidinum:** a very rare order (see on P. 44); it is just possible that *saeva* is felt to qualify both *Mater* and *Cupidinum* (see P. 52), and compare *Odes* 3. 15. 15 *flos purpureus rosae*. See too on *Odes* 3. 1. 42. Contrast *Odes* 4. 1. 4 *dulcium | mater saeva Cupidinum*, and P. 36.

et lasciva Licentia
finitis animum reddere amoribus.
urit me Glycerae nitor   5
splendentis Pario marmore purius,
urit grata protervitas
et vultus nimium lubricus aspici.
in me tota ruens Venus
Cyprum deseruit, nec patitur Scythas   10
et versis animosum equis
Parthum dicere nec quae nihil attinent.
hic vivum mihi caespitem, hic
verbenas, pueri, ponite turaque
bimi cum patera meri: 15
mactata veniet lenior hostia.

2. **Thebanae** (*ps*): the strained order seems to have no explanation save metrical convenience. But *Thebanae* may='from Thebes' (see on *Odes* I. 31. 9) in contrast to Venus from Cyprus.

Semelae puer: for the order see on P. 41.

3. **lasciva** (*p*): i.e. the wantonness (of Licentia); see on P. 27. But compare also on *Odes* I. 7. 5.

4. **finitis** (*ps*): i.e. that were finished and done for (so I thought); compare *relictos* at *Odes* I. 34. 5.

5. **Glycerae** (*p*): for the position see on P. 38.

6. **splendentis...purius** is an emphatic addendum ; see on P. 53.

Pario (*p*) i.e. the whitest and most brilliant of marbles.

purius has emphasis because placed after and far separated from *splendentis*.

7. **grata** (*p*): a woman's *protervitas* may easily be *ingrata* if carried too far ; but *grata* (*p*) may simply mean 'the charm (of coquetry)' ; see on P. 27.

9. **tota** is predicative with *ruens* i.e. swooping full on me.

11, 12. **versis...** | **Parthum:** for the grouping see on P. 9. But *animosum* naturally lies between *versis* and *equis* because the Parthian's courage comes out only as he flies away.

13. **vivum** (*ps*): ritual seems to have demanded that the sod should be fresh cut; hence the order.

15. **bimi cum patera meri:** for the grouping see on P. 20 a. New wine was required for sacrifices. See on *Odes* I. 31. 2, 3 and 3. 23. 3.

16. **mactata** (*ps*): a Roman in reading this word would think merely of the verbal idea i.e. slaughter and its completion (compare *explorato* etc.). Thus the line would be read by him ' after slaughter she will be more kindly by reason of my offering,' where *hostia* now becomes a causal ablative. See on P. 26, and compare *Odes* 4. 11. 7, 8. But the inevitable stress on *mactata*

XX.

Vile potabis modicis Sabinum
cantharis, Graeca quod ego ipse testa
conditum levi, datus in theatro
 cum tibi plausus,

care Maecenas eques, ut paterni   5
fluminis ripae simul et iocosa
redderet laudes tibi Vaticani
 montis imago.

is all to the point—a *slaughtered* victim is what Venus wants, not one *quae
nascitur* (*Odes* 3. 23. 9).

The ablative *hostia* perhaps confirms the view that *hostia* is also ablative
at *Odes* 3. 23. 18.

XX. 1. **Vile...modicis Sabinum | cantharis:** for the grouping see on
P. 9. Both *Vile* and *potabis* have interest i.e. 'cheap stuff you shall swill';
indeed *potabis* might be contrasted with the more elegent *bibes* of 1. 10.
Compare Cicero *Phil.* 2. 27. 67 *totos dies potabatur* (i.e. 'there was heavy
drinking all day') and the familiar *potus et exlex*.

The first three words *Vile potabis modicis* give us the picture 'cheap wine,
swilling, and from cheap (cups).'

2. **cantharis** has stress (see on *Odes* 4. 9. 26); *canthari* are large, wide-
bellied, and have handles. The implied antithesis is the less clumsy *poculum*
of 1. 12 below. For the grouping *modicis Sabinum | cantharis* see note at
Odes 4. 8. 33.

Graeca (*ps*): another abomination—something Greek! Happily it is only
the whiff of an empty jar. The bias of patriotism put Greek wines behind all
Italian wines, although Pliny esteemed them. Compare on *Odes* 3. 24. 57.

3. **datus in theatro:** these words have stress because they precede *cum*.
Possibly then *datus* equals *ultro datus*; Maecenas needed no *claqueurs*; and
in theatro draws attention to the public nature of the welcome.

5. **care** (*p*): the position, perhaps, emphasizes Horace's affection; but see
P. 36. Bentley's *clare* makes an excellent point, since *clarus* is used especially
of a senator, *splendidus* of a knight (see Duff on Juvenal *Sat.* 10. 95). Thus
the sense would be 'as glorious as a senator, Maecenas, though but a knight.'
See too on *Odes* 2. 17. 7, 8, 3. 24. 30.

paterni (*p*): Horace thus emphasizes the antiquity of Maecenas' family.
See *Odes* 1. 1. 1.

6. **fluminis** (*p*) i.e. 'the river (with its banks)'; see on P. 38.

simul by position ('*coniunctio*') belongs to both *ripae* and *montis imago*.

iocosa (*ps*) equals an adverb 'playfully'; see on P. 31.

7. **Vaticani** (*p*): the point is that even the more distant Vatican Hill
(more distant than the *mons Ianiculus*) threw back the echo of such loud
applause. See on *Odes* 3. 29. 38, 39.

8. **montis** (*p*) i.e. 'the hill (and its echo)'; see on P. 38.

Caecubum et prelo domitam Caleno
tu bibes uvam: mea nec Falernae   10
temperant vites neque Formiani
     pocula colles.

XXI.

Dianam tenerae dicite virgines,
intonsum, pueri, dicite Cynthium
    Latonamque supremo
     dilectam penitus Iovi.

vos laetam fluviis et nemorum coma,   5
quaecumque aut gelido prominet Algido,
    nigris aut Erymanthi
     silvis aut viridis Cragi.

9, 10. Caecubum...tu: the object comes first with emphasis; it is a first class wine.

prelo domitam Caleno | ...uvam: for the grouping see on P. 14.

Caleno (*s*): its position emphasizes the high quality of the wine.

tu is emphatic because inserted; contrast *mea* (*ps*), whose position seems to support the reading *tu*.

bibes may be a conative future i.e. 'you will be for drinking' (compare on *Odes* I. 15. 18). See however Mr L. H. Allen's paper *C.R.* Vol. XXV. p. 168. Gow, *C.R.* XXIX. p. 76, shows good reason for reading *iubes* ('you order up').

mea (*ps*): see above on *tu*. The possessive adjective merely sounds like 'as for me,' and is equivalent to an ethical dative. See note on *Odes* I. 13. 3.

10, 11. Falernae (*ps*): the position emphasizes (like *Caleno* above) the excellence of the wine; compare *Odes* 3. 1. 43, but see P. 21.

Formiani (*ps*): for its position compare *Falernae* above.

XXI. 1, 2. Dianam: note the chiasmus *Dianam...dicite...dicite Cynthium.*

tenerae (*ps*) i.e. because you are tender (sing to the tender maiden goddess); compare on *Odes* I. 1. 26, but see also P. 21.

intonsum (*ps*): Horace wishes to keep the adjective close to *pueri* i.e. the unshorn god ('unshorn' implies young) is to be worshipped by the young.

3, 4. Latonamque supremo | dilectam...Iovi: for the grouping see P. 14.

penitus, placed after *dilectam,* has emphasis.

5. nemorum (*p*) i.e. 'the groves (with their tresses of leaves)'; see on P. 38, and on *Odes* I. 1. 30.

6. gelido (*ps*) i.e. 'the snows (of Algidus)'; see on P. 27 and P. 21. For the phrase see *Odes* 3. 23. 9.

7. aut is placed before *Erymanthi,* not before *nigris,* because the names of the mountains are the ideas really connected together. See also note on *viridis* (*p*) in l. 8.

8. viridis (*p*): contrast the dark foliage (pines, holm-oaks etc.) of Erymanthus.

vos Tempe totidem tollite laudibus
natalemque, mares, Delon Apollinis   10
   insignemque pharetra
     fraternaque umerum lyra.

hic bellum lacrimosum, hic miseram famem
pestemque a populo et principe Caesare in
   Persas atque Britannos   15
     vestra motus aget prece.

XXII.

Integer vitae scelerisque purus
non eget Mauris iaculis neque arcu
nec venenatis gravida sagittis,
   Fusce, pharetra,

sive per Syrtis iter aestuosas   5
sive facturus per inhospitalem
   Caucasum vel quae loca fabulosus
     lambit Hydaspes.

9. **totidem**: for position see P. 21.

10. **natalem...Delon Apollinis**: for the grouping see P. 35. Compare on *Odes* 3. 4. 63.

11, 12. **insignemque pharetra | ...umerum**: the order is, of course, normal (see on *Odes* I. 7. 29) if *insignem* agrees with *umerum*. Editors, however, take *umerum* as an accusative of respect.

    fraterna (*ps*): his brother's, not his own; as if we had *aliena* (*non sua*).

    lyra: for its position see on P. 48.

13. **bellum lacrimosum...miseram famem**: note the chiasmus. But *miseram* (*p*) may equal 'the miseries (of famine)'; see on P. 27, and *Odes* 2. 14. 23.

14. **Caesare in**: for the position of *in* see on *Odes* I. 35. 39. Horace seems to forget that Romans will die even if war be transferred from Rome and Italy. See too on *Odes* I. 35. 39.

16. **vestra** (*ps*) equals *a vobis* (see on *Odes* I. 13. 3); subsequently *prece* means 'in answer to prayer' (see note on *Odes* I. 14. 10), and is heard with *aget* as well as with *motus*.

XXII. 1. **vitae scelerisque**: note the chiasmus.

2. **Mauris** (*p*): if we compare *Odes* 3. 10. 18 *nec Mauris animum mitior anguibus*, it seems a fair assumption that these darts were anointed with snake poison; hence the stress on *Mauris* in our passage. The same remarks apply to the reading *Mauri*.

3, 4. **venenatis...pharetra**: for the grouping see on P. 9.

5. **iter**: the noun equals a verb 'you go' and lies between *Syrtis* and *aestuosas*; see on P. 21.

namque me silva lupus in Sabina,
dum meam canto Lalagen et ultra   10
terminum curis vagor expeditis,
    fugit inermem,

quale portentum neque militaris
Daunias latis alit aesculetis
nec Iubae tellus generat, leonum   15
    arida nutrix.

aestuosas: the word includes two ideas—heat and boiling surge ; see on *Odes* 2. 6. 4.

6. **inhospitalem** (*p*) i.e. 'through the savagery, wildness (of the Caucasus)'; see on P. 27, and *Odes* 2. 14. 23. Horace repeats the words at *Epod.* 1. 12.

7. **fabulosus** (*ps*) equals *secundum fabulas* (see too on P. 21); it may be felt with both *loca* and *Hydaspes* (see on P. 52). Compare *Odes* 3. 4. 9.

9. **me silva lupus:** a beautiful instance of case relations grouped early; I was the object (*me*) in a forest of a wolf's attentions (see on *Odes* 1. 2. 17).

in Sabina merely equals a noun, as if we had e.g. *in Samnio*; see on *Odes* 1. 31. 9.

10, 11. **meam** (*ps*) may be predicative i.e. 'sing of her as mine,' or may equal 'my beloved' (see on *Odes* 1. 26. 8); but see also P. 21.

ultra | terminum has stress by separation from *vagor*. Horace is daydreaming and goes beyond his boundary fence.

curis vagor expeditis: see on P. 21 and P. 23. The contained subject *ego* may lie between *curis* and *expeditis* on the analogy of *dextra Hercules data* ; see on *Odes* 1. 10. 14.

12. **inermem:** a concessive addendum ; see on P. 53.

13. **militaris** (*p*): the soldiers of Apulia were famous, possessing the qualities of their native wolves (compare the 'martial' wolves of *Odes* 1. 17. 9, and see *Odes* 1. 33. 7). A wolf suckled the ancestors of the Roman people.

14. **latis** (*ps*) i.e. 'in the breadth (of its oak coppices).' See on P. 27 and P. 21.

15, 16. **Iubae** (*p*) is parallel to *militaris* (*p*) in l. 13 above. The name of Iuba at once suggests the fighting qualities of the Numidians. A country of such lions will produce lion-hearted men, and *leonum* stands outside *arida* and *nutrix* with stress in contrast to *luporum* implied with *portentum* (see on P. 43).

The words *arida nutrix* form a clever oxymoron : a *nutrix* should not be *arida* ; hence *arida* is preposited.

If instead of the grouping *leonum | arida nutrix* we had the normal *arida leonum nutrix*, we should lose the emphasis on both *arida* and *leonum*.

pone me pigris ubi nulla campis
arbor aestiva recreatur aura,
quod latus mundi nebulae malusque
    Iuppiter urget;   20

pone sub curru nimium propinqui
solis, in terra domibus negata:
dulce ridentem Lalagen amabo,
    dulce loquentem.

XXIII.

Vitas hinnuleo me similis, Chloe,
quaerenti pavidam montibus aviis
    matrem non sine vano
      aurarum et siluae metu.

nam seu mobilibus †veris inhorruit   5
adventus† foliis, seu virides rubum
    dimovere lacertae,
      et corde et genibus tremit.

17, 18. **pigris...nulla campis | arbor**: for the grouping see on P. 9. For *pigris* compare *iners* at *Odes* 2. 9. 5 and 4. 7. 12.

    aestiva (*ps*); see on P. 21. There is an antithesis to *pigris* (= *hibernis*) of l. 17.

    19. **malus** (*p*): see on *Odes* 2. 14. 23. The word is naturally placed near *nebulae*, and may well be in ἀπὸ κοινοῦ position (see on P. 33). Compare too *Odes* 3. 3. 56.

    21, 22. **propinqui** (*p*): compare *Odes* I. 24. 2. For *solis* see *Odes* 4. 9. 26.

    23, 24. **dulce ridentem** (*p*)**...loquentem**: the participles are not mere adjectives, but are causal.

    XXIII. 1. **hinnuleo me similis**: the order is as if Horace had written *hinnuleus me uti*, for which see on *Odes* I. 15. 29 and ll. 9, 10 of this *Ode*. For the early grouping of case relations see *Odes* I. 2. 17.

    2. **montibus aviis**: these words properly belong by order (see *Odes* I. 7. 29) to *pavidam* and *matrem*; the mother is terrified for her child's sake by the pathless mountains. Both mother and roebuck, however, are searching and therefore *montibus aviis* may be felt with both.

    5, 6. **mobilibus veris inhorruit | adventus foliis**: *veris* is the equivalent of *vernus* which Horace would, perhaps, have written but for the similar terminations of *mobilibus* and *vernus*; for the grouping see P. 10 and P. 12. For other readings see the commentators.

    virides (*ps*): the green (of the lizard); see P. 27. It is also the contrast of the bright green against the dark blackberry bush that startles.

    7. **lacertae**: for its position see on *Odes* I. 3. 16.

atqui non ego te tigris ut aspera
Gaetulusve leo frangere persequor: 10
  tandem desine matrem
  tempestiva sequi viro.

XXIV.

Quis desiderio sit pudor aut modus
tam cari capitis? praecipe lugubris
  cantus, Melpomene, cui liquidam pater
  vocem cum cithara dedit.

ergo Quintilium perpetuus sopor   5
urget? cui Pudor et Iustitiae soror,
  incorrupta Fides, nudaque Veritas
  quando ullum inveniet parem?

9, 10. **ego te tigris ut**: the case relations are grouped early; see on *Odes*
1. 2. 17. For the position of *ut* see on *Odes* 1. 15. 29.
  Note the chiasmus *tigris...aspera* | *Gaetulusve leo*.
  12. **sequi**: the position is startling. Is it only to give *viro* stress in contrast to *matrem*? But Horace seems to be saying two things in one expression (see *Odes* 1. 27. 23, 24, 1. 37. 18, 2. 4. 13, and 4. 4. 61) viz. 'cease to
follow your mother, you who are ripe for a husband to follow' i.e. *sequi* first
depends on *desine*, then on *tempestiva*. Observe that Horace could have
written *viro sequi*, and therefore metrical convenience has nothing to do with
the order; compare *Odes* 1. 14. 10.
  XXIV. 1, 2. desiderio and tam cari capitis are the important ideas: there
is nothing to be ashamed of in *regrets*, above all for *one so dear*. Hence
desiderio comes early and *tam cari capitis* is separated from it. Moreover
tam cari capitis may also be felt with *pudor* and *modus* i.e. 'in reference to
so dear a person.'
  tam cari (*p*): the sense demands stress; compare *Odes* 1. 22. 21.
  lugubris (*p*): a sad song from the Muse of Tragedy (*pace* Wickham).
See too on *Odes* 2. 14. 23.
  3. **liquidam** (*ps*) i.e. a *melting* voice, not merely *claram, argutam* etc.
In Vergil *Georg.* 1. 410 *liquida* seems to mean 'soft.'
  5. **Quintilium...sopor**: for the order see P. 51.
  perpetuus (*p*): *sopor* is the *vox propria* for unconsciousness; this unconsciousness lasts not for a few moments but *for ever*. English achieves
the same emphasis by making the adjective come after the noun—'the
sleep unbroken.'
  6. **urget**: the position makes the pressure all the heavier; see on *Odes*
4. 9. 26.
  Iustitiae (*p*): see on P. 41 *ad fin.*

multis ille bonis flebilis occidit,
nulli flebilior quam tibi, Vergili.   10
tu frustra pius heu non ita creditum
    poscis Quintilium deos.

quid, si Threicio blandius Orpheo
auditam moderere arboribus fidem?
num vanae redeat sanguis imagini,   15
    quam virga semel horrida,

non lenis precibus fata recludere,
nigro compulerit Mercurius gregi?
durum: sed levius fit patientia
    quicquid corrigere est nefas.   20

XXV.

Parcius iunctas quatiunt fenestras
iactibus crebris iuvenes protervi
nec tibi somnos adimunt, amatque
    ianua limen,

7. **incorrupta** (*p*): contrast the *fides* of *Odes* I. 18. 16.
nuda (*p*) is rightly stressed, as is *incorrupta*.
8. **ullum...parem**: both words have stress by mutual separation. See also P. 21.
9. **multis** (*s*) i.e. πολλοῖς μέν..., σοὶ δέ....
11. **non ita creditum** (*s*) is causal—because not so entrusted. See also P. 21.
13. **Threicio** (*ps*): for its position see on P. 24.
14. **auditam...fidem**: for the intrusive *moderere* see on P. 46. The effect is to stress *arboribus* i.e. 'heard and by trees.'
15. **num**: if *non* be read, it is emphatic because separated from *redeat*.
vanae (*ps*) i.e. 'to the emptiness (of the shade)'; see on P. 27.
16. **semel**: for its position see on P. 50 *c*. It has emphasis because it is far separated from *compulerit*.
17. **non lenis** (*ps*): see on P. 29.
18. **nigro** (*ps*) i.e. 'to the darkness (of his flock)'; see on P. 27.
20. **nefas** comes last with stress—'what to amend is *sin*.'
XXV. 1. **Parcius** (*s*) has emphasis; it is echoed chiastically by *minus et minus iam* of l. 6.
iunctas (*s*) i.e. 'because they are closed'; but see P. 21.
3. **amat** is emphatic because placed early; the door clings to the threshold instead of flying open.

quae prius multum.facilis movebat   5
cardines. audis minus et minus iam:
'me tuo longas pereunte noctes,
    Lydia, dormis?'

invicem moechos anus arrogantis
flebis in solo levis angiportu,   10
Thracio bacchante magis sub inter-
    lunia vento,

cum tibi flagrans amor et libido,
quae solet matres furiare equorum,
saeviet circa iecur ulcerosum,   15
    non sine questu,

laeta quod pubes hedera virenti
gaudeat pulla magis atque myrto,
aridas frondes hiemis sodali
    dedicet Hebro.   20

5. **prius** (*s*) is answered by the chiastic *iam* of l. 6—$\pi\rho\acute{o}\tau\epsilon\rho\sigma\nu$ $\mu\acute{\epsilon}\nu...\nu\nu\grave{\iota}$ $\delta\acute{\epsilon}$.

multum facilis: if *facilis* is nominative, it equals an adverb (see P. 31); if accusative plural, it may be classed under P. 21. In either case *facilis* suggests both literally 'moved with ease,' and metaphorically 'free and easy,' as in *facilis aditu*.

6. **cardines** should have stress (see on *Odes* 4. 9. 26); the position, perhaps, suggests the weight and immovability of a door.

minus...iam: both adverbs have stress by position.

7. **me tuo:** for the case relations see on *Odes* 1. 2. 17.

longas (*s*) i.e. 'the long long nights'; see also P. 21.

9. **moechos anus:** for the case relations see on *Odes* 1. 2. 17.

arrogantis (*s*) i.e. '(lament) the arrogance (of *moechi*)'; see on P. 27.

10. **in solo** (*ps*) i.e. 'in the loneliness (of an alley)'; see on P. 27. The words of this line should be read in their order viz. 'thou wilt weep in loneliness, of no account, in some lane.'

11, 12. **Thracio** (*ps*): perhaps to emphasize the bitter cold of the wind; compare *Epod.* 13. 3 *Threicio Aquilone.* But *Thracio* may be regarded as a second complement which stands outside *bacchante...vento* (see on P. 48).

magis placed after *bacchante* equals 'even more.'

13. **tibi** is an ethical dative i.e. 'when you feel the fire....'

flagrans (*p*) i.e. 'the fire (of passion)'; see on P. 27.

14. **equorum** (*s*): the stress makes this statement even more offensive.

15, 16. **circa...questu** are emphatic addenda; see on P. 53. Prose might write *saeviet idque circa* etc. Her heart is already diseased and needs no fresh onset of morbid passion.

17. **laeta** (*ps*) equals an adverb; see on P. 31.

XXVI.

Musis amicus tristitiam et metus
tradam protervis in mare Creticum
portare ventis, quis sub Arcto
rex gelidae metuatur orae,

quid Tiridaten terreat, unice   5
securus. o quae fontibus integris
gaudes, apricos necte flores,
necte meo Lamiae coronam,

18. **pulla** (*ps*): the order may be partly due to chiasmus (compare, for instance, *Odes* 2. 3. 9), partly to a desire to suggest that bright green ivy is best, and even (*atque*) dull green myrtle is preferable to dry leaves. In this case *magis* by its position equals 'far more' (compare l. 11 above) and qualifies *hedera gaudeat* and *gaudeat myrto* alike. But the hyperbaton is very harsh and has no parallel in the *Odes* and *Epodes*.

The order would be more tolerable if *atque* were taken in the sense of 'than' (see on *Epod.* 12. 14). Green ivy may symbolize youth; dark myrtle middle life: dry leaves old age. Thus we might translate by 'because gladly youth revels in green ivy, rather than in dusky myrtle; while withered leaves it dedicates....'

19, 20. **aridas** (*p*): contrast *viridis*. Note the chiasmus *hedera virenti... aridas frondes*.

hiemis (*p*): the sere and yellow leaf goes, naturally, to *winter's* comrade—the Hebrus. See on P. 43, if *sodali* be felt as quasi-adjectival.

sodali | dedicet Hebro: the order is a slight extension of the type noted at P. 21. The Hebrus suits *Thracio* of l. 11 above. Gow reads *Euro*.

XXVI. 2. **protervis** (*ps*): i.e. 'to the wildness (of the winds)'; see on P. 27. The order prepares us for the wildness of the Cretan sea. See on *Odes* I. 35. 7.

4. **rex** by position equals 'as king'; but see on *Odes* I. 27. 11, 12.

gelidae (*ps*) echoes *sub Arcto*. The order *gelidae metuatur orae* suggests that *gelidae orae* belongs first to *rex* and then, as dative of the agent, to *metuatur* (see P. 21, 22, 23).

6, 7. **securus** and **gaudes** have emphasis; see on *Odes* 4. 9. 26.

apricos (*ps*): see on P. 21. Horace passes from chill fear and terrors of the north to sunny climes and flowers.

8. **meo** (*p*) either equals 'my own beloved' or 'to pleasure me.' For the former compare Cicero *Verr.* 4. 1. 3 *apud tuos Mamertinos*; Livy 1. 16. 7 *mea Roma*; Catullus 3. 3 etc. *meae puellae*; Vergil *Ecl.* 3. 68 *parta meae Veneri sunt munera*; *Odes* 1. 22. 10, 3. 3. 13(?), 3. 3. 66, 3. 4. 73, 4. 5. 5, 4. 8. 2, 4. 11. 31, 32(?), 4. 15. 6(?), *Epod.* 13. 6. For the last, where *meo* is equivalent to *mihi*—an ethical dative—see on *Odes* I. 13. 3.

Pimplei dulcis. nil sine te mei
prosunt honores: hunc fidibus novis,   10
hunc Lesbio sacrare plectro
teque tuasque decet sorores.

XXVII.

Natis in usum laetitiae scyphis
pugnare Thracum est: tollite barbarum
morem verecundumque Bacchum
sanguineis prohibete rixis.

vino et lucernis Medus acinaces   5
immane quantum discrepat: impium
lenite clamorem, sodales,
et cubito remanete presso.

vultis severi me quoque sumere
partem Falerni? dicat Opuntiae   10
frater Megyllae, quo beatus
vulnere, qua pereat sagitta.

9. **Pimplei dulcis:** contrast on P. 36.

mei (*ps*) contains the subject (see on *Odes* I. 15. 33) as if we had *nil sine te ego prosum*. For case relations grouped together see on *Odes* I. 2. 17. See also P. 21.

10. **novis** is emphatic, because *novus* is normally preposited; see on *Odes* I. 2. 6.

11. **Lesbio** (*ps*) i.e. 'with *lyric* song,' a chiastic support to *novis*. Compare the position of *Aeolium* at *Odes* 3. 30. 13. See however P. 21.

12. **tuas** (*ps*): the grouping of pronoun (*te*) and possessive (*tuas*) is conventional; see however P. 21.

XXVII. 2, 3. **barbarum** (*p*): contrast *verecundum* (*p*) of l. 3 below, and see on *Epod.* 11. 13.

4. **sanguineis** (*ps*) i.e. 'from the blood-letting (of quarrels)'; see on P. 27 and P. 21.

5. **Medus** (*p*): the order reminds us that we have another βάρβαρος in addition to *Thracum* of l. 2 above.

6. **impium** (*ps*) i.e. 'because *impius*'; perhaps, too, the adjective suggests *impium bellum*—a civil war, a war among friends. See also P. 21.

8. **presso** (*s*) i.e. 'pressed into the cushions' (and not *sublato* for defence); see also P. 21.

9. **severi**: if the adjective goes with *Falerni*, it is *ps* and must be emphatic. Pliny speaks of a *tenue Falernum* which, presumably, is to be contrasted with the *ardentis* (*p*) *Falerni* of *Odes* 2. 11. 19, and the *forti...Falerno* of

cessat voluntas? non alia bibam
mercede. quae te cumque domat Venus,
   non erubescendis adurit   15
     ignibus ingenuoque semper

amore peccas. quicquid habes, age
depone tutis auribus. a miser,
   quanta laborabas Charybdi,
     digne puer meliore flamma!   20

Sat. 2. 4. 24. It is usually assumed that *severum Falernum* = Pliny's *austerum*, and the adjective is taken to mean 'rough, tart, and dry.' But the stress on *severi* remains unexplained. May not *severi* be contrasted with *ardentis* and *fortis*, seeing that *severus* is always associated with sobriety of behaviour? Horace then says 'Do you wish me to drink with you, but none of your fiery stuff?' Compare the *innocentis Lesbii* of *Odes* 1. 17. 21.

It is not impossible to take *severi* as nominative plural i.e. 'Do you wish to behave yourselves (*severi* = σωφρονοῦντες) and make me also take a share of Falernian?' Horace knew the value of a sudden change of topic when the party is growing quarrelsome, especially if the interruption concerns the love affairs of a guest.

For *severus* in the sense of 'sobered'(?) compare *Epod.* 11. 19.

10, 11. **Opuntiae | frater Megyllae**: for the grouping see on P. 20*a*.

11, 12. **quo beatus | vulnere, qua pereat sagitta**: such separation of relative or interrogative from its noun is common at all periods and in all authors; compare Cicero *Div. in Caec.* 2. 4 *quo ego adiumento sperabam*, and Horace *Odes* 1. 15. 9, 10, 1. 26. 4, 1. 35. 38, 2. 1. 36, 2. 7. 25, 3. 3. 53, 3. 20. 1, 3. 25. 2, 3. 27. 17, 3. 29. 25, 4. 3. 10, 4. 7. 8, 4. 11. 13, 14, 4. 14. 19, *Epod.* 2. 37, 6. 8, 12. 7, 17. 36, and ll. 19 and 22 below.

13. **cessat**, coming first, has stress i.e. 'do you falter in your will?'

non alia (*ps*) i.e. 'on these and no other terms'; see on P. 29, and compare *Odes* 1. 36. 8. See too P. 21.

14. **mercede** should have stress; see on *Odes* 4. 9. 26. Perhaps the implied antithesis is *vi* i.e. you may force me, but no other bribe will persuade me.

quae te cumque: for the grouping see on *Odes* 1. 2. 17, and for *cumque* on *Odes* 1. 6. 3.

Venus: for position see on *Odes* 1. 3. 16.

15. **non erubescendis** (*ps*): see on P. 29 and P. 21.

16. **ingenuo** (*ps*) has emphasis.

semper: for its position see on P. 50*b*. The word has stress by separation from *peccas*.

18. **tutis** (*p*): (ears) that are safe; contrast *infidis*.

19. **quanta...Charybdi**: see on l. 11 above.

20. **digne** (*p*): see on P. 36.

meliore (*p*): see on P. 28. For *meliore flamma* standing outside *digne* and *puer* see on P. 47.

quae saga, quis te solvere Thessalis
magus venenis, quis poterit deus?
    vix illigatum te triformi
        Pegasus expediet Chimaera.

XXVIII.

Te maris et terrae numeroque carentis harenae
    mensorem cohibent, Archyta,
pulveris exigui prope litus parva Matinum
    munera, nec quicquam tibi prodest

21, 22. **quis...Thessalis | magus venenis:** for the grouping one may compare P. 9. But *Thessalis* may be felt with both *magus* and *venenis* (see on P. 52); moreover *Thessalis magus venenis* can be read as 'a magician of Thessalian charms' (see *Odes* 3. 2. 32). For the interest of *Thessalis* compare *Marsis* (*ps*) at *Epod.* 5. 76.

quis poterit deus: *deus* comes last as a climax—witch, magician, god. But see also on l. 11 above.

23, 24. **vix:** for its position see note on *non* at *Odes* 2. 9. 13.

illigatum te triformi...Chimaera: what we hear in the first three words is 'a binding of you by a three-formed thing.' The word *Chimaera* comes late so that *triformi Chimaera* may be heard with both *illigatum* and *expediet*. For similar constructions see on *Odes* 1. 23. 12.

XXVIII. 1. Te...cohibent...munera: for the position of *Te* see on P. 51; but the pronoun is brought forward also to be parallel to *me quoque* of l. 21 below.

maris (*p*)...**terrae** (*p*)...**harenae** (*p*) are emphatic in contrast to *pulveris exigui* (*ps*).

numeroque carentis (*p*): the point is 'you, Archytas, thought in terms of sea and land, and of *infinity*, but now a few grains are enough for you.' The two words *numero carentis* form a compound adjective 'numberless, innumerable'; otherwise normal order would require *carentisque numero harenae*. See on *Odes* 3. 1. 24, and compare too on *Odes* 3. 26. 10.

2. **cohibent:** as Wickham says, the verb equals κατέχειν. Jebb on *Antigone* 409 πᾶσαν κόνιν σήραντες ᾗ κατεῖχε τὸν νέκυν translates κατεῖχε by 'covered.' May not κατέχειν and *cohibere* signify 'keep down,' 'prevent from wandering'?

3, 4. **pulveris exigui** (*ps*): the words are the real subject i.e. 'a little dust (as a meagre gift)'; see on P. 38. The antithesis of *maris...terrae* is also in mind.

exigui has stress; adjectives of number and quantity are normally preposited.

litus...munera: for the grouping see on P. 14. If we read *latum*, compare on P. 9. The juxtaposition of *latum* and *parva* is neat, even if artificial.

munera may have stress (see on *Odes* 4. 9. 26); perhaps the effect is

aerias temptasse domos animoque rotundum   5
   percurrisse polum morituro.
occidit et Pelopis genitor, conviva deorum,
   Tithonusque remotus in auras
et Iovis arcanis Minos admissus, habentque
   Tartara Panthoiden iterum Orco   10
demissum, quamvis clipeo Troiana refixo
   tempora testatus nihil ultra
nervos atque cutem morti concesserat atrae,
   iudice te non sordidus auctor
naturae verique. sed omnis una manet nox   15
   et calcanda semel via leti.

ironical. The word is frequently used of a ritual gift, cp. Catullus 101. 3 and 8, and *passim*.

   5. aerias (*ps*): 'air' is the point, not *domos*; see P. 27 and P. 21.

   animo may be in ἀπὸ κοινοῦ position with *temptasse* and *percurrisse*.

   rotundum (*ps*) i.e. 'the wheel (of the heavens)'; see on P. 27 and P. 21.

   6. morituro separated from *tibi* and coming last has great emphasis. Compare the preposited *moriture* of *Odes* 2. 3. 4, and *interitura* at *Odes* 4. 7. 10.

   7. occidit comes first to echo *morituro* and to emphasize the moral that all, even the greatest, must die. Compare *Odes* 3. 8. 18.

   Pelopis genitor, conviva deorum: there appears to be an artificial chiasmus. But *Pelopis* is regularly preposited in Horace (see *Odes* 2. 13. 37 and *Epod.* 17. 65). See however on P. 41.

   8. in auras: for the position of these words see on P. 47.

   9. Iovis (*p*): Minos is not merely *conviva deorum* but confidant of great Jove himself. Observe that Horace could have written *arcanisque Iovis* had he not wished to stress *Iovis*.

   Iovis arcanis Minos: for case relations grouped early see on *Odes* 1. 2. 17; the topic is Jove's secrets and Minos. The separation of *arcanis* from *admissus* gives *arcanis* stress: he is admitted *non cenis modo sed etiam arcanis* (see on P. 49).

   11, 12. demissum has some stress (see on *Odes* 4. 9. 26); contrast *remotus in auras* of l. 8.

   clipeo Troiana refixo | tempora: for the grouping see on P. 14. A Roman could, I fancy, feel *Troiana* with *clipeo* as well as with *tempora*; see on P. 52.

   13. atrae (*s*): see on P. 21. The effect is 'to death and darkness.'

   14. non sordidus (*p*): see on P. 29. In litotes we have, in effect, a stressed preposited epithet.

   15. naturae verique: for the position of these words see on P. 35.

   omnis: for its position see on P. 51.

   una (*s*) is brought close to *omnis*; this is a favourite collocation (compare *Odes* 3. 4. 48). See however the next note.

dant alios Furiae torvo spectacula Marti,
> exitio est avidum mare nautis;
mixta senum ac iuvenum densentur funera, nullum
> saeva caput Proserpina fugit.   20
me quoque devexi rapidus comes Orionis
> Illyricis Notus obruit undis.
at tu, nauta, vagae ne parce malignus harenae
> ossibus et capiti inhumato

16. **leti** may stand outside *calcanda...via* on the principle noted at P. 48, or because *via leti* is treated as one word—'Death road,' as Livy 34. 9. 6 has *pars tertia civium*. See also on P. 45. So far I assume that *manet* is to be supplied with *calcanda semel via*; but if with *calcanda* we may supply *est*, then *semel*, because postposited, is emphatic, and the *una* of l. 15 has stress, i.e. the road must be trodden once and once only; one night and one night only awaits all ; the stories of reincarnation are mere nonsense.

17. **torvo spectacula Marti**: *spectacula* is a poetic equivalent of *spectanda*, and thus *torvo...Marti* comes under P. 21.

18. **avidum** (*p*) i.e. 'the hunger (of the sea)'; see on P. 27, and compare *Odes* 2. 2. 1, 2, 3. 29. 61.

19. **mixta...funera**: for the intrusive *densentur* see on P. 46a. The insertion of *densentur* emphasizes the idea of *mixta*, somewhat like *opulenta* at *Odes* 1. 17. 16.

nullum has stress standing alone at the end of the line.

19, 20. **nullum | saeva caput Proserpina**: for the grouping see on P. 9.

21. **me quoque** must, so it seems to me, be antithetical to the *te* of l. 1. The interposition of ll. 19, 20 makes it unlikely that *me quoque* should refer to *nautis* of l. 18. The position of *me* is not necessarily due to the principle noted at P. 51, for, in all Latin, names of natural phenomena may be subjects to transitive verbs without any divergence from the normal order.

devexi...Orionis: for the grouping see on P. 10. For 'setting Orion' see *Odes* 3. 27. 18.

22. **Illyricis** (*ps*) **Notus**: these words are kept together because a south wind would drive the sailor from his due east course set to Corcyra (or from the more northern course to Dyrrhachium) on to the dangerous islands of the Illyrian coast.

23. **at tu**: here the ghost suddenly sees and hails a passing boat.

vagae (*ps*): the sand is scattered everywhere and therefore costs nothing. The case of *vagae* is dative with *parce*, genitive 'in point of which' with *malignus*, and genitive of definition with *particulam*. Compare *Liburnis*, *Odes* 1. 37. 30, *Afris* 2. 1. 26, *tibi* 2. 8. 1, *votis* 2. 8. 6, *consiliis* 2. 11. 12, *monstris* 3. 4. 73, *bobus* 3. 6. 43, *tibi* 3. 7. 22, *sibi* 3. 8. 19, 20, *tibi* 3. 27. 71, and *Peliae* in Ovid *Her.* 12. 129 *Quid referam Peliae natas pietate nocentes* (where *Peliae* is genitive with *natas* and dative with *nocentes*).

particulam dare: sic, quodcumque minabitur Eurus   25
    fluctibus Hesperiis, Venusinae
plectantur silvae te sospite, multaque merces,
    unde potest, tibi defluat aequo
ab Iove Neptunoque sacri custode Tarenti.
    neglegis immeritis nocituram   30
postmodo te natis fraudem committere? forset
    debita iura vicesque superbae
te maneant ipsum: precibus non linquar inultis,
    teque piacula nulla resolvent.
quamquam festinas, non est mora longa: licebit   35
    iniecto ter pulvere curras.

26. **Hesperiis, Venusinae:** the collocation seems to be intentional. Horace means the Italian (*Hesperiis*) coast on the side of Venusia. The word *Hesperiis* might be misleading but for the immediate definition supplied by *Venusinae*, which shows that *Hesperiis* here means eastern. Compare on *Odes* I. 36. 4.

Venusinae (*ps*): see on P. 21.

27. **te sospite** is an emphatic addendum (see on P. 53) i.e. 'while thou art safe.'

28. **aequo** (*ps*) i.e. 'from the kindness (of Jove)'; see on P. 27.

29. **sacri custode Tarenti:** for the grouping see on P. 20 a.

Tarenti: there is, to my mind, nothing unnatural in this reference. We may assume that the sailor started from Tarentum on his voyage to Greece and that the Eurus of l. 25 forced him into the Italian coast as soon as he rounded Calabria. The figure-head of his boat might show that he hailed from Tarentum. In any case, to a Roman living in the south east of Italy, Tarentum was *the* port *par excellence*, just as Hull would be to a Scarborough fisherman.

30, 31. **immeritis nocituram | postmodo-te-natis** (=posteris) **fraudem:** for the grouping see on P. 9. To take *te* as subject of *committere* is to play fast and loose with Latin order. See too on l. 33.

32. **debita iura vicesque superbae** is, perhaps, a chiasmus; but *debita* (*p*) has stress i.e. rights that are *debita*, *non soluta*. The *iura sepulchri*, says the ghost, may never be paid in your case.

33. **te...ipsum** is in emphatic contrast to *te natis* of l. 31.

inultis (*s*) has stress; see too on P. 21.

34. **te:** for its position see on P. 51.

35. **longa** forms part of the predicate. As an epithet *longa* would normally be preposited.

licebit perhaps has stress (see on *nullum* l. 19) i.e. 'you are perfectly free.'

XXIX.

Icci, beatis nunc Arabum invides
gazis et acrem militiam paras
non ante devictis Sabaeae
    regibus horribilique Medo

nectis catenas? quae tibi virginum   5
sponso necato barbara serviet?
puer quis ex aula capillis
    ad cyathum statuetur unctis,

doctus sagittas tendere Sericas
arcu paterno? quis neget arduis   10
pronos relabi posse rivos
    montibus et Tiberim reverti,

XXIX. 1, 2. **nunc** separated from *invides* has emphasis. The sense is, as Wickham says, 'What, *now*, after a lifetime spent in such different pursuits.' For the intrusive *nunc* and *invides* see P. 46 *b*. A Roman could read this line thus: 'What, Iccius, are the happy Arabians now your envy and—for their treasures?'

gazis by position (see on *Odes* 4. 9. 26) has interest. The sense is 'Do you, a kindly philosopher, envy the happy and for so sordid a reason—their wealth?'

acrem (*p*) i.e. the pains (of military service); see on P. 27, and on *Odes* 2. 14. 23. Compare *Odes* 1. 18. 5 *gravem* (*p*) *militiam*, and 3. 2. 2 *acri* (*p*) *militia*.

3, 4. **non ante...regibus:** unless we put a stop at *paras*, these words form an emphatic addendum; see on P. 53.

horribili (*p*) echoes *non ante devictis*. See too on *Odes* 2. 14. 23.

5. **quae tibi virginum:** for the early grouping of case relations see on *Odes* 1. 2. 17.

6. **barbara** seems to go with *serviet* i.e. like a barbarian, and no Roman, she will be your slave.

7. **puer** precedes *quis* in artificial contrast to *virginum* l. 5 above; cp. *prece qua* of *Odes* 1. 2. 26.

capillis: when a Roman reads this word, he at once thinks of *intonsus*, κομῶν.

8. **unctis** is little more than *unctus*; the boy will stand, smelling of perfume on his hair, and 'on his hair' is brought back to mind by the case-ending.

9. **Sericas** (*s*): we are reaching the extreme limit of the empire which Iccius is to conquer. We began modestly with Arabia; then came Parthia, and now it is China too. See also P. 21.

10. **arcu paterno:** as the phrase *sagittas tendere* may stand with or with-

cum tu coemptos undique nobilis
libros Panaeti, Socraticam et domum
   mutare loricis Hiberis,   15
    pollicitus meliora, tendis?

XXX.

O Venus regina Cnidi Paphique,
sperne dilectam Cypron et vocantis
   ture te multo Glycerae decoram
    transfer in aedem.

fervidus tecum puer et solutis   5
Gratiae zonis properentque Nymphae
et parum comis sine te Iuventas
   Mercuriusque.

out *arçu* or *cornu* (see *Aen.* 9. 606 and 9. 590), *arcu paterno* is, perhaps, an emphatic addendum (see on P. 53); the boy is a skilled archer like his fathers before him.

   10–12. **arduis...montibus:** for the grouping see on P.8. The juxtaposition of *arduis* and *pronos* is happy.

   13. **tu** is emphatic because inserted i.e. 'you of all people!'

   13, 14. **nobilis** is surely genitive. For the grouping *coemptos...nobilis | libros Panaeti* see on P. 9.

   coemptos undique: compare on *Odes* 1. 7. 7; but *undique*, by position, may go with both *nobilis* and *coemptos*.

   Socraticam (*ps*): the founder of the school is naturally mentioned before his disciples. Moreover there is artificial antithesis to *Panaeti*.

   XXX. 2, 3. **dilectam** (*p*) i.e. 'though dear to thee.'

   vocantis...Glycerae is preposited because it is the equivalent of an ablative absolute. The order, therefore, is the natural order of events: Glycera calls and Venus answers by coming.

   multo, being postposited and separated, is emphatic.

   te is object of *vocantis* and, later, of *transfer*.

   3, 4. **decoram** (*ps*): the adjective suggests both beauty and fitness (for the latter sense compare Livy *Pref.* §6, 2. 13. 10, 2. 24. 5, 36. 14. 5). Its position makes it mean 'because beautiful and worthy of thee.' See also P. 21.

   5. **fervidus tecum puer:** probably a Roman feels *se transferat* or the like with *tecum*, in which case *fervidus* is predicative. On the other hand it is tempting to read *tecum* first with *fervidus* (i.e. the *puer* is *fervidus* 'with thee,' just as in l. 7 *Iuventas* is *parum comis* 'without thee') and, later on, with *properent*; see P. 50 *e*.

   5, 6. **solutis | Gratiae zonis:** for the position of *Gratiae* see on *Odes* I. 10. 14.

XXXI.

Quid dedicatum poscit Apollinem
vates? quid orat de patera novum
  fundens liquorem? non opimae
    Sardiniae segetes feraces,

non aestuosae grata Calabriae   5
armenta, non aurum aut ebur Indicum,
  non rura, quae Liris quieta
    mordet aqua taciturnus amnis.

premant Calena falce quibus dedit
Fortuna vitem, dives ut aureis   10
  mercator exsiccet culullis
    vina Syra reparata merce,

properentque is short for *properent properentque*; compare *Odes* 2. 7. 25,
2. 17. 16, 2. 19. 28, 2. 19. 32, 3. 1. 12, 3. 4. 11, 3. 11. 6, 3. 21. 18, *C.S.* 22, *Epod.*
11. 22, and see on *Odes* 3. 4. 6,7.

XXXI. 1. **dedicatum** (*ps*) perhaps means 'because he is in his new
temple.' See too P. 21.

2, 3. **vates** has stress (see on *Odes* 4. 9. 26); as Wickham says, 'the bard
may fitly supplicate his inspirer.'

novum (*s*): see note at *Odes* 1. 19. 15, and on P. 21. Here *novus* means
'used for the first time' and approaches closely to the sense of *recens* ; compare *Odes* 4. 1. 32, 4. 4. 16, and *Epod.* 5. 65.

opimae (*p*) i.e. 'the bounty (of Sardinia)'; see on P. 27.

4. **Sardiniae** (*p*) i.e. Sardinia with its cornfields; see on P. 38. The reading *opimas Sardiniae segetes feracis* (a much more musical reading) gives
the order of P. 17.

5, 6. **aestuosae...armenta:** for the grouping see on P. 9. The juxtaposition of *aestuosae* and *grata* is happy : in spite of the heat it is a pleasant
sight.

armenta should have stress (see on *Odes* 4. 9. 26), perhaps in artificial
contrast to *aurum, ebur* etc.

7. **quieta** (*ps*): see on P. 21. The emphasis on *quieta* implies that, despite
its peaceful stream, it eats its way through. For the quiet flow of rivers on
the west of Italy see *Odes* 3. 29. 35, and *Epod.* 13. 13, 14.

8. **taciturnus** (*p*): see on *quieta* above. The words *taciturnus amnis*
form an emphatic addendum (see P. 53).

9. **Calena:** the adjective contains the subject, as if we had *Caleni* (see on
Odes 1. 15. 33). As Wickham says, 'at Cales' is the simple meaning. We
may compare (with Gow) *Cytherea* at *Odes* 1. 4. 5 ; *Sabina* at *Odes* 1. 22. 9 ;
Apulis(?) at *Odes* 1. 33. 7 ; *Bithyna* at *Odes* 1. 35. 7. Compare too *Odes* 2. 6. 3
(*Maura*), 2. 12. 2 (*Siculum*), 3. 4. 28 (*Sicula*), 3. 14. 3 (*Hispana*), 4. 2. 17

dis carus ipsis, quippe ter et quater
anno revisens aequor Atlanticum
    impune: me pascunt olivae,   15
      me cichorea levesque malvae.

frui paratis et valido mihi,
Latoe, dones et, precor, integra
    cum mente nec turpem senectam
      degere nec cithara carentem.   20

XXXII.

Poscimur. siquid vacui sub umbra
lusimus tecum, quod et hunc in annum
vivat et pluris, age dic Latinum,
    barbite, carmen,

(*Elea*), 4. 4. 17 (*Rhaetis*), 4. 4. 56 (*Ausonias*), 4. 12. 2 (*Thraciae*), 4. 14. 26 (*Apuli*), C.S. 65 (*Palatinas*), *Epod.* 1. 27 (*Calabris*), 14. 9 (*Samio*), 16. 59 (*Sidonii*). So Ovid *Her.* 12. 9 *cur umquam Colchi* (=in Colchis) *Magnetida vidimus Argon?* See also the note on *Odes* 1. 33. 16.

10, 11. **dives...aureis | mercator...culullis:** for the grouping see on P. 9.

aureis (*ps*) i.e. 'the gold (of his cups)'; see P. 27. It must also be remembered that the *culullus* was originally of clay.

exsiccet comes early to draw our attention to his greed.

12. **vina...merce:** for the grouping see on P. 14.

13. **dis...ipsis:** the ironic emphasis points to the contrast to *Fortuna* in l. 10 (Wickham).

15. **impune** (*pps*) is a very emphatic addendum; see on P. 53 and *Odes* 4. 9. 26.

me: for the position of this and the *me* of l. 16 see on P. 51.

16. **leves:** for its position see on P. 33.

17, 18. **et** may merely emphasize *valido*, like καί in καὶ καρτερῷ ἐμοὶ ὄντι. If however in l. 18 we read *et, precor, integra*, then the *et* of l. 17 would mean 'both.'

valido (*p*) i.e. strong, not weak.

integra (*p*) i.e. sound, not impaired.

19. **turpem** (*p*): Horace does not pray to avoid old age, but to avoid a disgusting, repulsive (*molestam*, ἐπίπονον, δύσκολον) old age. See too on *Odes* 2. 14. 23.

XXXII. 2. **tecum** placed last has stress. Only with the help of the lyric muse has the poet been able to achieve success as a lyrist.

hunc (*s*): contrast *pluris*.

3, 4. **Latinum** (*ps*): contrast *Lesbio* (*ps*) of l. 5. The juxtaposition of *Latinum* with the Greek word *barbite* is effective. Wickham cites *Odes* 4. 3. 23 *Romanae fidicen lyrae.* For the position of the vocative *barbite* see on *Odes* 1. 5. 3.

Lesbio primum modulate civi,   5
qui ferox bello tamen inter arma,
sive iactatam religarat udo
    litore navem,

Liberum et Musas Veneremque et illi
semper haerentem puerum canebat   10
et Lycum nigris oculis nigroque
    crine decorum.

o decus Phoebi et dapibus supremi
grata testudo Iovis, o laborum
dulce lenimen, mihi cumque salve   15
    rite vocanti!

XXXIII.

Albi, ne doleas plus nimio memor
immitis Glycerae, neu miserabilis
decantes elegos, cur tibi iunior
    laesa praeniteat fide.

5. **Lesbio** (*ps*): contrast *Latinum* l. 3.
civi coming last and separated has some stress ; see the commentators.
7, 8. **iactatam...navem**: for the grouping see on P. 10.
9, 10. **illi | semper haerentem** forms one idea 'her shadow.' Normal order would be *illi haerentem semper puerum*, or *semper haerentem illi puerum*.
11. **nigris** (*p*)**...nigro** (*p*): the colour is the point. So in *A. P.* 37 (quoted by Wickham) *spectandum nigris oculis nigroque capillo*. Compare too on *tenui* at *Odes* 1. 33. 5.
13, 14. **supremi | grata testudo Iovis**: for the grouping see on P. 10. The words *dapibus supremi grata* are read together i.e. 'to feasts of the Highest a gladness'; then *testudo* and *Iovis* fill in the sense with more detail: the gladness is the lyre, the Highest is Jove.
laborum stands outside *dulce* and *lenimen* in contrast to *dapibus* of l. 13. See on P. 43.
15. **cumque**: for this and other readings see the commentators.
16. **rite vocanti** is an emphatic addendum i.e. 'if I call duly'; see on P. 53.
XXXIII. 1. **plus nimio** by position qualifies both *doleas* and *memor*.
2. **immitis** (*p*) i.e. 'the unkindness (of Glycera)'; see on P. 27, and *Odes* 2. 14. 23. The position of the adjective also helps the oxymoron—πικρòν Γλυκέριον (see Wickham). Compare *insanientis* at *Odes* 1. 34. 2, and see note *Epod.* 5. 82.
miserabilis (*ps*) echoes *doleas* of l. 1. See also P. 21.

insignem tenui fronte Lycorida   5
Cyri torret amor, Cyrus in asperam
declinat Pholoen: sed prius Apulis
     iungentur capreae lupis,

quam turpi Pholoe peccet adultero.
sic visum Veneri, cui placet imparis   10
formas atque animos sub iuga aenea
     saevo mittere cum ioco.

ipsum me melior cum peteret Venus,
grata detinuit compede Myrtale
libertina, fretis acrior Hadriae   15
     curvantis Calabros sinus.

3, 4. **tibi iunior** | **laesa**: the case relations are grouped early i.e. you and a younger man and a wrong (*laesa*); see on *Odes* I. 2. 17.

laesa (*ps*): perhaps means 'by reason of a breach (of faith)'; see on P. 26 and P. 21.

5. **tenui** (*p*) i.e. 'the narrowness (of brow)'; see on P. 27, and compare *Epist.* I. 7. 26 *nigros angusta fronte capillos*. See too the note on *nigris* at *Odes* I. 32. 11.

6, 7. **Cyri** (*ps*): the genitive is thus placed to bring *Cyri* close to *Lycorida*. The same effect is produced by separation of *Cyrus* and *Pholoen*. Compare Livy I. 5. 7 *Romulus...Remus* and I. 6. 4 *Palatium Romulus, Remus Aventinum...capiunt*. But see also P. 38.

asperam (*ps*) is predicative, as Wickham says, i.e. 'only to find her cruel.' See too P. 21.

7. **Apulis** (*ps*) perhaps merely equals 'in Apulia'; compare *Calena* at *Odes* I. 31. 9. See also on l. 16 below. In any case Apulian wolves were, apparently, most fierce; see on *Odes* I. 22. 13.

9. **turpi** (*ps*) i.e. 'with a lover who is base.' Compare Livy *Pref.* § 13 *cum bonis potius ominibus* i.e. 'with omens that were good.'

10. **imparis** (*p*): inequality is the point.

12. **saevo** (*ps*): a jest may be *lascivus, protervus*; it should not be *saevus*. See too on *Odes* 2. 14. 23.

13. **ipsum me** i.e. 'to take my own case'; hence the words come early.

melior is predicative—εὐμενεστέρα οὖσα, in kindlier mood.

14. **grata** (*ps*): a fetter is normally *ingrata*. Compare *grata* (*p*) *compede* at *Odes* 4. 11. 23, and see note on *Epod.* 5. 82.

15, 16. **libertina** has stress; see on *Odes* 4. 9. 26. She is 'the common chit' of Martin's verse.

fretis...sinus is an emphatic addendum; see on P. 53.

Hadriae (*s*): the stress has point because Adriatic storms are notorious.

curvantis...sinus: the normal order would be *sinus Calabros curvantis*; but Hadria does not merely wash the bays of Calabria; it does more—it

XXXIV.

Parcus deorum cultor et infrequens,
insanientis dum sapientiae
    consultus erro, nunc retrorsum
        vela dare atque iterare cursus

cogor relictos: namque Diespiter,   5
igni corusco nubila dividens
    plerumque, per purum tonantis
        egit equos volucremque currum,

quo bruta tellus et vaga flumina,
quo Styx et invisi horrida Taenari   10
    sedes Atlanteusque finis
        concutitur. valet ima summis

'*curves* Calabria into bays,' and this is the sense which the order produces; for *curvantis* has special interest at the beginning of the line, *Calabros* (*p*) equals 'Calabria (and its bays),' and *sinus*, as Wickham points out, is 'accusative of the result.'

For *Calabros* (*p*)='Calabria (and its bays)' see on *Odes* I. 31. 9, and compare *Atlanteus*, *Odes* I. 34. 11, *Persicos* I. 38. 1, *Delmatico* 2. 1. 16, *Dauniae* 2. 1. 34, *Armeniis* 2. 9. 4, *Medum* 2. 9. 21, *Stygia* 2. 20. 8, *Scythicum* 3. 4. 36, *Pierio* 3. 4. 40, *Venafranos* 3. 5. 55, *Sabellis* 3. 6. 38, *Calabrae* 3. 16. 33, *Africis* 3. 29. 57, *Cecropiae* 4. 12. 6, *Argoo*, *Epod.* 16. 57. Compare too *patrios*, *Odes* 3. 27. 49.

XXXIV. 2. **insanientis** (*ps*): the position enforces the oxymoron; see on *Epod.* 5. 82.

sapientiae (*p*): see on P. 39.

3. **retrorsum** (*s*) i.e. back and not forward.

4. **iterare** is stressed by separation from *cogor*, and echoes *retrorsum*.

5. **relictos** (*s*): the stress echoes *iterare* (*s*) and *retrorsum* (*s*). Compare on *Odes* I. 19. 4.

7. **plerumque** postposited and alone at the commencement of the line has emphasis (see on *Odes* 4. 9. 26); the adverb thus means not merely 'often' (the weakened sense which it possessed in the prose of the time) but 'most often' (its original sense, as in Cicero).

per purum comes early for emphasis; it belongs to both *tonantis* and *egit*.

per purum tonantis (*ps*): the order emphasizes the marvel. See also P. 21.

8. **volucrem**: for its position see P. 33.

9. **bruta** (*p*) i.e. 'for all its mass.'

vaga (*p*) i.e. 'for all their speed.'

10, 11. **invisi...sedes**: for the grouping see on P. 9.

mutare et insignem attenuat deus,
obscura promens: hinc apicem rapax
   Fortuna cum stridore acuto   15
    sustulit, hic posuisse gaudet.

XXXV.

O diva, gratum quae regis Antium,
praesens vel imo tollere de gradu
   mortale corpus vel superbos
    vertere funeribus triumphos:

te pauper ambit sollicita prece   5
ruris colonus, te dominam aequoris
   quicumque Bithyna lacessit
    Carpathium pelagus carina;

Atlanteus (*p*) merely equals 'Atlas (at the boundary of the world)'; see on *Calabros*, *Odes* I. 33. 16.

12. **concutitur**: for the emphasis see *Odes* 4. 9. 26; compare *sustulit* l. 16.

13. **deus** coming last has stress. See also *Odes* I. 3. 16.

14. **obscura promens**: for the position of these words see on P. 53. The stress enforces the antithesis *insignem attenuat*.

rapax (*p*) is strongly verbal and may almost be felt to govern *apicem*; compare *castra vitabundus*, *haec contionabundus* and such Greek instances as ἄπορα πόριμος. See also on *Odes* 3. 1. 16. Horace is thinking of Livy's story at I. 34. 8.

XXXV. 1. **gratum** (*ps*): the adjective in sense and by position may, perhaps, qualify both *diva* and *Antium* (see P. 52). The *diva* is 'gracious' to Antium, and Antium is 'pleasing' to her (compare *Odes* I. 30. 2 *dilectam*), or 'grateful' for her protection (compare *Odes* 3. 26. 9 where *beatam divă* suggests 'blessed in its goddess'). If, however, we omit *quae*, the order is that of P. 21. (Compare *Odes* I. 38. 1.) Moreover *gratum...Antium* is equivalent to *grati regina Antii*, for which see on P. 20 a.

2. **imo** (*ps*) has stress even without *vel*. See too P. 21.

3, 4. **mortale** (*p*) i.e. 'even of mortal man.'

superbos: I cannot help feeling that a Roman would at first read *superbos* as 'the proud,' τοὺς ὑπερφρονοῦντας, and, in that case, the phrase is complete at *funeribus* (i.e. 'ready to overturn the proud by means of *funera*'); *triumphos* therefore comes as an emphatic addendum (see on P. 53) i.e. 'in the hour of their triumph,' and the juxtaposition of *funeribus* is effective enough. It is hard to believe that *vertere* is not the antithesis of *tollere*. Wickham compares *A.P.* 226 and takes *vertere* to equal *mutare*.

5. **te pauper**: note the case relations early, as in l. 9 below (see on *Odes* I. 2. 17).

te Dacus asper, te profugi Scythae
urbesque gentesque et Latium ferox   10
    regumque matres barbarorum et
        purpurei metuunt tyranni,

iniurioso ne pede proruas
stantem columnam, neu populus frequens
    ad arma cessantis, ad arma   15
        concitet imperiumque frangat:

te semper anteit saeva Necessitas,
clavos trabalis et cuneos manu
    gestans aena, nec severus
        uncus abest liquidumque plumbum: 20

pauper (*ps*) i.e. 'because he is poor'; therefore he courts Fortuna and with prayers that are anxious (*sollicita* preposited).

6. **ruris** (*p*) is contrasted with *aequoris*; landsman and sailor alike worship her.

7. **Bithyna...carina:** for the grouping see P. 10.

Bithyna practically equals 'from Bithynia' (see on *Calena* at *Odes* 1. 31. 9). There is point in both *Bithyna* (*ps*) and *Carpathium* (*p*): the trader from Bithynia challenges the open sea (*pelagus*) and the whole length of the dangerous Aegean. The worst part is the *Carpathium*, between Rhodes and Crete, where he cannot merely coast along. Compare *Myrtoum*, *Odes* 1. 1. 14 and *Creticum* 1. 26. 2.

9. **te Dacus:** see on l. 5 above.

profugi (*p*): contrast *asper* ('standing at bay,' as Wickham translates). See on *Odes* 4. 14. 42.

10, 11. **Latium ferox | regumque matres:** the sense is in parallel order i.e. free Latium in contrast to tyrants, and fiery warriors in contrast to weak women.

regumque matres barbarorum: for the grouping see on P. 20 β.

et: for its position see on l. 39 below.

12. **purpurei** (*ps*) i.e. 'for all their finery and luxuriousness.' See also P. 21.

13. **iniurioso** (*ps*) i.e. 'with contumely (of the foot)'; see P. 27, and *Odes* 2. 14. 23.

14. **stantem** (*p*) i.e. 'however firmly set up.'

15. **ad arma cessantis** may well go together i.e. those who are laggards 'at arming' may be aroused 'to arms.'

17. **saeva** (*p*): see on *Odes* 2. 14. 23. But the reading *serva* 'has the balance of manuscript authority' (Wickham), and, to my mind, yields a better sense. The question of questions is 'Does Fortuna (τύχη) or Necessitas (ἀνάγκη) rule?' Horace tells us the answer: Necessitas goes in front but

te Spes et albo rara Fides colit
velata panno nec comitem abnegat,
   utcumque mutata potentis
      veste domos inimica linquis.

at vulgus infidum et meretrix retro   25
periura cedit, diffugiunt cadis
   cum faece siccatis amici,
      ferre iugum pariter dolosi.

merely to carry out the bidding (*serva*) of Fortuna. If it is true that slaves ordinarily went behind, the fact only gives more point to *serva*. Compare *colit* at l. 21 below.

19. **aena** (*s*): this order helps to enforce the point of *severus* (*p*). We have a chiasmus *manu...aena* and *severus | uncus*. See also P. 21.

severus means inherently 'fixed,' 'rigid.' Thus, in Lucretius 5. 1190, *signa severa* probably signifies the fixed, unchanging constellations.

20. **liquidum** (*p*) is in somewhat artificial antithesis to *severus*—liquid versus solid.

21, 22. **te Spes**: see on l. 5. For the interpretation of ll. 21–28 see Appendix at the end of this Ode.

albo rara Fides...panno: for the grouping see on P. 10.

rara Fides...velata: for this grouping see on P. 34. Wickham says that *rara* means 'rarely found'; but the combination *albo rara panno* suggests the thin veil of *Fides* (see on *Odes* I. 18. 16, and compare the *rara tunica* of Ovid *Amor.* I. 5. 13); and in all other passages of Horace *pannus* has a contemptuous subaudition which ill accords with any complimentary meaning of *rara*.

23. **mutata potentis | veste domos**: for the grouping see on P. 9. To my mind the order makes it imperative to take *mutata veste* with *potentis domos*. A Roman on reading the words *mutata potentis veste* must feel *potentis* subject, as it were, of *mutata* (see on *Odes* I. 10. 14). Moreover the juxtaposition of *mutata potentis* sounds like 'there is change for the powerful,' and we need not find a difficulty in the fact that, when we reach *linquis*, *potentis* = τοὺς πρότερον κρατοῦντας. This clears away the scruples of Wickham, who refers *mutata veste* to Fortune.

25. **retro** (*s*) has emphasis.

26. **periura** (*s*) equals 'faithlessly'; see on P. 31.

(vulgus) cedit, diffugiunt...amici: note the chiasmus; the *vulgus* fall back, but *amici* scatter in every direction.

28. **ferre...dolosi**: these words are a causal addendum; see on P. 53.

pariter postposited and separated draws attention to the real point i.e. 'equally': some friends might go in harness with you, but, to use the language of rowing, would 'sugar' and shirk their share of the work.

serves iturum Caesarem in ultimos
orbis Britannos et iuvenum recens   30
    examen Eois timendum
        partibus Oceanoque rubro.

eheu, cicatricum et sceleris pudet
fratrumque. quid nos dura refugimus
    aetas? quid intactum nefasti   35
        liquimus? unde manum iuventus

metu deorum continuit? quibus
pepercit aris? o utinam nova
    incude diffingas retunsum in
        Massagetas Arabasque ferrum.   40

29, 30. **iturum** (*p*) i.e. '(make safe) the coming journey (of Caesar)'; see on P. 26.

in ultimos | orbis Britannos: for the position of this complement see on P. 47.

iuvenum (*p*) i.e. 'his warriors,' contrast *Caesarem*. The words *iuvenum recens examen* equal 'the warriors in new levy'; see on P. 38, and P. 43. The adjective *recens* may be felt to qualify both *iuvenum* and *examen* (see on *Odes* I. 19. 1).

31. **Eois** (*ps*) in contrast to *ultimos...Britannos*. See too P. 24. The word *Eois* covers the Massagetae and Arabes of l. 40.

33. **cicatricum et sceleris:** the genitives go with both *eheu* and *pudet*.

34. **fratrumque** has stress; see on *Odes* 4. 9. 26. The shame is that *brothers* were fighting against each other.

dura is felt with both *nos* and *aetas*; see P. 52.

35. **aetas** has stress (see on *Odes* 4. 9. 26) i.e. 'in our generation.' Compare Livy *Pref.* § 5 *mala quae nostra tot per annos vidit aetas*.

nefasti may be genitive with *quid* (for its position see on *Odes* I. 2. 1) or nominative plural, although the word is very rare of persons.

36. **liquimus** is read to be parallel to all the other perfects; but *linquimus* of the MSS justifies the position (see on *Odes* 4. 9. 26) i.e. 'we are still sinners.'

manum iuventus: see on *Odes* I. 2. 17.

37, 38. **quibus | pepercit aris:** for the separation of *aris* from *quibus* see on *Odes* I. 27. 11; *aris* has interest by its position: they did not spare even altars.

39, 40. **retunsum** (if we so read) **in | Massagetas...ferrum:** these words ought to mean 'the sword blunted against the Massagetae.' If Latin order has any significance, it seems impossible to take *in Massagetas* with *diffingas* (as all commentators, ancient and modern, do, although Porphyrion says there is ambiguity), especially in view of the fact that the words *retunsum in* coalesce (compare *Odes* 3. 1. 5). Moreover *diffingere* means only 'to change the form of' and is surely too strong a word for mere sharpening (see *Odes* 3. 29. 47). If the sense is 'sharpen our swords, blunted in civil war, against

XXXVI.

Et ture et fidibus iuvat
placare et vituli sanguine debito

eastern enemies,' what is the meaning of *nova* in *nova incude*? Presumably the anvil of imperial acquisition. But if we give *diffingas* its proper sense, the answer seems simpler; the 'new anvil' is the anvil of peace, upon which the sword is to 'change its form' and become the sickle. The reverse process is given by Vergil at *Georg.* 1. 508 *et curvae rigidum falces conflantur in ensem.* Horace longs for peace so soon as these new expeditions to the extreme West and East are over (compare on *Odes* 1. 21. 13–15).

retunsum in: for the position of the monosyllable compare *Odes* 1. 3. 19, 1. 7. 6, 1. 9. 13, 1. 21. 14, 1. 35. 11, 2. 6. 1, 2. 6. 2, 2. 13. 23, 2. 15. 5, 2. 16. 37, 3. 3. 71, 3. 4. 59, 3. 6. 3, 3. 8. 3, 3. 8. 26, 3. 8. 27, 3. 26. 9, 3. 27. 22, 3. 27. 29, 3. 29. 3, 3. 29. 7, 3. 29. 9, 3. 29. 49, 4. 6. 11.

APPENDIX ON ll. 21–28

Most commentators hold that Fortuna belongs permanently to the great house, the 'County family,' sometimes propitious, sometimes the reverse, and that Spes and Fides stay with her (*nec comitem abnegat*), while only the common people and the *meretrix* are faithless. But to this interpretation there are serious objections. How can Fortuna remain with the great house in view of *linquis* l. 24 (Bentley cheerfully altered to *vertis*), and, if Fortuna does not desert, in what sense can she be called *inimica* when Spes and Fides still accompany her? But elsewhere, when Fortune is adverse, she is a deserter, as in Ovid *Ex Ponto* 3. 2. 9 *ignoscimus illis | qui cum fortuna terga dedere fugae,* and *Trist.* 1. 5. 33 *vix duo tresve mihi de tot superestis amici; cetera fortunae, non mea, turba fuit.* In fact Fortune and Loyalty go away together as Ovid tells us at *Ex Ponto* 2. 3. 10 *et cum Fortuna statque caditque Fides,* and still more clearly and appositely *ib.* 1. 9. 15 *adfuit ille mihi, cum me pars magna reliquit, Maxime, fortunae nec fuit ipse comes,* i.e. 'Celsus did not go with Fortuna when she deserted me.' This last passage surely throws light on *nec comitem abnegat* (l. 22 of our Ode), which can hardly mean anything save that Spes and Fides, unlike Celsus, desert with the deserter Fortuna. Their behaviour indeed is illustrated by Ovid *Ex Ponto* 2. 3. 33 *diligitur nemo nisi cui fortuna secunda est,* and *ib.* 4. 3. 7 *nunc, quia contraxit vultum Fortuna, recedis.* Note especially Hor. *A. P.* 200, 201.

In view of these facts I would consider the sense of ll. 21–28 to be as follows: 'Hope and Loyalty are the submissive servants (*colit*) of Fortuna; they follow in her train (*nec comitem abnegat*) when the powerful go into mourning and Fortuna deserts them in enmity. But (*at*) what is true of the great is no less true of the common folk (*vulgus*) of both sexes (*meretrix*) there is no *Fides* to be found amongst them in the hour of misfortune, least of all amongst boon companions (*amici*).'

XXXVI. 2. **vituli** (*p*): even a calf is not a cheap victim for Horace (see on *Odes* 4. 2. 54, 55). For *vituli=vitulo* parallel to *ture* see P. 38; and for the grouping *vituli sanguine debito* see P. 35.

custodes Numidae deos,
 qui nunc Hesperia sospes ab ultima
caris multa sodalibus,   5
 nulli plura tamen dividit oscula
quam dulci Lamiae, memor
 actae non alio rege puertiae
mutataeque simul togae.

 Cressa ne careat pulchra dies nota, 10
neu promptae modus amphorae
 neu morem in Salium sit requies pedum,
neu multi Damalis meri
 Bassum Threicia vincat amystide,
neu desint epulis rosae   15
 neu vivax apium neu breve lilium.
omnes in Damalin putris
 deponent oculos, nec Damalis novo
divelletur adultero,
 lascivis hederis ambitiosior.   20

4. **ab ultima** (*s*): the stress shows that *Hesperia* is Spain, not Italy; compare on *Odes* I. 28. 26.

5, 6. **caris multa sodalibus...oscula:** for the grouping see on P. 9.
plura has stress by separation. See too on P. 28.

7. **dulci** (*p*) i.e. 'because so sweet.'

8. **non alio** (*p*): see on P. 29 and compare *Odes* I. 27. 13.

10. **Cressa** (*ps*): i.e. white, not black.
Cressa...pulchra dies nota: for the grouping see on P. 10.

11. **promptae modus amphorae:** for the order see on P. 20 *a*.

13. **multi Damalis meri:** for the order see on P. 20 *a*.

14. **Threicia vincat amystide:** for the grouping see P. 21. The early mention of Thrace tells us that they are going to make a night of it (compare *Odes* I. 27. 2).

16. **vivax** (*p*)**...breve** (*p*) are preposited merely for the sake of the antithesis.

17, 18. **omnes...oculos:** the alleged construction *in aliquem deponere oculos* is dubious. Elsewhere in Horace we find either *in* with the ablative, or the ablative alone. In other writers also the accusative with *in* seems to be a doubtful reading. If the sense 'fix on' is possible for *deponere*, we might supply *in ea* with *deponent*, and read *in Damalin putres* (compare Persius 5. 58 *in Venerem putris*). The word *putres* (*-is*) may be (1) nominative agreeing with *omnes* (i.e. all 'mashed on' Damalis); (2) if *in Damalin* belongs to *deponent*, accusative with *oculos* (i.e. languishing, melting); see on P. 21.

nec equals *nec tamen.*

XXXVII.

Nunc est bibendum, nunc pede libero
pulsanda tellus; nunc Saliaribus
   ornare pulvinar deorum
     · tempus erat dapibus, sodales.

antehac nefas depromere Caecubum   5
cellis avitis, dum Capitolio
   regina dementis ruinas
     funus et imperio parabat

contaminato cum grege turpium
morbo virorum, quidlibet impotens   10
   sperare fortunaque dulci
     ebria. sed minuit furorem

novo (*s*): i.e. 'because new'; such a woman as Damalis must have change. See also P. 21.

20. **lascivis** (*p*): Damalis is more wanton than 'the wantonness (of the ivy)'; see on P. 27. The ivy was associated with the dubious rites of Bacchus, quite apart from its clinging qualities.

XXXVII. This Ode, I venture to think, shows signs of the hasty workmanship of a Laureate writing to order, e.g. the awkward *nunc est...nunc... erat* of ll. 1–4; the exceptional metre of l. 5; the metre and order of l. 14; the order of *daret ut* (l. 20), and the strange *reparavit* of l. 24. See also on *Odes* 3. 14. 1 and 4. 14. 1.

2. **Saliaribus** (*ps*): i.e. with a banquet fit for the Salii, not with the meagre offerings of ordinary ritual. For generic adjectives preposited or separated see P. 37.

6, 7. **cellis avitis** is an addendum with stress (see on P. 53); it had been *nefas* to drink the oldest Caecuban.

Capitolio | regina: the juxtaposition of these words (see *Odes* 1. 2. 17) and the emphasis on *Capitolio* are effective. 'A Queen on the Capitol' is too awful to contemplate; a *rex* would be bad enough.

dementis (*p*): the epithet is felt, as Gow says, really with *regina* (see on P. 52). The *ruinae* are the dreams of madness.

9–12. **contaminato...ebria:** these words form an emphatic addendum (see on P. 53). She was preparing destruction for the empire and how? With a body of effeminate eunuchs, herself without control and—drunk!

9. **contaminato cum grege turpium:** for the grouping see on P. 34, and 35. Probably *contaminato* (*ps*) has emphasis i.e. 'utterly polluted.'

10. **quidlibet** has stress by separation from *sperare*: she has no control over expectations and those expectations are chimerical.

12. **ebria:** for the stress see on *Odes* 4. 9. 26.

vix una sospes navis ab ignibus,
mentemque lymphatam Mareotico
   redegit in veros timores   15
      Caesar, ab Italia volantem

remis adurgens, accipiter velut
mollis columbas aut leporem citus
   venator in campis nivalis
      Haemoniae, daret ut catenis   20

fatale monstrum. quae generosius
perire quaerens nec muliebriter
   expavit ensem nec latentis
      classe cita reparavit oras;

ausa et iacentem visere regiam   25
vultu sereno, fortis et asperas
   tractare serpentes, ut atrum
      corpore combiberet venenum,

13. **sospes** (*p*) i.e. 'the safety of...,' as if we had *servata*; see on P. 26.

ab ignibus, separated from *sospes*, has point (see on P. 49): after Antony's flight his captains fought desperately, and it was not until the ships were fired that the contest was decided.

14. **mentemque...Mareotico**: the metre is as exceptional as the order (for the latter see on P. 49); her hallucinations (*lymphatam*) are due to some mysterious Egyptian wine.

15. **veros** (*p*): contrast the imaginary horrors implied in *lymphatam*.

16. **Caesar**: for the stress (i.e. 'great Caesar') see on *Odes* 4. 9. 26, and compare *Odes* 1. 2. 44.

17. **accipiter velut**: for the order compare on *Odes* 1. 15. 29.

18. **mollis** (*p*): contrast the cruel strength of a hawk.

citus is felt, despite the case, with both *leporem* and *venator* (see P. 52); it is preposited with *venator* because a quick hunter is needed to catch a quick hare. Compare too on *Odes* 1. 23. 12.

19, 20. **nivalis**: the epithet is felt with both *campis* and *Haemoniae*; with the latter it is preposited because hares are most readily caught on the snow.

Haemoniae: there seems to be no point in its position; see on *Odes* 4. 9. 26.

20. **daret ut catenis**: the position of *daret* has no point. One might justify the order as a kind of tmesis, since *dare catenis* is equivalent to *vincire*; but Horace writes *ut* immediately after the verb at *Odes* 4. 13. 26, *Epod.* 16. 31, *Sat.* 1. 1. 26, 1. 4. 108, and 1. 5. 63. See too *Odes* 4. 2. 26. Ovid has many examples e.g. *Ex Ponto* 1. 3. 78, 1. 3. 83, 3. 6. 52, 4. 9. 74, 4. 10. 16, 4. 16. 50, etc.

21. **fatale** (*p*): see on *Odes* 2. 14. 23.

23. **latentis** (*ps*) i.e. 'a hiding-place (on the coast)'; see on P. 26.

deliberata morte ferocior,
saevis Liburnis scilicet invidens   30
  privata deduci superbo
  non humilis mulier triumpho.

XXXVIII.

Persicos odi, puer, apparatus,
displicent nexae philyra coronae:
mitte sectari, rosa quo locorum
  sera moretur.

simplici myrto nihil allabores   5
sedulus, curo: neque te ministrum
dedecet myrtus neque me sub arta
  vite bibentem.

25. **iacentem** (*ps*) i.e. 'the downfall (of her palace)'; see on P. 26, and P. 21.

26. **vultu sereno** is an emphatic addendum i.e. 'and that with equanimity'; see on P. 53.

asperas (*ps*) i.e. 'for all their angry hissing'; see also P. 21.

27. **atrum** (*ps*) i.e. 'the deadliness (of poison)'; see on P. 27, and *Odes* 2. 14. 23.

29. **deliberata** (*p*) i.e. 'by the determination (to die)'; see on P. 26.

30. **saevis** (*p*) emphasizes the cruelty in thus treating a woman; see also on *Odes* 2. 14. 23.

Liburnis is firstly dative with *invidens*, secondly ablative with *deduci*. Compare on *Odes* 1. 28. 23.

31, 32. **privata** is much more effective than the obvious *regina*: she is an ex-Queen.

superbo...triumpho: for the grouping see on P. 10, and on *Odes* 4. 8. 33.

superbo is well placed next to *non humilis*.

non humilis (*p*): see on P. 29.

XXXVIII. 1. **Persicos** (*ps*) i.e. 'Persia (and its luxury)'; see on *Odes* 1. 33. 16 *Calabros*; but if we omit *puer*, we have the grouping of P. 21 (compare *Odes* 1. 35. 1). One is reminded of Shakespeare's *Lear* 3. 6. 85 'I do not like the fashion of your garments—you will say | They are Persian.' Compare too *Odes* 3. 9. 4.

3. **rosa quo**: for the order, as if we had *rosam*, see on *Odes* 1. 4. 10.

4. **sera** goes with *moretur*—'late lingers.'

5. **simplici** (*p*): contrast *Persicos...apparatus* of l. 1.

6. **curo**: this awkward reading is, I suspect, due to the *o* of *myrto* above. It is satisfactory to read *sedulus cura* (abl.), an emphatic addendum (see on P. 53) i.e. 'in your sedulous care.'

te ministrum comes early in antithesis to *me...bibentem*.

7. **arta** (*p*) i.e. 'the close shade (of the vine)'; see P. 27.

BOOK II

I.

Motum ex Metello consule civicum
bellique causas et vitia et modos
    ludumque Fortunae gravisque
      principum amicitias et arma

nondum expiatis uncta cruoribus,   5
periculosae plenum opus aleae,
    tractas et incedis per ignis
      suppositos cineri doloso.

paulum severae Musa tragoediae
desit theatris: mox ubi publicas   10
    res ordinaris, grande munus
      Cecropio repetes coturno,

insigne maestis praesidium reis
et consulenti, Pollio, curiae,
    cui laurus aeternos honores   15
      Delmatico peperit triumpho.

I. 2. belli (*p*) echoes *motum* and equals 'war (and its causes)'; see on P. 38.

4, 5. **arma...cruoribus:** for the grouping see on P. 14.

6. **periculosae...aleae:** for the grouping see on P. 10.

8. **suppositos...doloso** is an addendum of interest (see on P. 53).
cineri doloso: for the position of these words see on P. 47.

9. **paulum** is emphatic because separated from *desit*.
severae...tragoediae: for the grouping see on P. 20 a.

10. **mox** is early in antithesis to *paulum*, as if we had *paulum* μὲν... *mox* δέ.

publicas (*p*) i.e. the history of our *state*, opposed to *regum facta* of Pollio's tragedies.

12. **Cecropio** (*ps*) i.e. the buskin of *Athens*; contrast your tale of *Rome's* tragedy. See also P. 21.

13. **insigne...reis:** for the grouping see on P. 9.

14. **consulenti** (*ps*) i.e. 'the counsels (of the Senate)'; see on P. 26. For the intervening vocative see *Odes* I. 5. 3.

15. **aeternos** (*p*) is emphatic. Horace in the *Odes* and *Epodes* always makes *aeternus* preposited.

iam nunc minaci murmure cornuum
perstringis auris, iam litui strepunt,
   iam fulgor armorum fugacis
      terret equos equitumque vultus.   20

audire magnos iam videor duces
non indecoro pulvere sordidos,
   et cuncta terrarum subacta
      praeter atrocem animum Catonis.

Iuno et deorum quisquis amicior   25
Afris inulta cesserat impotens
   tellure victorum nepotes
      rettulit inferias Iugurthae.

16. **Delmatico** (*ps*) i.e. 'in Dalmatia.' See on *Odes* I. 31. 9 and I. 33. 16, and compare P. 21.

17. **minaci...cornuum**: for the grouping see on P. 35.

18. **auris**: see on *Odes* I. 3. 16.

19. **fugacis** (*ps*) is proleptic with *terret* i.e. 'frighten into flight.' See on P. 30, and P. 21.

20. **equitum** (*p*): the order brings it close to *equos*, as in such familiar locutions as *teque tuamque manum*; but see also on P. 38.

21, 22. **audire** is emphatic because separated from *iam videor*. The effect is that of 'literally to hear.' I cannot see why a poet may not *hear* the shouts and the din of a world vanquished (*cuncta terrarum subacta*); both words ('shouts' and 'din') are implied by the context.

magnos (*s*) has emphasis. For the grouping *magnos...duces...sordidos* see on P. 34.

non indecoro (*ps*): see on P. 29.

24. **praeter...Catonis**: an emphatic addendum (see on P. 53); here is the one exception.

atrocem animum Catonis: for the grouping see on P. 35. But *Catonis* is almost generic and see therefore on P. 37 *ad fin.*

25. **deorum** (*p*): as if we had *Iuno et dei*; see on P. 38.

25–27. **quisquis...tellure**: if we omit *amicior Afris*, the grouping is that of P. 13.

Afris is dative with *amicior*, with *inulta* (to their vexation), and with *cesserat tellure* (to their sorrow).

impotens sc. ὤν, 'in impotence.'

victorum (*p*): contrast the *devicti Afri*. The Romans, in spite of their victory, had to suffer defeats in Africa. But *victorum* may be heard with *tellure* also; there is no need to put a comma before *victorum*.

28. **inferias** i.e. 'to be a funeral offering.'

Iugurthae comes as an emphatic addendum (see on P. 53) i.e. and that too to an African in the person of Iugurtha.

quis non Latino sanguine pinguior
campus sepulcris impia proelia　　　　　　　30
　　testatur auditumque Medis
　　　　Hesperiae sonitum ruinae?

qui gurges aut quae flumina lugubris
ignara belli? quod mare Dauniae
　　non decoloravere caedes?　　　　　　　35
　　　　quae caret ora cruore nostro?

sed ne relictis, Musa procax, iocis
Ceae retractes munera neniae,
　　mecum Dionaeo sub antro
　　　　quaere modos leviore plectro.　　　　40

II.

Nullus argento color est avaris
abdito terris, inimice lamnae
Crispe Sallusti, nisi temperato
　　splendeat usu.

29. **quis non** = *omnis* (*s*) emphatic.

Latino (*p*) anticipates *impia* in the next line. The blood is their own, shed in *civil* war.

30. **impia** (*p*) echoes *Latino* above. Compare on *Odes* 3. 24. 25, and see *Odes* 2. 14. 23.

32. **Hesperiae** (*p*) is set close to *Medis* with point; the East hears with joy of the fall of the West. But see also P. 20 *a*.

33, 34. **lugubris | ignara belli**: for the grouping we may compare on P. 20 β; but *lugubris* (*ps*) can equal 'the miseries (of war)'; see P. 27.

Dauniae (*ps*): the position makes it sound as if we had *Daunii...caedibus*; see on *Odes* I. 33. 16, and also on P. 21. I cannot see why the *pars pro toto* excuse should be dragged in. Horace is naturally proud of his own district. The Italian states, no doubt, still took pleasure in reminding Rome of the debt which she still owed them. A Scotch or Irish poet would do the same today.

36. **quae caret ora**: for the separation of *quae* and *ora* see on *Odes* I. 27. 11. The order helps to enforce the antithesis to *mare* l. 34.

37. **relictis, Musa...iocis**: for the position of *Musa* see on *Odes* I. 10. 14.

Musa procax: see P. 36. Gow reads comma after *Musa*, not after *procax*.

38, 39. **Ceae** (*ps*) is kept close to *iocis*; the very word *Ceos* suggests the dirges of Simonides, and prepares us for *Dionaeo* (*ps*), which at once calls up to the mind the joys of love, since Dione was mother of Venus. But for *Ceae...munera neniae* see also P. 20 *a*.

40. **leviore plectro** is an emphatic addendum; see on P. 53.

vivet extento Proculeius aevo,   5
notus in fratres animi paterni;
illum aget pinna metuente solvi
    Fama superstes.

latius regnes avidum domando
spiritum, quam si Libyam remotis   10
Gadibus iungas et uterque Poenus
    serviat uni.

crescit indulgens sibi dirus hydrops,
nec sitim pellit, nisi causa morbi
fugerit venis et aquosus albo   15
    corpore languor.

leviore (*p*): contrast *Ceae*, and compare *Dionaeo*. But comparatives are naturally preposited or separated; see on P. 28.

II. 1, 2. **Nullus** (*ps*) has emphasis = οὐδὲ εἷς. Compare *Epod.* 16. 17.

avaris abdito terris is a limiting addendum (see on P. 53) i.e. 'that is when the greed of earth hides it.'

avaris (*ps*) i.e. 'the greed (of earth)'; see on P. 27, and also on P. 24. Compare *Odes* 1. 28. 18, and 3. 29. 61.

3. **nisi...usu**: the clause qualifies *inimice*, just as in *Odes* 2. 3. 4 *moriture* is qualified by *seu...vixeris* and *seu...bearis*.

temperato (*ps*): the point lies here. Physical use of metal will keep it bright, but 'controlled' use implies an effort of mind and soul. See also on P. 21.

5. **extento Proculeius aevo**: for the position of *Proculeius* see on *Odes* 1. 10. 14, and compare *Odes* 1. 12. 45 *crescit occulto velut arbor aevo.*

6. **in fratres** belongs to both *notus* (known in regard to his brothers) and *paterni* (fatherly towards his brothers). See on P. 49, and note at *Odes* 3. 1. 5.

7. **illum**: for its position see on P. 51.

solvi probably has stress (but see on P. 47). The effect is 'with wing that fears only to be melted.' Fame will bear Proculeius aloft and aloft without fear save of repeating the performance of Icarus. Horace hints that greatness has its dangers, especially under a not yet stable monarchy.

9. **avidum** (*ps*) i.e. 'greed (of spirit)'; see on P. 27, and P. 21.

10. **spiritum** may have some stress (see on *Odes* 4. 9. 26): to conquer one's inner self is a greater achievement than to conquer provinces.

remotis by position is felt with both *Libyam* and *Gadibus*: each is 'remote' in reference to the other; compare *Odes* 1. 15. 29, 30.

11. **uterque** (*p*): contrast *uni* of the next line.

13. **dirus** (*p*) i.e. 'the horrors (of dropsy)'; see on P. 27, and on *Odes* 2. 14. 23.

15, 16. **venis**: for its position see on *Odes* 1. 3. 16.

aquosus...languor: for the grouping see on P. 10.

redditum Cyri solio Phraaten
dissidens plebi numero beatorum
eximit virtus populumque falsis
    dedocet uti   20

vocibus, regnum et diadema tutum
deferens uni propriamque laurum,
quisquis ingentis oculo irretorto
    spectat acervos.

III.

Aequam memento rebus in arduis
servare mentem, non secus in bonis
    ab insolenti temperatam
        laetitia, moriture Delli,

seu maestus omni tempore vixeris,   5
seu te in remoto gramine per dies
    festos reclinatum bearis
        interiore nota Falerni.

17. **Cyri** (*p*) is in artificial antithesis to *Phraaten*. Phraates is a bad king contrasted with the Xenophontic Cyrus.

18. **dissidens plebi** is causal, 'because differing from the mob.'

19. **falsis** (*ps*) is purposely kept close to *dedocet*: Virtue can unteach only what is false.

21. **vocibus** has stress (see on *Odes* 4. 9. 26); words and phrases half understood, catch-words, shibboleths are the bane of democracy.

22. **deferens uni:** the words lie in ἀπὸ κοινοῦ position between *diadema tutum* and *propriam laurum*.

propriam (*p*): the position emphasizes the idea of permanent possession.

23. **ingentis** (*s*) i.e. 'however vast.'

III. 1. **Aequam** (*ps*): contrast *arduis* i.e. a level mind in uphill circumstances.

2. **mentem:** see on *Odes* I. I. 14.

3. **insolenti** (*ps*) i.e. from a joy that is overdone. Greek would express the emphasis on *insolenti* by making the adjective predicative, ἀφ' ὑβριστικῆς τῆς χαρᾶς. But see also on P. 24.

4. **laetitia** should have emphasis (see on *Odes* 4. 9. 26); perhaps the purpose is to heighten the antithesis of joy and death (*moriture*).

moriture (*p*): see on P. 36, and compare *Odes* I. 28. 6.

5–8. **seu maestus...Falerni** is an emphatic addendum (see on P. 53). See also on *Odes* 2. 2. 3.

maestus comes early as if *seu iucundus* were following.

6, 7. **te...reclinatum:** observe how *all* the complements lie between *te* and *reclinatum* (see on *Odes* I. 7. 29, and contrast P. 48).

quo pinus ingens albaque populus
umbram hospitalem consociare amant,   10
   † ramisque et obliquo laborat
    lympha fugax .trepidare rivo, †

huc vina et unguenta et nimium brevis
flores amoenae ferre iube rosae,
   dum res et aetas et sororum   15
    fila trium patiuntur atra.

cedes coemptis saltibus et domo
villaque, flavus quam Tiberis lavit:
   cedes, et exstructis in altum
    divitiis potietur heres.   20

te in remoto i.e. 'yourself in your privacy'; see on *Odes* i. 2. 17.

remoto (*p*): the word has stress because retirement to the hills (e.g. to Tivoli) is part of the happiness.

8. **interiore nota Falerni** is an emphatic addendum (see on P. 53); for the grouping see on P. 35. The effect is to stress the age of the wine (*interiore* is like *reconditum* at *Odes* 3. 28. 2) and its high quality (*Falerni*). The normal order *interiore Falerni nota* would not bring out the points so clearly. For the position of *interiore* see also P. 28.

9. **pinus ingens albaque populus**: note the chiasmus and compare *Odes* I. 25. 17, 18, 19. In the word *ingens* (*pp*) lurks the idea of '*dark* shade' (contrast *alba* preposited).

11. **ramis**: the true reading of this line can scarcely be recovered. To take *ramis* with *consociare amant* is not easily defensible; for *ramis* would acquire a meaningless emphasis under P. 53 and under the principle noted at *Odes* 4. 9. 26. Compare *ventis* at *Odes* 3. 10. 7, 8.

One may accept provisionally a comma after *amant*, and a comma after *rivo*, reading *ramisque et obliquo*, and allowing the *huc* of l. 13 to pick up the *quo* of l. 9.

ramisque et obliquo (*ps*) i.e. the water struggles with fallen branches and the bend (see on P. 27) in the river. In fact a Roman would read the lines thus: 'with branches and the bend labours the speeding water to hasten down the stream.' Compare *Odes* 2. 5. 7.

13, 14. **nimium brevis | flores amoenae...rosae**: for the grouping see P. 35.

amoenae (*ps*) i.e. 'for all its beauty,' it too must die. A Roman may feel *amoenae* with *flores* also (see on P. 52).

15, 16. **sororum** (*p*) is the real subject; see on P. 38.

sororum | fila trium...atra: for the grouping see on P. 16 *a*. The position of *atra* at the end adds to the sombre colour of the line.

17. **coemptis** (*p*) i.e. '(you will abandon) the buying up of...' (see on P. 26). All his purchases of estates will come to nothing; he will have to leave them.

divesne prisco natus ab Inacho
nil interest an pauper et infima
    de gente sub divo moreris,
      victima nil miserantis Orci:

omnes eodem cogimur, omnium   25
versatur urna serius ocius
    sors exitura et nos in aeternum
      exilium impositura cumbae.

IV.

‚Ne sit ancillae tibi amor pudori,
Xanthia Phoceu! prius insolentem
serva Briseis niveo colore
    movit Achillem;

18. **flavus** (*ps*) i.e. 'yellow with flood waters.' The man of great wealth can afford (like Crispinus, Juv. *Sat.* 4. 7) a *villa* in town, so much in town that the Tiber, *when in flood*, washes past it. See on *Odes* 1. 2. 13.

20. **heres** comes last with point: you acquire all these good things only for the benefit of your heir, *o moriture Delli*.

21, 22. **prisco** (*ps*) is felt closely with *natus* i.e. 'of ancient lineage' (see too on P. 24); contrast *infima* (*ps*).

24. **victima...Orci** is an emphatic addendum (see on P. 53).

nil miserantis (*p*): the emphasis is natural. Compare *Odes* 2. 14. 6 *places illacrimabilem* (*p*) *Plutona*, and see on *Odes* 2. 14. 23.

25. **omnium** (*ps*) echoes *omnes* and is logical subject, 'all have their lots drawn' (see on P. 38). An ethical dative (*omnibus*) would give just the same effect.

26, 27. **serius ocius** belongs equally to *versatur* and *exitura*; hence its position between them.

27, 28. **aeternum** (*p*) i.e. 'for an eternity (—of exile)'; see on P. 27, and *Odes* 2. 1. 15.

exilium sounds like an emphatic addendum (see on P. 53); *in aeternum* by itself may mean 'for ever and ever'; then after the pause at the end of the line comes the mournful word 'exile.'

IV. 1. **ancillae** (*ps*): the point is love of a *slave-girl*.

2. **Xanthia Phoceu:** see on P. 36.

prius goes with the whole sentence i.e. 'long before you.'

insolentem (*ps*) is brought close to *serva* and enforces the antithesis of pride and slavery. ·

insolentem serva Briseis...Achillem: for the grouping see on P. 10.

3. **niveo** (*p*) i.e. 'the whiteness (of her complexion)'; see on P. 27, and compare *Epod.* 3. 9 *candidum* (*ps*), and *Odes* 1. 13. 9, 2. 5. 18.

4. **Achillem** comes last in contrast to the *serva Briseis*.

movit Aiacem Telamone natum   5
forma captivae dominum Tecmessae;
arsit Atrides medio in triumpho
    virgine rapta,

barbarae postquam cecidere turmae
Thessalo victore et ademptus Hector   10
tradidit fessis leviora tolli
    Pergama Grais.

nescias an te generum beati
Phyllidis flavae decorent parentes:
regium certe genus et penatis   15
    maeret iniquos.

crede non illam tibi de scelesta
plebe dilectam, neque sic fidelem,
sic lucro aversam potuisse nasci
    matre pudenda.   20

6. **forma...Tecmessae:** if *captivae* is an adjective, then the group *captivae dominum Tecmessae* comes under P. 20 *a*. But the order has two advantages: it allows *captivae...Tecmessae* to be heard with *forma* as well as with *dominum*, and it heightens the contrast of prisoner and master (compare note on *insolentem* l. 2 above).

7, 8. **medio...rapta:** these words are really emphatic addenda (see on P. 53); they carry the point viz. that in the very midst of his triumph the victor was vanquished and that by a captive maiden.

medio (*ps*) i.e. 'in the very midst of....' Compare Livy 34. 5. 8 *medio in foro*, 7. 19. 3, and 44. 35. 16.

9, 10. **barbarae** (*ps*) in contrast to *Thessalo* (*p*). The antithesis is 'foreigner and Greek.'

ademptus (*p*) i.e. 'the loss (of Hector)'; see on P. 26.

11, 12. **fessis...Grais:** for the grouping see on P. 10. The juxtaposition of *fessis* and *leviora* is happy: the weary have a lighter burden.

13. **te generum beati**: a Roman, probably, would first read these words together, as if we had *te genero beati*; indeed Horace is saying two things at once: the parents who are proud of you as son-in-law may bring honour to their son-in-law. See on *Odes* I. 23. 12.

14. **Phyllidis** (*p*) in artificial contrast to *te*, which is placed early in the preceding line.

decorent by position may have some stress i.e. κοσμοῦσι καὶ οὐκ αἰσχύνουσιν.

parentes comes last with point i.e. 'even her parents,' not to mention herself.

15. **regium** (*ps*) has emphasis: she is a descendant of *kings*.

bracchia et vultum teretisque suras
integer laudo: fuge suspicari,
cuius octavum trepidavit aetas
claudere lustrum.

V.

Nondum subacta ferre iugum valet
cervice, nondum munia comparis
aequare nec tauri ruentis
in venerem tolerare pondus.

circa virentis est animus tuae
campos iuvencae, nunc fluviis gravem
solantis aestum, nunc in udo
ludere cum vitulis salicto

5

16. **iniquos** (*s*) i.e. 'because ill-fated.' Note the chiasmus *regium genus...
penatis iniquos*; but see also P. 21.

17. **non**, of course, goes with *illam* i.e. μὴ ἐκείνην γε: not she, whatever
be the case with your other ladies.

illam tibi: note case relations grouped together; see on *Odes* 1.
2. 17.

scelesta (*p*): see on *Odes* 2. 14. 23. The position prepares us for and is
echoed by *pudenda* 1. 20.

21. **teretis** (*p*) i.e. 'the shapeliness (of her *suras*)'; see on P. 27.

23. **cuius** belongs first to *octavum* (sc. *lustrum*) and then to *aetas*.

octavum (*s*) i.e. his *quartum* or *quintum lustrum* might have been
dangerous, but not his *octavum*.

V. 1. **subacta**: one cannot help thinking that a Roman would read this
as nominative (assuming that a short vowel may stand here in arsis cp. *Odes*
1. 3. 36, 2. 6. 14, 2. 13. 16, 3. 5. 17, 3. 16. 26, 3. 23. 18); when *cervice* is
reached, he might resume *subacta* as ablative. The absence of any expressed
nominative feminine makes *valet* very obscure.

2. **cervice** may be taken as ἀπὸ κοινοῦ with *ferre* and *aequare*; this would
excuse its lonely position (see on *Odes* 3. 17. 15).

3. **tauri** (*ps*) i.e. 'the bull (and its weight)'; see on P. 38. There is also
the antithesis of *comparis* (ox) and bull.

4. **in venerem**: for the order see on P. 47.

5, 6. **virentis...tuae | campos iuvencae**: for the grouping see P. 9.

gravem (*ps*) i.e. 'the burden (of the heat)'; see on P. 27, and *Odes*
2. 14. 23; also on P. 21.

7. **in udo**: this can first be read as a noun ('in the wet'), as so often in
Livy e.g. *in sicco* 1. 4. 6; on reaching *salicto* a Roman may resume *udo* as an
adjective. Compare *obliquo laborat...rivo* at *Odes* 2. 3. 11, and see P. 27.

praegestientis. tolle cupidinem
immitis uvae: iam tibi lividos   10
  distinguet autumnus racemos
    purpureo varios colore.

iam te sequetur: currit enim ferox
aetas et illi, quos tibi dempserit,
  apponet annos: iam proterva   15
    fronte petet Lalage maritum,

dilecta, quantum non Pholoe fugax,
non Chloris albo sic umero nitens
  ut pura nocturno renidet
    luna mari, Cnidiusve Gyges: 20

9. **praegestientis** is a strong word in an emphatic position (see on *Odes* 4. 9. 26 and compare on *Odes* 3. 17. 3).

10–12. **immitis** (*p*): because 'unripe' is the point.

lividos (*ps*) is in contrast to *immitis*.

12. **varios** is Bentley's reading and gives, perhaps, the best sense. I suspect that three stages of colour are denoted in ll. 10–12: (1) the hard opaque green (*immitis*); (2) the semi-transparent grey-green (*lividos*) which gives a patchy effect (*distinguet*): (3) the deep purple which begins in the half of the grape furthest from the stem and thus makes the *racemus* look *varius* or *variatus* (i.e. 'striped'). In fact *varios* expresses the result of Autumn's action. The sense, therefore, seems to be 'soon you will find that Autumn speckles the early-ripening grey-green (*lividos*) of the grapes so that they become streaked (*varios*) with purple colour.' See Postgate on Propertius 5. 2. 13.

purpureo varios colore: for the grouping see on P. 24. If we read *varius*, these three words form a picturesque addendum describing Autumn as he would be dressed in some pageant.

13. **ferox** (*p*) equals an adverb with *currit*; see on P. 31.

14. **aetas:** for its position see on *Odes* 3. 17. 15.

15. **annos:** for its position see on *Odes* 1. 3. 16.

proterva (*p*) has stress: Lalage will 'rush you.'

18. **albo** (*ps*) i.e. 'with the whiteness (of her shoulder)'; see on P. 27, and note on *Odes* 2. 4. 3. The word *albo* is also brought close to *Chloris* for artificial antithesis of colouring. For the resultant position of *sic* see on P. 50 *d*, and for the whole grouping *Chloris albo...umero nitens* see P. 18.

19, 20. **pura...mari:** for the grouping see on P. 7. A Roman would read thus: 'clear in the night shines the moon upon the sea.'

Cnidius (*ps*): the position, perhaps, is meant to remind us of the effeminacy associated with the worship of Venus at Cnidos.

N. H.   6

quem si puellarum insereres choro,
mire sagacis falleret hospites
    discrimen obscurum solutis
      crinibus ambiguoque vultu.

VI.

Septimi, Gadis aditure mecum et
Cantabrum indoctum iuga ferre nostra et
barbaras Syrtis, ubi Maura semper
      aestuat unda:

Tibur Argeo positum colono   5
sit meae sedes utinam senectae,
sit modus lasso maris et viarum
      militiaeque.

21. **puellarum** (*ps*): among *girls* is the point; see on P. 38.
choro: for its position see on *Odes* 1. 3. 16.

22, 23. **mire** probably qualifies both *sagacis* and *falleret*.

sagacis contains the logical subject, if *falleret* be turned passively. For its position see on P. 51.

sagacis falleret hospites: for the grouping see on P. 21; but one feels that *sagacis* is substantival and that *hospites* comes as an afterthought i.e. 'if, of course, they are strangers.'

obscurum equals **obscuratum,** and we wait for the causal ablative; see on P. 47.

solutis (*p*) i.e. 'by the loosing (of his hair)'; see on P. 26.

24. **ambiguo** (*p*) i.e. 'by the ambiguity (of his face)'; see on P. 27.

VI. 1. **mecum** coming after *aditure* has stress i.e. 'with me you will go anywhere.'

mecum et: see on *Odes* 1. 35. 39.

2. **nostra** (*s*) i.e. '*our* yoke,' the *pax Romana* and its higher civilization. See too P. 21.

nostra et: see on *mecum et* in l. 1.

3. **barbaras** (*p*) i.e. 'the horrors (of the Syrtes)'; see on P. 27. Note too the chiasmus *Cantabrum indoctum...barbaras Syrtis.*

Maura (*ps*) i.e. 'in Mauretania'; see on *Odes* 1. 31. 9.

5. **Tibur...colono:** for the grouping see on P. 14.

Argeo (*ps*) may be heard first with *Tibur* (see on P. 52); but compare also P. 24.

6. **meae** (*ps*) i.e. '*my* old age,' whatever others may prefer. The possessive is equivalent to an ethical dative *mihi* (see on *Odes* 1. 13. 3); but as *utinam* is really parenthetic, like *precor* between commas, the grouping *meae sedes... senectae* is that of P. 20 *a*.

7, 8. **maris...militiaeque:** these words are heard with *modus* and *lasso*.

unde si Parcae prohibent iniquae,
dulce pellitis ovibus Galaesi   10
flumen et regnata petam Laconi
    rura Phalantho.

ille terrarum mihi praeter omnis
angulus ridet, ubi non Hymetto
mella decedunt viridique certat   15
    baca Venafro,

ver ubi longum tepidasque praebet
Iuppiter brumas et amicus Aulon
fertili Baccho minimum Falernis
    invidet uvis.   20

ille te mecum locus et beatae
postulant arces, ibi tu calentem
debita sparges lacrima favillam
    vatis amici.

9. **iniquae** (*s*) i.e. 'because cruel'; the adjective amounts to an adverb (see on P. 31 and also P. 21).

10, 11. **dulce pellitis ovibus...flumen:** for the grouping see on P. 10.
Galaesi belongs to *dulce flumen* and lies between (see on *Odes* 1. 7. 29).
flumen need not have stress (see on *Odes* 4. 9. 26): there is no real pause.

11, 12. **regnata...Phalantho:** for the grouping see on P. 9.

13. **terrarum:** the position after *ille* makes the genitive quasi-partitive, as if we had *ibi terrarum*.

praeter omnis has stress because separated from *ridet*.

14. **angulus** by separation from *ille* gains in point i.e. 'a quiet corner.' Compare *Epist.* 1. 7. 45 *vacuum Tibur*.

non goes with *Hymetto*, as the order shows, and is equivalent to *ne Hymetti quidem mellibus*.

15. **viridi** (*ps*) i.e. 'the green (of Venafrum)' = the green olives of Venafrum; see on P. 27.

17, 18. **ver...longum** (*s*), **tepidas** (*p*)...**brumas:** length and warmth are the points ; note also the chiasmus.

18, 19. The reading **amicus Aulon fertili Baccho** is unsatisfactory: (1) *fertilis* is not a normal epithet of Bacchus, who cannot, like Ceres, be said 'to give fertility'; (2) the order should be *amicus Baccho fertili Aulon*. Good manuscripts read *fertilis*, and we may accept Bentley's *apricus*, for *amicus*; the prepositied *apricus* echoes *tepidas* (*p*) of l. 17.

minimum qualifies *Falernis* (compare *non* in l. 14) and the phrase amounts to *ne Falernis quidem*. See too on P. 21.

21. **ille te mecum locus:** note the case relations grouped together ('the you-with-me place'); see on *Odes* 1. 2. 17.

VII.

O saepe mecum tempus in ultimum
deducte Bruto militiae duce,
   quis te redonavit Quiritem
     dis patriis Italoque caelo,

Pompei, meorum prime sodalium,   5
cum quo morantem saepe diem mero
   fregi coronatus nitentis
     malobathro Syrio capillos?

tecum Philippos et celerem fugam
sensi, relicta non bene parmula,   10
   cum fracta virtus et minaces
     turpe solum tetigere mento.

beatae (*ps*) i.e. 'the blessedness (of the heights)'; see on P. 27 and P. 21.

22, 23. **calentem...favillam**: for the grouping see on P. 8.

24. **vatis**: see P. 35.

VII. 2. **deducte**: observe the adverbial equivalents, *saepe...ultimum* and *Bruto...duce*, on either side of this word; see P. 34 *ad fin.*

3. **Quiritem** by position is quasi-proleptic i.e. 'to be a civilian, a man of peace.'

4. **dis patriis Italoque caelo**: note the chiasmus, which keeps the patriotic words together.

5. **Pompei...sodalium**: for the grouping see on P. 14.

6, 7. **saepe** belongs first to *morantem...diem*, as the order suggests, and then to *fregi*; see P. 50 *a*.

fregi: the meaning is uncertain. May it not be a metaphor from a wild beast who 'crushes and swallows'? Compare *Odes* 1. 23. 10, and Statius *Theb.* 11. 28. So we talk of 'killing time,' and Latin has *consumere tempus.*

coronatus...capillos: these are emphatic addenda (see on P. 53). Not only, says Horace, did we have wine, but all the *Persicos apparatus*—garlands and unguents.

7, 8. **nitentis...capillos**: for the grouping see on *Odes* 1. 7. 29.

9. **celerem** (*p*) i.e. 'the swiftness (of the flight)'; see on P. 27 and compare *Odes* 2. 13. 17.

10. **sensi**: a comma is not needed after this word.

relicta...parmula: for the ablative absolute after the verb compare on *Odes* 3. 1. 34.

11. **fracta**: supply *est.*

12. **turpe** may be (1) a preposited adjective (see on *Odes* 2. 14. 23); (2) interjectional and parenthetic, equalling *pro pudor!* (3) a quasi-adverb emphatic by separation from *tetigere.*

mento: for its position see on *Odes* 1. 3. 16.

sed me per hostis Mercurius celer
denso paventem sustulit aere:
   te rursus in bellum resorbens   15
    unda fretis tulit aestuosis.

ergo obligatam redde Iovi dapem,
longaque fessum militia latus
   depone sub lauru mea nec
    parce cadis tibi destinatis.   20

oblivioso levia Massico
ciboria exple, funde capacibus
   unguenta de conchis. quis udo
    deproperare apio coronas

curatve myrto? quem Venus arbitrum   25
dicet bibendi? non ego sanius
   bacchabor Edonis: recepto
    dulce mihi furere est amico.

13, 14. **me** coming early has emphasis; contrast *te* of l. 15 below.

me per hostis Mercurius: for grouping of case relations see on *Odes* I. 2. 17.

denso paventem sustulit aere: *denso (ps)...aere* does double duty, for the words are first heard with *paventem* i.e. 'terrified by the thickness (see on P. 27) of the mist'; then they are heard with *sustulit* i.e. 'Mercury carried me off in the thickness of the mist.' Compare Vergil *Georg.* I. 298 *et medio tostas aestu terit area fruges,* where *medio...aestu* goes first with *tostas* i.e. 'parched *by* the midday heat,' and then with *terit* i.e. 'the threshing-floor bruises them *in* the midday heat.'

15. **te** comes early in contrast to *me* of l. 13. But see also on P. 51.

16. **aestuosis** (*s*): shallow waters with sandy bottom are harmless enough, but *aestuosis* implies breakers. See also on P. 21.

17. **obligatam** (*ps*) i.e. 'your debt (of a feast)'; see on P. 26.

18. **longa...latus:** for the grouping see on P. 9.

21, 22. **oblivioso...ciboria:** for the grouping see on P. 9.

capacibus (*ps*) has stress i.e. μεγάλαις καὶ οὐ σμικραῖς.

23. **udo** (*ps*) seems to mean, 'wet, not dry,' i.e. who will freshen up the parsley which has been flagging in the heat of midday? See also P. 21, and compare *Sat.* 2. 4. 22, 23. Page takes *udo* to mean 'pliant,' but is there evidence for such a sense? The πολύγναμπτον σέλινον of Theocritus 7. 68 clearly means 'curling.' Had Horace ὑγρός in mind with its secondary meaning of 'pliant'?

25. **curatve:** see on *Odes* I. 30. 6 *properentque.*

quem Venus arbitrum: for the separation of *quem* from *arbitrum* see on *Odes* I. 27. 11.

VIII.

Ulla si iuris tibi peierati
poena, Barine, nocuisset umquam,
dente si nigro fieres vel uno
    turpior ungui,

crederem: sed tu simul obligasti   5
perfidum votis caput, enitescis
pulchrior multo iuvenumque prodis
    publica cura.

expedit matris cineres opertos
fallere et toto taciturna noctis   10
signa cum caelo gelidaque divos
    morte carentis.

26. **bibendi** (*s*): the effect of the position is a loving stress on 'drinking, drinking, drinking!'

27, 28. **Edonis** has stress by separation from *sanius*.

recepto is at first substantival i.e. 'I will get lively for one who has safely returned,' and then *amico* comes as an emphatic addendum (see on P. 53) i.e. 'above all for one who is a friend.'

VIII. 1, 2. Ulla (*ps*) has great emphasis.

tibi is first dative of the agent with *peierati*, then later object of *nocuisset*. See note on *vagae* at *Odes* I. 28. 23.

umquam (*pp*) has emphasis.

3, 4. **dente** comes first in contrast to *ungui* last.

nigro has some stress because separated from *dente* by *si*.

uno (*s*) i.e. 'if only one (nail)'; see too on P. 24. Editors speak of *uno* as belonging to both *dente* and *ungui*, but the case is different from those cited at P. 33. See also Conway's article in the *C.R.* vol. 14, p. 358.

5. **crederem** is emphatic; see on *Odes* 4. 9. 26.

tu is emphatic because inserted.

6. **perfidum votis caput**: the word *votis* is ablative in point of which with *perfidum*, and ablative of the means with *obligasti*; compare on *tibi* l. 1 above.

7. **pulchrior multo**: these words are emphatic addenda; see on P. 53.

multo (*pp*) has emphasis by position.

iuvenum (*ps*): this is a kind of pendent genitive (common in Greek) and signifies loosely 'as for the youths'; ultimately it is construed with *cura*. See on P. 40.

8. **publica** (*p*) i.e. 'open to all,' like a star for all to behold and enjoy (compare Ovid *Her.* 18. 150 *publica...sidera*, *Met.* 6. 351, and *ib.* 2. 35); but the emphasis on *publica* is a left-handed compliment.

9. **expedit** comes first with stress i.e. 'it positively pays you,' λυσιτελεῖ καὶ οὐ βλάπτει.

ridet hoc, inquam, Venus ipsa, rident
simplices Nymphae, ferus et Cupido
semper ardentis acuens sagittas   15
    cote cruenta.

adde quod pubes tibi crescit omnis,
servitus crescit nova, nec priores
impiae tectum dominae relinquunt,
    saepe minati.   20

te suis matres metuunt iuvencis,
te senes parci, miseraeque nuper
virgines nuptae, tua ne retardet
    aura maritos.

matris (*p*) i.e. even a mother's ashes. But see also P. 35.

10, 11. **toto taciturna...signa cum caelo:** for the grouping see on P. 10.

11, 12. **gelidaque...carentis:** for the grouping see on P. 17.

14. **simplices** (*p*) i.e. 'for all their simplicity' (Wickham); contrast *ferus* (*p*) 'fierce and rough.'

15. **semper** seems to belong to *ferus* as well as to *acuens*; it therefore has emphasis by separation from both words.

ardentis (*ps*) is usually taken to mean 'burning (arrows)'; but if 'burning' be taken in a literal sense the picture is unsatisfactory. To my ear *ardentis* is proleptic (see on P. 30) and one may compare *Odes* 3. 20. 10 *dentes acuit timendos*. We may therefore choose between (1) 'till the points send out sparks,' (2) 'to make them sting,' as if we had *urentes*. The word *ardere*, in poetry, might easily pass into the sense of 'stinging'; compare *caecus*=making one blind, and 'dizzy precipices,' 'sleeping beds' etc. For the order, however, see P. 21.

16. **cote cruenta** is an emphatic addendum (see on P. 53) i.e. 'and on a whetstone stained with blood.' His arrows are stained with the blood of hourly victims and have stained the whetstone itself.

17. **omnis** (postposited and separated) means 'yes, all of it.'

18. **nova** (*s*)='and those never before existent,' 'an altogether new lot' in colloquial English. Moreover as *novus* is usually preposited, it here acquires added emphasis (see on *Odes* 1. 2. 6).

19. **impiae tectum dominae:** for the grouping see on P. 20 a. The force of *impiae* (*ps*) is 'though faithless.' The word *pius* signifies 'loyal affection'; when used of women it amounts to *pudicus*. Compare Ovid *Her.* 13. 78, 14. 49, 14. 64, and note 1. 85 *ille tamen pietate mea precibusque pudicis* | *frangitur.*

20. **saepe minati** is an emphatic addendum (see on P. 53) i.e. 'for all their threats.'

21. **te suis matres:** note the early grouping of case relations (see on *Odes* 1. 2. 17). It should be observed that *suis* may be felt as a substantive and

IX.

Non semper imbres nubibus hispidos
manant in agros aut mare Caspium
 vexant inaequales procellae
  usque, nec Armeniis in oris,

amice Valgi, stat glacies iners   5
menses per omnis aut Aquilonibus
 querceta Gargani laborant
  et foliis viduantur orni:

tu semper urges flebilibus modis
Mysten ademptum, nec tibi Vespero   10
 surgente decedunt amores
  nec rapidum fugiente solem.

that consequently *iuvencis* comes as an unpleasant and unexpected (therefore emphatic) addendum.

22, 23. parci, miseraeque: note the chiasmus.

miserae (*p*): contrast the normal *felicitas* of new brides.

nuper belongs, I suspect, to *virgines* (like Livy's *deinceps reges* 3. 34. 9), and *nuptae* is a substantive with which *miserae* agees; in fact *nuper virgines* may be placed between commas.

tua (*ps*) as if *tu* with *ne retardes aurā* following. 'Any but that girl' say the mothers. See on *Odes* 1. 15. 33.

24. aura was taken by Servius to mean 'flash,' 'glitter' as at *Aen.* 6. 204. See on *Odes* 3. 29. 64.

IX. 1. Non semper (*s*): this is the emphatic moral of the whole Ode. Compare *usque* (*pps*) at l. 4, *omnis* (*pps*) at l. 6, *omnis* (*s*) at l. 14, *semper* (*pp*) at l. 17, and *tandem* (*pps*) at l. 18. Compare *Odes* 2. 10. 11 on *summos*.

hispidos (*ps*) is proleptic i.e. 'so that the fields become roughened and tangled'; see on P. 30.

3. inaequales (*p*) goes with *vexant* i.e. 'harass by their gusts'; see also P. 27.

4. usque (*pps*): see on l. 1, and on *Odes* 4. 9. 26.

Armeniis (*ps*) i.e. 'in Armenia (and its coasts)'; see on *Odes* 1. 33. 16. Horace thus passes from the extreme east (Caspian Sea), to Armenia (Black Sea), and then to south east Italy (*Mons Garganus*). Compare *Odes* 3. 4. 28.

6. menses per omnis is an adverb phrase postposited and separated; it therefore has emphasis. See l. 1.

omnis (*pps*): for the emphasis see on l. 1.

Aquilonibus by position is logical subject, as if we had *Aquilones querceta... faciunt ut laborent.*

8. orni: for position see on *Odes* 1. 3. 16.

9. tu is emphatic because inserted i.e. 'but you—you....'

at non ter aevo functus amabilem
ploravit omnis Antilochum senex
   annos, nec impubem parentes   15
     Troilon aut Phrygiae sorores

flevere semper. desine mollium
tandem querellarum, et potius nova
   cantemus Augusti tropaea
     Caesaris et rigidum Niphaten   20

flebilibus (*p*) i.e. 'with tears (in your music)'; see on P. 27.

10. **Vespero** is, apparently, used for 'the stars rising after sunset' with *surgente*, and, when *fugiente* is reached, signifies 'the stars disappearing in the sunrise.' A Roman poet has no difficulty in saying that 'Evening rises' when he means that night begins. So Vergil *Aen.* 2. 8, in hinting that it is high time for bed, says that 'the falling (setting) stars urge us to sleep' (*suadentque cadentia sidera somnos*) i.e. 'dawn is not far off.'

12. **rapidum** (*ps*) i.e. (1) 'before the speed (of the sun)'; (2) 'before the burning heat (of the sun)'; the poet feels both ideas at once. For the position of *rapidum* see on P. 27 and P. 21.

13, 14. **non** (*s*) means 'it is not the case that...' and qualifies the whole sentence. Compare *Odes* 1. 17. 1, 2 *saepe*, 1. 27. 23 *vix*, 2. 10. 9 *saepius*, 2. 10. 17 *non*, 2. 11. 13 *non*, 2. 13. 21 *quam paene*, 2. 13. 30 *magis*, 2. 14. 5 *non*, 2. 17. 9 *non*, 2. 20. 13 *iam*, 3. 2. 31 *raro*, 3. 15. 7 *non*, 3. 24. 34 *non*, 4. 1. 9 *tempestivius*, 4. 4. 61 *non*, 4. 8. 13 *non*, 4. 9. 5 *non*, 4. 9. 45 *non*, 4. 11. 17 *iure*, *C. S.* 13 *rite*, *Epod.* 14. 11 *persaepe*, 17. 54 *non*.

ter-aevo-functus amabilem...omnis Antilochum senex annos: for the elaborate grouping see on P. 6.

amabilem (*ps*) is concessive i.e. 'though so beloved.'

14. **omnis** (*s*): see on l. 1.

15. **annos** is in a somewhat emphatic position (see on *Odes* 4. 9. 26). One wonders why Horace did not put *annos* in l. 14; for *omnis* is the more suitable word to carry the emphasis here. He may have been offended by the assonance *annos Antilochum*; or he may have wished to preserve the artificial grouping *functus amabilem omnis Antilochum senex annos*; or again, having written *menses per omnis* in l. 6, he may have desired the variety of *omnis annos*. But compare *Odes* 1. 8. 10, 11, and *Sat.* 1. 2. 114.

impubem (*ps*) is concessive i.e. 'though young.'

16. **Phrygiae** (*ps*) i.e. if 'barbarians' could control their sorrow, surely a civilized Roman ought to do so.

17. **semper** postposited and last is emphatic; see on l. 1.

mollium (*ps*) has stress.

18. **tandem** (*pps*) is emphatic (see l. 1). The pause at the end of l. 17 prevents the necessity of grouping *tandem* with *mollium* and *querellarum* (see on P. 50 *b*). It is possible to take *tandem* as if in a bracket with the sense 'I pray'; compare *Epod.* 17. 6 *parce vocibus tandem sacris*.

Medumque flumen gentibus additum
victis minores volvere vertices,
 intraque praescriptum Gelonos
  exiguis equitare campis.

X.

Rectius vives, Licini, neque altum
semper urgendo neque, dum procellas
cautus horrescis, nimium premendo
  litus iniquum.

auream quisquis mediocritatem   5
diligit, tutus caret obsoleti
sordibus tecti, caret invidenda
  sobrius aula.

saepius ventis agitatur ingens
pinus et celsae graviore casu   10
decidunt turres feriuntque summos
  fulgura montis.

potius goes partly with *nova* i.e. 'rather let us have something new (in place of perpetual dolorousness)'; partly with *cantemus.*

18, 19. **nova...Augusti tropaea Caesaris:** for the grouping see on P. 9, and compare on *Odes* 4. 1. 10, 11.

nova | cantemus Augusti tropaea: for the intrusive *cantemus* see on P. 46 *a.*

20. **rigidum** (*p*) i.e. 'the frosts (of Niphates)'; see on P. 27.

21. **Medum** (*p*) i.e. 'the Mede (and his river),' or 'in Media (the river...)'; see on *Odes* 1. 33. 16.

flumen...victis: for the grouping see on P. 16 *a.*

22. **minores** (*s*) i.e. 'less and not greater'; see also P. 21, and P. 28.

23. **intra...praescriptum:** the adverbial phrase is separated from its verb *equitare* for emphasis.

24. **exiguis** (*s*) is predicative i.e. (as Wickham says) 'and find them all too narrow'; see also P. 21.

X. 3. **cautus**=*caute*; see on P. 32.

5, 6. **auream** (*ps*) i.e. 'the gold (of a middle course)'; not the gold of a miser's dream (see on P. 27).

6. **tutus:** read a comma after this word (so Bentley), not after *diligit,* which has no stress (see on *Odes* 4. 9. 26). The adjective *tutus*=*tuto,* 'securely'; see on P. 32.

6, 7. **obsoleti...tecti:** for the grouping see on P. 20 *a.*

invidenda (*ps*) i.e. 'the envy (excited by a palace)'; see on P. 27.

9. **saepius** (*s*) i.e. 'more often is it the case that...'; see on *non* at *Odes* 2. 9. 13.

ventis comes early, being the logical subject, as if we had *venti agitant.*

sperat infestis, metuit secundis
alteram sortem bene praeparatum
pectus. informis hiemes reducit   15
    Iuppiter, idem

summovet. non, si male nunc, et olim
sic erit: quondam citharae tacentem
suscitat Musam neque semper arcum
    tendit Apollo.   20

rebus angustis animosus atque
fortis appare: sapienter idem
contrahes vento nimium secundo
    turgida vela.

ingens has some stress because it comes last in the line.

10. **pinus** may have emphasis (see on *Odes* 4. 9. 26) to mark the idea of tallness; but there is no real pause after it.

celsae (*ps*) echoes the possible emphasis on *ingens* l. 9.

graviore (*p*): see on P. 28.

11. **summos** (*ps*) also echoes *ingens* and *celsae*. For the iteration of an idea, compare on *non semper* at *Odes* 2. 9. 1.

14. **alteram** i.e. 'a change (of fortune)'; see on P. 27.

bene praeparatum (*p*) has emphasis i.e. 'if well-balanced.'

15. **pectus** should, perhaps, have stress (see on *Odes* 4. 9. 26); there is nothing either good or bad but the *pectus* makes it so. Compare *Epist.* I. 11. 30.

informis (*p*) i.e. 'the repulsiveness (of winter)'; see on P. 27, and *Odes* 2. 14. 23. In Horace *informis* appears to have the one sense of 'ugly.' Others here translate by 'shapeless.'

17. **summovet** has stress (see on *Odes* 4. 9. 26); contrast *reducit*. The celestial policeman 'moves them on.'

non (*s*): see on *Odes* 2. 9. 13.

18, 19. **quondam** (*s*): contrast *neque semper* (*s*).

citharae; *cithara* is the reading of the best MSS; it goes first with *tacentem* (silent in point of the lyre), then with *suscitat* (awakes by the lyre). If *citharae* be read, we may still take it as a genitive in point of which with *tacentem*; it can hardly go with *Musam*: the separation seems to have no point.

tacentem (*ps*) is causal; see also P. 21.

22. **idem** is merely a strong *autem* i.e. 'but on the other hand'; hence *sapienter* is very slightly separated from the verb.

23, 24. **vento...secundo | turgida vela**: note the chiasmus. The words *vento...secundo* are in the ablative of attendant circumstances. Horace is not writing abnormally the normal *turgida vento secundo vela*; what he says is 'since the wind is too strong behind, you will be wise to furl *swelling* (*turgida* preposited) sails.' Compare on *Odes* 3. 13. 4, 5.

XI.

Quid bellicosus Cantaber et Scythes,
Hirpine Quincti, cogitet Hadria
   divisus obiecto, remittas
     quaerere nec trepides in usum

poscentis aevi pauca: fugit retro   5
levis iuventas et decor, arida
   pellente lascivos amores
     canitie facilemque somnum.

non semper idem floribus est honor
vernis neque uno luna rubens nitet   10
   vultu: quid aeternis minorem
     consiliis animum fatigas?

XI. 1. **bellicosus** (*p*) has stress; it is *war* in Cantabria, *war* in Scythia that Hirpinus fears. Compare on P. 27.

2, 3. **Hadria...obiecto** is an emphatic addendum (see on P. 53). As Page says, the point is 'even if the Scythian were separated from us by nothing more than the Adriatic.'

obiecto (*s*) is predicative i.e. 'as a barrier,' as if Horace had written *obice*. See on P. 24 and compare P. 26.

4. **quaerere** should have stress (see on *Odes* 4. 9. 26); perhaps the effect is 'ask, ask, ask.'

5. **pauca** would normally lie between *poscentis* and *aevi*; it should therefore have emphasis (see however on P. 47).

retro (*pp*) i.e. not merely speeds, but speeds *back*, retreats before the advance of age; compare *Odes* 1. 35. 25 *meretrix retro | periura cedit.*

6. **lēvis** (*p*): contrast *rugosa senectus* which is here expressed by *arida* (*ps*) *canitie*.

arida (*ps*) contrast *levis*; the adjective is also causal.

7. **lascivos** (*p*) i.e. 'the *lasciviam* (of love)'; see on P. 27.

8. **facilem** (*p*) i.e. 'the *facilitatem* (of sleep)'; see on P. 27.

9, 10. **idem...vernis:** for the grouping see on P. 17.

vernis: the position of stress (see on *Odes* 4. 9. 26) at once reminds us that spring soon passes.

10, 11. **uno...vultu:** for the grouping see on P. 15.

uno (*s*) is emphatic; it echoes *semper* (*s*) of l. 9.

rubens: does Horace refer to the red colour of the moon when rising and its change to silver when it mounts the sky? In *Sat.* 1. 8. 35 the moon 'blushes' behind the tombs, evidently as it rises. But in Propertius 1. 10. 8 the moon is said to 'blush' (at lovers' embraces?) even when it is high in the heavens.

cur non sub alta vel platano vel hac
pinu iacentes sic temere et rosa
    canos odorati capillos,   15
        dum licet, Assyriaque nardo

potamus uncti? dissipat Euhius
curas edacis. quis puer ocius
    restinguet ardentis Falerni
        pocula praetereunte lympha?   20

quis devium scortum eliciet domo
Lyden? eburna dic age cum lyra
    maturet, incomptum Lacaenae
        more comae religata nodum.

vultu by position, perhaps, has stress (see on *Odes* 4. 9. 26); it may emphasize the transitoriness of facial expression.

11, 12. **aeternis...animum:** for the grouping see on P. 9.

consiliis is comparative ablative with *minorem*, and instrumental ablative with *fatigas* (see on *Odes* 1. 28. 23).

13. **non:** for its position see on *Odes* 2. 9. 13.

alta (*ps*): height implies shade; thus the sense is 'under the shadow (of the plane)'; see on P. 27. The adjective, as is shown by *vel...vel*, belongs to both *platano* and *pinu*.

14. **sic temere:** the words go, by *coniunctio*, with *potamus* as well as *iacentes*.

15. **canos** (*ps*) i.e. 'in spite of our white hairs.' See also on P. 24.

16. **dum licet** belongs, by *coniunctio*, to the preceding lines and also to *potamus*.

Assyria (*p*): in contrast, perhaps, to the inferior *saliunca* or Celtic nard (see Vergil *Ecl*. 5. 17). Horace would 'do it in style' with *Syrian* nard (hence the separation from *uncti*) and *Falernian* wine.

19. **ardentis** (*p*): the word is purposely kept close to *restinguet*, as if we had *ardorem Falerni* (see on P. 27). See also on *Odes* 1. 27. 9.

Falerni (*p*): contrast cheaper wines. See also on P. 38.

20. **praetereunte lympha:** a picturesque addendum (see on P. 53) reminding us that the dinner is out of doors. See too on *Odes* 3. 1. 34.

21. **devium** (*p*): her *shyness* is the point; otherwise she would need no enticing. But see emendations.

22. **Lyden:** the position seems to be without point (see on *Odes* 4. 9. 26), and it is tempting therefore to read *eburnam* with *Lyden* i.e. 'white as ivory'; compare Ovid *Am*. 3. 7. 7 *bracchia eburnea*, *Her*. 20. 50 *cervix eburnea*, and Propertius 2. 1. 9 *eburni digiti*. The reading *eburna* (*ps*) presents other difficulties; a *scortum*, especially if shy, could hardly afford a lyre of ivory, whether this means 'inlaid with ivory' or 'having ivory horns to support the cross-piece,' and the only justification for the position of *eburna* (*ps*) is that our attention is drawn to more 'swagger,' like *Syrian* nard and *Falernian* wine.

XII.

Nolis longa ferae bella Numantiae
nec dirum Hannibalem nec Siculum mare
Poeno purpureum sanguine mollibus
    aptari citharae modis,

nec saevos Lapithas et nimium mero   5
Hylaeum domitosque Herculea manu
Telluris iuvenes, unde periculum
    fulgens contremuit domus

23. **maturet** perhaps has stress (see on *Odes* 4. 9. 26).

23, 24. The reading of these lines is very uncertain. If we accept Bentley's *incomptam Lacaenae more comam religata nodo*, then the position of *Lacaenae more* almost compels us to take these words with *incomptam...comam* i.e. her hair is untidy like that of a *Spartan* (*Lacaenae* is preposited) damsel, and she is bidden to tie it up hastily in a *knot* (note the stress on *nodo* coming last). Propertius (4) 3. 14. 28 implies that a Spartan maiden took no great care of her coiffure. I am assured on good feminine authority that knotting the hair on the top is quite the quickest way of making it look 'respectable.' For this hasty knot compare *Odes* 3. 14. 21, 22.

The same sense can be obtained from the reading *incomptum Lacaenae more comas religata nodum*, where *comas* is accusative after *religata* (middle voice), and *incomptum...nodum* is an accusative of 'result' or quasi-internal and proleptic. In this reading both *incomptum* (*ps*) and *nodum* (placed last) have their proper stress. On the other hand if we read *in comptum Lacaenae more comas religata nodum*, there is great stress on *comptum* (*ps*), and we are driven to assume that the *neat* knot was essentially Spartan. But there is a further difficulty: Horace has bidden the lady to make haste and then adds, in effect, 'by taking time over an elaborate coiffure': indeed the words that follow *maturet* form an emphatic addendum (see P. 53).

Another possibility is that *comptum* is a noun='coiffure' (see Lucretius I. 88) and that *nodum* is an accusative of result in apposition with *comptum* and *comas* i.e. so as to make a knot.

XII. 1. **longa...Numantiae**: for the grouping see on P. 9.

2, 3. **dirum** (*p*) i.e. 'the horrors (associated with Hannibal)'; see on P. 27, and on *Odes* 2. 14. 23. Compare also on *Odes* 4. 4. 49. If we read *durum*, the position prepares us for the antithesis *mollibus* (*ps*).

Siculum (*p*) amounts to 'near Sicily' (see on *Odes* I. 31. 9). Horace passes from Spain and Italy to Sicily and its seas. Compare *Odes* 3. 4. 28.

mare...sanguine: for the grouping see on P. 14.

3, 4. **mollibus...modis**: for the grouping, with *aptari* intrusive, see on P. 46 a. The soft measures of the lyre do not suit *dura belli*.

5. **saevos** (*p*) i.e. 'the cruelties (of the Lapithae)'; see on P. 27 and on *Odes* 2. 14. 23.

Saturni veteris: tuque pedestribus
dices historiis proelia Caesaris,   10
Maecenas, melius ductaque per vias
      regum colla minacium.

me dulcis dominae Musa Licymniae
cantus, me voluit dicere lucidum
fulgentis oculos et bene mutuis   15
      fidum pectus amoribus;

quam nec ferre pedem dedecuit choris
nec certare ioco nec dare bracchia
ludentem nitidis virginibus sacro
      Dianae celebris die.   20

6. **Herculea** (*p*): the adjective is like a preposited genitive equivalent to 'tamed by Hercules by his hand'; see on P. 38, and compare the note at *Odes* I. 3. 36. For the grouping see also P. 10.

8. **fulgens** (*ps*): the order suggests that *fulgens* is more than a mere epithet of *domus*, and that it is a true participle i.e. 'all ablaze there trembled...'; but see P. 21, and *Odes* 3. 3. 10, and 3. 3. 33.

9. **pedestribus** (*ps*): contrast *poeticis*; see also P. 21.

11, 12. **melius** (*pps*) has emphasis and equals *idque melius*.

ducta...minacium: for the grouping see on P. 17.

13, 14. **me** is emphatic by position; contrast *tu* of l. 9.

dulcis (*ps*) i.e. 'the charms (of her singing)'; see on P. 27, and contrast *ferae* and *bella* of l. 1. Two points are to be noted: (1) the position of *Musa* between *dominae* and *Licymniae*; (2) the stress on *cantus* (see on *Odes* 4. 9. 26). The word *cantus* thus prepares us for the antithesis *fulgentis oculos* and *fidum pectus*. Horace is bidden to sing of Licymnia's music, flashing eye, and fidelity. Next, the group *dominae Musa Licymniae* ought, as Wickham says, to mean 'the Muse of your lady Licymnia' (see for the grouping P. 20 a), and compare *Odes* 2. 1. 9 *severae Musa tragoediae*). The expression 'Muse of Licymnia' is possible enough in Horace; it is implied at *Odes* 1. 17. 13, 14 *pietas mea et Musa*, and *Epist.* 1. 19. 28 **temperat Archilochi Musam pede mascula Sappho*. The sense therefore may well be as follows: 'The Muse of Licymnia (for Licymnia composes her own songs) bids me sing of her poetry, her eyes, and her faithful affection.'

14, 15. **lucidum | fulgentis** is a quasi-compound i.e. 'brightly-gleaming'; see on *Odes* 3. 1. 24.

15. **fulgentis** (*p*) i.e. 'the flash (of her eyes)'; see on P. 27.

* I cannot resist a word of comment on this line. Wilkins translates thus: 'Masculine Sappho moulds her muse by the measure of Archilochus.' But if Latin order means anything, we cannot well separate the group *Archilochi musam pede*. May we not render by 'Sappho keeps within control the muse of Archilochus while using the measure of Archilochus'?

num tu quae tenuit dives Achaemenes
aut pinguis Phrygiae Mygdonias opes
  permutare velis crine Licymniae,
    plenas aut Arabum domos,
cum flagrantia detorquet ad oscula   25
cervicem, aut facili saevitia negat,
quae poscente magis gaudeat eripi,
    interdum rapere occupet?

XIII.

Ille et nefasto te posuit die,
quicumque primum, et sacrilega manu
  produxit, arbos, in nepotum
    perniciem opprobriumque pagi;

bene must go first with *mutuis*; it may be felt later with *fidum* also.

mutuis...amoribus: for the grouping see on P. 10.

17. **choris** comes last and prepares us for *ioco*, which also follows its verb. She can *dance*, and she can *jest*.

19, 20. **nitidis** (*p*): 'Oh then they're dressed in all their best,' because it is, as it were, a Sunday ; for *sacro*, early in its group and at the end of the line, explains while it echoes, the preposited *nitidis*.

21–24. The preposited adjectives (see on P. 27) all have point i.e. not the wealth (*dives*) of *Achaemenes*, not the fertility (*pinguis*) of Phrygia, not the fulness (*plenas*) of unlooted Arabian homes are worth one lock of Licymnia's hair.

22. **aut pinguis...opes:** a Roman would read the line thus : 'or fertile Phrygia with a Mygdon's wealth.'

pinguis (*p*) i.e. 'the wealth (of Phrygia)'; see on P. 27.

Phrygiae (*p*): for its position see on P. 38, and 43.

Mygdonias (*p*): for the preposited generic adjective see on P. 37. Compare too *Odes* 3. 16. 41.

24. **plenas** (*ps*) i.e. 'the fulness (of houses)'; see on P. 27. The adjective is made emphatic by putting *aut* after it. If *aut* preceded, the order would be normal (see on *Odes* 1. 7. 29). Observe that either position of *aut* suits the metre.

25. **flagrantia** (*p*) is causal, 'because they are full of passion.' See also P. 21.

26. **cervicem** by position should have stress (see on *Odes* 4. 9. 26); perhaps 'neck' instead of 'lips' echoes the passion of *flagrantia*.

facili (*p*) i.e. '(a cruelty) that yields easily'; the position of *facili* heightens the oxymoron (see on *Epod.* 5. 82).

27. **magis** (*pp*) goes with *poscente* i.e. '*even more* than her suitor.'

28. **interdum** belongs to both *rapere* and *occupet*.

illum et parentis crediderim sui   5
fregisse cervicem et penetralia
  sparsisse nocturno cruore
    hospitis; ille venena Colcha

et quicquid usquam concipitur nefas
tractavit, agro qui statuit meo   10
  te triste lignum, te caducum
    in domini caput immerentis.

quid quisque vitet, numquam homini satis
cautum est in horas. navita Bosphorum
  Thynus perhorrescit neque ultra   15
    caeca timet aliunde fata,

XIII. 1, 2. **nefasto** (*ps*)...**sacrilega** (*p*): such words of indignation
are naturally stressed. Compare *triste* (*p*) at l. 11, and see on *Odes* 2.
14. 23.

die: for its position see on *Odes* I. 3. 16.

3, 4. **nepotum | perniciem opprobriumque pagi:** note the chiasmus.

5. **parentis** (*ps*): a father's neck, not to mention a less important
person.

sui (*s*): his own father, not to mention his neighbour's.

7. **nocturno** (*p*): the murder *at night* adds to the horror (compare
Epod. 5. 20). Horace always has *nocturnus* preposited or separated. See also
P. 31.

8. **hospitis** very properly has emphasis (see on *Odes* 4. 9. 26). For the
grouping *nocturno cruore hospitis* see on P. 35.

9. **nefas:** for its separation from *quicquid* see on *Odes* I. 27. 11, 12, and
for its position I. 3. 16.

10. **tractavit** should have stress (see on *Odes* 4. 9. 26)='has had constant
dealings with....'

agro qui statuit meo: the order, perhaps, gives interest to both *agro* and
meo. A farm (not the wilds of Colchis) should have been spared, says Horace,
and *my* farm above all, because I do not deserve any punishment (compare
immerentis separated at l. 12).

11. **triste** (*p*): see on P. 36, and also on *Odes* 2. 14. 23.

12. **domini** (*p*) and **immerentis** (*s*): the two enormities are (1) that it
should fall on the owner's head ; (2) that the sufferer was an innocent man.
See too P. 42. For the position of the group *domini...immerentis* after
caducum see on P. 47.

14. **in horas** (*pp*): the point is that man has not warning *from hour to
hour*. Certain definite dangers he dreads and avoids.

15. **Thynus** (*s*); the sense is: 'the *Bithynian* sailor fears the *Bosporus*,'
as we might say 'the *Breton* fisherman fears the *Channel*' i.e. each man dreads

miles sagittas et celerem fugam
Parthi, catenas Parthus et Italum
    robur: sed improvisa leti
        vis rapuit rapietque gentis.   20

quam paene furvae regna Proserpinae
et iudicantem vidimus Aeacum
    sedesque discriptas piorum et
        Aeoliis fidibus querentem

Sappho puellis de popularibus,   25
et te sonantem plenius aureo,
    Alcaee, plectro dura navis,
        dura fugae mala, dura belli.

the dangers of his own corner of the world. *Poenus (s)* of the MSS = 'even though a skilled sailor' (if *Poenus* can mean 'Phoenician').

15. **ultra:** *sc. Bosphorum.*

16. **caeca…fata:** for the grouping with intrusive *timet* see on P. 46 *a*.

17. **celerem** (*p*) i.e. 'the swiftness (of flight)'; see on P. 27. It may be that *celerem* is ἀπὸ κοινοῦ with *sagittas* and *fugam* (see on P. 33), but the phrase looks like an awkward reminiscence of *Odes* 2. 7. 9, and Bentley's *reducem* is tempting, for the preposited adjective gives point to the oxymoron (see on *Epod.* 5. 82).

17, 18. **celerem fugam | Parthi:** for the grouping see on P. 35.

18. **Parthi,** by position, has stress (see on *Odes* 4. 9. 26); its position helps out this curious series of artificial antitheses i.e. the Poenus fears the Bosporus, the Roman fears the Parthian, and the Parthian fears a Roman prison. For a similar but terser effort see *Odes* 3. 6. 46–48.

18, 19. **Italum** is ἀπὸ κοινοῦ with *catenas* and *robur*; see on P. 33.

19. **robur** has stress (see on *Odes* 4. 9. 26). Its very position seems to suggest the finality of a life sentence. Compare *custos* at *Odes* 3. 4. 79.

20. **gentis:** for its position see on *Odes* 1. 3. 16.

21. **quam paene** goes with the whole sentence (see on *Odes* 2. 9. 13). Contrast *paene* at *Odes* 3. 6. 13.

furvae regna Proserpinae: for the grouping see on P. 20 *a*.

22. **iudicantem** is predicative i.e. 'on his judgement-seat.'

23. **piorum** has a half comic stress; Horace imagines himself in the place where a great gulf is fixed, but (he adds) on the right side of it. Probably *discriptas* colours both *sedes* and *piorum*. Compare on *Odes* 1. 19. 1, and see P. 49.

piorum et: see on *Odes* 1. 35. 39.

24, 25. **Aeoliis** (*p*): the order may draw attention to the fact that Sappho, though a Lesbian, wrote in Aeolic. Note the adverbial phrases *Aeoliis fidibus* and *puellis de popularibus* placed on either side of *querentem*. Compare *Odes* 2. 7. 1, 2, and see on P. 34 *ad fin.*

utrumque sacro digna silentio
mirantur umbrae dicere: sed magis   30
  pugnas et exactos tyrannos
    densum umeris bibit aure vulgus.

quid mirum, ubi illis carminibus stupens
demittit atras belua centiceps
  auris et intorti capillis   35
    Eumenidum recreantur angues?

quin et Prometheus et Pelopis parens
dulci laborem decipitur sono,
  nec curat Orion leones
    aut timidos agitare lyncas.   40

XIV.

Eheu fugaces, Postume, Postume,
labuntur anni nec pietas moram
  rugis et instanti senectae
    afferet indomitaeque morti;

26. **plenius** (*pp*): contrast the less vigorous muse of Sappho.
aureo (*ps*): contrast the, comparatively speaking, silvern music of Sappho.
27. **Alcaee:** for this intervening vocative see on *Odes* I. 5. 3.
29. **sacro** (*ps*): a silence not of interest merely but of awe. See also P. 24.
30. **magis** goes with the whole sentence. See on *Odes* 2. 9. 13.
31. **exactos** (*p*) i.e. 'the driving out (of tyrants)'; see on P. 26.
32. **densum umeris** (*p*) equals *frequens* and goes adverbially (see on P. 31) with *bibit aure*, i.e. the mob crowds to hear Alcaeus.
33. **illis carminibus:** the words come early as if we had *illa carmina obstupefaciunt*.
34, 35. **atras...auris:** for the grouping see P. 15.
35. **auris** may have some stress (see on *Odes* 4. 9. 26) in artificial contrast to *capillis*; but there is no real pause.
35, 36. **intorti...angues:** for the grouping, with *recreantur* intrusive, see on P. 46 *a*.
37. **Pelopis** (*p*): see on *Odes* I. 28. 7.
38. **dulci** (*ps*) i.e. 'by the sweetness (of the sound)'; see on P. 27.
40. **timidos** (*ps*): contrast *feros* implied with *leones*. Compare *Odes* 2. 14. 12, and see also P. 21.
XIV. 1. **fugaces** (*ps*) equals an adverb; see on P. 31.
2. **anni:** for its position see *Odes* I. 3. 16.
3. **instanti** (*p*) i.e. 'the onset (of age)'; see on P. 27, and compare *instantis tyranni* of *Odes* 3. 3. 3.

non, si trecenis, quotquot eunt dies,   5
amice, places illacrimabilem
    Plutona tauris, qui ter amplum
    Geryonen Tityonque tristi

compescit unda, scilicet omnibus,
quicumque terrae munere vescimur,   10
    enaviganda, sive reges
    sive inopes erimus coloni.

frustra cruento Marte carebimus
fractisque rauci fluctibus Hadriae,
    frustra per autumnos nocentem   15
    corporibus metuemus Austrum.

visendus ater flumine languido
Cocytos errans et Danai genus
    infame damnatusque longi
    Sisyphus Aeolides laboris.   20

4. **indomitae** (*p*) i.e. 'the invincibility (of death)'; see on P. 27.

5. **non** goes with the whole sentence; see on *Odes* 2. 9. 13.

trecenis (*s*): the hyperbole is natural enough. Compare *Odes* 3. 4. 79 *trecentae* (*ps*).

6. **illacrimabilem** (*p*) i.e. 'the heartlessness (of Pluto)'; see on P. 27.

8. **tristi** (*ps*): see P. 21, and the note on *invisas* l. 23 below.

10. **terrae** (*p*) i.e. 'by earth (and its bounty)'; see on P. 38.

11. **enaviganda** has stress (see on *Odes* 4. 9. 26); it is a long word for a long thing (see on *Odes* 3. 17. 3).

12. **inopes** (*ps*): contrast *divites* implied with *reges* (compare *timidos* at *Odes* 2. 13. 40); and see P. 21. The words *sive reges...coloni* (indeed *scilicet... enaviganda* also) are emphatic addenda; see on P. 53.

13. **cruento** (*p*) i.e. 'the blood (of battle)'; see on P. 27.

14. **fractis...Hadriae**: for the grouping see on P. 9.

15, 16. **nocentem...Austrum**: for the grouping and the intrusive *metuemus* see on P. 46 *a*.

17, 18. **visendus** comes early with stress i.e. 'we must see with our own eyes' (ἐφορᾶν δεῖ); contrast *linquenda* of l. 21.

ater...Cocytos: the grouping is like that of instances quoted at P. 15.

Danai (*p*) **genus** i.e. the Danaides. For the position of *Danai* see on P. 41.

19, 20. **damnatusque longi | Sisyphus...laboris**: for the grouping see on P. 11.

21. **linquenda** comes early with some stress; see on *visendus* l. 17.

placens (*p*) lies in ἀπὸ κοινοῦ position with *domus* and *uxor* (see on P. 33). It may also signify 'the charms (of wife)'; see on P. 27.

linquenda tellus et domus et placens
uxor, neque harum, quas colis, arborum
    te praeter invisas cupressos
      ulla brevem dominum sequetur.

absumet heres Caecuba dignior   25
servata centum clavibus et mero
    tinguet pavimentum superbo,
      pontificum potiore cenis.

22. **uxor** has pathetic emphasis (see on *Odes* 4. 9. 26) i.e. 'yes, even your wife.'

harum...arborum (*ps*): these words form the logical subject (see on P. 38) i.e. 'nor shall these trees..., not one of them (*ulla*) follow....'

23. **invisas** (*p*): adjectives expressing strong emotions of dislike and pain tend to be preposited or separated (see P. 36 on *povera donna*). Compare *acer* 1. 29. 2, 3. 2. 2, *Epod.* 12. 25, *ater* 1. 37. 27, 3. 1. 40, 3. 14. 13, 4. 11. 35, *Epod.* 6. 15, *barbarus* 3. 5. 49, *damnosus* 3. 6. 45, *deformis Epod.* 13. 18, *devotus* 3. 4. 27, *dirus* 1. 2. 1, 2. 2. 13, 2. 12. 2, *Epod.* 13. 10, *durus* 3. 11. 31, 4. 4. 57, 4. 9. 49, *Epod.* 4. 4, *famosus* 3. 3. 26, *fatalis* 1. 37. 21, 3. 3. 19, *gravis* 1. 2. 5, 1. 2. 22, 1. 15. 16, 1. 18. 5, 2. 5. 6, 2. 19. 8, 3. 3. 30, 3. 5. 4, 4. 9. 22, *horribilis* 1. 29. 4, 2. 19. 24, *horridus Epod.* 13. 1, *immanis* 3. 4. 43, 4. 14. 15, *immitis* 1. 33. 2, *impius* 2. 1. 30, 3. 4. 42, 3. 24. 25, *Epod.* 3. 1, *importunus* 3. 16. 37, *impudicus Epod.* 16. 58, *incestus* 3. 3. 19, 3. 6. 23, *incontinens* 3. 4. 77, *infamis* 1. 3. 20, *Epod.* 17. 42, *informis* 2. 10. 15, *inhospitalis* 1. 22. 6, *Epod.* 1. 12, *iniuriosus* 1. 35. 13, *invidus* 1. 11. 7, 4. 5. 9, *invisus* 3. 3. 31, 3. 14. 23, *lugubris* 1. 24. 2, *male ominatis* 3. 14. 11, *malignus* 2. 16. 39, *malus* 1. 22. 19, *Epod.* 3. 7, 16. 16, *miser* 1. 21. 13, *mordax* 1. 18. 4, *nefastus* 2. 13. 1, *nil miserans* 2. 3. 24, *obscenus Epod.* 5. 98, *pallidus* 1. 4. 13, *perfidus* 3. 5. 33, *sacrilegus* 2. 13. 2, *saevus* 1. 12. 43, 1. 16. 11, 1. 33. 12, 1. 35. 17, 1. 37. 30, 2. 12. 5, 3. 11. 45, 3. 16. 16, *scelestus* 2. 4. 17, *tristis* 1. 3. 14, 1. 16. 9, 2. 13. 11, 2. 14. 8, 3. 3. 62, 3. 16. 3, 3. 24. 33, *Epod.* 10. 10, *turpis* 1. 31. 19, 2. 7. 12, 3. 5. 6, 3. 27. 39.

24. **brevem** (*p*) has stress to emphasize the oxymoron (see on *Epod.* 5. 82); he is absolute owner (*dominus*) on a short tenure. See Page's note.

25. **dignior** (*s*) i.e. *isque dignior*, whether ironically said or not; see also P. 28.

26. **servata centum clavibus:** these words sound like an emphatic addendum (see P. 53) i.e. your hundred keys will not avail you then. It is possible, however, to regard *heres Caecuba dignior servata* as a grouping after the type of those quoted at P. 16.

27. **superbo** (*s*): the purpose of the position is to emphasize the magnificent prodigality of the heir. It may even be a partial compliment with reference to the pouring of libations. We may suspect that most people used *vin ordinaire* for this purpose, not the oldest Pommery.

28. **pontificum** (*ps*) has emphasis i.e. even than a Lord Mayor's banquet. The position of the genitive may be due to the generic sense, as if we had *pontificalibus* (*ps*); see on P. 37 *ad fin.* Compare *Saliaribus* at *Odes* 1. 37. 2.

XV.

Iam pauca aratro iugera regiae
moles relinquent, undique latius
    extenta visentur Lucrino
        stagna lacu platanusque caelebs

evincet ulmos: tum violaria et   5
myrtus et omnis copia narium
    spargent olivetis odorem
        fertilibus domino priori,

tum spissa ramis laurea fervidos
excludet ictus, non ita Romuli   10
    praescriptum et intonsi Catonis
        auspiciis veterumque norma.

privatus illis census erat brevis,
commune magnum: nulla decempedis
    metata privatis opacam   15
        porticus excipiebat Arcton,

XV. 1. **pauca** (*s*) is emphatic i.e. 'few, too few.'

regiae (*p*): the contrast is found in the rustic simplicity suggested by *aratro* and *pauca...iugera*. Compare a Cincinnatus who *quattuor iugerum colebat agrum* (Livy 3. 26. 8).

2, 3. **undique latius | extenta**: these words, as the order shows, go closely with the predicate *visentur*.

3, 4. **Lucrino** (*ps*) **| stagna lacu**: there is an antithesis between *Lucrino* and *stagna*, for *Lucrino* is not only *ps*, but has a slight pause after it at the end of the line. *Lucrinus* suggests a huge *public* work; *stagna* (=*piscinae*) a poor piece of private luxury. As *Lucrinus* can stand alone in the sense of 'the Lucrine lake,' the addition of *lacu* reinforces the antithesis i.e. fishponds (*stagna*) wider than a lake.

5. **ulmos**: see on *Odes* 1. 3. 16. For *violaria et* see *Oaes* 1. 35. 39.

6. **omnis copia narium**: for the grouping see on P. 35; but it is possible to regard *copia narium* as a quasi-compound (see on P. 45).

8. **fertilibus...priori**: the sentence is grammatically complete at *odorem*; these words therefore are emphatic addenda (see on P. 53), and *fertilibus* is concessive 'though productive.'

9. **fervidos** (*ps*) i.e. 'the heat (of the rays)'; see on P. 27, and also on P. 21.

10–12. **Romuli** (*ps*)...**Catonis** (*p*)...**veterum** (*p*): the genitives are logical subjects (see on P. 38), as if 'Not so did Romulus, or Cato, or the men of old days.'

11. **intonsi** (*p*) i.e. the Cato who died in B.C. 149 (when beards were worn), not the modern Cato of *Odes* 2. 1. 24.

nec fortuitum spernere caespitem
leges sinebant, oppida publico
   sumptu iubentes et deorum
     templa novo decorare saxo.   20

XVI.

Otium divos rogat in patenti
prensus Aegaeo, simul atra nubes
   condidit lunam neque certa fulgent
     sidera nautis;

otium bello furiosa Thrace,   5
otium Medi pharetra decori,
   Grosphe, non gemmis neque purpura ve-
     nale neque auro.

non enim gazae neque consularis
summovet lictor miseros tumultus   10
   mentis et curas laqueata circum
     tecta volantis.

13. **privatus** (*ps*): contrast *commune* l. 14. Compare *proprio* at *Odes* I. I. 9.

14–16. **nulla** (*ps*), as often in Cicero, equals *non, nunquam*. But if we comma off *decempedis metata privatis* we have *nulla...opacam porticus... Arcton* (see on P. 9).

decempedis | metata privatis: for the grouping see on P. 24.

privatis (*s*) echoes *privatus* of l. 13.

15. **opacam** (*ps*) i.e. 'the shade (of the northern side)'; see on P. 27.

17. **fortuitum** (*ps*): contrast *novo* of l. 20. See also P. 21.

18. **publico** (*p*): contrast *privatis* of l. 15.

19. **deorum** (*p*): the order emphasizes their piety. See too Conway's article *C. R.* Vol. XIV. p. 358.

20. **novo** (*ps*) i.e. 'new-fangled, recherché, never seen before'; the word does not mean 'new-cut' (*recenti*). See also on P. 21.

XVI. I. **patenti** (*ps*) i.e. caught ἐν τῷ πελάγει, μετέωρος, not coasting along ἐν τῇ θαλάττῃ. See also on P. 24.

2. **atra** (*p*) i.e. 'the blackness (of the cloud)'; see on P. 27.

3. **certa** (*ps*) is predicative with *fulgent* i.e. 'shine clear and steady'; but see too P. 21.

5. **bello furiosa** (*p*): the words form a compound (Ἀρειμανής, as Wickham says); hence *bello* does not stand between *furiosa* and *Thrace* (see on *Odes* 3. I. 24). The adjective *bello furiosa* is concessive i.e. 'though mad in war.' The juxtaposition of *otium* and *bello* has point: the Thracian, though his heart is in war, professes to want peace.

vivitur parvo bene, cui paternum
splendet in mensa tenui salinum
nec levis somnos timor aut cupido　　　　　　　15
　　sordidus aufert.

quid brevi fortes iaculamur aevo
multa? quid terras alio calentis
sole mutamus? patriae quis exul
　　se quoque fugit?　　　　　　　　　　　　20

scandit aeratas vitiosa navis
cura nec turmas equitum relinquit,
ocior cervis et agente nimbos
　　ocior Euro.

7. **venale** is concessive 'though to be purchased.' Note its ἀπὸ κοινοῦ position between *purpura* and *auro*.

9. **consularis** (*ps*) i.e. nor even the *consul's* lictor, much less the lictor of a subordinate official. See also on P. 21.

10, 11. **miseros tumultus mentis**: for the grouping see on P. 35. There is some stress on *mentis* (we are half expecting *plebis*) because it stands outside *miseros* and *tumultus*. Further *mentis* lies in ἀπὸ κοινοῦ position with *tumultus* and *curas*.

laqueata (*ps*): contrast the *paupere tecto* of *Epist.* 1. 10. 32.

13, 14. **parvo bene**: both adverbs are emphatic because postposited.

paternum (*ps*) goes closely with *splendet*, as if we had *a patre traditum*; it sounds almost like a noun (heirloom), and both *tenui* and *salinum* come as a kind of paraprosdokian: his heirloom is a salt-cellar on a humble table. See *Odes* 2. 18. 26, 27.

15. **levis** (*p*) i.e. 'light,' 'easy,' 'natural'; contrast the *gravis somnus* of over weariness (often due to anxiety) or of narcotics and drunkenness. Compare *Epod.* 2. 28.

17. **brevi** (*ps*): contrast *multa* of l. 18.

18, 19. **multa**: for the stress of its position see on *Odes* 4. 9. 26.

terras...sole: for the grouping see on P. 14 and compare on P. 48.

19, 20. **patriae** (*ps*) prepares us for *se quoque* i.e. τίς τῆς γε πόλεως φυγὰς ὢν καὶ ἑαυτὸν φεύγει;

21, 22. **aeratas...cura**: for the grouping see on P. 9. The juxtaposition of the adjectives is, I believe, of importance with regard to the interpretation. Horace says that things of bronze (*aeratas*) are the objects of something *vitiosa* i.e. 'full of flaws,' 'producing flaws,' 'cankering'; compare *Odes* 1. 18. 4 *mordaces...sollicitudines*, and 2. 11. 18 *curas edacis*. Orelli translates *vitiosa* by 'morbid.' For the position of *cura* see on *Odes* 3. 17. 15.

23, 24. **ocior cervis...Euro**: these words are emphatic addenda (see on P. 53).

agente...Euro: for the grouping with intrusive *ocior* see on P. 46 *a*.

laetus in praesens animus, quod ultra est,   25
oderit curare et amara lento
temperet risu: nihil est ab omni
    parte beatum.

abstulit clarum cita mors Achillem,
longa Tithonum minuit senectus,   30
et mihi forsan, tibi quod negarit,
    porriget hora.

te greges centum Siculaeque circum
mugiunt vaccae, tibi tollit hinnitum
apta quadrigis equa, te bis Afro   35
    murice tinctae

vestiunt lanae: mihi parva rura et
spiritum Graiae tenuem Camenae
Parca non mendax dedit et malignum
    spernere vulgus.   40

26. **lento** (*ps*): the phrase *lento* ('patient') *risu* has no parallel. Bentley suggested *leni* (*ps*) in contrast to *amara* i.e. sweeten the bitter with a not sour smile. See too P. 21.

29. **clarum** may be heard proleptically with *abstulit* i.e. carried him off to fame (see on P. 30).

clarum...Achillem: for the grouping see P. 10.

cita (*p*): contrast *longa* (*ps*) of l. 30, and compare *Sat.* I. I. 8 *momento cita mors venit aut victoria laeta.*

30. **longa** (*s*): contrast *cita* (*p*) above, and compare on *Odes* 3. 11. 38.

31. **tibi** precedes the relative in contrast to *mihi*.

32. **hora**: for its position see on *Odes* I. 3. 16.

33. **te** comes early in contrast to *mihi* of l. 37.

te greges: note the case relations grouped early (see on *Odes* I. 2. 17). A Roman can wait for some word like *cingunt* or *circumdant*. Ultimately Horace governs *te* by *circum*. The method has its dangers, as Pope shows when he writes, 'See Pan with flocks, with fruits Pomona crowned.'

greges centum (*pp*) **Siculaeque...vaccae**: note the chiasmus giving stress to both adjectives. Large pastures in *Sicily* imply great wealth. Moreover *Siculae* is felt with both *greges* and *vaccae*. See on P. 33.

34. **vaccae**: for the position see on *Odes* I. 3. 16.

35. **bis** (*s*) has emphasis. For the value and method of twice dipping see Mayor on Juvenal I. 27.

Afro (*p*) has stress: the Gaetulian purple was famous.

36, 37. **tinctae | vestiunt lanae**: see on P. 21.

37. **mihi** comes early in contrast to *te* of l. 33.

rura et: see on *Odes* I. 35. 39.

XVII.

Cur me querellis exanimas tuis?
nec dis amicum est nec mihi te prius
    obire, Maecenas, mearum
        grande decus columenque rerum.

a, te meae si partem animae rapit   5
maturior vis, quid moror altera,
    nec carus aeque nec superstes
        integer? ille dies utramque

ducet ruinam. non ego perfidum
dixi sacramentum: ibimus, ibimus,   10
    utcumque praecedes, supremum
        carpere iter comites parati.

me nec Chimaerae spiritus igneae,
nec, si resurgat, centimanus Gyas
    divellet umquam: sic potenti   15
        Iustitiae placitumque Parcis.

38. **spiritum...Camenae:** for the grouping see on P. 14.

39. **Parca non mendax:** see on P. 29.

malignum (*ps*) i.e. 'the jealousy (of the *vulgus*)'; see on P. 27, P. 21, and *Odes* 2. 14. 23.

    XVII. 1. **tuis** (*s*) is, perhaps, in artificial contrast to *me*; but see P. 21.

3, 4. **mearum...rerum:** for the grouping see P. 10.

5. **meae** (*ps*): so placed to keep it close to the antithetical *te*.

6. **maturior** (*p*): see on P. 28.

7, 8. **carus** sc. ὤν. The sense is *quippe qui nec carus sim...nec, quamvis superstes, integer*. Editors supply *mihi* with *carus*; but why not *amicis (meis tuisque)*? A satisfactory word would be *clarus* (see on *Odes* 1. 20. 5).

aeque seems to be in ἀπὸ κοινοῦ position with *carus* and *integer*; compare on *Odes* 3. 7. 26, and 27.

8. **integer** should have stress; see on *Odes* 4. 9. 26.

8, 9. **utramque:** the position is as if we had *utrique*. See also P. 21.

non belongs to the whole sentence; see on *Odes* 2. 9. 13.

perfidum (*ps*) i.e. an oath *that is going to be broken*; see also P. 21.

11. **supremum** (*ps*) i.e. the *last* journey shall find us companions as we have always been in life. See also P. 21.

13. **me nec Chimaerae:** note the case relations grouped early (see on *Odes* 1. 2. 17).

me is brought forward on the principle noted at P. 51.

Chimaerae (*p*) is logical subject; see on P. 38.

Chimaerae spiritus igneae: for the grouping see on P. 20 *a*.

seu Libra seu me Scorpios aspicit
formidulosus, pars violentior
   natalis horae, seu tyrannus
      Hesperiae Capricornus undae,   20

utrumque nostrum incredibili modo
consentit astrum. te Iovis impio
   tutela Saturno refulgens
      eripuit volucrisque fati

tardavit alas, cum populus frequens   25
laetum theatris ter crepuit sonum:
   me truncus illapsus cerebro
      sustulerat, nisi Faunus ictum

14. **resurgat** is followed by a future *divellet*; compare *Odes* 3. 3. 7, 8.
centimanus (*p*) i.e. 'the hundred hands (of Gyas)'; see on P. 27.
15. **umquam** (*pp*) has emphasis.
potenti (*p*) i.e. powerful, not feeble.
16. **placitumque**: for its position see on *Odes* 1. 30. 6.
17. **me**: note the ἀπὸ κοινοῦ position.
18. **formidulosus** is a long word in a position of stress (see on *Odes* 4. 9. 26)
to describe a fearsome thing; compare on *Odes* 3. 17. 3. See too P. 21.
18, 19. **pars violentior | natalis horae**: the grouping is rare (see on P. 44,
45). It is just possible that *pars violentior*, like *pars tertia* etc., may be felt
as one word.
natalis (*p*): in Horace this word is always preposited, as it is, with somewhat rare exceptions, in all Latin where the words *hora* and *tempus* occur.
19, 20. **tyrannus** is a quasi-adjective (τυραννεύων), as at *Odes* 3. 17. 9;
the grouping *tyrannus...undae* is therefore that of P. 9.
21. **utrumque nostrum**: these words are put early for emphasis; we go
as a pair, says Horace, through life, and beyond.
incredibili (*p*) has emphasis.
22. **astrum**: for its position see on *Odes* 1. 3. 16.
te Iovis impio: note the early grouping of case relations (see on *Odes*
1. 2. 17). The persons concerned are you, Jove, and the evil one.
te: for its position see on P. 51. It is also in contrast to *me* of l. 27.
Iovis (*p*): see on P. 38.
22, 23. **impio...refulgens**: for the grouping see on P. 27.
Saturno goes first with *refulgens* and then with *eripuit*.
24, 25. **volucrisque...alas**: for the grouping with the intrusive verb see
on P. 46 *a*.
26. **laetum** (*ps*) is in effect an emphatic adverb (see on P. 31). A Roman
would read thus: 'the thronging populace all joyously in the theatre....'
sonum: for its position see on *Odes* 1. 3. 16.

dextra levasset, Mercurialium
    custos virorum. reddere victimas   30
      aedemque votivam memento:
         nos humilem feriemus agnam.

XVIII.

Non ebur neque aureum
      mea renidet in domo lacunar,
non trabes Hymettiae
      premunt columnas ultima recisas
Africa, neque Attali   5
      ignotus heres regiam occupavi,
nec Laconicas mihi
      trahunt honestae purpuras clientae.
at fides et ingeni
      benigna vena est, pauperemque dives   10

27. **me** is placed early in contrast to *te* of l. 22.

cerebro: for its position outside *truncus* and *illapsus* see on P. 47.

29, 30. **Mercurialium | custos virorum:** for the grouping see on P. 20 β. With *custos* supply ὤν causal i.e. 'because he is the guardian....' See note at *Odes* 2. 18. 14.

virorum is perhaps half comic, like our 'gentlemen' in 'gentlemen of the road,' 'gentlemen of the pen.'

reddere = ἀποδιδόναι 'to give what is due'; hence it comes early with stress.

32. **humilem** (*ps*): contrast the expensive *victima* of l. 30, *quae nivali pascitur Algido* (*Odes* 3. 23. 9). See also P. 21.

XVIII. This ode is apparently an experiment in metre; not always a successful experiment, if one may judge by certain obscurities of expression and abnormalities of construction.

1, 2. **aureum...lacunar:** for the grouping see on P. 8.

4, 5. **columnas...Africa:** for the grouping see on P. 14.

Africa should have stress; see on *Odes* 4. 9. 26.

5, 6. **Attali** (*p*) belongs to *regiam* as well as to *heres*. Its position makes it generic i.e. 'an Attalus'; compare *Attalicis* (*p*) at *Odes* 1. 1. 12; and see P. 37 *ad fin.*, and P. 43.

ignotus (*p*) on the analogy of *novus* (*p*) *homo*.

7, 8. **Laconicas** (*ps*), because Laconian purple was one of the most expensive purples. For the grouping *Laconicas...honestae purpuras clientae* see on P. 9.

9, 10. **at fides et ingeni | benigna vena est:** a Roman would read these words thus: 'But loyalty and ability I have, and a rich vein of the latter.'

me petit: nihil supra
    deos lacesso nec potentem amicum
largiora flagito,
    satis beatus unicis Sabinis.
truditur dies die   15
    novaeque pergunt interire lunae:
tu secanda marmora
    locas sub ipsum funus et sepulcri
immemor struis domos,
    marisque Bais obstrepentis urges   20
summovere litora,
    parum locuples continente ripa.
quid quod usque proximos
    revellis agri terminos et ultra

Horace hastens to tell us his two outstanding qualities; hence *ingeni* is placed outside *benigna* and *vena*. See on P. 38 and P. 43. It is possible also that *ingeni* is a quasi-objective genitive with *benigna*; if so, see on P. 39.

    pauperem (*ps*) i.e. 'though poor indeed.'

    12. **potentem** (*p*) i.e. 'though powerful.'

    14. **satis beatus** sc. ὤν i.e. *quod satis beatus sum.* Causal clauses may always follow the principal clause (compare on *custos Odes* 2. 17. 30).

    unicis (*p*): the order is that of numeral adjectives. Horace has the word again only at *Odes* 3. 14. 5. The adverb occurs at *Odes* 1. 26. 5.

    16. **novae** (*ps*) i.e. 'although new (they at once begin to go the way of other moons).' The ancient poet still professes to believe that each new moon is a newly created thing i.e. *nova*, not merely *recens*.

    17. **secanda** (*p*): see on P. 26. The cutting of marble into slabs was regarded as a fashionable luxury. See Wickham *ad loc.*

    18, 19. **sub ipsum funus** is a postposited adverb and has stress i.e. '*and that too* with death before you.' .

    sepulcri is preposited partly to echo *funus*, partly because *sepulcri* is an objective genitive (see P. 39).

    domos: for its position see on *Odes* 1. 3. 16.

    20. **maris** (*ps*) is logical object of *submovere* i.e. the sea (and its shores); see on P. 38. Moreover Horace wishes to keep *maris* close to the antithetic *terram* implied in *domos*.

    22. **continente ripa** may well be nothing but an ablative absolute i.e. 'because the shore confines you.' For the ablative absolute placed late see on *Odes* 3. 1. 24.

    23. **usque** goes partly with *proximos* (τοὺς ἀεὶ ὁμόρους as Wickham says), partly with the whole sentence i.e. *semper*, συνεχῶς ἀεί.

    23, 24. **proximos...terminos:** for the grouping see on P. 46 *a*.

limites clientium   25
    salis avarus? pellitur paternos
in sinu ferens deos
    et uxor et vir sordidosque natos.
nulla certior tamen
    rapacis Orci fine destinata   30
aula divitem manet
    erum. quid ultra tendis? aequa tellus
pauperi recluditur
    regumque pueris, nec satelles Orci
callidum Promethea   35
    revexit auro captus: hic superbum

26, 27. **avarus** goes with *salis* i.e. 'in your greed.'

paternos is kept near to *pellitur* purposely, and does double duty: he is evicted from his ancestral home and carries away ancestral gods; he has no valuable heirlooms and his simple piety is well contrasted with the impious greed of the rich man. Thus *deos*, at least to your millionaire, comes as something of a paraprosdokian. See on *Odes* 2. 16. 13, 14.

28. **et uxor et vir:** the words lie in ἀπὸ κοινοῦ position between *deos* and *sordidosque natos.*

sordidos (*p*): their unkempt, uncared for condition heightens the picture of misery.

29. **nullă** (*ps*) **certior** (*ps*): both words are emphatic.

30. **rapacis** (*p*) i.e. 'the greed (of Orcus)'; see on P. 27.

Orci (*p*): Orcus is the agent and therefore important. It is as if Horace had written in a parenthesis *rapax enim Orcus finem iam destinavit* (see on P. 38). The genitive is subjective i.e. 'the limit *set by* the greed of Orcus.'

fine destinata is, I believe, merely an ablative absolute. The sense of the passage may be stated thus: The poor have been evicted and now possess no *certa sedes*; but the wealthy *rex* is little better off in his palace, for *his* landlord, greedy Orcus, has fixed the limit of his tenancy. But see the editors.

31. **aula:** we are expecting some such word as *sedes*, of which *aula* is a picturesque and ironical equivalent.

divitem (*ps*) i.e. 'though rich,' 'however rich.' See too P. 21.

32. **erum** has stress (see on *Odes* 4. 9. 26) and is ironical. He thinks he is master, but *vita mancipio nulli datur* and 'this night thy soul shall be required of thee.'

aequa (*p*) i.e. 'equally'; see on P. 31.

34. **regum** (*p*): contrast *pauperi* of l. 33. See also P. 41.

35. **callidum** (*p*) i.e. 'although cunning,' 'for all his cunning.'

36. **auro captus:** the words are an emphatic addendum (see on P. 53). The antithesis implied, if we knew the story, would, perhaps, be *sed a Iove iussus.*

Tantalum atque Tantali
   genus coercet, hic levare functum
pauperem laboribus
   vocatus atque non vocatus audit.   40

XIX.

Bacchum in remotis carmina rupibus
vidi docentem, credite posteri,
   Nymphasque discentis et auris
   capripedum Satyrorum acutas.

euhoe, recenti mens trepidat metu   5
plenoque Bacchi pectore turbidum
   laetatur: euhoe, parce Liber,
   parce gravi metuende thyrso!

fas pervicacis est mihi Thyiadas
vinique fontem, lactis et uberes   10
   cantare rivos atque truncis
   lapsa cavis iterare mella:

superbum (*p*) i.e. 'the pride (of Tantalus)'; see on P. 27.

37. **Tantali** (*p*): see on P. 41.

38, 39. **levare functum | pauperem laboribus**: the word *laboribus* may stand outside *functum* and *pauperem* because it is felt with *levare* as well as with *functum* (see on P. 49 and the note there on *Odes* 1. 2. 23). It is possible that *functum* (*p*) may, like *defunctus*, mean 'dead'; if so, there is an additional note of bitterness i.e. 'it is only when dead that the poor man finds relief.'

XIX. 1, 2. **Bacchum...docentem**: the stress is on *remotis* (*ps*). A Roman reads the topics in their order i.e. Bacchus in the wilds (*in remotis*), hymns among the rocks (*carmina rupibus*). The collocation of *remotis carmina* draws attention to the wild mise-en-scène of Bacchic song and dance.

2. **docentem** comes last to prepare us for the antithesis *discentis*.

4. **capripedum** (*p*): the position helps to remind us that the ears are ears of *beasts* and therefore can be pricked up (*acutas*).

5. **recenti** (*p*)=*recenter* (*s*): the word belongs as much to *trepidat* as to *metu*. See on P. 31.

metu: for its position see on *Odes* 1. 3. 16.

7. **laetatur** has stress (see on *Odes* 4. 9. 26); the word comes as a surprise: we are expecting something like *turbatur, confunditur*. The poet is in a whirl, but a whirl of *gladness*, not of pain.

8. **gravi** (*ps*) i.e. 'by reason of the fearsomeness (of the thyrsus)'; see on P. 27 and also on P. 24. Compare too on *Odes* 2. 14. 23.

9. **pervicacis** (*ps*) i.e. 'the persistence (of the Thyiads)'; see on P. 27.

fas et beatae coniugis additum
stellis honorem tectaque Penthei
   disiecta non leni ruina,   15
     Thracis et exitium Lycurgi.

tu flectis amnes, tu mare barbarum,
tu separatis uvidus in iugis
   nodo coerces viperino
     Bistonidum sine fraude crinis.   20

tu, cum parentis regna per arduum
cohors Gigantum scanderet impia,
   Rhoetum retorsisti leonis
     unguibus horribilique mala,

10. **vini** (p)...**lactis** (ps): these are the antithetical parts of the description; hence the position of the words. Greek would write τοῦ μὲν οἴνου...τοῦ δὲ γάλακτος.

10, 11. **lactis et uberes | rivos:** see on P. 43.

uberes (ps) i.e. 'the richness of (streams)'; see on P. 27 and also on P. 21.

11, 12. **truncis | lapsa cavis...mella:** for the grouping see on P. 14.

13. **beatae** (p) i.e. 'the apotheosis (of the wife)'; see on P. 27.

coniugis (p) is the primary logical object (see on P. 38). Moreover a complement *stellis* already stands between *additum* and *honorem*; hence the second complement *beatae coniugis* may lie outside (see on P. 48).

15. **non leni ruina:** for the position of these words see on P. 48.

non leni (p): see on P. 29.

16. **Thracis et exitium Lycurgi:** for the grouping see on P. 20 β.

18. **tu...iugis:** for the grouping see on P. 14.

19. **viperino** (s): one does not see a snake used as a hair-ribbon every day; compare on *aureo* l. 29 below. See also P. 21.

20. **Bistonidum** (ps) i.e. 'the Bistonides (on their locks)'; see P. 38. The genitive seems to depend on both *fraude* and *crinis*. The order does not favour taking *sine fraude* with the subject of *coerces*.

21, 22. **parentis** (p) is brought forward next to *tu* in order to group the topics together viz. 'you, your father, and his realm.' See on *Odes* I. 2. 17.

per arduum: the phrase is felt ἀπὸ κοινοῦ with *regna, cohors,* and *scanderet*.

22. **cohors...impia:** for the grouping and intrusive verb see on P. 46 a.

23. **leonis** (p): the order emphasizes his miraculous aspect.

24. **horribili** (p): the adjective may go with *unguibus* also (see on P. 33); but compare too *Odes* 2. 14. 23.

25–28. **quamquam** is usually taken as 'and yet'; but it might well go with *dictus* (καίπερ δοκῶν) i.e. 'Though called more fitted for the dance...you were accounted ill suited to battle; but you were the same (*sed idem* is surely more

quamquam choreis aptior et iocis   25
  ludoque dictus non sat idoneus
    pugnae ferebaris; sed idem
      pacis eras mediusque belli.

te vidit insons Cerberus aureo
  cornu decorum, leniter atterens   30
    caudam, et recedentis trilingui
      ore pedes tetigitque crura.

XX.

Non usitata nec tenui ferar
  pinna biformis per liquidum aethera
    vates, neque in terris morabor
      longius, invidiaque maior

than *idem* alone) amid peace and war,' i.e. you were as capable in war as you were in the dance.

aptior: note its ἀπὸ κοινοῦ position between *choreis* and *iocis*.

28. **pacis...belli:** the antithesis is emphasized by placing one word at the beginning and the other at the end of the line.

mediusque=*medius mediusque*: see on *Odes* 1. 30. 6.

29, 30. **insons** goes closely with *vidit* i.e. 'without attempting to injure.'

aureo cornu decorum: these words are a concessive addendum (see on P. 53) i.e. 'though adorned with a golden horn.' Cerberus might well have taken him for an animal, and a strange one too.

aureo (*p*): the epithet is part of the miraculous; compare *viperino* (*s*) l. 19 above, and *trilingui* (*p*) l. 31 below.

31. **caudam** has some stress (see on *Odes* 4. 9. 26); Cerberus rubs his tail, not his muzzle, against the stranger; he does not sniff him suspiciously.

recedentis (*ps*): is the main object (see on P. 38). Moreover the *re* is important: Cerberus might let men *into*, but not *out of* Hades.

trilingui (*p*): see on *aureo* l. 29 above.

32. **tetigitque:** see on *Odes* 1. 30. 6.

XX. 1. **Non usitata** (*p*) **nec tenui** (*p*): for the preposited adjectives see on P. 29. Compare *Epod.* 5. 73.

2, 3. **pinna** may be read as instrumental ablative with *ferar*, and as causal ablative with *biformis*.

biformis...vates: for the grouping see on P. 10.

liquidum (*p*): we may contrast the *crassum aera* of *Epist.* 2. 1. 244, and *udam...humum* of *Odes* 3. 2. 23.

3. **vates** has stress (see on *Odes* 4. 9. 26); he is no mere versifier but an inspired person.

4. **longius** (*pp*) has emphasis; see also on *Odes* 4. 9. 26.

N. H.   8

urbes relinquam. non ego pauperum   5
sanguis parentum, non ego quem vocas,
   dilecte Maecenas, obibo
      nec Stygia cohibebor unda.

iam iam residunt cruribus asperae
pelles et album mutor in alitem   10
   superne nascunturque leves
      per digitos umerosque plumae.

iam Daedaleo notior Icaro
visam gementis litora Bosphori
   Syrtisque Gaetulas canorus   15
      ales Hyperboreosque campos.

5. **non** separated from its verb and repeated is very emphatic and amounts
to *numquam.*

pauperum (*ps*): the pause at the end of the line adds to the emphasis;
but see also P. 20 a.

6. **quem vocas:** everything depends upon the tone of the Ode. Those
who take it seriously must admit that the third stanza is perilously near the
ridiculous. Fancy the tubby Horace 'dolled up' as a bird! In this line an
attempt is made to put an elevated interpretation on *vocas* (e.g. 'dost summon
to poetic endeavour'). But such an attempt introduces an idea opposed to
the demands of the context. Horace says 'I, though of low descent, I whom...,
shall never die,' and the blank space can be filled only by some depreciatory
notion e.g. 'whom men despise'; hence Bentley's *quem vocant* (sc. *pauperum
sanguinem*), and Gow's *iocas*='banter' (see *C. R.* vol. XXIX p. 26).

But if the tone of the Ode is half-jesting, we obtain a satisfactory sense
from the reading *quem vocas*, viz. 'I who am of humble origin, I whom you
ask to your table, I a poor client, I a solid piece of flesh, fond of my dinner,
I, *moi qui parle*, shall never die, but suffer a sky-change.'

7. **dilecte** (*p*) i.e. 'dear, dear Maecenas'; but see on P. 36.

8. **Stygia** (*ps*) i.e. 'by Styx (and its waters)'; see on *Odes* I. 33. 16. Compare too on P. 21.

9. **asperae** (*p*): contrast *lēves* of l. 11. In any case the human leg should
be smooth, not wrinkled and rough.

10. **pelles** has stress (see on *Odes* 4. 9. 26); contrast *cutis*, the human
skin. Compare too Juvenal 10. 92 *deformem pro cute pellem.*

album (*ps*) i.e. 'into the whiteness (of a swan)'; see on P. 27 and P. 21.

11. **superne** (*pps*): placed late and alone at the beginning of the line (see
on *Odes* 4. 9. 26), it is in artificial contrast to *cruribus*, as if Horace had
written κάτω μὲν μέλας...ἄνω δὲ ἀργός.

leves: the slight pause at the end of the line gives stress in contrast to
asperae of l. 9. The adjective goes closely with *nascuntur* i.e. 'there are born
smooth over fingers and shoulders the feathers.'

me Colchus et qui dissimulat metum
Marsae cohortis, Dacus et ultimi
    noscent Geloni, me peritus
        discet Hiber Rhodanique potor.   20
absint inani funere neniae
luctusque turpes et querimoniae:
    compesce clamorem ac sepulcri
        mitte supervacuos honores.

13. **iam** goes with the whole sentence; see on *Odes* 2. 9. 13.

Daedaleo notior Icaro: for the grouping see on P. 24 and compare *Odes* 4. 5. 11. In any case Daedalus, the inventor, is to be stressed rather than the unfortunate son.

14. **gementis litora Bosphori**: for the grouping see on P. 20 β. At the same time the *roar* of the breakers has point. Horace no longer fears them.

15, 16. **Syrtisque Gaetulas...Hyperboreosque campos**: note the chiasmus of south and north.

canorus (*p*): the picture is of *music* in strange places and of *wings* (*ales*) to take him there; hence *canorus ales* lies ἀπὸ κοινοῦ between *Syrtis Gaetulas* and *Hyperboreosque campos*.

17. **me Colchus**: case relations grouped early; see on *Odes* 1. 2. 17.

18. **Marsae** (*p*): the Marsian mountaineers were among the finest fighters in the Roman army.

ultimi (*ps*): a Roman would read thus: 'men most distant will honour me—the Geloni.' See too on P. 21.

19. **peritus** (*ps*): contrast the barbarian *Colchus* and *Dacus*. See too on P. 21.

20. **Rhodani** (*p*): contrast *Hiberi* (of the Ebro) implied in *Hiber*.

21. **inani** (*p*) i.e. 'because the *funus* is *inane*'; the coffin, so to speak, is empty now that the body, magically changed, has flown away.

22. **turpes** is probably ἀπὸ κοινοῦ with *luctus* and *querimoniae*.

23. **sepulcri**: the position sounds like 'and as for burial'; see on *Odes* 2. 8. 7, and P. 40. Let us have no burial (says Horace), for there is no body to inter (*inani* preposited l. 21), and let us have no honours, for they are superfluous (*supervacuos* preposited).

BOOK III

I.

Odi profanum vulgus et arceo.
favete linguis! carmina non prius
   audita Musarum sacerdos
      virginibus puerisque canto.

regum timendorum in proprios greges,   5
reges in ipsos imperium est Iovis,
   clari Giganteo triumpho,
      cuncta supercilio moventis.

est ut viro vir latius ordinet
arbusta sulcis, hic generosior   10
   descendat in campum petitor,
      moribus hic meliorque fama

I. 1. **profanum** (*p*) i.e. 'the unhallowedness (of the *vulgus*)'; see on
P. 27. Note the ἀπὸ κοινοῦ position of *vulgus* between the two verbs.

3. **Musarum** (*p*): contrast *Iovis, Iunonis* etc.

5. **regum** (*ps*): contrast *Iovis* l. 6.

in proprios greges might first be felt with *timendorum* (see on *Odes*
1. 35. 39, and 2. 2. 6) i.e. tyrants who spread fear over their subjects ; later,
of course, the phrase is governed by *imperium*, as in *facile est imperium
in bonos* (Plautus *Miles* 3. 1. 17). Compare also *Odes* 4. 4. 2 *regnum in
avis*.

proprios (*p*) i.e. their sway is limited (Wickham).

6. **Iovis** comes last, contrast *regum* l. 5.

7, 8. **clari...moventis**: these words are an emphatic addendum : see on
P. 53.

Giganteo (*p*) i.e. 'because over giants'; but see P. 37.

10. **sulcis** has interest because the sentence is constructionally complete
at *arbusta*. Horace is thinking of a vineyard, on a large scale, where the
vines would be planted in long rows (*sulcis*) with uprights joined by a support
(see Shuckburgh on *De Senect.* 15. 52). Small holders would use no support
or trellis-work.

generosior sc. ὤν i.e. 'because he is of nobler birth'; the order prepares
us for *moribus* and *fama*.

12. **meliorque**: see on *Odes* 1. 30. 6.

13. **contendat** has some stress (see on *Odes* 4. 9. 26); even the man of
character and repute still struggles and is the slave of ambition.

contendat, illi turba clientium
sit maior: aequa lege necessitas
   sortitur insignis et imos, 15
     omne capax movet urna nomen.

destrictus ensis cui super impia
cervice pendet, non Siculae dapes
   dulcem elaborabunt saporem,
     non avium citharaeque cantus 20

somnum reducent: somnus agrestium
lenis virorum non humilis domos
   fastidit umbrosamque ripam,
     non Zephyris agitata Tempe.

desiderantem quod satis est neque 25
tumultuosum sollicitat mare
   nec saevus Arcturi cadentis
     impetus aut orientis Haedi,

14. **aequa** (*p*): contrast *iniqua*.

16. **omne...nomen:** for the grouping see on P. 8. The juxtaposition of *omne* and *capax* gives the effect of a compound adjective 'all-embracing.' See also *Odes* I. 34. 14.

17. **destrictus ensis** precedes the relative because all important: the drawn sword ruins everything.

destrictus (*p*): a sheathed sword would be no terror.

impia (*p*): it is only the wicked man who has such fears.

18. **Siculae** (*p*): these feasts were almost as celebrated as those of the Sybarites; contrast *humilis* (*p*) l. 22. The adjective *Siculae* may be quasi-generic (see on P. 37).

19. **dulcem** (*ps*) goes closely with *elaborabunt* i.e. 'will not make sweet'; see too P. 21.

20. **avium** (*p*) **citharaeque** (*p*): these are the logical subjects; see on P. 38.

21, 22. **somnus...virorum:** for the grouping see on P. 14. The words *agrestium virorum* are heard first with *somnus* and later with *domos*.

non is emphatic because separated from *fastidit* i.e. 'does *not* disdain.'

humilis (*p*): contrast *Siculae* (*p*) l. 18.

23. **umbrosam** (*p*) i.e. 'the shade (of a bank)'; see on P. 27.

24. **Zephyris agitata** is a quasi-compound, like 'wind-swept.' The words are preposited because the open air life (already suggested by *umbrosam* of l. 23) is emphasized. For similar quasi-compounds compare *Odes* I. 28. I *numero carentis*; 2. 12. 14 *lucidum fulgentis*; 2. 16. 5 *bello furiosa*; 3. 24. 17 *matre carentibus*; 3. 25. 10 *nive candidam*; 3. 26. 10 *carentem nive*; 4. 14. 51 *caede gaudentes*. Add *Epod.* 12. 21, 16. 6, and see on P. 49.

25. **desiderantem...sollicitat mare:** for the order see on P. 51.

non verberatae grandine vineae
fundusque mendax, arbore nunc aquas   30
    culpante, nunc torrentia agros
        sidera, nunc hiemes iniquas.

contracta pisces aequora sentiunt
iactis in altum molibus: huc frequens
    caementa demittit redemptor   35
        cum famulis dominusque terrae

fastidiosus: sed Timor et Minae
scandunt eodem quo dominus, neque
    decedit aerata triremi et
        post equitem sedet atra Cura.   40

quodsi dolentem nec Phrygius lapis
nec purpurarum sidere clarior
    delenit usus nec Falerna
        vitis Achaemeniumque costum:

26. **tumultuosum** (*ps*) i.e. 'the tumult (of the sea)'; see on P. 27 and P. 21.

28. **orientis** (*p*): contrast *cadentis* l. 27.

33. **contracta** (*ps*) i.e. 'the straitening (of the water space)'; see on P. 26.

34. **iactis...molibus** is probably an ablative absolute after the principal verb, as often in Livy. So ll. 30, 31 *arbore...culpante.*

frequens (*ps*) is equal to an adverb; see P. 31.

36, 37. **cum famulis** goes, probably, as the position suggests, with both *redemptor* and *dominus.*

terrae depends first on *dominus*, then on *fastidiosus.* The adjective has stress (see on *Odes* 4. 9. 26); he is sick and weary of the land, though lord of it.

39. **aerata** (*p*) i.e. 'for all its bronze plates.' See Gow *ad loc.* and compare *Odes* 2. 16. 21. For *triremi et* see *Odes* 1. 35. 39.

40. **atra** (*p*): see on *Odes* 2. 14. 23.

41. **dolentem...lapis...usus:** for the order of *dolentem* see on P. 51.

Phrygius (*p*): the order reminds us that it is an expensive imported marble.

42. **purpurarum** (*p*) is the logical subject; see on P. 38.

sidere clarior is read first as if we had *clariorum* agreeing with *purpurarum* (see on P. 52). Consult Page's note, and see too Wilkins on *Epist.* 2. 2. 199 *pauperies immunda domus*, where *immunda* colours both *pauperies* and *domus.* Compare the note on *Odes* 1. 19. 1.

43. **Falerna** (*p*): see on *Odes* 1. 20. 10, 11.

44. **Achaemenium** (*p*): like *Phrygius* (*p*) *lapis* of l. 41, it is costly and mported.

cur invidendis postibus et novo 45
sublime ritu moliar atrium?
   cur valle permutem Sabina
     divitias operosiores?

II.

Angustam amice pauperiem pati
robustus acri militia puer
   condiscat et Parthos ferocis
     vexet equés metuendus hasta

vitamque sub divo et trepidis agat 5
in rebus. illum ex moenibus hosticis
   matrona bellantis tyranni
     prospiciens et adulta virgo

45. **invidendis** (p) has natural emphasis. See too on *Odes* 2. 14. 23.

45, 46. **novo...atrium**: for the grouping see on P. 9.

47. **Sabina** (s) is brought next to *divitias* as a reminder of the *disciplina tetrica ac tristis veterum Sabinorum* (Livy 1. 18. 4). See also P. 21.

II. 1. **Angustam** (ps) i.e. 'the pinch (of humble circumstances)'; see on P. 27.

amice: this adverb has stress by separation from *pati* i.e. ῥᾳδίως καὶ οὐ χαλεπῶς. But its position between *Angustam* and *pauperiem* is awkward, and perhaps we should accept *amici* (vocative); for the position of which see on *Odes* 1. 5. 3.

2. **acri** (p) i.e. 'the hardships (of warfare)'; see on P. 27, and on *Odes* 2. 14. 23. Compare too on *Odes* 1. 29. 2. But the grouping *robustus...puer* may be classified under P. 10.

4. **hasta** lies outside *eques* and *metuendus* because it modifies *vexet* also. See on P. 49, and compare *Odes* 2. 18. 38, 39.

5. **trepidis** (ps) i.e. in peril, not security. Compare Nietzsche's 'Live dangerously.' See too P. 21.

6. **in rebus** has emphasis (see on *Odes* 4. 9. 26) i.e. in action, not in idleness.

illum...matrona: the picture is made vivid by the order; the Roman *iuvenis* is the object (as shown by the case) from the enemy's walls of the mother's gaze (see on *Odes* 1. 2. 17).

7. **bellantis** (p) by chiasmus echoes *hosticis*.

8. **prospiciens** by its position qualifies both *matrona* and *virgo*.

adulta (p): she is old enough to feel the stir of sexual emotion, as *suspiret eheu* shows.

suspiret, eheu, ne rudis agminum
sponsus lacessat regius asperum   10
    tactu leonem, quem cruenta
        per medias rapit ira caedes.

dulce et decorum est pro patria mori:
mors et fugacem persequitur virum
    nec parcit imbellis iuventae   15
        poplitibus timidove tergo.

virtus repulsae nescia sordidae
intaminatis fulget honoribus
    nec sumit aut ponit securis
        arbitrio popularis aurae.   20

virtus recludens immeritis mori
caelum negata temptat iter via
    coetusque vulgaris et udam
        spernit humum fugiente pinna.

est et fideli tuta silentio   25
merces: vetabo, qui Cereris sacrum
    vulgarit arcanae, sub isdem
        sit trabibus fragilemque mecum

10. **regius** goes with *lacessat* i.e. let him not provoke in his royal pride ; *regius* almost equals *superbus*.

11, 12. **cruenta | ...caedes**: for the grouping see on P. 7.

medias (*ps*) i.e. right through, in the very midst of. Compare *Odes* 3. 16. 9 etc.

14. **fugacem** (*ps*): the *et* preceding adds to the emphasis of the epithet. See too on P. 21.

15. **imbellis** (*p*) echoes *fugacem* i.e. even if he runs away.

imbellis iuventae: the preposited genitive is the real object of *parcit*; see on P. 38.

16. **timido**: for its position see on P. 33.

17. **sordidae** is an emphatic addendum (see on P. 53); Virtue may be repulsed, but never dishonourably.

18. **intaminatis** (*ps*) is contrasted with the preceding *sordidae*. See too P. 21.

20. **arbitrio...aurae** is an emphatic addendum (see on P. 53).

popularis (*p*): for generic adjectives preposited see on P. 37.

22. **negata** (*ps*) i.e. 'though closed'; Virtue pays no attention to the sign-boards of the conventional world.

23. **udam** (*ps*) equals 'misty,' 'dank'; contrast *liquidum* (*p*) *aethera* at *Odes* 2. 20. 2. See also P. 21.

solvat phaselon. saepe Diespiter
neglectus incesto addidit integrum;   30
   raro antecedentem scelestum
     deseruit pede Poena claudo.

III.

Iustum et tenacem propositi virum
non civium ardor prava iubentium,
   non vultus instantis tyranni
     mente quatit solida neque Auster,

dux inquieti turbidus Hadriae,   5
nec fulminantis magna manus Iovis:
   si fractus illabatur orbis,
     impavidum ferient ruinae.

24. **fugiente pinna** is an emphatic addendum (see on P. 53).

fugiente (*p*) i.e. by swift flight (of her wing); see on P. 26.

25, 26. **fideli...** | **merces**: for the grouping see on P. 9.

26. **merces** should have stress (see on *Odes* 4. 9. 26) i.e. reward, not punishment.

26, 27. **Cereris** (*p*): to divulge the mystery of this particular goddess is the unpardonable sin.

Cereris sacrum | **vulgarit arcanae**: for the grouping see on P. 20 β.

27. **sub isdem**: for the separation see on P. 21.

28. **fragilem** (*ps*): the pinnace is frail *per se*, but more frail with a Jonah on board; hence the emphasis by separation.

31. **raro**, like *saepe* in l. 29, goes with the whole sentence (see on *Odes* 2. 9. 13) and, also like *saepe*, is emphatic by separation from the verb.

antecedentem (*p*) i.e. 'though keeping in front.'

32. **claudo** (*s*) i.e. 'though limping.' Moreover *Poena* is rightly set between the words which describe her. Compare *Odes* 1. 12. 41 *incomptis Curium capillis*, 1. 27. 21, 22 *Thessalis magus venenis*, 3. 4. 28 *Sicula Palinurus unda*, 3. 4. 54 *minaci Porphyrion statu*, 4. 2. 33 *maiore poeta plectro*, *Epod.* 17. 35 *venenis officina Colchicis*. See also note on *Odes* 4. 8. 33 *viridi tempora pampino*, and compare *Odes* 1. 2. 41.

III. 1, 2. **Iustum** (*p*)...**tenacem** (*p*): the topics are Justice and Constancy; hence the preposited adjectives.

virum...ardor...quatit: for the order see P. 51.

civium (*p*) is logical subject (see on P. 38), as if we had *cives ardenter prava iubentes*. See also P. 20 α.

3. **instantis** (*p*): the position makes the picture of the wrathful tyrant 'towering over' his victim more vivid; compare *Odes* 2. 14. 3 *instanti senectae*.

4. **solida** (*s*) i.e. because it is fixed like a rock. See too P. 21.

5. **dux...Hadriae**: for the grouping see on P. 14.

hac arte Pollux et vagus Hercules
enisus arces attigit igneas: 10
   quos inter Augustus recumbens
     purpureo bibet ore nectar;

hac te merentem, Bacche pater, tuae
vexere tigres indocili iugum
   collo trahentes; hac Quirinus   15
     Martis equis Acheronta fugit,

gratum elocuta consiliantibus
Iunone divis: 'Ilion, Ilion
   fatalis incestusque iudex
     et mulier peregrina vertit   20

in pulverem, ex quo destituit deos
mercede pacta Laomedon, mihi
   castaeque damnatum Minervae
     cum populo et duce fraudulento.

6. fulminantis...Iovis: for the grouping see on P. 10.

7, 8. fractus goes closely with *illabatur* i.e. in fragments; it equals *si fractus sit et illabatur*; see on *Epod.* 5. 32.

illabatur...ferient: compare on *Odes* 2. 17. 14.

impavidum sc. ὄντα.

ruinae: for its position see on *Odes* 1. 3. 16.

9, 10. vagus (*p*) is a titular and ritual epithet (see on *Odes* 1. 7. 5)— 'Hercules the Wanderer.'

vagus Hercules | enisus: for the grouping see on P. 34.

10. igneas (*s*): this is no mere earthly citadel; compare *lucidas* (*ps*) l. 33 below, and see on P. 21. Compare also *Odes* 2. 12. 8.

12. purpureo (*ps*): see on P. 21. Wickham sees the rosy light of divinity in *purpureo*; but compare Keats *Nightingale* l. 17, 'And purple-stained mouth.'

13. tuae (*ps*): perhaps we may contrast *Martis* (*p*) *equis* l. 16 below; or *tuae* equals 'thy beloved' (see on *Odes* 1. 26. 8). The position has also the merit of combining all the case relations in one line (see on *Odes* 1. 2. 17). Compare too P. 21.

14, 15. indocili...trahentes: an emphatic addendum (see on P. 53).

iugum is well placed between *indocili* and *collo*; it goes with both *indocili* (untaught in respect of the yoke) and with *trahentes*.

16. Martis (*p*): perhaps contrast *tuae* l. 13 above, but *Martis* is naturally kept close to his son.

17, 18. elocuta...divis: for the grouping see on P. 9.

19, 20. fatalis incestusque: the epithets of invective are emotionally preposited; see on *Odes* 2. 14. 23.

iam nec Lacaenae splendet adulterae   25
famosus hospes nec Priami domus
   periura pugnacis Achivos
     Hectoreis opibus refringit,

nostrisque ductum seditionibus
bellum resedit. protinus et gravis   30
   iras et invisum nepotem,
     Troica quem peperit sacerdos,

Marti redonabo; illum ego lucidas
inire sedes, discere nectaris
   sucos et adscribi quietis   35
     ordinibus patiar deorum.

peregrina: note the chiasmus.

23. **castae** (*ps*): contrast *incestus* of l. 19; but the adjective is also ritual (see on *Odes* I. 7. 5). For the grouping *castae damnatum Minervae* see on P. 24 *ad fin.*

25. **Lacaenae** (*ps*): see on P. 21. The case is surely dative i.e. 'in the eyes of.'

26, 27. **famosus** (*p*): see on *Odes* 2. 14. 23.

Priami...periura: for the grouping see on P. 35.

pugnacis (*p*) i.e. 'the prowess (of the Achivi)'; see on P. 27.

28. **Hectoreis** (*p*) i.e. 'even of Hector'; or the adjective may be generic 'of a Hector' (see on P. 37).

29, 30. **nostris...bellum**: for the grouping see on P. 9.

30, 31. **gravis** (*p*)...**invisum** (*p*): equal *gravitatem* (*irarum*) and *invidiam* (*nepotis*) respectively; see on P. 27. But compare also on *Odes* 2. 14. 23.

32. **Troica** (*ps*): the emphasis of detestation: whom a priestess bore and she of Trojan descent.

33, 34. **illum ego**: see on *Odes* I. 2. 17. Both pronouns are emphatic i.e. 'him even I....'

lucidas (*ps*): compare on *igneas* l. 10 above, and see P. 21.

34. **nectaris** (*p*) is preposited because like *lucidas* it describes a characteristic feature of the divine dwelling-place. Moreover *nectaris* is the logical object; see on P. 38.

35. **sucos**: the position, perhaps, suggests long sips (see on *Odes* 4. 9. 26).

quietis (*p*): the last ranks in which a son of Mars might be expected to stand. The epithet has also ironic emphasis in view of l. 29 above.

36. **deorum** is emphatic because it stands outside and is separated from *quietis ordinibus*. Its position echoes the stress on *lucidas* and *nectaris*, and allows *quietis* to have emphasis. But see also on P. 35.

dum longus inter saeviat Ilion
Romamque pontus, qualibet exules
   in parte regnanto beati;
     dum Priami Paridisque busto   40

insultet armentum et catulos ferae
celent inultae, stet Capitolium
   fulgens triumphatisque possit
     Roma ferox dare iura Medis.

horrenda late nomen in ultimas   45
extendat oras, qua medius liquor
   secernit Europen ab Afro,
     qua tumidus rigat arva Nilus,

aurum irrepertum et sic melius situm,
cum terra celat, spernere fortior   50
   quam cogere humanos in usus,
     omne sacrum rapiente dextra.

---

37. **longus** (*ps*) i.e. in all its length, a length (of sea); see on P. 27.

inter is purposely set next to *longus*, as if we had *longum intervallum*. Contrast *Odes* 3. 15. 5.

38. **exules** lying between *qualibet* and *in parte* has stress i.e. (anywhere) provided they are exiles from Troy.

39. **beati** goes with *regnanto* and almost equals an adverb (see on P. 31) i.e. 'with my blessing upon them.'

40, 41. **Priami Paridisque** (*p*): as if we had *Priamo Paridique in busto iacentibus* (I presume that *insultare* here governs the dative); see on P. 38.

armentum: for its position see on *Odes* 1. 3. 16.

catulos ferae: see on *Odes* 1. 2. 17.

42. **inultae** goes adverbially with *celent*. See on P. 31.

stet is emphatic by position. Compare Cicero *Acad. Pr.* 2. 1. 3 *ut hodie stet Asia Luculli institutis servandis*—'Asia owes her stability to maintaining the ordinances of Lucullus.'

43. **fulgens** i.e. 'in all its brilliancy'; see on *Odes* 4. 9. 26.

45, 46. **late** qualifies both *horrenda* and *nomen* (for the latter compare *Odes* 3. 17. 9 *late tyrannus* and Livy 3. 39. 4 *deinceps reges*, etc.), and, ultimately, the verb *extendat*.

in ultimas (*ps*) has emphasis i.e. 'to the very ends of the world'; see also P. 21.

medius (*p*) i.e. 'the interposition (of water)'; see on P. 27.

48. **tumidus** (*ps*) i.e. 'the swelling (of the Nile)'; see on P. 27.

51, 52. **humanos** (*ps*): Horace means that gold might be used for *divine* purposes, for decorating temples etc. Hence *omne sacrum* is placed early

quicumque mundo terminus obstitit,
hunc tanget armis, visere gestiens,
    qua parte debacchentur ignes,   55
      qua nebulae pluviique rores.

sed bellicosis fata Quiritibus
hac lege dico, ne nimium pii
    rebusque fidentes avitae
      tecta velint reparare Troiae.   60

Troiae renascens alite lugubri
fortuna tristi clade iterabitur,
    ducente victrices catervas
      coniuge me Iovis et sorore.

ter si resurgat murus aeneus   65
auctore Phoebo, ter pereat meis
    excisus Argivis, ter uxor
      capta virum puerosque ploret.'

outside *rapiente* and *dextra* (see on P. 49), and the phrase *humanos in usus* goes with *rapiente* as well as with *cogere*. For the late ablative absolute see on *Odes* 3. 1. 34.

53. **mundo** is, perhaps, felt first with *quicumque terminus* as if *mundi*, and then with *obstitit*; but Bentley's *quacumque* is tempting. See however on *Odes* 1. 27. 11, 12.

55. **ignes** comes last to prepare us for the antithesis *nebulae*.

56. **pluvii** (*ps*) i.e. 'the rain (of dew)'; see P. 27. The phrase is a good description of a Scotch mist. But *pluvii*, by position, may qualify both *nebulae* and *rores*; see on P. 33. Compare *Odes* 1. 22. 19.

57. **bellicosis** (*ps*) i.e. despite their prowess in war I dictate terms to them.

59, 60. **avitae | tecta...Troiae:** for the order see on P. 20 *a*. But a Roman may feel *avitae* with *tecta* (see on P. 52). The stress on *avitae* brings out the point: Rome must not think of restoring the past. The position of *Troiae* emphasizes the particular object of the prohibition.

61. **Troiae** (*ps*) is really subject (see on P. 38), and picks up the previous *Troiae* as a sort of rhetorical connective.

62. **tristi** (*p*) reiterates chiastically the *lugubri* of l. 61. See also on *Odes* 2. 14. 23.

63. **victrices** (*p*) is heard with *ducente* as if *in victoriam*.

64. **Iovis**, by position, qualifies both *coniuge* and *sorore*.

65. **ter** (*s*) is emphatic.

66, 67. **meis** (*ps*): perhaps 'my beloved'; see on *Odes* 1. 26. 8. But compare also on P. 24.

non hoc iocosae conveniet lyrae:
quo, Musa, tendis? desine pervicax
referre sermones deorum et
magna modis tenuare parvis.

70

IV.

Descende caelo et dic age tibia
regina longum Calliope melos,
seu voce nunc mavis acuta,
seu fidibus citharave Phoebi.

auditis, an me ludit amabilis
insania? audire et videor pios
errare per lucos, amoenae
quos et aquae subeunt et aurae.

5

69. **iocosae** (*ps*) is rightly brought close to *hoc* which implies *triste*. These themes will not suit the playfulness (see on P. 27) of the lyre. See also on P. 21.

70. **pervicax** equals an adverb 'presumptuously' (compare on P. 31), but it may, of course, be vocative.

71. **deorum et**: see on *Odes* I. 35. 39.

72. **parvis**, postposited and separated, is put last in contrast to *magna*. See also P. 21.

IV. 2. **longum** (*s*): contrast the shortness of the average lyric.

Calliope: for the intervening vocative see on *Odes* I. 5. 3.

3, 4. **acuta** (*s*): whether we read *seu, si*, or *et*, and whatever be the general interpretation, *acuta*, by position, expresses a contrast to the quieter music of the *cithara*.

For the general interpretation see the commentators. If I may comment myself, I would say that *acuta* seems to be a most ungallant adjective when applied to a lady's voice (compare the 'ear-piercing cymbals' of *Odes* I. 16. 7). At *Odes* I. 12. 2 we find the alternative *lyra vel acri tibia*. The same alternative, I believe, is intended here; for *vox* is used of the sound of strings at *A. P.* 216, *Sat.* I. 3. 8, *Aen.* 646, and even of oars at *Aen.* 3. 669, and therefore why may it not be used of the *tibia*? Supposing we read *si* for *seu* before *voce* (though it is not necessary), all is simple enough viz. 'sing a melody to the flute if you now prefer (to sing) to its *shrill* note, or (sing) if (you so prefer) to the lyre.' If we read *seu voce* the interpretation is the same, for the first *seu* = εἰ μέν, and the second εἰ δέ. Contrast the *seu* of l. 22 below.

5, 6. **me**: for its position see on P. 51.

amabilis (*p*): the order heightens the oxymoron; see on *Epod.* 5. 82. But *amabilis* may equal *amabiliter* (see on P. 31).

6. **insania** has stress as a paraprosdokian (see on *Odes* 4. 9. 26).

me fabulosae Vulture in Apulo
nutricis extra limina Pulliae   10
   ludo fatigatumque somno
     fronde nova puerum palumbes

texere, mirum quod foret omnibus,
quicumque celsae nidum Acherontiae
   saltusque Bantinos et arvum   15
     pingue tenent humilis Forenti,

ut tuto ab atris corpore viperis
dormirem et ursis, ut premerer sacra
   lauroque collataque myrto,
     non sine dis animosus infans.   20

6, 7. **videor:** note its ἀπὸ κοινοῦ position with *audire* and *errare*, as if we had *audire videor et videor errare*. Not unlike is *properentque* of *Odes* 1. 30. 6 (see note *ad loc.*).

pios (*ps*): groves that are hallowed—ἱεροὺς καὶ οὐ βεβήλους. See too P. 21.

amoenae (*ps*) i.e. the charms (of stream and breeze); see on P. 27.

8. **subeunt:** note the *coniunctio* position.

9. **me fabulosae:** this collocation sounds like 'about me there is a romance'; see note on *Odes* 1. 2. 17, and compare on 1. 15. 33, and 1. 22. 7.

10. **nutricis extra limina Pulliae:** whatever be the true reading, the words are grouped on the analogy of P. 20 β.

11. **fatigatumque:** see on *Odes* 1. 30. 6.

12. **nova** i.e. wondrous, miraculous, never seen before; see on *Odes* 1.2.6.

puerum palumbes: these words resume and complete the grammatical relations of *me fabulosae* l. 9 above.

13. **texere** perhaps has stress (see on *Odes* 4. 9. 26); the covering of the child is the main part of the miracle.

mirum: note the emphasis; it stands outside its clause.

14. **celsae** (*ps*): contrast *humilis* (*p*) of l. 16 below. But see too on P. 20 a.

16. **humilis Forenti:** the genitive phrase is separated from *arvum pingue* to heighten the contrast of Bantia's wooded slopes and of Acherontia, perched far away on the topmost crags.

humilis (*p*): contrast *celsae* l. 14 above. The word reminds us that agriculture begins only when the low-lying lands are reached.

17. **tuto...viperis:** for the grouping see on P. 9.

18. **dormirem:** for its position see on *subeunt* l. 8 above.

ut premerer coming early has stress i.e. actually buried under.

sacra (*p*): the stress draws attention to the divine inspiration implied; the adjective belongs to *myrto* also. See Conway *C. R.* vol. XIV. p. 358.

19. **collata** (*p*) i.e. 'a heap (of myrtle)'; see on P. 26. The participle, by position, qualifies both *lauro* and *myrto*; see on P. 33.

vester, Camenae, vester in arduos
tollor Sabinos, seu mihi frigidum
    Praeneste seu Tibur supinum
        seu liquidae placuere Baiae.

vestris amicum fontibus et choris   25
non me Philippis versa acies retro,
    devota non extinxit arbor,
        nec Sicula Palinurus unda.

utcumque mecum vos eritis, libens
insanientem navita Bosphorum   30
    temptabo et urentis harenas
        litoris Assyrii viator:

20. **non...infans:** the line is an emphatic addendum (see on P. 53). As to *animosus* one can only say that elsewhere in Horace it means 'courageous.' The child did wander away by itself into the woods (l. 10 *extra limina*) and thereby showed courage for an infant (*infans* comes last with stress), but such courage in a babe was divinely sent (*non sine dis*). The stress, by position, on both *non sine dis* and *animosus* (*p*) is natural enough.

21. **arduos** (*ps*) i.e. 'to the heights (of Sabine land)'; see on P. 27, and P. 21.

22. **seu:** supply *vester sum* i.e. 'or, I am yours, if Praeneste has pleased me, or Tibur....' For *seu* = or if, compare *Odes* 1. 6. 19.

frigidum i.e. 'the coolness (of Praeneste)'; see on P. 27.

24. **liquidae** (*ps*) i.e. 'the brightness, bright air (of Baiae)'; see P. 27, and P. 21.

25. **vestris** (*ps*) echoes *vester* of l. 21.

amicum i.e. because your friend, ἅτε φίλον ὄντα.

26. **non me:** these words go together i.e. not me (whatever happened to others).

me: for its position compare on P. 51.

versa (*p*) i.e. 'the turning (of the line)'; see on P. 26.

retro is emphatic; it should lie between *versa* and *acies*. Horace does not conceal the fact that it was an utter rout. See on P. 49, and compare *Epod.* 5. 80.

27. **devota** (*ps*): 'thrice damned'; see on *Odes* 2. 14. 23.

28. **Sicula** (*ps*) may mean 'near Sicily' (compare on *Odes* 1. 31. 9). Horace passes from danger at home to Sicily and its seas (compare on *Odes* 2. 9. 4, and 2. 12. 2). Furthermore *Palinurus* may be felt to be qualified by the words between which it lies; compare on *Odes* 3. 2. 32 *pede Poena claudo*.

29, 30. **libens** amounts to an adverb (see on P. 31); but for the grouping of *libens...Bosphorum* see on P. 9.

30. **insanientem** (*ps*) i.e. 'the raging (of the Bosporus)'; see on P. 27.

visam Britannos hospitibus feros
et laetum equino sanguine Concanum,
   visam pharetratos Gelonos 35
     et Scythicum inviolatus amnem.

vos Caesarem altum, militia simul
fessas cohortes addidit oppidis,
   finire quaerentem labores
     Pierio recreatis antro. 40

vos lene consilium et datis et dato
gaudetis, almae. scimus ut impios
   Titanas immanemque turbam
     fulmine sustulerit caduco,

navita: the noun may be read as if *navigans* i.e. 'sailing over,' as at *Aen.* 1. 67 etc., and its position prepares us for the antithesis *viator* l. 32 below.

31. **temptabo:** note the ἀπὸ κοινοῦ position of the verb governing both *Bosphorum* and *harenas.*

urentis (*p*) i.e. 'the heat (of sands)'; see on P. 27.

32. **litoris Assyrii:** the words are in ἀπὸ κοινοῦ position with *harenas* and *viator.*

34. **laetum...Concanum:** for the grouping see on P. 10.

equino has some stress; see on P. 37.

35. **pharetratos** (*p*) i.e. 'the quivers (of the Geloni)'; see on P. 27. So we might say 'the assagais of the Zulus.'

36. **Scythicum** (*p*) i.e. Scythia (and its river); see on *Odes* 1. 33. 16.

Scythicum...amnem: the grouping is as if we had *et Scythicum visam amnem Scythico inviolatus amne* (compare on P. 21 and P. 24).

37, 38. **vos Caesarem altum, militia simul | fessas cohortes addidit (?) oppidis:** this reading gives *militia* a position of emphasis as extreme as it is pointless. I venture to think that we should accept *fessus,* omitting the comma after *altum,* and take *militia* ἀπὸ κοινοῦ with *altum* and *fessus* i.e. 'raised to fame by war but weary of it.' Even if we read *fessas,* we may still take *militia* with both *altum* and *fessas.*

40. **Pierio** (*ps*) i.e. 'Pieria (and its cave)'; see on *Odes* 1. 33. 16. See too P. 21.

41. **lene** (*p*) i.e. *lene, non bellicosum.*

42, 43. **almae** is causal by position i.e. 'because you are kindly, you rejoice in gentle counsel.'

impios (*p*)...**immanem** (*p*): the words of invective are naturally stressed; see on *Odes* 2. 14. 23.

44. **caduco** (*s*): see on P. 21. Horace seems to be translating καταιβάτης κεραυνός.

N. H. 9

qui terram inertem, qui mare temperat   45
ventosum et urbes regnaque tristia
   divosque mortalisque turmas
    imperio regit unus aequo.

magnum illa terrorem intulerat Iovi
fidens iuventus horrida bracchiis,   50
   fratresque tendentes opaco
    Pelion imposuisse Olympo.

sed quid Typhoeus et validus Mimas,
aut quid minaci Porphyrion statu,
   quid Rhoetus evulsisque truncis   55
    Enceladus iaculator audax

contra sonantem Palladis aegida
possent ruentes? hinc avidus stetit
   Vulcanus, hinc matrona Iuno et
    numquam umeris positurus arcum,   60

46. **ventosum** (*s*) equals ἀκατάστατον in contrast to *inertem* (l. 45),
βέβαιον. For its position see on *Odes* 4. 9. 26.

47. **mortalis** (*p*): contrast *divos*.

48. **aequo** (*s*): the epithet is brought close to *unus*; though he stands alone,
he rules all, not like a tyrannical monarch, but with impartial sway—εἰς
πάντας ὁμοίως. Compare *Odes* 1. 28. 15.

49, 50. **magnum illa terrorem...iuventus:** for the grouping see on P. 9.
fidens (*p*)='confident,' 'emboldened.' The grouping *fidens iuventus
horrida* is that noted at P. 34. The order is all against taking *fidens* with
bracchiis. The line may be translated just as it stands—'those confident
warriors bristling with arms.' We may say, of course, that *horrida* explains
fidens i.e. 'confident because bristling with....' Except for χείρεσσι πεποιθότες,
would anyone have desired to take *fidens* with *bracchiis*?

51. **opaco** (*ps*): commentators quote εἰνοσίφυλλον and *frondosum Olympum*, but *opaco*, by its position, is surely more than a standing epithet. If we
take it first with *tendentes*, then with *Olympo* we have a fine picture—'striving
in the darkness (of Olympus) to set Pelion upon Olympus.'

53. **validus** (*p*) i.e. 'for all his strength'; compare *centimanus* (*p*) l. 69
below. But see also on P. 33.

54. **minaci** (*ps*) i.e. 'with the threat (of his size)'; see on P. 27. For
Porphyrion lying between *minaci* and *statu* (as if 'Porphyrion of threatening
mien') see on *Odes* 3. 2. 32.

58. **ruentes** coming last equals *si ruerent*.
avidus sc. ὤν i.e. 'eager for the fray.'

59. **Vulcanus:** there may be stress (see on *Odes* 4. 9. 26) due to artificial
antithesis to the matron Juno.

qui rore puro Castaliae lavit
crinis solutos, qui Lyciae tenet
    dumeta natalemque silvam,
        Delius et Patareus Apollo.

vis consili expers mole ruit sua: 65
vim temperatam di quoque provehunt
    in maius; idem odere viris
        omne nefas animo moventis.

testis mearum centimanus Gyas
sententiarum, notus et integrae   70
    temptator Orion Dianae,
        virginea domitus sagitta.

iniecta monstris Terra dolet suis,
maeretque partus fulmine luridum
    missos ad Orcum; nec peredit   75
        impositam celer ignis Aetnen,

Iuno et: see on *Odes* I. 35. 39.

60. **numquam** has emphasis by separation from *positurus*.

61, 62. **Castaliae**: its position outside *rore* and *puro* prepares us, like μέν, for the succeeding *Lyciae*, which is separated and preposited. For the grouping *rore puro Castaliae* see on P. 44.

63. **natalem** (*p*) i.e. (the woods) of his *birth*, opposed to the woods of Lycia. See *Odes* I. 21. 10.

64. **Delius** (*p*)...**Patareus** (*p*): for ritual epithets, preposited to give dignity and impressiveness, see on *Odes* I. 7. 5.

65. **sua** (*s*): compare Livy *Pref.* § 4 *ut iam magnitudine laboret sua*.

67. **in maius** has stress being postposited and standing alone at the beginning of the line; see on *Odes* 4. 9. 26.

odere has emphasis because it comes early in contrast to *provehunt in maius*.

69, 70. **testis mearum** (*ps*): the possessive equals *mihi*; see on *Odes* I. 13. 3 *vae meum*.

centimanus (*p*) i.e. 'for all his hundred hands'; compare *validus* l. 53 above.

70. **sententiarum**: there is no point in the position if we read a comma before *notus* (see on *Odes* 4. 9. 26); it seems better, therefore, to accept *sententiarum notus, et* (Lambinus), in which case the grouping *testis mearum... sententiarum notus* is that of P. 18.

70, 71. **integrae...Dianae**: for the grouping see on P. 10; *temptator* is quasi-adjectival (compare *amatorem* l. 79).

72. **virginea** (*ps*): a weak maiden kills a giant; see also P. 24, and P. 37

73. **monstris** is first dative with *iniecta*, then ablative with *dolet* (compare on *Odes* I. 28. 23).

incontinentis nec Tityi iecur
reliquit ales, nequitiae additus
　　custos; amatorem trecentae
　　　　Pirithoum cohibent catenae.　　　　　　　　　80

V.

Caelo tonantem credidimus Iovem
regnare: praesens divus habebitur
　　Augustus adiectis Britannis
　　　　imperio gravibusque Persis.

milesne Crassi coniuge barbara　　　　　　　　　5
turpis maritus vixit et hostium
　　(pro curia inversique mores!)
　　　　consenuit socerorum in armis

suis (*s*) probably equals 'her beloved' (see on *Odes* 1. 26. 8); compare also
l. 65 above.

74, 75. **fulmine** must be read with both *luridum* and *missos* i.e. Orcus is
ghastly wan in the flash of the lightning, and the *partus* are sent to Orcus
by the lightning.

luridum | missos ad Orcum: for the grouping see on P. 21.

76. **impositam...Aetnen**: for the grouping see on P. 10.

77. **incontinentis** (*p*): see on *Odes* 2. 14. 23.

Tityi (*p*) is logical object; see on P. 38. Moreover the genitive may be
pendent i.e. 'as for unchaste Tityus'; compare on P. 40.

78. **ales**: for its position see *Odes* 1. 3. 16.

79, 80. **custos** has stress (see on *Odes* 4. 9. 26); the bird was to be gaoler,
as the chains of l. 80 were to imprison. Compare *robur* at *Odes* 2. 13. 19.

amatorem...catenae: for the grouping see on P. 9. For *amatorem* see on
temptator l. 71 above.

V. 1. **Caelo** goes first with *tonantem*, and then is heard again with
regnare.

2. **regnare** has stress (see on *Odes* 4. 9. 26) i.e. is absolute monarch.

praesens (*p*): contrast *caelo* above.

4. **imperio**: for its position see on P. 47.

gravibus (*p*): see on *Odes* 2. 14. 23.

6. **turpis** (*p*): see on *Odes* 2. 14. 23.

hostium (*ps*): the genitive may be read first as possessive with the subject of the awaited verb i.e. 'and, belonging to the enemy, at the orders of the
enemy'; ultimately it is constructed with *socerorum* and *armis* l. 8.

7. **inversi** (*p*) i.e. 'the inversion (of morals)'; see on P. 26, but see also
P. 33.

8. **consenuit** has emphasis by position i.e. 'has actually grown old!'

socerorum (*ps*): they have even married the daughters of the enemy!

sub rege Medo Marsus et Apulus,
anciliorum et nominis et togae   10
   oblitus aeternaeque Vestae,
     incolumi Iove et urbe Roma?

hoc caverat mens provida Reguli
dissentientis condicionibus
   foedis et exemplo trahenti   15
     perniciem veniens in aevum,

si non periret immiserabilis
captiva pubes. 'signa ego Punicis
   adfixa delubris et arma
     militibus sine caede' dixit   20

'derepta vidi; vidi ego civium
retorta tergo bracchia libero
   portasque non clausas et arva
     Marte coli populata nostro.

Indeed from *hostium* (l. 6) to *armis* is a crescendo: with the enemy he has grown old—with the enemy's daughters—under the enemy's flag! But there is much to be said for *arvis* (see on l. 24 below).

9. **sub rege...Apulus** is an emphatic addendum of indignation; see on P. 53. Notice the collocation of *Medo* and *Marsus* (Hun and Highlander), and the offensiveness of *rege*—a sensual eastern potentate.

10–12. These lines are further emphatic addenda; see on P. 53.

11. **aeternae** i.e. 'the eternal fires (of Vesta)'; see on P. 27, and *Odes* 2. 1. 15. For the preposited ritual epithet see on *Odes* 1. 7. 5.

12. **incolumi...Roma**: see on *Odes* 3. 1. 34.

13. **mens provida Reguli**: for the abnormal grouping see on P. 44. But *mens provida* may be regarded as one word 'prescience'; see on P. 45.

14. **condicionibus**: for its position see on P. 47.

15. **foedis** probably has stress (see on *Odes* 4. 9. 26) i.e. 'because dishonourable.' Moreover such adjectives are more often preposited (see on *Odes* 2. 14. 23).

trahenti: for other readings see the commentators.

16. **perniciem**: for its position see on P. 47.

veniens (*ps*) i.e. not for the moment only, but for the future (*veniens*) and for centuries (*aevum*).

17. **immiserabilis** goes with *periret* i.e. 'unpitied.'

18. **captiva** (*p*) i.e. 'because taken prisoner'; this gives the reason for *immiserabilis*.

signa ego Punicis: see on *Odes* 1. 2. 17.

Punicis (*ps*) i.e. on Punic shrines, not Roman. See too on P. 24.

21. **vidi ego civium**: see on *Odes* 1. 2. 17.

auro repensus scilicet acrior　　　　　　　　　　25
miles redibit. flagitio additis
　　　damnum: neque amissos colores
　　　　lana refert medicata fuco,

nec vera virtus, cum semel excidit,
curat reponi deterioribus.　　　　　　　　　　30
　　　si pugnat extricata densis
　　　　cerva plagis, erit ille fortis,

qui perfidis se credidit hostibus,
et Marte Poenos proteret altero,
　　　qui lora restrictis lacertis　　　　　　　　35
　　　　sensit iners timuitque mortem.

hic, unde vitam sumeret inscius,
pacem duello miscuit. o pudor!
　　　o magna Carthago, probrosis
　　　　altior Italiae ruinis!'　　　　　　　　40

civium (*ps*): the genitive is logical object of *vidi* i.e. I have seen my fellow-citizens, their arms bound etc. (see on P. 38); it belongs to both *tergo* and *bracchia*.

22. **retorta...libero:** for the position of *libero* see on P. 48. It helps to echo *civium*, free citizens.

24. **Marte coli populata:** the order, I venture to think, makes it necessary to take *Marte* first with *coli*, and then with *populata* i.e. 'fields being cultivated by our soldiers—fields which these same soldiers had laid waste.' Compare Bentley's *in arvis* l. 8 above, and see l. 45 below; also *Odes* 3. 6. 7.

nostro (*s*) i.e. '*our* soldiers'; there lies the shame of it.

25. **auro** is, by position, logical subject: gold has redeemed him and will doubtless bring him back a braver man.

acrior is predicative with *redibit*.

27. **damnum** has ironical emphasis (see on *Odes* 4. 9. 26).

amissos (*p*) echoes *damnum*.

28. **medicata fuco:** a causal addendum (see on P. 53).

29. **vera** (*p*): contrast *medicata fuco*.

31, 32. **pugnat** comes early with stress i.e. 'shows fight.'

extricata...plagis: for the grouping see on P. 9.

33. **perfidis** (*ps*) i.e. 'to the perfidy (of the foe)'; see on P. 27 and *Odes* 2. 14. 23.

34. **altero** postposited and separated has emphasis i.e. 'in a *second* war.'

36. **iners** sc. ὤν, and equals *idque iners*, 'and that without a protest.'

mortem comes last with bitter emphasis—*mortem, non flagitium*.

39, 40. **probrosis...ruinis:** for the grouping see on P. 46 *a*; *altior=altior facta*.

fertur pudicae coniugis osculum
parvosque natos ut capitis minor
   ab se removisse et virilem
     torvus humi posuisse vultum,

donec labantis consilio patres   45
firmaret auctor numquam alias dato,
   interque maerentis amicos
     egregius properaret exul.

atqui sciebat quae sibi barbarus
tortor pararet: non aliter tamen   50
   dimovit obstantis propinquos
     et populum reditus morantem,

quam si clientum longa negotia
diiudicata lite relinqueret,
   tendens Venafranos in agros   55
     aut Lacedaemonium Tarentum.

41. **pudicae** (*p*): in contrast to such wives as those of *Odes* 3. 6. 25–32.
coniugis (*p*): see on P. 38.

43. **virilem** (*ps*) equals (1) 'because he was brave,' (2) 'though a brave man,' (3) 'though a husband.' For (2) compare Lucan 8. 107 *duri* (*ps*) *flectuntur pectora Magni*. But see also on P. 37.

44. **torvus** equals 'sternly'; see on P. 31.
vultum: for its position see on *Odes* 1. 3. 16.

45, 46. **consilio** goes first with *labantis* as an ablative in point of which, secondly with *firmaret* as an ablative of the means. Compare on l. 24 above.
auctor almost equals *per auctoritatem*.

47. **maerentis** (*p*) i.e. 'the tears (of his friends)'; see on P. 26.

48. **egregius** (sc. ὤν) goes with *inter...amicos*, as if 'standing out among his friends'; he was calm, they were weeping. Later on *egregius* may be felt with *exul* by oxymoron (see on *Epod.* 5. 82). Compare also P. 21.
exul as if *in exilium*.

49. **barbarus** (*p*) i.e. 'the brutality (of the torturer)'; see on P. 27, and also on *Odes* 2. 14. 23.

51. **obstantis** (*p*) i.e. 'the opposition (of his kindred)'; see on P. 26. Compare *Odes* 4. 9. 43, and *Epod.* 2. 32.

53. **clientum** is the logical object of *relinqueret* i.e. 'his clients and their long drawn out suits'; see on P. 38.

55, 56. **Venafranos** (*p*) i.e. Venafrum (and its fields); see on *Odes* 1. 33. 16. The stress suggests a holiday near at hand in the country; contrast *Lacedaemonium* (*p*) *Tarentum*, which implies a longer journey to a town with semi-oreign surroundings.

VI.

Delicta maiorum immeritus lues,
Romane, donec templa refeceris
   aedisque labentis deorum et
     foeda nigro simulacra fumo.

dis te minorem quod geris, imperas.   5
hinc omne principium, huc refer exitum!
   di multa neglecti dederunt
     Hesperiae mala luctuosae.

iam bis Monaeses et Pacori manus
non auspicatos contudit impetus   10
   nostros et adiecisse praedam
     torquibus exiguis renidet.

paene occupatam seditionibus
delevit urbem Dacus et Aethiops,
   hic classe formidatus, ille   15
     missilibus melior sagittis.

VI. 3. **deorum** has emphasis because it lies outside *aedis* and *labentis*. Horace bids the Roman restore not private houses, but the dwellings of the *gods*. The genitive is also in ἀπὸ κοινοῦ position with *aedis* and *simulacra*. The emphasis of *deorum* is echoed by *dis* of l. 5.

    deorum et: for the elision see on *Odes* 1. 35. 39.

    4. **foeda...fumo**: for the grouping see on P. 9.

    5. **dis te minorem**: see on *Odes* 1. 2. 17. The ideas, thus early expressed, are the gods, and you, and your submission (*minorem*) to them. Note the stress on *dis* by separation from *minorem* (a Roman must know no superior but God), and the emphasis on the whole group because it lies outside *quod geris*. Contrast the normal *quod te minorem dis geris*, which, be it observed, would scan perfectly, and bring out none of the points. The line is a fine motto for any empire.

    7. **multa** must be read first with *neglecti* as an internal accusative; later it may be felt with *mala* (compare on *Odes* 3. 5. 24, and 4. 4. 46 *impio*).

    8. **luctuosae** if dative is proleptic, 'so that she is full of sorrows' (see on P. 30); if genitive, see on P. 20 a.

    9. **iam bis** is emphatic by separation from *contudit*.

    Pacori (*p*) i.e. 'Pacorus (and his hosts)'; see on P. 38.

    10. **non auspicatos** (*ps*) i.e. 'because unblest, unsanctioned.' See also on P. 29 and P. 21.

    11. **nostros** has stress by position (see on *Odes* 4. 9. 26) i.e. '*even our* assaults.'

fecunda culpae saecula nuptias
primum inquinavere et genus et domos:
 hoc fonte derivata clades
  in patriam populumque fluxit.   20

motus doceri gaudet Ionicos
matura virgo et fingitur artibus
 iam nunc et incestos amores
  de tenero meditatur ungui.

mox iuniores quaerit adulteros   25
inter mariti vina neque eligit,
 cui donet impermissa raptim
  gaudia luminibus remotis,

13, 14. **paene** is emphatic because separated from *delevit.* Contrast *Odes* 2. 13. 21. It may possibly colour *occupatam* also.

occupatam...urbem: for the grouping see on P. 46 *a*.

16. **missilibus** (*ps*) i.e. 'in shooting (of arrows)'; see on P. 27. Compare too on P. 24.

19. **hoc fonte** has stress by position (see on P. 49) i.e. 'from this source and this only.'

21, 22. **Ionicos** (*s*) is emphatic i.e. the loose dances of Asia Minor, not the natural dancing of a mere child (contrast *matura* (*p*) *virgo*).

23. **iam nunc** may go ἀπὸ κοινοῦ with both *fingitur* and *meditatur*; if we put a stop after *artibus*, then *iam nunc* (*s*) equals καὶ ἤδη in contrast to *mox.*

incestos (*p*): to ponder on *pure* loves is innocent enough; see also *Odes* 2. 14. 23.

24. **tenero** (*ps*): the position of *tenero* does not help to decide between the two interpretations viz. (1) 'from tenderest years' (*meditatur* then means 'has been pondering'); (2) 'from the very heart.' Cicero *Fam.* 1. 6. 2 *a teneris, ut Graeci dicunt, unguiculis* has the same separation, and the adjective appears, by position, to mean 'when tender.' The same may be true of our passage, but see P. 21. The second interpretation makes *tenero* equal 'from the tenderness (of the nail) i.e. the quick'; see on P. 27.

25. **mox** (*s*) contrast *iam nunc* of l. 23 above.

iuniores (*ps*) i.e. 'that are younger (than her husband)'; see too P. 28 and P. 21.

26. **inter mariti vina:** for the position of *mariti* see on P. 42.

27, 28. **donet** comes early with point; contrast *emptor* l. 32.

impermissa raptim | gaudia: i.e. 'forbidden hasty joys.' For the adverb compare Livy 3. 2. 13 *multas passim manus,* 'many scattered bands,' and frequently elsewhere.

luminibus remotis: an emphatic addendum; see on P. 53.

sed iussa coram non sine conscio
surgit marito, seu vocat institor　　　　　　　　　　30
　　seu navis Hispanae magister,
　　　　dedecorum pretiosus emptor.

non his iuventus orta parentibus
infecit aequor sanguine Punico
　　Pyrrhumque et ingentem cecidit　　　　　　35
　　　　Antiochum Hannibalemque dirum;

sed rusticorum mascula militum
proles, Sabellis docta ligonibus
　　versare glaebas et severae
　　　　matris ad arbitrium recisos　　　　　　40

portare fustis, sol ubi montium
mutaret umbras et iuga demeret
　　bobus fatigatis, amicum
　　　　tempus agens abeunte curru.

29. **coram** is ἀπὸ κοινοῦ with *iussa* and *surgit*.

30. **marito** comes last with emphasis; even her husband is party to it.

31. **navis** (*p*) at once suggests sailor in contrast to the land-lubber *institor*.

32. **dedecorum** has emphasis since it stands outside *pretiosus emptor* (see on P. 43); the captain is canny enough and close-fisted enough in buying from natives, but he is positively extravagant in buying a woman's *dishonour*.

33. **non his** (*s*) has emphasis i.e. 'not like *these*.'

35, 36. **ingentem** (*s*): the adjective is almost titular, like 'Alexander the Great' (see on *Odes* 1. 7. 5), and see also P. 21. Observe too the chiasmus *ingentem...Antiochum Hannibalem...dirum*.

37, 38. **rusticorum...proles**: for the grouping see on P. 9.

proles: there is no real pause here; the word is read straight on with *Sabellis docta* etc., and we need not include it among the examples cited at *Odes* 4. 9. 26.

Sabellis (*ps*) may mean 'among the Sabines' (see on *Odes* 1. 33. 16); it can also colour both *proles* and *ligonibus* (see on P. 52). For the grouping *Sabellis docta ligonibus* see P. 24.

39. **severae** (*p*): a mother is not usually *severa* to her boys. See on *Odes* 3. 1. 47.

40, 41. **matris** (*p*): they obeyed their mother, not their father only.

recisos portare i.e. 'to cut and carry'; see on *Epod.* 5. 32.

41–44. Most commentators appear to assume that the time is evening. It is surely possible that the hour of siesta is meant. The early position of *sol* seems to suggest the hot sun. We are in a deep mountain valley; the topic is the sun and the mountains (*sol...montium*; see on *Odes* 1. 2. 17); the

damnosa quid non imminuit dies?   45
aetas parentum, peior avis, tulit
    nos nequiores, mox daturos
       progeniem vitiosiorem.

VII.

Quid fles, Asterie, quem tibi candidi
primo restituent vere Favonii
    Thyna merce beatum,
       constantis iuvenem fidei

Gygen? ille Notis actus ad Oricum   5
post insana Caprae sidera frigidas
    noctes non sine multis
       insomnis lacrimis agit.

shadows are beginning to change (*mutaret* is inceptive imperfect) to the eastern side; the sun is passing the zenith; his chariot no longer *adit* but *abit* (hence l. 44 *abeunte* is preposited, and the phrase *abeunte curru* comes as an addendum of interest; see P. 53).

Since writing this note I came across Dr Frazer's article in *C. R.* vol. II. p. 260, where he takes the same view as I. Mr Rogers in his translation of the *Birds* in an additional note on l. 1500 adversely criticizes the view of Dr Frazer, but does not, in my opinion, compel conviction. The passage in Horace's *Epistles* I. 16. 5–7 seems to bear out Frazer's interpretation.

41. **montium** (*ps*) is logical object (see on P. 38) i.e. 'was changing the mountains in respect of shadow.'

42. **mutaret...demeret**: the mood is, I venture to think, Livian frequentative subjunctive.

umbras: see on *Odes* I. 3. 16.

43. **amicum** (*p*) i.e. τὸν φίλον καὶ οὐ χαλεπὸν καιρόν. The words *bobus fatigatis* may be read with it as well as with *demeret*. Compare on I. 28. 23.

45. **damnosa** (*ps*) i.e. 'the thefts (of time)'; see on P. 27 and *Odes* 2. 14. 23.

dies: see on *Odes* I. 3. 16.

47. **mox...vitiosiorem** is an unpleasant addendum (see on P. 53). The whole stanza is a neat 'This-is-the-house-that-Jack-built' piece of work.

VII. 1, 2. **candidi...Favonii**: for the grouping see on P. 8. In speaking of *Favonius* Horace thinks merely of spring, not of the most suitable wind to bring Gyges home.

3–5. **Thyna...Gygen**: these lines are emphatic addenda; see on P. 53. There is a crescendo: he has been prosperous, he is true, he is your Gyges. Compare Livy 34. 5. 2 *vir gravissimus, consul, M. Porcius.*

3. **Thyna** (*p*) emphasizes the distance of his travels.

4. **constantis...fidei**: for the grouping see on P. 20 β.

5. **Gygen**: the position shows that here is the climax (see on *Odes* 4 9. 26).

atqui sollicitae nuntius hospitae,
suspirare Chloen et miseram tuis   10
   dicens ignibus uri,
     temptat mille vafer modis.

ut Proetum mulier perfida credulum
falsis impulerit criminibus nimis
   casto Bellerophontae   15
     maturare necem refert;

narrat paene datum Pelea Tartaro,
Magnessam Hippolyten dum fugit abstinens;
   et peccare docentis
     fallax historias monet.   20

frustra: nam scopulis surdior Icari
voces audit adhuc integer. at tibi
   ne vicinus Enipeus
     plus iusto placeat cave,

6. **frigidas** (*p*): he is cold because he is faithful and therefore alone.

7, 8. **non sine...lacrimis:** for the grouping see on P. 24.

9. **sollicitae...hospitae:** for the grouping see on P. 20 *a*.

10. **tuis** (*ps*) i.e. 'fires like thine (Asterie's)'; the stress, in its appeal to Asterie, emphasizes the fidelity of Gyges.

12. **mille...modis:** for the grouping see on P. 24.

13. **Proetum...credulum:** for the grouping see on P. 16 β.

14, 15. **falsis** (*ps*) has stress; see also on P. 21.

nimis by its position at the end of the line has emphasis—'too (chaste) altogether.'

casto (*p*) i.e. 'because (too) chaste.'

17. **Tartaro:** for its position see P. 47.

18. **Magnessam** (*p*): the order distinguishes her from Hippolyte, the wife of Theseus; but the adjective may be regarded as titular (see on *Odes* I. 7. 5).

Hippolyten is brought before *dum* so that the persons contained in the story may be grouped more closely; see on *Odes* I. 2. 17.

abstinens i.e. ἅτε σώφρων ὤν.

19, 20. **peccare docentis | fallax historias:** the order suggests that *docentis...historias* is first an accusative of respect with *fallax* (see on P. 24 *ad fin.*) and then object of *monet.*

21. **frustra:** compare *Odes* 3. 13. 6.

Icari (*s*): the position makes in favour of Orelli's view that we have here the genitive of *Icarus=Icaria.* All rocks are deaf, but most deaf the cruel rocks of a dangerous sea.

22. **tibi** comes early with the sense of 'as for you' (contrast Gyges); it construes later with *vicinus* and *placeat.* See on *Odes* I. 28. 23.

quamvis non alius flectere equum sciens 25
aeque conspicitur gramine Martio,
   nec quisquam citus aeque
    Tusco denatat alveo.

prima nocte domum claude neque in vias
sub cantu querulae despice tibiae, 30
   et te saepe vocanti
    duram difficilis mane.

VIII.

Martiis caelebs quid agam Kalendis,
quid velint flores et acerra turis
   plena miraris positusque carbo in
    caespite vivo,

docte sermones utriusque linguae. 5
voveram dulcis epulas et album
   Libero caprum prope funeratus
    arboris ictu.

26. **aeque** may be taken ἀπὸ κοινοῦ with *sciens* and *conspicitur* (see l. 27); compare *Odes* 2. 17. 7.

gramine Martio is an addendum of interest (see on P. 53) i.e. although no one is more admired *here*, now that Gyges is absent. So *Tusco* (*ps*) emphasizes the thought 'here *in Rome.*'

27. **aeque,** if qualifying *citus* alone, has stress because postposited (not half as swiftly), but it may be ἀπὸ κοινοῦ with *denatat* (compare *aeque* of l. 26).

28. **Tusco** (*ps*): see on P. 21 and also on l. 26 above.

30. **querulae:** the adjective colours both *cantu* and *tibiae* (see on P. 52); hence, perhaps, its position. The insertion of *despice* avoids the cacophony of *querulae tibiae* (see on P. 19).

VIII. 1. **Martiis** (*ps*) is intentionally kept close to *caelebs*, for Juvenal 9. 53 calls these Kalends *femineae*. See too on *Odes* 3. 18. 10.

3, 4. **carbo in:** for the position of *in* see on *Odes* 1. 35. 39.

in caespite vivo: for the position of this group see on P. 47.

6. **dulcis** (*p*) i.e. 'the sweetness, daintiness, dainties (of the feast)'; see on P. 27.

album (*ps*) i.e. white, not black, because for Liber.

7. **Libero:** for its position compare on P. 50 *b*.

prope funeratus is a causal addendum; see on P. 53.

8. **arboris:** preposited because 'tree' is more important than 'the blow'; see on P. 38.

hic dies anno redeunte festus
corticem adstrictum pice demovebit   10
amphorae fumum bibere institutae
    consule Tullo.

sume, Maecenas, cyathos amici
sospitis centum, et vigilis lucernas
perfer in lucem; procul omnis esto   15
    clamor et ira.

mitte civilis super urbe curas:
occidit Daci Cotisonis agmen,
Medus infestus sibi luctuosis
    dissidet armis,   20

servit Hispanae vetus hostis orae
Cantaber sera domitus catena.
iam Scythae laxo meditantur arcu
    cedere campis.

neglegens, ne qua populus laboret,   25
parce privatus nimium cavere et
dona praesentis cape laetus horae ac
    linque severa.

10. **pice**: for its position see on P. 47. The word may also be ἀπὸ κοινοῦ with *demovebit*.

12. **consule Tullo** is an addendum emphasizing the age of the wine; see on P. 53. Compare *Odes* 3. 14. 28, and see also on P. 48.

14. **centum** being postposited gains stress.

vigilis (*p*) is predicative with *perfer* as if 'keep the lamps awake.' Compare *Odes* 3. 21. 23.

15. **omnis** (*s*) has stress.

18. **occidit** comes early with emphasis, like *servit* l. 21. Compare *Odes* 1. 28. 7.

Daci is substantival, like *Medus* l. 19.

Cotisonis (*ps*) i.e. 'Cotiso and his hosts'; see on P. 38, and compare *Odes* 3. 16. 11.

19, 20. **sibi** goes with (1) *infestus*, (2) *luctuosis*, (3) *dissidet*; compare on *Odes* 1. 28. 23.

luctuosis: see on P. 21.

21. **servit**: see on *occidit* l. 18 above.

Hispanae...orae: for the grouping see P. 10.

22. **sera** (*ps*) i.e. 'at last, though late'; compare on *Odes* 3. 11. 28. See too P. 24.

IX.

Donec gratus eram tibi
      nec quisquam potior bracchia candidae
cervici iuvenis dabat,
      Persarum vigui rege beatior.
'donec non alia magis   5
      arsisti neque erat Lydia post Chloen,
multi Lydia nominis
      Romana vigui clarior Ilia.'
me nunc Thressa Chloe regit,
      dulcis docta modos et citharae sciens,   10
pro qua non metuam mori,
      si parcent animae fata superstiti.
'me torret face mutua
      Thurini Calais filius Ornyti,

23. **laxo** (*ps*): contrast *intento, adducto*. See too P. 21.

25. **ne qua...laboret** probably depends on both *neglegens* and *cavere*.

26. **cavere et**: see on *Odes* I. 35. 39.

27. **praesentis**: (*ps*) has emphasis.

laetus equals an adverb; see on P. 32.

horae has stress because separated so far from *dona* i.e. 'if for a short hour only.'

horae ac: see on *Odes* I. 35. 39.

28. **severa** is last in contrast to *laetus*.

IX. 2. **candidae** (*p*) i.e. 'whiteness (of thy neck)'; see on P. 27. There is an implied contrast of 'brown' with *bracchia*.

3. **iuvenis** is an emphatic addendum (see on P. 53); the speaker has no objection to a boy, an old man, or one of the fair sex, but a *iuvenis*—no!

4. **Persarum** (*ps*): Persia suggests the height of luxurious and sensuous pleasure (compare *Odes* I. 38. 1). Contrast too *Romana* of l. 8 below.

6. **arsisti** perhaps has stress (see on *Odes* 4. 9. 26); the force of the aorist (contrast *ardebas*, which would have scanned) is 'burst into a sudden flame of passion.'

7. **multi...nominis**: for the grouping see on P. 20 β.

8. **Romana** (*ps*): see on l. 4 above. There is also the antithesis of the foreigner from Ilium.

9. **me nunc Thressa**: see on *Odes* I. 2. 17. The proper name is preposited implying some ultra-foreign slave girl; compare *Odes* 3. 10. 15.

10. **dulcis docta modos**: see on P. 24 *ad fin.* There is stress on the sweetness of her music.

citharae: see on P. 39.

12. **superstiti** (*s*) i.e. 'so that it survives'; see on P. 30.

pro quo bis patiar mori, 15
    si parcent puero fata superstiti.'
quid si prisca redit venus,
    diductosque iugo cogit aeneo?
si flava excutitur Chloe,
    reiectaeque patet ianua Lydiae? 20
'quamquam sidere pulchrior
    ille est, tu levior cortice et improbo
iracundior Hadria,
    tecum vivere amem, tecum obeam libens.'

X.

Extremum Tanain si biberes, Lyce,
saevo nupta viro, me tamen asperas
porrectum ante fores obicere incolis
    plorares Aquilonibus.

audis quo strepitu ianua, quo nemus 5
inter pulchra satum tecta remugiat
ventis, et positas ut glaciet nives
    puro numine Iuppiter?

13. **me** is early in contrast to the *me* of l. 9 above.

14. **Thurini...Ornyti**: for the grouping see P. 15 *ad fin.*

16. **superstiti**: see on l. 12 above.

17. **prisca** (*ps*): contrast *nova*; compare *Odes* 3. 21. 11, 4. 2. 40, *Epod.* 2. 2. See too P. 21.

18. **aeneo** (*s*) i.e. not *fragili*. See too P. 21.

19. **flava** (*ps*) i.e. for all her golden hair. See also P. 21. Compare too *Odes* 1. 5. 4.

20. **reiectaeque...Lydiae**: for the grouping see on P. 20 *a*. The order supports Gow's view that *Lydiae* is genitive.

21, 22. **pulchrior | ille est, tu levior**: note the chiasmus.

22, 23. **improbo | iracundior Hadria**: see on P. 24.

24. **libens** equals *libenter* (see on P. 32) and, being postposited, has stress.

X. 1. **Extremum** (*p*) and **Tanain** preceding *si* both emphasize the outlandish environment.

2, 3. **saevo** (*ps*): contrast the self-indulgent and (probably) complacent *vir* of l. 15. Scythian morality with regard to the marriage bond was high.

me...fores: for the grouping see on P. 14.

3, 4. **incolis** is a quasi-adjective; for its position see on P. 21.

6. **pulchra** (*ps*): contrast *foeda, inculta* i.e. you do not live in some barbarian hut, but in a lovely home; you are cosy and I am freezing; you enjoy the sound of the wind, I do not.

ingratam Veneri pone superbiam,
ne currente retro funis eat rota: 10
non te Penelopen difficilem procis
    Tyrrhenus genuit parens.

o quamvis neque te munera nec preces
nec tinctus viola pallor amantium
nec vir Pieria paelice saucius   15
    curvat, supplicibus tuis

parcas, nec rigida mollior aesculo
nec Mauris animum mitior anguibus.
non hoc semper erit liminis aut aquae
    caelestis patiens latus.   20

7, 8. **ventis:** the objections to this reading are clearly stated by Bentley. Another objection is the position of *ventis* (see on *Odes* 4. 9. 26). The zeugma of *audis…ut glaciet* is unparalleled for harshness. The *audire* of *Odes* 2. 1. 21 is not similar, nor is it quite relevant to quote *Aen.* 4. 490 *mugire videbis | sub pedibus terram,* since you can *see*, as well as *hear*, an earthquake ; in any case *videre* equals both to see with the eye and to perceive with the mind (compare *Odes* 1. 14. 3–6, and *Prop.* 2. 16. 49). I should therefore vote for *sentis*, with a comma after *remugiat.* See on *ramis*, *Odes* 2. 3. 11.

    positas (*ps*): *fallen* snow under a clear frosty (*puro* preposited) sky is a much colder proposition than *falling* snow.

    9. **ingratam Veneri:** the words are causal (ἅτε ἀηδῆ οὖσαν), hence their position ; see too P. 46 *a*.

    10. **retro,** as Wickham says, is ἀπὸ κοινοῦ with *currente* and *funis eat.* That the order is intentional is obvious enough ; for Horace could easily have interchanged *retro* and *rota.* The separation of *currente retro* from *rota* makes the first two words causal (compare *ingratam Veneri* above) i.e. because the wheel runs *back*, the rope also runs *back*. See too P. 46 *b*.

    rota: see on *Odes* 1. 3. 16.

    11. **procis:** for its position see on P. 47.

    12. **Tyrrhenus** (*ps*) : because the Etruscans were notoriously lax in morals. See too P. 21.

    13. **te munera:** see on P. 51.

    14. **amantium:** for its position see on P. 48.

    15. **Pieria** (*p*): compare on *Thressa*, *Odes* 3. 9. 9.

    16. **curvat** should have stress (see on *Odes* 4. 9. 26) i.e. 'bend not, much less break.'

    17. **parcas** has stress i.e. 'spare, oh spare!' ; again see on *Odes* 4. 9. 26, and compare *sospitum* at *Odes* 3. 14. 10.

    rigida…aesculo: for the grouping see on P. 24.

    18. **Mauris…anguibus:** the grouping is that noted at P. 24, since *animum*

N. H.   10

XI.

Mercuri (nam te docilis magistro
movit Amphion lapides canendo)
tuque testudo, resonare septem
    callida nervis,

nec loquax olim neque grata, nunc et   5
divitum mensis et amica templis,
dic modos, Lyde quibus obstinatas
    applicet auris:

quae velut latis equa trima campis
ludit exultim metuitque tangi,   10
nuptiarum expers et adhuc protervo
    cruda marito.

tu potes tigris comitesque silvas
ducere et rivos celeris morari;
cessit immanis tibi blandienti   15
    ianitor aulae

mitior is a quasi-compound adjective, like φρενοθελγής, φρενοτερπής κ.τ.λ. For *Mauris* (*ps*) see on *Odes* 1. 22. 2.

19. **hoc** (*s*) i.e. not *this* side (others may endure his torments, if they are fools enough).

liminis...aquae: for the position of the objective genitive see on P. 39.

XI. 1, 2. **te docilis magistro:** for the grouping see on P. 25.

canendo is an emphatic addendum; see on P. 53. The order is the same at *A. P.* 395.

3. **septem** (*s*): contrast the tetrachord. The words *septem nervis* are heard with both *resonare* and *callida*; for the latter see P. 24.

5. **olim** is ἀπὸ κοινοῦ with *loquax* and *grata*; its abnormal position also prepares us for the antithesis *nunc*, as if we had πρότερον μέν...νυνὶ δέ.

6. **divitum** (*p*) i.e. 'the wealthy (at their banquets)'; see on P. 38.

amica is, by position, ἀπὸ κοινοῦ with *mensis* and *templis*. See on *Odes* 1. 30. 6.

7. **Lyde** precedes the relative for emphasis i.e. 'even Lyde.'

obstinatas (*ps*) i.e. 'though stubbornly closed'; but see P. 21.

9. **latis...campis:** for the grouping see P. 15. See too on *Odes* 4. 8. 33.

10. **exultim** seems by position to be ἀπὸ κοινοῦ with *ludit* and *metuit* i.e. the mare jumps in sport and in fear.

11, 12. **nuptiarum** (*p*): see on P. 39, since *expers=inscia*; compare on *Odes* 4. 14. 7.

adhuc has stress by separation from *cruda* i.e. 'so far at least.'

protervo...marito: for the grouping see on P. 24.

[Cerberus, quamvis furiale centum
muniant angues caput eius atque
spiritus taeter saniesque manet
    ore trilingui.] 20

quin et Ixion Tityosque vultu
risit invito, stetit urna paulum
sicca, dum grato Danai puellas
    carmine mulces.

audiat Lyde scelus atque notas 25
virginum poenas et inane lymphae
dolium fundo pereuntis imo,
    seraque fata,

quae manent culpas etiam sub Orco.
impiae (nam quid potuere maius?), 30
impiae sponsos potuere duro
    perdere ferro.

13. **comitesque** goes with *tigris* as well as *silvas*; see on P. 33.

15, 16. **immanis** must, I think, belong to *ianitor* and equal 'for all his monstrous might.' The words *ianitor aulae* form a compound—'doorkeeper' (compare Tennyson's 'silent Opener of the Gate'). It is hard to see how the phrase 'monstrous doorkeeper,' after the mention of Amphion, could be understood of any doorkeeper save Cerberus, but, if we accept Bentley's *exeatque* in l. 18, there is nothing not Horatian about the next stanza. On the other hand if *immanis* is taken with *aulae*, there is no parallel to such a pointless separation of the adjective; and, seeing that *immanis* is so obscure in form (there is nothing to suggest that it is either genitive or feminine), we are compelled to think of it as subject to *cessit*. Contrast *grato* in l. 23 below.

17, 18. **furiale...caput**: for the grouping see on P. 8.

20. **ore trilingui**: this is not necessarily an emphatic addendum (see on P. 53), for we still await the source from which the blood drips.

22. **invito** (*s*): as if we had *invitus* i.e. 'and that too against his will'; but see on P. 21.

stetit is put early for emphasis; usually the Danaides were running with the vessel.

22, 23. **paulum** is in ἀπὸ κοινοῦ position with *stetit* and *sicca*.

sicca has stress i.e. 'actually dry!'; see on *Odes* 4. 9. 26.

23, 24. **grato...carmine**: the grouping is as if we had *Danai puellis*, dative with *grato*.

Danai puellas=*Danaidas*; hence *Danai* is preposited. See on P. 41.

27. **pereuntis** is causal by position i.e. 'since it runs through.'

imo (*s*): see on P. 21.

una de multis face nuptiali
digna periurum fuit in parentem
splendide mendax et in omne virgo   35
    nobilis aevum,

'surge' quae dixit iuveni marito,
'surge, ne longus tibi somnus, unde
non times, detur; socerum et scelestas
    falle sorores,   40

quae, velut nanctae vitulos leaenae,
singulos eheu lacerant: ego illis
mollior nec te feriam neque intra
    claustra tenebo.

me pater saevis oneret catenis,   45
quod viro clemens misero peperci;
me vel extremos Numidarum in agros
    classe releget.

i, pedes quo te rapiunt et aurae,
dum favet nox et Venus, i secundo   50
omine et nostri memorem sepulcro
    scalpe querellam.'

28. **sera** (*p*) i.e. 'at last, though late'; compare *Odes* 3. 8. 22. In Horace *serus* is never a postposited adjective.

30. **maius**, separated and last, has emphasis.

31. **duro** (*ps*): see on *Odes* 2. 14. 23, and P. 21.

34. **periurum** (*ps*) i.e. 'because he was perjured'; the word justifies her *splendidum mendacium*.

35, 36. **in omne...aevum**: for the grouping see on P. 15.

38. **longus** (*s*) is emphatic i.e. the sleep that knows no waking. Compare *Odes* 2. 16. 30.

tibi begins by being ethical ('lest you find yourself given...') and ends by being indirect object.

39. **scelestas** (*ps*) is ἀπὸ κοινοῦ with *socerum* and *sorores* (see on P. 33); compare too on P. 21.

42. **ego illis**: see on *Odes* 1. 2. 17.

45. **me pater**: compare note on l. 42.

saevis (*ps*): see on *Odes* 2. 14. 23, and P. 21.

46. **misero** (*s*) i.e. 'because in misery,' ὡς ἀθλίῳ ὄντι. See also P. 24. The dative goes first with *clemens*, then with *peperci*.

47. **extremos...agros** is a slight modification of the normal *in extremos Numidarum agros*; the effect is to stress *extremos*.

XII.

Miserarum est neque amori dare ludum neque dulci
mala vino lavere aut examinari metuentis
    patruae verbera linguae.

tibi qualum Cythereae puer ales, tibi telas
operosaeque Minervae studium aufert, Neobule,   5
    Liparaei nitor Hebri,

simul unctos Tiberinis umeros lavit in undis,
eques ipso melior Bellerophonte, neque pugno
    neque segni pede victus;

catus idem per apertum fugientis agitato   10
grege cervos iaculari et celer arto latitantem
    fruticeto excipere aprum.

49. **pedes** precedes *quo* to heighten the antithesis of *aurae* i.e. on land and sea. Compare *Epod.* 16. 21.

50. **secundo** (*ps*): contrast *malo, infelici, infausto.*

51. **omine**: there is no real pause, and therefore no stress (but see on *Odes* 4. 9. 26).

nostri: for the position of the objective genitive see P. 39.

nostri memorem (*ps*) is proleptic; see on P. 30.

XII. 1. **Miserarum**: the first word indicates ·the topic—'Unhappy Woman.' As Gow says 'the emphasis is on the gender.'

dulci (*ps*) i.e. 'the sweetness (of .wine)'; see on P. 27. For *dulce vinum* compare *Odes* 3. 13. 2, and *Epod.* 9. 38.

3. **patruae verbera linguae**: see on P. 20 *a*, and P. 37.

4. **Cythereae** (*p*): for its position see on P. 41.

Cythereae puer ales: for the grouping see on P. 35.

5. **operosae** (*p*) i.e. 'the toils (of Minerva)'; see on P. 27.

Minervae is preposited in artificial contrast to *Cythereae* of l. 4.

6. **Liparaei...Hebri**: for the grouping see on P. 20 *a*.

7. **unctos...undis**: for the grouping see on P. 9.

8. **ipso** (*s*) is emphatic; Greek uses καί e.g. καὶ αὐτοῦ τοῦ Β. ἀμείνων. See too P. 24.

9. **segni** goes with both *pugno* and *pede*; see on P. 33.

10, 11. **per‧apertum...cervos**: the complement *agitato grege* lies, as usual, between *fugientis* and *cervos*, and the other complement *per apertum* can therefore stand outside; this is its natural position since it is an adverb equivalent (see on P. 48).

fugientis...cervos: for the grouping see P. 10. Note how Horace sets together the words implying fear.

11, 12. **arto...aprum**: for the grouping see P. 9.

XIII.

O fons Bandusiae, splendidior vitro,
dulci digne mero non sine floribus,
    cras donaberis haedo,
        cui frons turgida cornibus

primis et venerem et proelia destinat.   5
frustra: nam gelidos inficiet tibi
    rubro sanguine rivos
        lascivi suboles gregis.

te flagrantis atrox hora Caniculae
nescit tangere, tu frigus amabile   10
    fessis vomere tauris
        praebes et pecori vago.

fies nobilium tu quoque fontium,
me dicente cavis impositam ilicem
    saxis, unde loquaces   15
        lymphae desiliunt tuae.

XIII. 2. **dulci** (*p*) i.e. 'the sweetness (of wine)'; see on P. 27, and compare *Odes* 3. 12. 1. See too P. 24.

dulci digne mero: for the intervening vocative see on *Odes* 1. 5. 3.

4, 5. **cui...primis:** I am not convinced that this must be translated as if we had *cui frons cornibus primis turgida* (for a similar instance see on *Odes* 2. 10. 23, 24). To assume this is needlessly to abandon rules of order and to neglect the necessary emphasis on *primis* which is abnormally postposited; compare *paucorum* at *Odes* 3. 16. 30, and see on *Odes* 4. 9. 26. I should prefer to take *cornibus primis* either as ablative ἀπὸ κοινοῦ with *turgida* and *proelia destinat*, or as dative of the part in apposition with the whole *cui*, and, like it, constructed with *destinat*. We may then translate 'whose swelling brow destines love and battles for his *first* horns'; i.e. he will begin young. The stress on 'first' is due to the position of *primis*.

6, 7. **frustra:** compare *Odes* 3. 7. 21.

gelidos (*ps*) i.e. 'the coldness (of thy stream)'; see on P. 27. The epithet thus suggests the antithesis of limpid and cold to opaque and warm suggested by *rubro* (*p*) *sanguine*.

8. **lascivi...gregis:** for the grouping see on P. 20 β.

9. **te...hora:** see on P. 51.

flagrantis...Caniculae: for the grouping see on P. 10.

13. **nobilium** (*ps*) has emphasis i.e. famous, not obscure.

14–16. **me dicente:** these words and the following are a causal addendum see on P. 53) i.e. '(you shall be famous) because *I sing of*....'

14, 15. **cavis...saxis:** for the grouping see on P. 10.

XIV.

Herculis ritu modo dictus, o plebs,
morte venalem petiisse laurum
Caesar Hispana repetit penatis
    victor ab ora.

unico gaudens mulier marito   5
prodeat iustis operata divis,
et soror clari ducis et decorae
    supplice vitta

virginum matres iuvenumque nuper
sospitum. vos, o pueri et puellae,   10
iam virum expectate. male ominatis
    parcite verbis.

hic dies vere mihi festus atras
eximet curas: ego nec tumultum
nec mori per vim metuam tenente   15
    Caesare terras.

15, 16. **loquaces** (*p*) i.e. 'the babbling (of thy rills)'; see on P. 27.
loquaces | lymphae...tuae: for the grouping see on P. 34.
lymphae desiliunt tuae: for the grouping see on P. 21.

XIV. This Ode, of laureate workmanship obviously, is also, like *Ode* 1. 37, 'good in parts.' The same may be said of *Ode* 4. 14. Horace does not seem to have got into his stride until the fourth stanza.

   1. **Herculis** (*p*) is equivalent to *Herculeo*—a preposited generic epithet (see on P. 37 *ad fin.*) i.e. 'like a Hercules.' Naturally the thing or person compared is named first, and this is always the case with *ritu* in Horace (see *Odes* 3. 29. 33, 34, *Sat.* 2. 1. 29, 2. 3. 268, and *A. P.* 62).

   2. **morte venalem** (*ps*) is concessive i.e. 'though it be bought even at the price of death'; see too P. 21.

   3, 4. **Caesar...ora:** a Roman reads the lines thus: 'Caesar in Spain (see on *Odes* 1. 31. 9) is about to return home victorious from its shores.'

   5. **unico...marito:** for the grouping see on P. 10. For *unico* see on *Odes* 2. 18. 14.

   6. **iustis** (*ps*) is causal i.e. 'because they have been true to their promises' (if we read *divis*); if *sacris* be read, then *iustis* will equal 'that are deserved, that are due'; but see on P. 24.

   7. **clari** (*p*) has emphasis and equals *clarissimi* of prose.

   7–9. **decorae supplice vitta...matres:** for the grouping see on P. 10.
virginum matres iuvenumque: note the ἀπὸ κοινοῦ position of *matres*.

   10. **sospitum** has stress (see on *Odes* 4. 9. 26) expressing ecstasy of emotion; compare on *parcas* at *Odes* 3. 10. 17.

i, pete unguentum, puer, et coronas
et cadum Marsi memorem duelli,
Spartacum siqua potuit vagantem
   fallere testa.   20

dic et argutae properet Neaerae
murreum nodo cohibere crinem;
si per invisum mora ianitorem
   fiet, abito.

lenit albescens animos capillus   25
litium et rixae cupidos protervae;
non ego hoc ferrem calidus iuventa
   consule Planco.

11, 12. Amid the welter of various readings and emendations there is little
use in discussing order; but whether we accept *male ominatis* or *male
inominatis* the epithet has some stress by separation. See on *Odes* 2. 14. 23,
and P. 21.

13, 14. **atras | eximet curas:** for the position of *atras* (prettily kept close
to its antithesis *festus*) see on P. 21, and *Odes* 2. 14. 23.

15, 16. **per vim** (*pp*) has stress.

tenente | Caesare terras: *terras* may stand outside according to the prin-
ciple noted at P. 47. The effect is to stress *terras* somewhat i.e. 'while Caesar
is master of *the world.*' For the position of *terras* compare *Odes* 4. 14. 22
Pleiadum choro scindente nubes, and for the ablative absolute last see on *Odes*
3. 1. 34.

18, 19. **cadum...duelli:** for the grouping see on P. 14.

Marsi (*ps*): its position emphasizes the age of the wine, as does the position of *Spartacum.* See also P. 21, since *memorem* is the equivalent of a verb;
compare *cupidos* l. 26 below.

21. **argutae** (*ps*)**...Neaerae:** although datives, the words are also logical
subject of *properet*, and the grouping is that of P. 21; for similar examples
see P. 23.

22. **murreum:** unless we read *cohibente* (for grouping see P. 15), the order
of *murreum* seems pointless; but the meaning of *murreum* is too uncertain
for dogmatism.

nodo: see on *Odes* 2. 11. 24.

23. **invisum** (*ps*) i.e. 'the disagreeableness (of the doorkeeper)'; see on
P. 27, and *Odes* 2. 14. 23.

25. **lenit** comes early with stress i.e. *lenit, non irritat.*

25, 26. **albescens...cupidos:** for the grouping see on P. 17. The stress is
on *albescens*, which suggests the antithesis *iuventa proterva.*

litium et rixae: see on P. 39.

rixae cupidos protervae: as *cupidos* is equal to *cupientes*, the grouping
comes under P. 21; compare *memorem* l. 18 above.

XV.

Uxor pauperis Ibyci,
    tandem nequitiae fige modum tuae
famosisque laboribus:
    maturo propior desine funeri
inter ludere virgines   5
    et stellis nebulam spargere candidis.
non, siquid Pholoen satis,
    et te, Chlori, decet: filia rectius
expugnat iuvenum domos,
    pulso Thyias uti concita tympano.   10
illam cogit amor Nothi
    lascivae similem ludere capreae:
te lanae prope nobilem
    tonsae Luceriam, non citharae decent
nec flos purpureus rosae   15
    nec poti vetulam faece tenus cadi.

28. **consule Planco:** the addendum (see on P. 53) emphasizes the length of time; compare *Odes* 3. 8. 12.

XV. 1. **pauperis** (*p*) implies that Ibycus cannot afford her extravagances.

2. **tuae** (*s*): contrast *filiae*; if you won't restrain your daughter, at least restrain yourself.

3. **famosis** (*p*): contrast the *obscuris laboribus* of *lanificium*.

4. **maturo** (*ps*): contrast *immaturo*.
funeri comes last as an offensive surprise for *aevo* or the like.

5. **inter ludere virgines:** the tmesis emphasizes *virgines*. Contrast *Odes* 3. 3. 37.

6. **candidis** (*s*): the position gives *candidis* great emphasis i.e. 'no matter how bright.' In fact *candidis* comes as a surprise; we are half expecting a proleptic *obscuris*.

7. **non** i.e. 'It is not the case that...'; *non* qualifies the whole sentence (see on *Odes* 2. 9. 13).

9. **iuvenum** (*p*): contrast *senum*, who are more fitted for Chloris.

10. **pulso...tympano:** for the grouping see on P. 15; *pulso* equals 'the beat (of the drum)'; see on P. 26.
uti: for its position see on *Odes* 1. 15. 29, 30.

11. **illam:** for its position see P. 51.

12. **lascivae...capreae:** for the grouping see on P. 20 *a, ad fin.*
capreae: the further separation of this word by *ludere* makes the simile even more offensive; compare *funeri* l. 4 above.

13, 14. **te lanae:** for the order see on P. 51.
lanae...Luceriam: for the grouping see on P. 14.

XVI.

Inclusam Danaen turris aenea
robustaeque fores et vigilum canum
tristes excubiae munierant satis
    nocturnis ab adulteris,

si non Acrisium virginis abditae   5
custodem pavidum Iuppiter et Venus
risissent: fore enim tutum iter et patens
    converso in pretium deo.

aurum per medios ire satellites
et perrumpere amat saxa potentius   10
ictu fulmineo: concidit auguris
    Argivi domus, ob lucrum

15. **flos purpureus rosae:** for the abnormal order see on P. 44; but *purpureus* may colour both *flos* and *rosae*; compare *Odes* I. 19. 1, and see P. 52 *ad fin.*

16. **vetulam:** the interposition of this word in the normal group *poti faece tenus cadi* gives it appropriate and most unpleasant emphasis; the two words *poti vetulam* at once bring up the picture of a drunken old beldame. But the reading *vetula* (*p*) with *faece* has point; because the wine is old, she drinks it to the dregs.

XVI. 1, 2. **Inclusam Danaen turris aenea | robustaeque fores:** note the chiastic grouping of epithets and nouns.

Danaen turris: see on P. 51.

vigilum (*p*) has stress; contrast 'somnolent.'

vigilum canum: the preposited genitive is the logical subject; see on P. 38.

3. **tristes** (*p*) i.e. 'the sternness, implacability (of their watch)'; see on P. 27, and *Odes* 2. 14. 23.

satis (*pp*) i.e. 'more than enough.'

4. **nocturnis** (*ps*) equals an adverb 'at night'; see on P. 31, and *Odes* 2. 13. 7.

5, 6. **Acrisium** is logical subject and is placed early to give us, as soon as possible, the other important person in the story.

6. **pavidum:** for the second complement outside see on P. 48.

7. **risissent** has stress; see on *Odes* 4. 9. 26.

tutum is either predicative or its position is due to the fact that *iter* lies ἀπὸ κοινοῦ between the two epithets. Compare Milton's 'in this dark world and wide,' and see too P. 34.

8. **converso...deo** is an emphatic proviso; see on P. 53, and also *Odes* 3. 1. 34.

9. **medios** (*ps*) i.e. 'the very midst (of guards)'; compare *Odes* 3. 2. 12 etc., but see also P. 21.

demersa exitio; diffidit urbium
portas vir Macedo et subruit aemulos
reges muneribus; munera navium 15
saevos illaqueant duces.

crescentem sequitur cura pecuniam
maiorumque fames: iure perhorrui
late conspicuum tollere verticem,
Maecenas, equitum decus. 20

quanto quisque sibi plura negaverit,
ab dis plura feret: nil cupientium
nudus castra peto et transfuga divitum
partis linquere gestio,

contemptae dominus splendidior rei, 25
quam si quicquid arat impiger Apulus
occultare meis dicerer horreis,
magnas inter opes inops.

10, 11. **potentius...fulmineo** is an emphatic addendum; see on P. 53.

11, 12. **auguris** (*p*)...**domus** i.e. 'the augur and his house'; see on P. 38, and compare *Odes* 3. 8. 18.

12, 13. **ob lucrum...exitio** is an emphatic addendum; see on P. 53.

urbium (*p*) i.e. 'cities (and their gates)'; see on P. 38. The order also prepares us for the antithesis *navium* (*ps*) in l. 15.

14. **aemulos** (*p*) i.e. 'because they were rivals'; the *vir Macedo* '*divisit et imperavit.*'

15. **muneribus** comes last with emphasis (see on P. 53) to remind us of *ob lucrum* l. 12, and *aurum* l. 9; *munera* following heightens the emphasis.

navium (*ps*): contrast *urbium* l. 13; the antithesis is land and sea. See too P. 43.

16. **saevos** (*ps*) i.e. 'the brutality (of captains)'; see P. 27, P. 21, and *Odes* 2. 14. 23.

17. **crescentem** (*ps*) is emphatic; the *growth* of money means care (see on P. 27).

18. **maiorum** (*p*) is emphatic i.e. for *more*.

19. **conspicuum** (*p*) is proleptic; see on P. 30, and P. 21.

20. **equitum** (*p*) emphasizes the fact that Maecenas preferred the lower rank.

22. **nil cupientium** (*ps*): contrast *divitum*.

23. **divitum** may be ἀπὸ κοινοῦ with *transfuga* and *partis*.

25. **contemptae...rei**: for the grouping see on P. 15.

26. **impiger** (*p*) i.e. 'the energy, vigour (of the Apulian)'; see on P. 27.

27. **meis** (*ps*) is emphatic 'my very own'; see on *Odes* I. 1. 9, and P. 21.

28. **magnas** (*s*): contrast *inops*.

purae rivus aquae silvaque iugerum
paucorum et segetis certa fides meae   30
fulgentem imperio fertilis Africae
    fallit sorte beatior.

quamquam nec Calabrae mella ferunt apes,
nec Laestrygonia Bacchus in amphora
languescit mihi, nec pinguia Gallicis   35
    crescunt vellera pascuis,

importuna tamen pauperies abest,
nec, si plura velim, tu dare deneges.
contracto melius parva cupidine
    vectigalia porrigam,   40

quam si Mygdoniis regnum Alyattei
campis continuem. multa petentibus
desunt multa: bene est, cui deus obtulit
    parca quod satis est manu.

29. **purae rivus aquae:** for the grouping see on P. 20 *a.*

30. **paucorum** has stress i.e. 'only a few'; adjectives of quantity are normally preposited, and, moreover, *paucorum* looks somewhat lonely at the commencement of the line (see on *Odes* 4. 9. 26); compare too *primis* at *Odes* 3. 13. 5.

segetis...meae: for the grouping see on P. 18. The stress on *certa* and *meae* is sound i.e. I can *rely* on *my* crops.

31. **fertilis** (*p*): contrast the desert portion.

33. **Calabrae** (*ps*): the honey of Calabria was famous; but see also on *Odes* 1. 33. 16, for the sense is 'Calabria (and its bees).'

apes: see on *Odes* 1. 3. 16.

34. **Laestrygonia** (*ps*): the wine of Formiae was famous.

35, 36. **mihi** comes last with stress—ἔμοιγε.

pinguia...pascuis: for the grouping see on P. 7.

37. **importuna** (*ps*) i.e. 'the sting (of *pauperies*)'; see on P. 27, and *Odes* 2. 14. 23.

39, 40. **contracto...vectigalia:** for the grouping see on P. 9. The early position of *contracto* prepares us for the antithesis *porrigam.*

melius belongs partly to *contracto*, partly to the whole sentence.

41. **Mygdoniis** (*ps*): see on *Odes* 2. 12. 22, and P. 37. The position of the adjective also prepares us for *Alyattei*. But *Mygdoniis* (*ps*) may equal 'Mygdonia (and its plains)'; see on *Odes* 1. 33. 16.

43. **multa** comes last to echo the *multa* of l. 42.

44. **parca** (*ps*) has stress i.e. 'sparing, not lavish.'

XVII.

Aeli vetusto nobilis ab Lamo,
quando et priores hinc Lamias ferunt
   denominatos et nepotum
     per memores genus omne fastos,

auctore ab illo ducis originem,   5
qui Formiarum moenia dicitur
   princeps et innantem Maricae
     litoribus tenuisse Lirim

late tyrannus. cras foliis nemus
multis et alga litus inutili   10
   demissa tempestas ab Euro
     sternet, aquae nisi fallit augur

XVII. An unsatisfactory Ode in both meaning and order. Editors may well reject it.

1. **Aeli...Lamo:** for the grouping see on P. 14; and compare on P. 24 for *vetusto...Lamo.*

2–4. The order throws no light on these obscure lines.

2. **priores hinc Lamias:** these words may be grouped together i.e. 'the earlier Lamiae descended from him,' and *hinc* may then be repeated with *denominatos.* See on P. 50 *a.*

ferunt: as verbs taking the acc. and inf. normally come early, *ferunt,* coming late, has the stress of incredulity.

3. **denominatos:** the ponderosity of the word in a position of stress (see on *Odes* 4. 9. 26) is, perhaps, satirical; compare *sermonibus* at *Odes* 3. 21. 10, *praegestientis* 2. 5. 9, *enaviganda* 2. 14. 11, *formidulosus* 2. 17. 18, and *obliviones* 4. 9. 34.

nepotum (*ps*) may be contrasted with *priores* above, and represents descendants of whom there is written record (*memores...fastos*) in opposition to the semi-mythical *priores*; but it is also the logical subject of the infinitive and therefore comes early (see on P. 38).

4. **per memores...fastos:** for the grouping see on P. 15.

omne (*pp*) i.e. 'the *whole* race'=*universum.*

5. **auctore** by position equals 'as founder.'

6. **Formiarum** (*p*) i.e. 'Formiae (and its walls)'; see on P. 38.

7, 8. **princeps** lies ἀπὸ κοινοῦ between *moenia* and *Lirim.*

innantem...Lirim: for the grouping see on P. 46 *a.*

Maricae | litoribus: perhaps 'Marica (and her shores)'; see on P. 38. Marica seems to equal *lucus Maricae.*

9. **late tyrannus:** see on P. 53, and on *Odes* 2. 17. 19.

10. **multis** may have stress (see on *Odes* 4. 9. 26), perhaps to emphasize the violence of the storm.

annosa cornix. dum potes, aridum
compone lignum: cras Genium mero
   curabis et porco bimenstri ·   15
      cum famulis operum solutis.

XVIII.

Faune, Nympharum fugientum amator,
per meos finis et aprica rura
lenis incedas abeasque parvis
      aequus alumnis,

si tener pleno cadit haedus anno,   5
larga nec desunt Veneris sodali
vina craterae, vetus ara multo
      fumat odore.

litus: the position of this word, like that of *nemus* between *foliis* and *multis*, makes a vivid picture of a shore covered with seaweed; see the note at *Odes* 4. 8. 33. Latin love of parallelism may also be at work; after *foliis nemus multis* it was inevitable to write *alga litus inutili*. Compare *Odes* 3. 25. 11, 12.

11. **demissa** (*p*) i.e. 'the downrush (of the storm)'; see on P. 26.

ab Euro by its position outside *demissa* and *tempestas* ought to have emphasis. Compare *Odes* 4. 6. 10, P. 34 *ad fin.*, and P. 49.

12. **sternet:** there is little point in its position (see on *Odes* 4. 9. 26).

aquae (*ps*): the *cornix* is augur of *rain*, if of nothing else.

13. **annosa** (*p*) i.e. with all his years of experience he ought to know something about the weather.

aridum (*ps*) i.e. before it is drenched with the rain. See too P. 21.

15. **curabis:** its position (see on *Odes* 4. 9. 26) may be justified because it is ἀπὸ κοινοῦ with *mero* and *porco* (compare *Odes* 2. 5. 2, 2. 5. 14, 2. 16. 22, 3. 19. 3, 3. 20. 13, 3. 24. 11, 3. 24. 38, 3. 27. 2, 4. 6. 3).

16. **cum famulis...solutis** is an emphatic addendum (see on P. 53) and a last hit, perhaps, at one who, claiming high lineage, sits *more maiorum* with farm-hands in the kitchen.

XVIII. 1. **Faune...amator:** for the grouping see on P. 16, *ad fin.*

2. **meos** (*p*) i.e. whatever you do to others—selfish, but very Roman!

aprica (*p*): the epithet 'sunny' implies the golden grain and verdure of the meadow; these Faunus might ruin by his tread. So *Epist.* 1. 14. 30 *aprico* (*ps*), where the flood may wash away the produce.

3. **lenis** equals an adverb; see on P. 32.

incedas abeasque: note the juxtaposition of the verbs i.e. if you do come, go quickly.

parvis (*s*) has emotional emphasis i.e. 'poor little things!' See also P. 24.

ludit herboso pecus omne campo,
cum tibi Nonae redeunt Decembres;   10
festus in pratis vacat otioso
    cum bove pagus;

inter audaces lupus errat agnos,
spargit agrestis tibi silva frondes,
gaudet invisam pepulisse fossor   15
    ter pede terram.

XIX.

Quantum distet ab Inacho
    Codrus, pro patria non timidus mori,
narras et genus Aeaci
    et pugnata sacro bella sub Ilio:

5. **tener...anno**: for the grouping see P. 7.

6. **larga** goes with the predicate *nec desunt* i.e. 'in plenty,' as if we had *et larga adsunt*.

Veneris (*p*) **sodali** is (so Ritter) Faunus. You, says Horace, are the comrade of *Venus*, and therefore shall have wine in plenty. It is the old combination of Wein, Weib, Gesang.

7. **vina craterae** i.e. wine in a mixing-bowl, no meagre drop from some *patera*. The order is against taking *craterae* in apposition with *sodali*.

vetus (*p*): this altar has served you many a year, and with much, not little (*multo* separated) incense. But for *multo* see also P. 21.

9. **herboso...campo**: for the grouping see on P. 15, and for *omne* (*pp*) see on *Odes* 3. 17. 4.

10. **Decembres** (*s*): the month is, perhaps, more important than the day. Compare *Odes* 3. 8. 1 *Martiis* (*ps*) *caelebs quid agam Kalendis*, and see P. 21.

11, 12. **festus...pagus**: for the grouping see on P. 10. A Roman would read these charming lines thus: 'There is holiday in the meads, all is rest (*vacat*) and peace (*otioso*), for man and beast.'

13. **audaces** (*ps*): contrast *timidos* which would be the natural and expected epithet. The order says 'boldness in front of the wolf.'

14. **agrestis** (*ps*) equals *in agros*, 'over the fields.' Compare *Odes* 1. 22. 9 *in Sabina*.

15. **invisam** (*ps*) i.e. 'because hated'; hence his delight. The participle is almost a noun, 'his hated enemy,' the object of his contumely.

16. **ter pede terram**: notice the effective crowding of explosive consonants (t, p, d, t) at the close. We hear the thud of his dance.

XIX. 3. **narras**: for its position see on *Odes* 3. 17. 15.

4. **pugnata...Ilio**: for the grouping see on P. 9.

quo Chium pretio cadum 5
    mercemur, quis aquam temperet ignibus,
quo praebente domum et quota
    Paelignis caream frigoribus, taces.
da lunae propere novae,
    da noctis mediae, da, puer, auguris 10
Murenae. tribus aut novem
    miscentur cyathis pocula commodis.
qui Musas amat imparis,
    ternos ter cyathos attonitus petet
vates: tris prohibet supra 15
    rixarum metuens tangere Gratia

5. **quo...cadum:** again see on P. 9.

6. **mercemur** has stress (see on *Odes* 4. 9. 26) i.e. who is going to do the *buying*?—that's what interests me.

7. **quo...domum:** *domum* lying outside *quo praebente* perhaps has some stress. What I want, says Horace, is a roof over my head. See *Odes* 3.14. 15,16.

8. **Paelignis** (*ps*): the adjective is probably generic. See on P. 37, but also on P. 21. The effect of the order is much as if one wrote 'a cold Antarctic' for 'an Antarctic cold.'

9. **propere novae:** both words are emphatic because they are unexpected addenda (see on P. 53) i.e. 'drink to the moon—at once—because it is new.' The haste is necessary, for the new moon quickly disappears after the sun. See too P. 50 *c*, and *Odes* 2. 18. 16.

11. **Murenae** has stress (see on *Odes* 4.9. 26); the effect is grandiose—the great Murena.

11, 12. **tribus aut novem** (*s*): the choice is three or nine (but see also P. 21); Horace playfully takes the post of *arbiter bibendi*, and slyly lays down that the inspired poet (*vates* l. 15) may have nine *cyathi*, but hot-heads, like Murena, are safer with three only. I humbly agree with Page that the *size* of the bumper is the point, not the proportion of water and wine.

commodis is an addendum (see on P. 53) i.e. 'as best suits each.' Note that the grouping *tribus aut novem...cyathis...commodis* is that of P. 34.

13. **imparis** (*s*): see on P. 21. The epithet merely equals *novem* and prepares us for *ternos ter*.

14, 15. **ternos ter:** the order is due to the desire of avoiding the jingle *ter ternos*.

attonitus (*ps*) is causal, 'because frenzied.'

15. **vates** is emphatic (see on *Odes* 4.9. 26) i.e. 'because an inspired seer.'

tris...supra: both words are emphasized, *tris* by being first (in order to enforce the contrast *ternos ter*), *supra* by being separated.

16, 17. **rixarum:** for the position of the objective genitive see on P. 39.

Gratia...sororibus: for the grouping see on P. 14.

nudis iuncta sororibus.

insanire iuvat: cur Berecyntiae

cessant flamina tibiae?

cur pendet tacita fistula cum lyra?   20

parcentis ego dexteras

odi: sparge rosas; audiat invidus

dementem strepitum Lycus

et vicina seni non habilis Lyco.

spissa te nitidum coma,   25

puro te similem, Telephe, Vespero

tempestiva petit Rhode;

me lentus Glycerae torret amor meae.

XX.

Non vides, quanto moveas periclo,

Pyrrhe, Gaetulae catulos leaenae?

dura post paulo fugies inaudax

proelia raptor,

18. **Berecyntiae** (*ps*): see note on *Odes* 1. 18. 13, and also on P. 20 *a*.

20. **tacita** may colour both the nouns; see on P. 52.

21. **parcentis** (*ps*) has stress.

22, 23. **odi**.is emphatic; see on *Odes* 4. 9. 26.

sparge comes early for stress i.e. 'scatter freely.'

invidus equals an adverb, 'with envy'; see on P. 31.

invidus...Lycus: for the grouping see on P. 10.

24. **vicina...Lyco**: for the grouping see on P. 14.

25. **spissa...coma**: for the grouping see on P. 15.

26. **puro...Vespero**: see previous note.

27. **tempestiva** (*ps*) is causal, 'because she is fitted for you.' See also P. 21.

28. **me...torret amor**: see on P. 51. But *me* is also contrasted with *te* ll. 25, 26.

lentus (*ps*) equals 'slowly'; see on P. 31.

Glycerae (*ps*) is in contrast to *Rhode* l. 27.

Glycerae...meae: for the grouping see on P. 20 *a*. But the grouping from *lentus* down to *meae* may be classified under P. 17.

XX. A most obscure Ode *pace* the commentators. It seems to be a translation from the Greek (see on *Odes* 3. 26).

1. **quanto moveas periclo**: see on P. 21, and compare *Odes* 3. 27. 17 and note on *Odes* 1. 27. 11, 12.

2. **Gaetulae...leaenae**: for the grouping see on P. 20 *a*.

3, 4. **dura...raptor**: for the grouping see on P. 9.

cum per obstantis iuvenum catervas   5
ibit insignem repetens Nearchum:
grande certamen, tibi praeda cedat,
    maior an illa.

interim, dum tu celeris sagittas
promis, haec dentes acuit timendos,   10
arbiter pugnae posuisse nudo
    sub pede palmam

fertur et leni recreare vento
sparsum odoratis umerum capillis,
qualis aut Nireus fuit aut aquosa   15
    raptus ab Ida.

XXI.

O nata mecum consule Manlio,
seu tu querellas sive geris iocos
    seu rixam et insanos amores
        seu facilem, pia testa, somnum,

6. **insignem** (*ps*) i.e. 'because outstanding'; as Wickham says 'easily found among them all.' But see too P. 21.

7. **tibi** placed early prepares us for the antithesis *illi* or *illa* (whichever be read).

8. **maior**: as there is no parallel to *maior=magis*, we may accept *illa* (*sit*) *maior* i.e. 'or she is to be the winner' (see *Epist.* 1. 10. 35).

9. **celeris** (*p*): the stress can only mean that he selects the arrows that are undamaged and are newly feathered.

10. **promis** should have stress (see on *Odes* 4. 9. 26); the taking out of the arrows implies immediate use.

timendos (*s*) is proleptic i.e. 'so as to make them dreaded.' See on P. 30, and compare on *Odes* 2. 8. 15. See too P. 21.

11. **nudo** (*ps*): he is cooling himself (see l. 13) and his sensuous charm is emphasized by the implied nakedness of his person.

13. **fertur** is in ἀπὸ κοινοῦ order with *posuisse* and *recreare*; see note on *Odes* 3. 17. 15.

leni (*ps*): i.e. 'the gentleness (of the wind)'; see on P. 27 and P. 21.

14. **sparsum...capillis**: for the grouping see on P. 9.

15, 16. **aquosa...Ida**: there is no point in *aquosa* (*ps*); see, however, P. 21.

XXI. 1. **O nata mecum**: these words come early in order to emphasize the age of the wine.

2. **geris** is in ἀπὸ κοινοῦ position with *querellas* and *iocos*.

3. **insanos** (*p*) may (1) be ἀπὸ κοινοῦ with *rixam* and *amores* (see on P. 33), or may (2) equal 'the madness (of love)'; see on P. 27.

quocumque lectum nomine Massicum   5
servas, moveri digna bono die,
   descende, Corvino iubente
    promere languidiora vina.

non ille, quamquam Socraticis madet
sermonibus, te negleget horridus: 10
   narratur et prisci Catonis
    saepe mero caluisse virtus.

tu lene tormentum ingenio admoves
plerumque duro; tu sapientium
   curas et arcanum iocoso   15
    consilium retegis Lyaeo;

4. **facilem...somnum:** the grouping is that of P. 10. The collocation of *facilem* and *pia* is happy i.e. ease (of sleep) is due to your sense of duty and kindliness (*pietas*). For the preposited epithet with the vocative see on P. 36.

5. **quocumque...Massicum:** for the grouping see on P. 9.

6. **servas** is emphatic (see on *Odes* 4. 9. 26) i.e. you still preserve through all these years.

moveri may perhaps be felt with *servas* also, i.e. you save it for being moved, worthy to be moved etc. There is an antithesis of keeping still and of moving.

bono die is an addendum (see on P. 53) i.e. 'but only on a *happy* (*bono* preposited) day.'

7. **Corvino iubente** equals *Corvinus enim iubet*; see on *Odes* 3. 1. 34.

8. **languidiora** (*p*): for its position see on P. 28.

9. **non ille:** the negative goes with *ille*.

Socraticis (*ps*) i.e. ' of a Socrates '; see on P. 37, and P. 21.

10. **sermonibus:** the lonely position (see on *Odes* 4. 9. 26) suits the ponderousness of the topic; compare *denominatos* at *Odes* 3. 17. 3.

horridus: the adjective equals an adverbial phrase (see on P. 31) i.e. (1) like a churl (2) with a shudder (compare Ovid *Am.* 2. 16. 19).

11. **prisci** (*p*) i.e. for all his old-fashioned austerity; compare *Odes* 3. 9. 17.

prisci Catonis: the genitive, thus brought forward, is felt as subject (see on P. 38).

12. **saepe** separated from *caluisse* has stress, 'many a time and oft.'

virtus coming last echoes the *severitas* implied in *prisci* l. 11.

13, 14. **lene** (*p*): for the preposited adjective in oxymoron see on *Epod.* 5. 82.

plerumque duro i.e. 'although stern by wont'; the words form an emphatic addendum (see on P. 53).

tu sapientium: case relations grouped early (see on *Odes* 1. 2. 17).

15, 16. **curas:** a Roman is inevitably forefeeling a verb such as *solvis*.

arcanum...Lyaeo: for the grouping see on P. 9.

tu spem reducis mentibus anxiis
viresque et addis cornua pauperi,
    post te neque iratos trementi
        regum apices neque militum arma.   20

te Liber et si laeta aderit Venus
segnesque nodum solvere Gratiae
    vivaeque producent lucernae,
        dum rediens fugat astra Phoebus.

XXII.

Montium custos nemorumque virgo,
quae laborantis utero puellas
    ter vocata audis adimisque leto,
        diva triformis,

imminens villae tua pinus esto,   5
quam per exactos ego laetus annos
    verris obliquum meditantis ictum
        sanguine donem.

18. **viresque** may be object of (1) *reducis* (2) *addis*; if of the latter see on *Odes* 1. 30. 6. But see Gow.

19, 20. **iratos...apices:** for the grouping with *trementi* intrusive see on P. 46 *a*. Perhaps *iratos* belongs mainly to *regum* (see on P. 52). We may supply *irata* before *militum*.

21. **te Liber:** see on *Odes* 1. 2. 17 and compare l. 14 above.

laeta (*ps*) goes closely with *aderit* and equals 'with smiles'; see on P. 31, and also P. 21.

23. **vivae** (*ps*): sc. οὖσαι i.e. 'being unextinguished....' Compare *Odes* 3. 8. 14, and see P. 21.

24. **dum rediens fugat** merely equals *dum redit et simul fugat.*

XXII. Is not this a little hymn of gratitude written for a friend whose wife had come safely through her confinement?

1. **Montium custos nemorumque:** for the grouping see on P. 34. Compare *Odes* 3. 25. 14, 15 *Naiadum potens Baccharumque.*

4. **triformis:** contrast on *Odes* 1. 7. 5.

5. **tua** (*p*) is predicative i.e. 'be thine.'

6. **exactos...annos:** for the grouping see on P. 15. Moreover *ego* may be felt as subject of *exactos* (see on *Odes* 1. 10. 14).

7, 8. **verris** (*ps*) is the gift i.e. 'with a boar and its blood'; see on P. 38. **verris...ictum:** for the grouping see on P. 14.

XXIII. 1. **supinas** (*ps*) i.e. 'in prayer'; compare Vergil *Aen.* 4. 205 *multa Iovem manibus supplex orasse supinis* (*s*). To hold up the hands to

XXIII.

Caelo supinas si tuleris manus
nascente luna, rustica Phidyle,
   si ture placaris et horna
     fruge Lares avidaque porca,

nec pestilentem sentiet Africum   5
fecunda vitis nec sterilem seges
   robiginem aut dulces alumni
     pomifero grave tempus anno.

nam quae nivali pascitur Algido
devota quercus inter et ilices   10
   aut crescit Albanis in herbis
     victima, pontificum securis

heaven might be a sign of mere irritation or despair, as *Sat.* 2. 5. 97 shows. Hence the word *supinas* is important.

manus: see on *Odes* I. 3. 16.

2. **nascente** i.e. 'at the birth (of the moon)'; see on P. 26.

nascente luna: these words stand in ἀπὸ κοινοῦ position with both *tuleris* and *placaris*.

rustica (*p*): see on P. 36. The word enforces the moral that being simple herself she should be simple in her offerings. For the sense of *rustica* (homely) see Ovid *Heroid.* 14. 132, 16. 285 (287), 17. 12, 13, 17. 186 etc.

3. **placaris:** note the ἀπὸ κοινοῦ position between *ture* and *horna fruge*.

horna (*p*): see on *Odes* I. 19. 15 (*bimi*).

4. **Lares:** note the ἀπὸ κοινοῦ position between *horna fruge* and *avida porca*.

avida (*p*) implies, presumably, that the *porca* was no skinny offering.

5. **pestilentem** i.e. 'the bane (of Africus)'; see on P. 27 and on P. 21.

6. **fecunda** (*p*): the stress is due to the sense of l. 5. There has been no hot wind; therefore the vine bears well.

sterilem (*ps*) i.e. 'the blight (of rust)'; see on P. 27.

7. **dulces** (*p*) i.e. 'your pets (the younglings)'; see on P. 27.

8. **pomifero...anno:** for the grouping see on P. 10.

9. **nivali** (*ps*) i.e. 'the snows (of Algidus)'; see on P. 27 and on P. 21, and compare *Odes* I. 21. 6.

11. **Albanis** (*ps*) is in artificial contrast to *Algido* l. 9.

12, 13. **victima:** if we write a comma after this word it has some emphasis (see on *Odes* 4. 9. 26) i.e. 'it is fattened (*crescit* comes early) only to be a victim,' as if we had *moritura* (see note on *Odes* I. 28. 6).

pontificum (*p*): contrast *rustica Phidyle* and *te*, which comes early to enforce the antithesis. At the same time *pontificum* may be felt as ἀπὸ κοινοῦ with both *victima* and *securis*.

cervice tinguet: te nihil attinet
temptare multa caede bidentium
   parvos coronantem marino   15
      rore deos fragilique myrto.
immunis aram si tetigit manus,
non sumptuosa blandior hostia
   mollivit aversos Penatis
      farre pio et saliente mica.   20

XXIV.

Intactis opulentior
   thesauris Arabum et divitis Indiae,

14. **multa caede bidentium:** for the grouping see on P. 35.

15, 16. **parvos** (*ps*) is very emphatic; contrast the *magni dei* to which the *pontifices* make sacrifice.

marino rore: Columella calls this plant either *marinus ros* or *ros marinus*. Horace chooses what is metrically convenient. Since the *ros* is *marinus*, as opposed to *terrenus*, the preposited order is natural.

deos is governed by both *temptare* and *coronantem*; Latin makes this obvious by placing *parvos* between them.

fragili (*p*) i.e. 'by fragments, sprigs (of myrtle)'; see on P. 27 *ad init*.

17–20. **immunis** (*ps*) must be emphatic whether we translate by 'giftless,' 'lay,' or 'guiltless.' For the many interpretations of these lines see the commentators. I venture to add one more, because it seems to me simple and supported by the order of the words viz. 'If a *giftless* (or 'lay') hand has touched the altar, *not* a hand more flattering with its *sumptuous* (*sumptuosa* preposited) victim, yet it has softened...' Any who think the idea too lofty for Horace should read Ovid *Ex Ponto* 3. 4. 81. The position of both *immunis* and *aram* before *si* suggests that the antithesis 'lay' and 'altar' is intended to be brought out.

17. **manus:** see note on l. 1 above.

18. **non** equals 'and not.'

sumptuosa blandior hostia: for the grouping see on P. 24, and for the form of the line compare *Odes* 1. 19. 16. The sense of *blandior* is 'wheedling' as at *Sat.* 1. 1. 25.

19. **aversos** (*p*) i.e. 'the displeasure (of the Penates)'; see on P. 26, and *Epod.* 10. 18.

20. **farre...mica:** these words form an emphatic addendum (see on P. 53); i.e. 'and that with only *farre pio....'*

Note the chiasmus *farre pio* and *saliente mica*.

saliente (*p*) may equal 'jumping, crackling (of *mica*)'; see on P. 27.

XXIV. 1. **Intactis** (*ps*) has stress; a *thesaurus* would be of little value after plunderers had gone over it. But see also P. 24.

2. **Arabum...Indiae:** for the position of the genitive see on P. 35.

caementis licet occupes
   Tyrrhenum omne tuis et mare †publicum†,
si figit adamantinos   5
   summis verticibus dira Necessitas
clavos, non animum metu,
   non mortis laqueis expedies caput.
campestres melius Scythae,
   quorum plaustra vagas rite trahunt domos,   10
vivunt et rigidi Getae,
   immetata quibus iugera liberas
fruges et cererem ferunt,
   nec cultura placet longior annua,

divitis (*p*) echoes the wealth implied in *thesauris*; it may also be ἀπὸ κοινοῦ with *Arabum* (see on P. 33).

3, 4. caementis...Tyrrhenum (terrenum) omne tuis: for the grouping see on P. 16 β.

mare publicum (?): Lachmann's *terrenum* is supported by *Odes* 2. 18. 28; and that *publicum* is tolerable may be shown by Ovid *Heroid.* 18. 150, and *Met.* 6. 351-3. But see on *Odes* 4. 2. 42. Gow now suggests *Metaponticum* (*C. R.* XXIX. p. 78).

omne (*pp*) has emphasis i.e. καὶ τὸ πᾶν.

5. figit (-et, -at) comes early with stress.

5-7. adamantinos | summis verticibus... | clavos: for the grouping (with intrusive words) see on P. 10.

7. clavos is emphatic (see on *Odes* 4. 9. 26). The word implies the idea of fixedness and immutability (see Wickham on *Odes* 1. 35. 18), and echoes *figit* (early) and *adamantinos* (separated) of l. 5.

8. mortis (*p*) i.e. 'death (and his noose)'; see on P. 38.

caput: see on *Odes* 1. 3. 16; but the word is also in artificial contrast to *animum* l. 7.

9. campestres (*ps*) i.e. living in the free open plains; contrast the rich man anchored to his palace.

melius: a Roman forefeels some verb of loose meaning such as *agunt*; indeed he requires no verb at all.

10. vagas (*ps*) echoes *campestres* (*ps*); it may also be felt with *plaustra* (see on P. 52).

domos: see on *Odes* 1. 3. 16.

11. vivunt perhaps has stress (see on *Odes* 4. 9. 26) i.e. they do more than exist, they *live*. But see also on *Odes* 3. 17. 15.

rigidi (*p*) is causal, 'because austere.'

12. immetata (*ps*) and **liberas** (*p*) emphasize the fact that private property in land or produce is unknown. The interposition of *quibus* heightens the effect of the quasi-oxymoron *immetata...iugera* (compare on *Epod.* 5. 82).

defunctumque laboribus　　　　　　　　　　　　　15
　　　aequali recreat sorte vicarius.
illic matre carentibus
　　　privignis mulier temperat innocens,
nec dotata regit virum
　　　coniux nec nitido fidit adultero.　　　　　20
dos est magna parentium
　　　virtus et metuens alterius viri
certo foedere castitas,
　　　et peccare nefas aut pretium est mori.
o quisquis volet impias　　　　　　　　　　　　25
　　　caedes et rabiem tollere civicam,
si quaeret 'pater urbium'
　　　subscribi statuis, indomitam audeat
refrenare licentiam,
　　　clarus postgenitis: quatenus, heu nefas!　　30

14. **longior annua** is a restrictive addendum (see on P. 53)—'*that is* tillage beyond a year's space.'

16. **aequali** (*ps*): this is the important word, like *aequo* in *aequo animo*, and therefore comes early. See also on P. 21.

17, 18. **matre carentibus** is a compound, ἀμήτωρ, 'motherless.' Hence *matre* need not lie between *carentibus* and *privignis* (see *Odes* 3. 1. 24). The preposited position of *matre-carentibus* may make it (1) concessive, (2) causal, but the latter sounds too much like Christian ethics.

innocens goes with *temperat*, and may surely mean 'controls without causing them hurt.' Horace uses *innocens* in one other passage only (*Odes* 1. 17. 21), where it has the same meaning. This is also Gow's view. See too P. 31.

19. **dotata** (*ps*) i.e. 'because she has a dowry.'

20. **coniux** probably has stress (see on *Odes* 4. 9. 26) i.e. 'a true helpmate, *con-iuncta.*'

nitido (*ps*) i.e. 'the sleekness (of a lover)'; see on P. 27 and P. 21.

21. **parentium** is ἀπὸ κοινοῦ with *dos* and *virtus* i.e. 'the dowry from the parents is the parents' *virtus.*'

22. **virtus** has emphasis (see on *Odes* 4. 9. 26); their great dower is not money but *virtus*.

23. **certo** (*p*) i.e. not lax but trustworthy.

25, 26. **impias** (*p*) equals *contra pietatem*, unpatriotic (with reference to civil war), and prepares us for the stress on *civicam* (*s*)=*inter cives*. For this use of *impius* compare *Odes* 2. 1. 30. See too on *Odes* 2. 14. 23.

28. **indomitam** (*ps*) i.e. 'though untamed.'

30. **clarus postgenitis** is an addendum of result (see on P. 53), ὥστε

virtutem incolumem odimus,
    sublatam ex oculis quaerimus invidi.
quid tristes querimoniae,
    si non supplicio culpa reciditur,
quid leges sine moribus   35
    vanae proficiunt, si neque fervidis
pars inclusa caloribus
    mundi nec Boreae finitimum latus
durataeque solo nives
    mercatorem abigunt, horrida callidi   40
vincunt aequora navitae?
    magnum pauperies opprobrium iubet
quidvis et facere et pati,
    virtutisque viam deserit arduae.
vel nos in Capitolium,   45
    quo clamor vocat et turba faventium,

κλεινὸς γενέσθαι. Here *carus* is a variant, and seems to have point; he is hated in his life-time, but loved by posterity. See on *Odes* I. 20. 5.

32. **invidi** coming last is causal i.e. 'because we are captious.'

33. **tristes** (*p*) i.e. 'the bitterness (of lamentation)'; see on P. 27, and *Odes* 2. 14. 23.

34. **si non** i.e. 'if it is the case that...not'; see on *Odes* 2. 9. 13.

supplicio is the logical subject and is therefore put early i.e. 'if punishment do not cut back crime.' Compare Livy 3. 62. 2 *consilio collegae, virtute militum victoria parta est*='the tactics of my colleague, and the bravery of the soldiers won the day.' So *passim* in Livy.

36, 37. **fervidis...caloribus**: for the grouping see on P. 15. The position of *fervidis* prepares us for the antithesis *Boreae* l. 38.

38. **mundi** stands in ἀπὸ κοινοῦ position with *pars* and *latus*. See on *Odes* 3. 17. 15.

Boreae (dative) is put early and outside *finitimum* and *latus* to express the contrast to *fervidis* in l. 36. See on P. 49.

40, 41. **horrida...navitae**: for the grouping see on P. 7.

42. **magnum** (*s*) equals *maximum*.

magnum pauperies opprobrium: as if we had *magnum pauperiei opprobrium*; for this order compare *Odes* 4. 8. 31 *clarum Tyndaridae sidus*, and Vergil *Aen.* 1. 435 *ignavum fucos pecus*, and *Epist.* 1. 18. 104 *gelidus Digentia rivus*.

44. **virtutis** (*p*) i.e. 'virtue (and its path)'; see on P. 38.

arduae (*s*) i.e. 'because it is difficult'; the adjective is felt with *viam* also (compare on P. 52).

virtutis...arduae: for the whole grouping see P. 20 β.

vel nos in mare proximum
    gemmas et lapides, aurum et inutile,
summi materiem mali,
    mittamus, scelerum si bene paenitet.   50
eradenda cupidinis
    pravi sunt elementa, et tenerae nimis
mentes asperioribus
    formandae studiis. nescit equo rudis
haerere ingenuus puer   55
    venarique timet, ludere doctior,
seu Graeco iubeas trocho,
    seu malis vetita legibus alea,
cum periura patris fides
    consortem socium fallat et hospites,   60

45. **nos** is emphatic because it is inserted and equals *nos ipsi*, 'with our own hands.' Some verb of general meaning e.g. *feramus* is forefelt.

47. **proximum**: I marvel that someone has not tried to improve Horace by emending (particular for general) to *Apulicum!* See on *Odes* I. I. 14.

49. **summi...mali**: for the grouping see on P. 20 *a*.

50. **mittamus** should have stress (see on *Odes* 4. 9. 26); perhaps it means 'to turn out of the house' as one would a divorced wife. See Terence *Phorm.* 4. 3. 70, and Suetonius *Calig.* 25.

scelerum is emphatic because it precedes *si*. The sense is 'if we regret our *sins*, and not our poverty only.' This weaker meaning of *paenitet* is common enough.

51. **cupidinis** (*ps*): passion is *the* vice which must be checked *a puero*.

52. **tenerae** (*ps*) has stress in contrast to *asperioribus* l. 53.

nimis (*pp*) has emphasis.

53. **asperioribus** (*ps*): see l. 52 above. For comparatives preposited or separated see on P. 28, and consult also P. 24.

54. **equo** is ἀπὸ κοινοῦ with *rudis* (ablative in point of which) and *haerere*.

55. **ingenuus** (*p*): contrast *plebeius, agrestis*, who would have learnt to ride and 'rough it.'

57. **Graeco** (*ps*): anything Greek was anathema, at any rate to the man in the street. The Greeks were already beating Romans in the trade of the Levant, and 'Made in Greece' was not a popular brand; although, as usual, everyone bought the articles (compare on *Odes* I. 20. 2). For the order see also P. 21.

60. **consortem** (*p*) emphasizes the fact that the partnership is one of capital, not of friendship (*hospitem*).

61. **indigno** (*ps*): he is piling up wealth only that his heir may have it, and that heir worthless. Compare on *Odes* 4. 7. 19, 20.

indignoque pecuniam
    heredi properet. scilicet improbae
crescunt divitiae: tamen
    curtae nescio quid semper abest rei.

XXV.

Quo me, Bacche, rapis tui
    plenum? quae nemora aut quos agor in specus
velox mente nova? quibus
    antris egregii Caesaris audiar
aeternum meditans decus   5
    stellis inserere et consilio Iovis?
dicam insigne, recens, adhuc
    indictum ore alio. non secus in iugis

62, 63. **improbae** (*ps*) seems to go with the predicate *crescunt* i.e. 'grow to shameless bulk,' and is quasi-proleptic (see on P. 30); or the adjective may equal an adverb 'insatiably' (see on P. 31). Compare also P. 21.

64. **curtae** (*ps*) is very emphatic. A Roman would read the line thus 'yet defectiveness there is—something always lacking to his fortune.' See on P. 27.

XXV. 1, 2. **tui | plenum** is an emphatic addendum (see on P. 53) i.e. 'and that too full of thyself.'

2. **plenum** has further stress by its position (see on *Odes* 4. 9. 26) and equals *plenissimum*.

quae nemora: a Roman on hearing *quae nemora* can keep an open mind about its case. He feels it definitely accusative when he reaches the *in* of *in specus*.

quos agor in specus: for the order see on *Odes* 1. 27. 11.

3. **velox mente nova** are emphatic addenda (see on P. 53).

nova is in its frequent sense of 'strange,' 'unwonted,' 'mystic,' 'mysterious.' On the order of *novus* see *Odes* 1. 2. 6.

4. **egregii** (*p*): see on *Odes* 1. 6. 11.

egregii Caesaris (*ps*) is a 'pendent' genitive, more or less with *audiar*, and equals '...on the topic of peerless Caesar shall I be heard...'; ultimately the genitive belongs to *decus*. For this Greek pendent genitive, meaning 'in the matter of,' as if with περί, see on P. 40.

5. **aeternum** (*ps*) is predicative, as Wickham says, i.e. 'so as to be eternal' (see on P. 30, and P. 21).

7. **recens** is in its proper sense of 'fresh,' 'having existed a short time only'; the next phrase *adhuc indictum ore alio* is a periphrasis for *novum* (for the adverb and adverbial equivalent on either side of *indictum* see on P. 34 *ad fin.*).

exsomnis stupet Euhias,
  Hebrum prospiciens et nive candidam   10
Thracen ac pede barbaro
  lustratam Rhodopen, ut mihi devio
ripas et vacuum nemus
  mirari libet. o Naiadum potens
Baccharumque valentium   15
  proceras manibus vertere fraxinos,
nil parvum aut humili modo,
  nil mortale loquar. dulce periculum est,
o Lenaee, sequi deum
  cingentem viridi tempora pampino.   20

XXVI.

Vixi puellis nuper idoneus
et militavi non sine gloria:
  nunc arma defunctumque bello
  barbiton hic paries habebit,

9. **exsomnis** sc. οὖσα. Presumably the all-night festivals were held at the full moon, when the country would be seen clearly enough, especially as the plain is covered with snow. This does away with Bentley's objection that one could not *prospicere Hebrum* at night.

10. **nive candidam** forms one word νιφαργής; hence *nive* need not lie between *candidam* and *Thracen* (see on *Odes* 3. 1. 24). The preposited *nive-candidam* equals 'the snow-whiteness (of Thrace)'; see on P. 27.

11. **Thracen**: its position (see on *Odes* 4. 9. 26) is, perhaps, in artificial contrast to *Rhodopen*.

11, 12. **pede...Rhodopen**: the position of *pede barbaro* is abnormal (see on P. 49), but Latin love of parallelism is doubtless the cause. Having written *nive candidam Thracen*, Horace inevitably continued *pede barbaro lustratam Rhodopen* (compare on *Odes* 3. 17. 10).

13. **vacuum** is in ἀπὸ κοινοῦ position with *ripas* and *nemus*; see on P. 33.

14, 15. **Naiadum potens Baccharumque**: for the grouping compare *Odes* 3. 22. 1 *montium custos nemorumque*, and see on P. 34.

15, 16. **valentium...fraxinos** is a pointed addendum: Bacchus is lord of worshippers with such wondrous powers; how mighty, therefore, must he himself be!

proceras (*ps*) i.e. no mere saplings.

17. **parvum** (*pp*) and **humili** (*p*) have stress.

18. **dulce** (*p*) is predicative.

laevum marinae qui Veneris latus   5
custodit. hic, hic ponite lucida
   funalia et vectes et arcus
     oppositis foribus minacis.

o quae beatam diva tenes Cyprum et
Memphin carentem Sithonia nive,   10
   regina, sublimi flagello
     tange Chloen semel arrogantem.

20. **cingentem...pampino** is an emphatic causal addendum (see on P. 53) and = *quippe qui cingat.*

viridi (*ps*) i.e. 'the greenery (of the vine leaves)'; see on P. 27, and also note on *Odes* 4. 8. 33.

XXVI. This Ode is, I suspect, a translation from the Greek, and, like *Odes* 3. 20, is not a complete success.

1. **Vixi** comes early with emphasis i.e. 'It is all over'; compare Vergil *Aen.* 2. 325 *fuimus Troes.*

2. **non sine gloria:** the postposited adverb-phrase = *maxima cum gloria.*

5. **laevum...latus:** for the grouping see on P. 10.

6. **custodit** should have stress (see on *Odes* 4. 9. 26). The left side is, conventionally, the unprotected side. Compare *latus claudere* i.e. *in sinistra ambulare* (see Duff on Juvenal 3. 131).

lucida (*p*): perhaps 'the gleam (of waxened ropes)'; see on P. 27.

7, 8. **arcus...minacis:** for the grouping see on P. 18.

oppositis (*p*) i.e. 'the opposition (of doors)'; see on P. 26, and compare *Odes* I. 11. 5.

9. **quae...Cyprum:** for the grouping see on P. 9.

beatam diva: a Roman might feel these words to mean 'blessed in its goddess'; see on *Odes* I. 35. 1.

Cyprum et: see on *Odes* I. 35. 39.

10. **carentem...nive:** this is, apparently, an artificial rendering of Bacchylides' ἀχείμαντον Μέμφιν. The preposited *Sithonia* is somewhat pointless, even though the snows of Chalcidice might be proverbial. To speak of a place where snow never falls as 'free from *Arctic* snows' is worthy of our eighteenth century versifiers.

The words *Sithonia nive* may stand outside *Memphin* and *carentem* because we still wait for the object of *carentem*; see on P. 47, and compare *Odes* I. 28. 1.

11, 12. **sublimi** (*p*) makes *tange* a paraprosdokian for *caede.* Compare *Odes* 3. 29. 63, 64. The adverb *semel* postposited and separated goes with *tange* and heightens the paraprosdokian i.e. 'touch her and once only.'

arrogantem (*s*) is causal, 'for her disdain' (ἅτε σεμνὴν γενομένην); or it might be concessive. The grouping *Chloen semel arrogantem* need not, of necessity, mean 'Chloe once disdainful'; see on P. 50 *c.*

XXVII.

Impios parrae recinentis omen
ducat et praegnas canis aut ab agro
rava decurrens lupa Lanuvino
    fetaque volpes.

rumpit et serpens iter institutum,   5
si per obliquum similis sagittae
terruit mannos. ego cui timebo
    providus auspex,

antequam stantis repetat paludes
imbrium divina avis imminentum,   10
oscinem corvum prece suscitabo
    solis ab ortu.

XXVII. 1, 2. **Impios...omen | ducat:** for the order see on P. 51.

parrae (*p*) i.e. 'the owl (and its omen)'; see on P. 38. The position also prepares us for *canis, lupa, volpes.*

2. **ducat** may be emphatic (see on *Odes* 4. 9. 26); the poet wishes that the omen may not merely terrify for the moment, but attend the *impios* on their way. See however on *Odes* 3. 17. 15.

praegnas (*p*): 'pregnancy (of the *canis*)'; see on P. 27.

2, 3. **ab agro...Lanuvino:** for the grouping see on P. 18.

rava decurrens probably sounds like 'a dun streak as it speeds down.'

4. **feta** (*p*): see on *praegnas* l. 2 above.

6. **per obliquum:** sc. *veniens* or the like.

7. **mannos:** for its position see on *Odes* 1. 3. 16.

8. **providus** (*p*): the ordinary *auspex* judges after the flight, but Horace will arrange things beforehand. Before the *divina avis* can (*repetat* is subjunctive of purpose prevented) give warning of storm, he will prearrange on the east, the propitious side if you turn north, the cry of a *corvus*.

9. **stantis** (*ps*): Horace, if a friend is to travel (*timebo* is future), will have him go in summer, when the voyage to Greece would be safest. The *running* waters are then dried up, and the *divina avis* (probably the *cornix*) seeks '*standing* waters' in the marshes. There it utters its *raucisonos cantus* (Lucretius 5. 1083), *caput spargens undis, velut occupet imbrem* (Lucretius 5. 556), and *pluviam vocat...et sola...spatiatur* (Vergil *Georg.* 1. 389). Cicero *Progn.* 223 speaks of it as *cursans per litora* before a storm and adds *demersit caput et fluctum cervice recepit.* But see also P. 21.

10. **imbrium...imminentum:** for the grouping see on P. 18.

11. **oscinem** (*p*): (1) 'the cry (of a *corvus*)'; see on P. 27; (2) proleptic (so Wickham); compare on P. 30.

12. **solis ab ortu:** an emphatic addendum (see P. 53) and equals *idque solis ab o tu,* the favourable side (see on l. 8 above). Perhaps *solis* is pre-

sis licet felix, ubicumque mavis,
et memor nostri, Galatea, vivas,
teque nec laevus vetet ire picus   15
    nec vaga cornix.

sed vides, quanto trepidet tumultu
pronus Orion: ego quid sit ater
Hadriae novi sinus et quid albus
    peccet Iapyx.   20

hostium uxores puerique caecos
sentiant motus orientis Austri et
aequoris nigri fremitum et trementis
    verbere ripas.

posited because of the preposition (compare on P. 42). See too *Odes* 4. 4. 14 *matris ab ubere*; 4. 6. 20 *matris in alvo*. We have the same order in l. 58 of this *Ode* (*hac ab orno*).

15. **teque:** the pronoun coming first has emphasis i.e. whatever may happen to others.

laevus (*ps*) i.e. by being on the left and unlucky side.

16. **vaga** (*p*) i.e. 'the pacing up and down (of the *cornix*)'; see on P. 27, and compare Vergil's *spatiatur* (a sign of coming rain) quoted at l. 9 above.

17. **quanto trepidet tumultu:** see on P. 21; compare *Odes* 3. 20. 1, and see note on *Odes* I. 27. 11, 12.

18, 19. **pronus** (*p*) sc. ὤν. Orion is head downwards (*pronus*) towards the western horizon just before dawn in the latter half of November; and the sailor, anxiously waiting for sunrise, would not be likely to forget the fact. See on *Odes* I. 28. 21 and *Epod.* 10. 10, 15. 8. •

ater Hadriae novi sinus: for the grouping with the intrusive *novi* see on P. 46 *a*. But the position of *novi* makes it mean 'I have known only too well.'

albus (*ps*) i.e. 'for all its clear skies'=καίπερ λαμπρὸς ὤν. See also P. 21.

21. **hostium** (*p*) is emphatic; compare the position of *impios* l. 1.

caecos (*ps*) equals 'mysterious,' 'unexpected'; the shift from W. to S. has occurred suddenly. See on P. 21.

22. **orientis** (*p*): i.e. 'the rising (of the wind)'; see on P. 26. Contrast *orti*; for when *Auster* has once risen, the motions are anything but *caeci*.

22, 23. **motus...fremitum:** note the chiastic orders—*motus* answered by *fremitum*, *orientis* by *nigri*, and *Austri* by *aequoris*. This elaborate performance is an excuse for not placing *orientis Austri* between *caecos* and *motus* (see on P. 43).

Austri et: see on *Odes* I. 35. 39.

23. **aequoris:** see on *Odes* I. 14. 9.

sic et Europe niveum doloso   25
credidit tauro latus et scatentem
beluis pontum mediasque fraudes
    palluit audax.

nuper in pratis studiosa florum et
debitae Nymphis opifex coronae,   30
nocte sublustri nihil astra praeter
    vidit et undas.

quae simul centum tetigit potentem
oppidis Creten, 'pater, o relictum
filiae nomen pietasque' dixit   35
    'victa furore!

unde quo veni? levis una mors est
virginum culpae. vigilansne ploro
turpe commissum, an vitiis carentem
    ludit imago   40

vana, quae porta fugiens eburna
somnium ducit? meliusne fluctus
ire per longos fuit, an recentis
    carpere flores?

25, 26. **niveum...latus:** for the grouping see on P. 8.

27. **pontum mediasque fraudes:** *medias* is preposited, as if Horace had written *mediasque ponti fraudes*. See too P. 33.

28. **audax** sc. καίπερ οὖσα, 'for all her boldness.'

29. **florum et:** see on *Odes* 1. 35. 39.

30. **debitae...coronae:** for the grouping see on P. 20 *a*.

32. **vidit:** note how the verb lies between the two objects of *praeter*, which is itself in ἀπὸ κοινοῦ position.

33, 34. **centum...Creten:** for the grouping see on P. 9, and compare *Epod.* 9. 29 *centum nobilem Cretam urbibus.*

35. **nomen:** compare Ovid *Her.* 10. 70.

36. **furore** is an emphatic addendum (see on P. 53) i.e. 'duty vanquished —by *madness*!' She will not say '*amore*.'

37. **levis** is predicative and emphatic.

38. **virginum** (*p*) has stress i.e. 'for *maidens* who sin.'

39. **turpe** (*p*): sinful is the point. See also on *Odes* 2. 14. 23.

41. **vana:** we may agree with Page, who puts a comma at *imago* l. 40, and takes *vana* adverbially with *fugiens* i.e. 'idly flying'; see P. 31.

    eburna (*s*): contrast *cornea* (Verg. *Aen.* 6. 894), and see also P. 21.

43. **per longos** (*s* and postposited) i.e. 'over the length (of sea)'; see on P. 27 and P. 21. Compare too *Odes* 3. 3. 37.

siquis infamem mihi nunc iuvencum   45
dedat iratae, lacerare ferro et
frangere enitar modo multum amati
    cornua monstri.

impudens liqui patrios penatis:
impudens Orcum moror: o deorum   50
siquis haec audis, utinam inter errem
    nuda leones!

antequam turpis macies decentis
occupet malas teneraeque sucus
defluat praedae, speciosa quaero   55
    pascere tigris.

vilis Europe, pater urget absens,
quid mori cessas? potes hac ab orno
pendulum zona bene te secuta
    laedere collum.   60

recentis (*ps*): see on P. 21. The epithet suggests fresh flowers in the dewy morning, contrasted with *nocte sublustri* of l. 31 above.

45, 46. **infamem...iuvencum**: the position of *mihi nunc* requires that the words should go with *infamem* and *iuvencum* i.e. 'the bull now infamous in my eyes' (compare *tibi invisus* l. 71 below). When *dedat* is reached, both words, *mihi* and *nunc*, are felt again with it.

iratae (*s*) i.e. 'to my wrath'; see on P. 27.

ferro et: see on l. 22 *Austri et*.

47. **modo multum amati**: the group is preposited and separated in contrast to *infamem mihi nunc* of l. 45. See too P. 20 a.

49. **patrios** (*p*): perhaps equals 'land (of my home)'; see on P. 27. We might render by 'fatherland and home' (see on *Calabros, Odes* I. 33. 16).

50, 51. **o deorum | siquis**: a Roman would read thus: 'o ye gods, if any....' For the partitive genitive early compare *Epod.* 5. 1 *At o deorum quicquid in caelo regit | terras.* Horace may have πρὸς θεῶν in mind.

inter errem: Livy (6. 7. 3) has *interequitare* transitive, and there seems no reason why we should not read *intererrem*. But see on *A.P.* 424 and the note of Wilkins *ad loc.*

53. **turpis** (*p*): contrast *decentis* (*ps*); but for the latter see also P. 21.

54. **teneraeque** (*ps*) echoes the stress of *decentis*.

57. **vilis** (*p*): see on P. 36.

absens (*s*) i.e. 'though absent.'

58. **hac ab orno**: the order makes *hac* deictic, ἀπὸ ταυτησί. Compare *solis ab ortu* l. 12 above.

sive te rupes et acuta leto
saxa delectant, age te procellae
crede veloci, nisi erile mavis
    carpere pensum

regius sanguis dominaeque tradi   65
barbarae paelex.' aderat querenti
perfidum ridens Venus et remisso
    filius arcu.

mox, ubi lusit satis, 'abstineto'
dixit 'irarum calidaeque rixae,   70
cum tibi invisus laceranda reddet
    cornua taurus.

uxor invicti Iovis esse nescis.
mitte singultus, bene ferre magnam
disce fortunam: tua sectus orbis   75
    nomina ducet.'

59, 60. **pendulum...collum:** for the grouping with *laedere* intrusive see on P. 46 *a*, and P. 15.

61. **te rupes:** see on P. 51.

63. **veloci** (*s*) i.e. 'swift though it be'; see on P. 21.

erile (*ps*): a Roman would read thus: 'unless you prefer a mistress (*era, domina*) and the task enjoined by her.' Hitherto Europa has spun wool of her own (*suum, non erile pensum*) or given wool out for others to spin. The position of *erile* prepares us for *regius* (*p*) in l. 65.

66. **barbarae paelex:** both words are emphatic addenda (see on P. 53), i.e. '(to a mistress) who is a foreigner, the wife of some eastern potentate, while you are a concubine.'

67. **remisso** (*ps*) i.e. unstrung, because his work is over (Wickham). Cupid goes normally *intento arcu*. But see also on *Odes* 1. 10. 14.

69. **satis** (*pp*) i.e. 'had jested her *fill*,' 'was *tired* of teasing.'

70. **calidae** lies in ἀπὸ κοινοῦ position with *irarum* and *rixae*; see on P. 33.

71, 72. **cum tibi**=ἐπεί τοι, 'since let me tell you'; *tibi* begins by being ethical dative, and then is felt successively with *invisus, laceranda,* and *reddet* (compare *vagae* of *Odes* 1. 28. 23). For *cum* equalling ἐπεί=γάρ with a future indicative see Livy 34. 4. 17 *miserum illum virum..., cum, quod ipse non dederit, datum ab alio videbit.*

invisus...taurus: for the grouping see on P. 8.

73. **invicti** (*p*) suggests the antithesis of Europa who is *victa furore*. But *invicti* (*p*) may be due to the emphasis of compliment; see on *Odes* 1. 6. 11.

74. **magnam** (*s*) i.e. 'a fortune that is glorious'; see too on P. 21.

75, 76. **tua...nomina:** for the grouping see on P. 10

XXVIII.

Festo quid potius die
 Neptuni faciam? prome reconditum,
Lyde, strenua Caecubum,
 munitaeque adhibe vim sapientiae.
inclinare meridiem   5
 sentis ac, veluti stet volucris dies,
parcis deripere horreo
 cessantem Bibuli consulis amphoram?
nos cantabimus invicem
 Neptunum et viridis Nereidum comas;   10
tu curva recines lyra
 Latonam et celeris spicula Cynthiae:
summo carmine, quae Cnidon
 fulgentisque tenet Cycladas et Paphum
iunctis visit oloribus;   15
 dicetur merita Nox quoque nenia.

XXVIII. 1, 2. **Festo** (*ps*): the sense is 'What better can I do on a *feast-day*, and that the feast-day of Neptune?' *Neptuni* has stress because it lies outside *festo* and *die* (see on P. 35). As the date of Neptune's festival was July 23rd, it would be 'thirsty' weather.

 reconditum (*ps*) i.e. the oldest wine; compare *interiore* at *Odes* 2. 3. 8.

 3. **strenua** equals an adverb (so our colloquial 'quick and lively').

 4. **munitae** (*ps*) i.e. 'the fortress (of wisdom)'; see on P. 26.

 6. **stet,** coming early, is emphatic and prepares us for the antithesis *volucris* (*p*).

 11. **curva** (*ps*): compare on *Odes* 1. 10. 6, and see P. 21.

 12. **celeris spicula Cynthiae:** for the grouping see on P. 20 β. But a Roman may read the group 'swift in her arrows Cynthia.' Compare *Odes* 3. 29. 11, 12.

 13, 14. **summo** (*p*) i.e. 'last and best.' The order is natural for a superlative.

 fulgentis (*ps*): the epithet may be ἀπὸ κοινοῦ with *Cnidon* and *Cycladas* (see on P. 33); then the reference will be to the bright gleam of marble and of doves in flocks. But if *fulgentis* belong to *Cycladas* only, see P. 21.

 15. **iunctis** (*ps*) i.e. 'with team (of swans)'; see on P. 26, and also on P. 21.

 16. **dicetur:** to place a comma after this word and omit the semicolon after *oloribus* is to give *dicetur* a meaningless stress (see on *Odes* 4. 9. 26).

 merita Nox quoque nenia: i.e. 'night shall be sung because she has deserved a lullaby'; it is as if we had *meritā...neniam* (see on *Odes* 1. 10. 14).

XXIX.

Tyrrhena regum progenies, tibi
non ante verso lene merum cado
    cum flore, Maecenas, rosarum et
      pressa tuis balanus capillis

iamdudum apud me est; eripe te morae,   5
ne semper udum Tibur et Aefulae
    declive contempleris arvum et
      Telegoni iuga parricidae.

fastidiosam desere copiam et
molem propinquam nubibus arduis;   10
    omitte mirari beatae
      fumum et opes strepitumque Romae.

plerumque gratae divitibus vices,
mundaeque parvo sub lare pauperum
    cenae sine aulaeis et ostro   15
      sollicitam explicuere frontem.

XXIX. 1. **Tyrrhena** is doubtless felt by a Roman with both *regum* and *progenies*; see on P. 52.

2. **verso...cado**: for the grouping see on P. 10.

3. **rosarum et**: see on *Odes* 1. 35. 39.

4. **pressa...capillis**: for the grouping see on P. 9.

5. **iamdudum** (*s*): the emphasis prepares us for *eripe te morae*.

6. **semper** (*s*) is emphatic.

udum (*p*) i.e. 'the waters, waterfalls (of Tivoli)'; see on P. 27. Compare *Odes* 4. 2. 30 *uvidi Tiburis*, and 1. 7. 13 *praeceps Anio*.

Aefulae (*p*) i.e. 'Aefula (and its slopes)'; see on P. 38.

7. **declive** (*ps*) i.e. 'the slope (of its fields)'; see on P. 27 and P. 21.

arvum et: see on *Odes* 1. 35. 39.

8. **Telegoni...parricidae**: for the grouping see on P. 20 β.

9. **fastidiosam** (*ps*) i.e. 'because it brings only weariness'; see too P. 21.

copiam et: see on *Odes* 1. 35. 39.

10. **nubibus arduis**: for the position of these words see on P. 47.

11, 12. **beatae | fumum...Romae**: for the grouping see on P. 20 a. But a Roman may read the words thus: 'blest in smoke and wealth and noise—Rome'; as if we had *beatam fumo et opibus strepituque Romam*. See too on *Odes* 3. 28. 12.

13. **gratae**: supply *sunt* probably.

14, 15. **mundae...pauperum**: these words form an epithet in front of *cenae*, and *sine aulaeis et ostro* an epithet behind it. This is merely an

iam clarus occultum Andromedae pater
ostendit ignem, iam Procyon furit
    et stella vesani Leonis,
        sole dies referente siccos;   20

iam pastor umbras cum grege languido
rivumque fessus quaerit et horridi
    dumeta Silvani caretque
        ripa vagis taciturna ventis.

tu civitatem quis deceat status   25
curas, et urbi sollicitus times,
    quid Seres et regnata Cyro
        Bactra parent Tanaisque discors.

extension of the simple *dulce decus meum*. See on P. 34, and compare ll. 55, 56 below. The same is true of the group *parvo sub lare pauperum*; but *pauperum* may be heard with both *lare* and *cenae*.

16. **sollicitam** (*ps*) equals *sollicitudines* (*frontis*), like *explicuit...seria frontis* of *Sat.* 2. 2. 125. See too on P. 27 and P. 21.

17. **clarus occultum**: note the juxtaposition of antithetical adjectives ('bright from the darkness'). In latitude 41°, *a* Cephei has an altitude of 13° at lower transit, and, even in the clearer skies of summer, cloud-banks on the horizon might often obscure him.

17, 18. **clarus occultum...pater | ostendit ignem**: for the grouping see on P. 9.

Andromedae pater: see on P. 41 *ad fin.*

ignem: for its position see on *Odes* 1. 3. 16.

19. **stella** is used rather than *sidus* because Regulus is so conspicuous a member of the constellation.

vesani (*p*) echoes *furit* of l. 18. It is probably felt with *stella* also.

20. **sole...siccos**: for the ablative absolute see on *Odes* 3. 1. 34.

siccos (*s*) i.e. 'that are *dry*'; see too P. 21 and P. 48.

22, 23. **fessus** equals an adverb; see on P. 31.

horridi...Silvani: for the grouping see on P. 20 *a*. The epithet may be felt with *dumeta* also.

24. **ripa...ventis**: for the grouping see on P. 14. The words *vagis...ventis* may be heard both with *caret*, and, as an 'ablative in point of which,' with *taciturna*.

25. **tu civitatem**: see on *Odes* 1. 2. 17 for the case relations grouped early; the topic is 'you and the state'; hence *civitatem* precedes its clause.

tu, because inserted, is emphatic i.e. 'but thou' (contrast *pastor* l. 21).

quis...status: for the separation see on *Odes* 1. 27. 11.

26. **curas** perhaps has stress (see on *Odes* 4. 9. 26) i.e. 'art over anxious.'

prudens futuri temporis exitum
caliginosa nocte premit deus   30
  ridetque, si mortalis ultra
    fas trepidat. quod adest memento
componere aequus: cetera fluminis
ritu feruntur, nunc medio alveo
  cum pace delabentis Etruscum   35
    in mare, nunc lapides adesos
stirpesque raptas et pecus et domos
volventis una, non sine montium
  clamore vicinaeque silvae,
    cum fera diluvies quietos   40

29. **prudens** may be absolute 'in his providence,' as at *Odes* I. 3. 22; but the position of *futuri temporis* between *prudens* and *exitum* suggests that the genitive is ἀπὸ κοινοῦ i.e. 'God, though he knows the future, hides its issue.' The word *futuri* is preposited because it is the important element of the phrase.

30. **caliginosa** (*p*) i.e. 'the blackness (of night)'; see on P. 27.

deus: for its position see on *Odes* I. 3. 16.

32. **fas**: note the emphasis on this word; there is a slight pause after *ultra*.

33. **aequus** equals an emphatic adverb, 'with perfect calmness'; see P. 31 and P. 32.

fluminis (*p*): see on *Odes* 3. 14. 1.

34. **medio** (*p*) i.e. not overflowing (its bed, *alveo*); compare *Odes* I. 2. 18 and 4. 7. 3. If *aequore* be read, then *medio aequore* is literally 'its smooth waters being in the middle (between the banks).'

35. **Etruscum** (*ps*): the rivers on the west of Italy, e.g. the Umbro, Tiber, Liris, Volturnus, glide through level plains and marshes to the sea. The *synapheia* well expresses the unbroken quietude of these rivers. See on *Odes* I. 31. 7. We may compare the absence of caesura in Horace's *labitur et labetur in omne volubilis aevum*, and Homer's κύματα μακρὰ κυλινδόμενα προτὶ χέρσον.

The words *Etruscum in mare* are not necessarily an emphatic addendum for the reasons stated at P. 47 and P. 48.

38, 39. **una** (*pp*) is emphatic and equals 'in one confusion.'

montium...silvae: for the grouping compare *Odes* 3. 22. 1 *montium custos nemorumque*, and see on P. 34.

vicinae (*p*) suggests the antithesis *distantium* implied with *montium*. See note on *Odes* I. 20. 7.

40. **fera** (*p*) i.e. 'the fury (of the flood)'; see on P. 27. Contrast too *quietos*.

quietos (*ps*) i.e. 'the peace, sleep (of the waterways)'; see on P. 27 and P. 21.

irritat amnis. ille potens sui
laetusque deget, cui licet in diem
   dixisse 'vixi: cras vel atra
      nube polum pater occupato,

vel sole puro; non tamen irritum,   45
quodcumque retro est, efficiet neque
   diffinget infectumque reddet,
      quod fugiens semel hora vexit.'

Fortuna, saevo laeta negotio et
ludum insolentem ludere pertinax,   50
   transmutat incertos honores,
      nunc mihi, nunc alii benigna.

laudo manentem: si celeris quatit
pinnas, resigno quae dedit et mea
   virtute me involvo probamque   55
      pauperiem sine dote quaero.

non est meum, si mugiat Africis
malus procellis, ad miseras preces
   decurrere et votis pacisci,
      ne Cypriae Tyriaeque merces   60

42. **in diem** is read with both *licet* and *dixisse*.

43. **dixisse**: the tense has point: 'he has said,' when the day is over.
atra (p): contrast *puro* of l. 45.

48. **fugiens** i.e. 'in its flight.'
semel is, probably, ἀπὸ κοινοῦ with *fugiens* and *vexit*; see P. 50 *a*.

49. **saevo** (ps): Fortune delights *saevo, non benigno negotio*; but see P. 24 and P. 14.
negotio et: see on *Odes* I. 35. 39.

51. **incertos** (p) is proleptic i.e. ὥστε ἀβεβαίους εἶναι. See on P. 30.

53. **celeris** (ps) is proleptic i.e. '(shakes) into swiftness.' See on P. 30 and P. 21.

54. **pinnas** should have stress (see on *Odes* 4. 9. 26). The mention of wings implies flight and is in contrast to *manentem*.
mea (p) is emphatic i.e. 'what is my own—my virtues,' not the advantages of wealth and success brought by Fortuna.

55, 56. **probam...dote**: for the grouping compare ll. 14, 15 above, and see P. 34.

57. **Africis** (ps): see on *Odes* I. 33. 16 *Calabros*. The words sound like 'if there groan off Africa.'

addant avaro divitias mari:
tunc me biremis praesidio scaphae
tutum per Aegaeos tumultus
aura feret geminusque Pollux.

XXX.

Exegi monumentum aere perennius
regalique situ pyramidum altius,
quod non imber edax, non Aquilo impotens
possit diruere aut innumerabilis
annorum series et fuga temporum.
non omnis moriar, multaque pars mei
vitabit Libitinam: usque ego postera
crescam laude recens, dum Capitolium

5

58. **miseras** (*p*): the stress suggests want of dignity i.e. 'piteous, abject, servile (prayers).'

59. **decurrere** may have stress (see on *Odes* 4. 9. 26): the frightened merchants *rush* to prayers.

60. **Cypriae** (*p*) **Tyriaeque** (*p*): the position of the adjectives emphasizes the value of the cargo—copper from Cyprus, purple from Tyre.

61. **addant**, coming early, has stress; they bring fresh wealth to a sea already over-rich.

avaro (*ps*) i.e. 'the greed (of the sea)'; see on P. 27, and compare *Odes* 1. 28. 18 and 2. 2. 1.

62–64. **me...aura feret:** for the order see on P. 51; *me* is also contrasted with the other passengers.

biremis (*ps*) i.e. 'with only two oars'; see also P. 20 β.

63. **tutum** (*s*) equals an adverb, 'in safety'; see on P. 31.

Aegaeos (*p*) i.e. 'even Aegean storms'; see on *Odes* 1. 1. 14, 15.

64. **aura** may be part of the miracle and come as a paraprosdokian after *tumultus*, like *tange* after *sublimi flagello* at *Odes* 3. 26. 11, 12. If not, *aura*, despite French *orage*, is far too weak after *procellis* and *tumultus*. Have we here the *aura* (gleam) of Vergil *Aen.* 6. 204? Servius suspected it at *Odes* 2. 8. 24. If Horace is using this *aura*, the reference is to the gleam of Castor and Pollux, and *aura* forms with *geminusque Pollux* a kind of hendiadys i.e. 'the fires of twin Pollux' (see on *Odes* 1. 3. 2); then too *geminus* is ἀπὸ κοινοῦ with *aura* and *Pollux* (see on P. 33). If *aura* means 'breeze,' we must justify the preposited *geminus* by calling it a ritual epithet (see on *Odes* 1. 7. 5).

XXX. 2. **regali...pyramidum:** for the grouping see on P. 35.

6. **multaque pars mei:** *multa pars* may be felt as one word (see on P. 45); but compare on P. 35. Juvenal 3. 193 *magna parte sui* is similar (see Duff's note *ad loc.*).

7, 8. **usque...recens:** a Roman would read the words thus: 'always *I* in

scandet cum tacita virgine pontifex.
dicar, qua violens obstrepit Aufidus   10
et qua pauper aquae Daunus agrestium
regnavit populorum, ex humili potens
princeps Aeolium carmen ad Italos
deduxisse modos. sume superbiam
quaesitam meritis et mihi Delphica   15
lauro cinge volens, Melpomene, comam.

time to come shall grow in praise ever fresh'; i.e. *laude* belongs partly to
crescam, partly to *recens*.

usque is emphatic by separation from *crescam*.

postera (*ps*) i.e. 'in the future,' though, at present, I may be of little
account. See too P. 21.

crescam coming early probably has stress i.e. *crescam, non minuar*.

recens is an emphatic addendum (see on P. 53) i.e. 'as if just published';
contrast *novus* 'never before existent.'

9. **tacita** (*p*): the stress on the epithet perhaps suggests to the mind the
solemn silence which reigned during religious ceremonials; compare *favete
linguis* and εὐφημεῖτε. Perhaps, too, Vestals were ceremonially dumb when
they came out of the seclusion of the *Atrium Vestae*.

10. **violens** (*ps*): like *longe sonantem* of *Odes* 4. 9. 2, the epithet describes
that part of the river nearest Venusia. The Aufidus would be noisy in the
hills, but not in the plain. See also P. 21.

qua...obstrepit: these words ought to go with *dicar*; if they went with
princeps deduxisse, we should have *obstrepat*. If Shakespeare had said 'men
will ever talk of me at Stratford,' he would not be belittling himself: he would
merely imply that all the world was going to visit his birth-place as if some
sacred shrine.

11, 12. **agrestium** (*ps*): Horace is speaking of *Apulia Daunia* in the
north (contrast Venusia in the south), and these Daunii would be pastoralists
(*agrestes*) of the plains opposed to the mountaineers of Venusia and of the
upper Aufidus. See also P. 21.

12-14. **ex humili potens | princeps...deduxisse**: the construction seems
to be '(I shall be spoken of where...) as being *ex humili potens* and *princeps...
deduxisse*.' But see the editors.

Aeolium (*p*) prepares us for the antithesis *Italos* (*ps*). See on *Odes*
1. 26. 11 *Lesbio* (*ps*): see also P. 21.

15. **meritis** has stress; it should lie between *superbiam* and *quaesitam*.
See on P. 49.

mihi equals 'if you please'; it is a quasi-ethical dative and therefore
comes early, as so often. Compare Greek καί μοι λαβὲ τὴν μαρτυρίαν.

Delphica (*p*) i.e. not the laurel of victory in war, not *Parthica, Indica,
Sarmatica* etc., but *Delphica*. Compare *Apollinari* (*s*) at *Odes* 4. 2. 9, and
contrast *Deliis...foliis* at *Odes* 4. 3. 6.

BOOK IV

I.

Intermissa, Venus, diu
    rursus bella moves? parce precor, precor.
non sum, qualis eram bonae
    sub regno Cinarae. desine, dulcium
mater saeva Cupidinum,   5
    circa lustra decem flectere mollibus
iam durum imperiis: abi,
    quo blandae iuvenum te revocant preces.
tempestivius in domum
    Pauli purpureis ales oloribus   10

I. The strained order of the Ode suggests that Horace was rusty after some ten years' abstinence from writing this form of poetry.

1, 2. **Intermissa...moves?** If *intermissa* and *diu* belong to *moves*, we must classify the grouping under P. 46 *b*, with the vocative *Venus* quasi-parenthetic (see on *Odes* 1. 5. 3). Bentley says that to take *intermissa* and *diu* with *Venus* is a *puerilis error*, but on grounds of order, at least, there is no objection. We may compare *Odes* 3. 4. 26 *versa acies retro* and other instances quoted at P. 49. It is just possible that *intermissa* is felt first with *Venus* and subsequently with *bella* (see on P. 52).

rursus (*s*) has emphasis; contrast *intermissa...diu* (*pps*).

3, 4. **bonae | sub regno Cinerae:** for the grouping see on P. 20 *a*.

4, 5. **dulcium...Cupidinum:** for the grouping see on P. 15. Contrast *Odes* 1. 19. 1, and P. 36.

6. **decem** (*pp*) has emphasis.

mollibus (*ps*): contrast *durum*. As Gow says, *mollibus* is felt first with *flectere*, then with *durum*.

8. **blandae...preces:** for the grouping with intrusive words see on P. 46 *b*. The effect is to stress *iuvenum*, and to make *blandae* (*ps*) sound like *blanditiae* (see on P. 27).

9. **tempestivius** belongs to the whole sentence (see on *Odes* 2. 9. 13), but also has stress by position.

10, 11. **Pauli...Maximi:** the extraordinary separation of *Maximi* from *Pauli* has no real parallel in the *Odes*, *C.S.*, or *Epodes*, if we except the dubious *Raeti...Vindelici* of *Odes* 4. 4. 17, 18, and *nova...Augusti tropaea Caesaris* at 2. 9. 18, 19, where the conventional order of P. 9 is illustrated. In the *C.S.* l. 70 Horace writes *quindecim Diana preces virorum*; but the position of *quindecim* gives the effect of 'the XV' (in Ovid *Ex Ponto* 3. 5. 23

comissabere Maximi,
   si torrere iecur quaeris idoneum:
namque et nobilis et decens
   et pro sollicitis non tacitus reis
et centum puer artium   15
   late signa feret militiae tuae,
et quandoque potentior
   largi muneribus riserit aemuli,

sedissem forsitan unus | de centum iudex in tua verba viris, the antithesis of
unus and *centum*, quite apart from P. 9, justifies the order). At *Epod.* 4. 7
sacram metiente te viam there is appropriate stress on *sacram*, and we have
also the grouping of P. 10; so Martial uses the grouping of P. 8 at 1. 70. 5
sacro veneranda petes Palatia clivo.

   The nearest approach to our present passage is *Epist.* 1. 8. 1 *Celso gaudere
et bene rem gerere Albinovano | Musa rogata refer.* Here the second verb
eases the construction. Moreover Horace seems to be poking fun at the
sonorous *Albinovano* of a rather conceited young man. The intention may
be the same in thus placing *Maximi.* See too *Sat.* 1. 10. 28, and 1. 10. 80.

   Other examples, with clearer justification, are *Epist.* 1. 12. 26 *Claudi
virtute Neronis*, and *Sat.* 2. 3. 243 *Quinti progenies Arri* (compare *Odes*
2. 9. 18 quoted above, and see P. 20 a, β); *Epist.* 1. 15. 2, 3 *nam mihi Baias |
Musa supervacuas Antonius (facit)*, which may be classified under P. 16 a;
Vergil, *Aen.* 1. 271 *longam multa vi muniet Albam*, and *Aen.* 6. 766 *unde
genus Longa nostrum dominabitur Alba* (in both passages a small 'l' might
be read, and the stress would be equivalent to 'over all its length'; moreover
1. 271 is a case of P. 10, and 6. 766 of P. 14). Martial's *Argi nempe soles
subire letum* (1. 117. 9) is a mere *tour de force.*

   In view of the confusion in MSS over *comissabere* one might venture to
alter the punctuation and emend. Why not a comma after *preces* (l. 8),
another after *Pauli* (l. 10), and a semicolon after *oloribus?* Then read *comissare
ibi maxime* with postposited emphasis on both adverbs. In l. 10 there would
be some stress on *Pauli* (see on *Odes* 4. 9. 26).

   purpureis ales oloribus: for the grouping see on P. 24.

   12. **idoneum** (*s*) i.e. *tale ut idoneum sit*; see also P. 21.

   14. **pro sollicitis non tacitus reis:** we may regard *sollicitis* as substantival
i.e. 'for anxious men he is not silent when they are accused (*reis*).' See too
P. 24.

   15. **centum puer artium:** for the grouping see on P. 20 a.

   16. **late** (*s*) has emphasis.

   militiae (*s*) **tuae:** the stress is, perhaps, due to the contrast of the peaceful
toga implied in l. 14. Paulus sees military service—under the banner of
Venus.

   17. **potentior** sc. ὤν i.e. 'when conqueror,' 'when triumphant over.'

   18. **largi** (*ps*) i.e. 'however lavish.'

Albanos prope te lacus
    ponet marmoream sub trabe citrea.   20
illic plurima naribus
    duces tura, lyraeque et Berecyntiae
delectabere tibiae
    mixtis carminibus non sine fistula;
illic bis pueri die   25
    numen cum teneris virginibus tuum
laudantes pede candido
    in morem Salium ter quatient humum.
me nec femina nec puer
    iam nec spes animi credula mutui   30

largi muneribus riserit aemuli: for the grouping see on P. 20 a.

muneribus may first be read as ablative of comparison with *potentior*, but, when *riserit* is reached, the order is all in favour of taking it as causal ablative.

19, 20. **Albanos prope te lacus | ponet marmoream:** the order, at first sight, is extremely harsh. As, however, *prope* may follow its case, we really have the grouping *prope Albanos te lacus...marmoream*, for which compare on P. 17. See also *Odes* 4. 15. 24.

sub trabe citrea is, perhaps, an emphatic addendum (see on P. 53) i.e. you shall have a temple and that with a roof of expensive wood.

21. **plurima** (*s*) equals an adverb e.g. *largissime*, ἀφθονώτατα. See on P. 31.

22. **tura:** for its position see on *Odes* 1. 3. 16.

22, 23. **lyrae** (*ps*) i.e. 'the lyre (and its music)'; see on P. 38 and P. 43. For the abnormal order compare on *Odes* 1. 1. 23 *lituo tubae | permixtus sonitus*. The genitive may, however, be pendent i.e. 'and as for the lyre... you shall be gladdened by the mingled music' (see on P. 40). But the ablatives *lyra...Berecyntia...tibia* have good MS authority. Others take *lyrae* as dative.

Berecyntiae (*ps*): see on *Odes* 1. 18. 13 and 3. 19. 18. Compare too on P. 21.

25. **bis pueri die:** perhaps both *bis* and *die* have stress, the former by separation from *laudantes*, the latter by separation from *bis*. The meaning of *bis* is, I presume, 'morning and evening,' in honour of Venus as a morning and evening star. The stress on *die* may be intended to emphasize the idea that these pure children had no part in midnight orgies.

26. **numen cum teneris virginibus tuum:** the grouping may be that of P. 18. But see too P. 50 c.

teneris (*p*) adds to the sensuous picture; see too *Odes* 1. 21. 1.

28. **humum:** for its position see on *Odes* 1. 3. 16.

29. **me** comes early in contrast to *illic* of l. 25.

nec certare iuvat mero
    nec vincire novis tempora floribus.
sed cur heu, Ligurine, cur
    manat rara meas lacrima per genas?
cur facunda parum decoro   35
    inter verba cadit lingua silentio?
nocturnis ego somniis
    iam captum teneo, iam volucrem sequor
te per gramina Martii
    campi, te per aquas, dure, volubilis.   40

II.

Pindarum quisquis studet aemulari,
Iulle, ceratis ope Daedalea
nititur pinnis, vitreo daturus
    nomina ponto.

30. **spes...mutui**: for the grouping see on P. 16 *a*.

31. **mero** has stress because separated from *certare*. Horace could have scanned with *mero iuvat*.

32. **novis** (*ps*): there is almost nothing to justify the order, if *novis* is no more than *recentibus* (see on *Odes* I. 31. 2). Perhaps *novis* and *floribus* may be felt to go with *tempora*: the temples are surrounded by fresh flowers, in sense and in order; compare *Odes 4. 8. 33 viridi tempora pampino*, and see on 3. 2. 32.

34. **rara...genas**: for the grouping see on P. 9.

35, 36. **facunda parum decoro...cadit lingua silentio**: for the grouping see on P. 7.

37. **nocturnis** (*ps*) equals *noctu*; see on P. 31, and compare *Epod.* 5. 92.

38. **captum** and **volucrem** are at first intentionally vague in their reference; we are surrounded by the dim uncertainties of dreamland.

39, 40. **te...volubilis**: these lines form an emphatic addendum (see P. 53), and the effect is something like this: 'In my dreams I hold, I follow the flight...it is thou, it is thou!'

Martii (*p*) is perhaps felt with *gramina* and *campi*; see on P. 52.

40. **campi** has stress (see on *Odes 4. 9. 26*); contrast *per aquas*.

aquas, dure, volubilis: for the intervening vocative see on *Odes* I. 5. 3.

volubilis probably means 'that roll past' (compare *Epist.* I. 2. 43).

II. 1. **Pindarum** comes first because it is *the* topic.

2, 3. **ceratis...pinnis**: for the grouping and the intrusive verb see on P. 46 *a*.

vitreo (*ps*) i.e. 'to a *glassy* sea.' Most men are lost in a stormy sea. Icarus doubtless chose a calm day for flying but was nevertheless drowned.

monte decurrens velut amnis, imbres					5
quem super notas aluere ripas,
fervet immensusque ruit profundo
    Pindarus ore,

laurea donandus Apollinari,
seu per audacis nova dithyrambos					10
verba devolvit numerisque fertur
    lege solutis,

seu deos regesve canit, deorum
sanguinem, per quos cecidere iusta
morte Centauri, cecidit tremendae					15
    flamma Chimaerae,

sive, quos Elea domum reducit
palma caelestis, pugilemve equumve
dicit et centum potiore signis
    munere donat;					20

5. **monte decurrens** is placed first in contrast to the *taciturnus amnis* of the plains.

imbres is brought in front of the relative that it may stand by *amnis* and thus suggest 'swollen by rains.' See on l. 26 below.

6. **notas** (*ps*): see on P. 21, and compare *Odes* I. 2. 10.

7, 8. **immensus** goes closely with *ruit*.

immensus...ore: for the grouping see on P. 9.

9. **Apollinari** (*s*): compare on *Delphica* at *Odes* 3. 30. 15. See also P. 24.

10, 11. **audacis...verba**: for the grouping see on P. 9.

12. **lege solutis** (*s*): the order heightens the oxymoron; see on *Epod.* 5. 82.

13, 14. **deorum** (*p*) echoes *deos*; also it forms with *sanguinem* a patronymic (see on P. 41) and translates θεόγονοι.

14. **sanguinem** should have stress (see on *Odes* 4. 9. 26); perhaps it suggests human as opposed to divine beings.

iusta (*p*) has emphasis; it is almost equivalent to *iure* (see on P. 31).

15, 16. **tremendae | flamma Chimaerae**: for the grouping see on P. 20 a. See also on *Epod.* 6. 9.

17. **Elea** (*ps*) i.e. 'from Elis'; see on *Odes* I. 31. 9. But as *domum reducit* is merely a compound verb we may classify under P. 21.

18. **caelestis** is proleptic (see on P. 30) i.e. ὥστε δοκεῖν εἶναι θεούς. Compare *Odes* I. I. 6 *evehit ad deos*.

19, 20. **centum...munere**: for the grouping see on P. 9.

21, 22. **flebili sponsae iuvenemve raptum**: the first three words form one

flebili sponsae iuvenemve raptum
plorat et viris animumque moresque
aureos educit in astra nigroque
    invidet Orco.

multa Dircaeum levat aura cycnum,   25
tendit, Antoni, quotiens in altos
nubium tractus: ego apis Matinae
    more modoque

grata carpentis thyma per laborem
plurimum circa nemus uvidique   30
Tiburis ripas operosa parvus
    carmina fingo.

picture—the tearful widow of the warrior—and thus the position of *ve* may be justified. We have passed from ἐπινικία to θρῆνοι, and, appropriately, the first word we hear is *flebili* (*p*) i.e. 'tears (of a widow).'

    plorat has stress (see on *Odes* 4. 9. 26) and echoes *flebili* (*p*).

    23. **aureos** goes with *educit* proleptically (see on P. 30), and its sense is echoed by *in astra*.

    nigro (*ps*): contrast *aureos*; but see also P. 21.

    25. **multa...cycnum**: for the grouping see on P. 7.

    26. **tendit** has emphasis because it precedes *quotiens* i.e. 'strains all his powers.' Compare *imbres* l. 5 above, and see *Odes* 4. 9. 28, *Epod.* 1. 9, 10, and *Odes* 1. 37. 20.

    27. **ego** is emphatic because inserted; contrast Pindar.

    ego apis: the genitive *apis* is, very properly, kept close to *ego* in order that the objects compared may lie together (compare on *Odes* 1. 15. 29). See too *Odes* 1. 2. 17.

    29, 30. **grata** (*ps*) i.e. 'the sweets (of thyme)'; see on P. 27, and also on P. 21.

    per laborem is an emphatic addendum (see on P. 53), and equals *idque per laborem.* Horace implies that Pindar writes with the ease of a great inspiration, whereas he himself is compelled to *work*; his *felicitas* is *curiosa* indeed. As if to make the point more obvious still, he adds *plurimum* (*pp*) in a position of emphasis (see on *Odes* 4. 9. 36), and at l. 31 speaks of his *carmina* as *operosa* (*ps*).

    30, 31. **uvidi** (*p*) i.e. 'the falls (of Tibur)'; see on P. 27, and compare *Odes* 3. 29. 6 *udum* (*p*) *Tibur.*

    Tiburis goes with both *nemus* and *ripas* as its order shows.

    operosa (*ps*): the stress echoes *per laborem* and *plurimum* in ll. 29, 30 above.

    parvus comes happily next to *operosa* i.e. small but hard-working, like the bee.

concines maiore poeta plectro
Caesarem, quandoque trahet ferocis
per sacrum clivum merita decorus 35
  fronde Sygambros:

quo nihil maius meliusve terris
fata donavere bonique divi
nec dabunt, quamvis redeant in aurum
  tempora priscum. 40

concines laetosque dies et urbis
publicum ludum super impetrato
fortis Augusti reditu forumque
  litibus orbum.

33. **maiore** (*ps*): the position is natural with comparatives; see on P. 28.
poeta is qualified by the words between which it lies (see on *Odes* 3. 2. 32), but *maiore...plectro* is heard with *concines* also.

34. **Caesarem** has stress (see on *Odes* 4. 9. 26) i.e. 'Great Caesar'; the position moreover prepares us for the antithesis of his doughty foes, the Sygambri.
ferocis (*ps*) i.e. 'for all their valour'; the poet laureate wisely emphasizes the valour of the enemy.

35. **sacrum** (*p*): the adjective comes first, usually, with *clivus*. Martial 1. 70. 5 has *sacro veneranda petes Palatia clivo*.

35, 36. **merita** (*ps*): the triumph was no formal compliment; Augustus had conducted the campaign in person.
merita decorus | fronde: for the grouping see on P. 24.

38. **fata...bonique divi**: the adjective may be ἀπὸ κοινοῦ (see on P. 33), or may, as Page says, be emphatic i.e. 'in their goodness.'

39. **redeant** comes early with emphasis i.e. 'go *back*.'

40. **priscum** (*s*): the order echoes the stress on *redeant* i.e. 'back to the good old times.' See also the note on *Odes* 3. 9. 17.

41, 42. **laetos** (*p*) i.e. 'the gladness (of the days)'; see on P. 27.
dies et urbis | publicum ludum: the genitive *urbis* belongs to both *dies* and *ludum*; hence its position (see P. 43). But *urbis* may be emphatic in contrast to the rest of Italy.

publicum (*p*) is kept near to *urbis* and emphasizes the fact that the whole *populus* was concerned. In Horace however, with one somewhat doubtful exception (*Odes* 3. 24. 4), the adjective *publicus* is either preposited or separated from its noun.

42, 43. **impetrato | fortis Augusti reditu**: the grouping may be classified under P. 10; but both *impetrato* and *fortis* have interest. The former = 'fulfilment of prayer (for his return)'; see on P. 26. The latter is a compliment stressed.

tum meae, siquid loquar audiendum,   45
vocis accedet bona pars, et 'o sol
pulcher, o laudande!' canam recepto
    Caesare felix.

'*io*'que dum procedis, 'io triumphe!'
non semel dicemus 'io triumphe!'   50
civitas omnis, dabimusque divis
    tura benignis.

te decem tauri totidemque vaccae,
me tener solvet vitulus, relicta
matre, qui largis iuvenescit herbis   55
    in mea vota,

45. **meae** (*ps*) i.e. 'then comes *my* turn.' A Roman feels *meae* as if it were *ego* (see on *Odes* 1. 15. 33), contrasted with *tu* of *concines* in l. 41 above.

    audiendum (*s*) has modest stress, ἄξιόγγε τοῦ ἀκούειν. See too P. 21.

46. **vocis** (*ps*) is placed early as if subject (see on P. 38 and P. 43). A Roman reads thus: 'my voice shall be added—a good part of it.' When *bonus* equals *magnus*, like all adjectives of quantity, it is preposited.

47. **pulcher** should have stress (see on *Odes* 4. 9. 26). Compare too on P. 36.

    recepto (*p*) i.e. 'at the coming back (of Caesar)'; see on P. 26.

49, 50. Order throws no light on the vexed question of the reading.

51. **omnis** (*pp*) has emphasis and equals *universa, cuncta*.

52. **benignis** (*s*) is causal i.e. 'for their goodness.'

53, 54. **te...tauri..., me...solvet vitulus**: the order expresses the antithesis of σὲ μὲν...ἐμὲ δὲ....

    tener (*ps*): the idea of tenderness placed early suggests at once something small, in contrast to the solid massiveness of ten bulls and ten cows. See too P. 21.

54, 55. **relicta | matre**: there is some stress on *matre* (see on *Odes* 4. 9. 26), and one cannot help feeling that the words mean more than 'just weaned' of the *vitulus*. In any case the phrase is quasi-parenthetic and thus the (otherwise) ugly collocation *matre qui* is less noticeable. Horace seems to say 'you, Antonius, send ten bulls and ten cows; I send one male calf and no cow (lit. leaving behind the *mother*)—a calf which....' The poet cannot afford to give up the cow; if he does, where is he to get other victims, not to mention his milk? In his *Epist.* 1. 3. 36 Horace is plainly promising a rich sacrifice when he writes *pascitur in vestrum reditum votiva iuvenca*. See too *Odes* 1. 36. 2 *et vituli sanguine*.

    This interpretation of *relicta matre* avoids the objection that a calf recently weaned has no horns which could be described as crescent-shaped. Vergil at *Georg.* 4. 299, is nearer the truth in saying *Tum vitulus bima curvans iam*

fronte curvatos imitatus ignis
tertium lunae referentis ortum,
qua notam duxit, niveus videri,
　　cetera fulvus.　　　　　　　　　　　　　60

III.

Quem tu, Melpomene, semel
　　nascentem placido lumine videris,
illum non labor Isthmius
　　clarabit pugilem, non equus impiger
curru ducet Achaico　　　　　　　　　　5
　　victorem, neque res bellica Deliis
ornatum foliis ducem,
　　quod regum tumidas contuderit minas,
ostendet Capitolio;
　　sed quae Tibur aquae fertile praefluunt　10

cornua fronte | *quaeritur*, and Horace's *iuvenescit* at l. 55 scarcely implies a baby calf.

　　largis (*ps*): see on P. 21.

　　56. **mea** (*p*): contrast *tua* i.e. you can give so much, I so little.

　　57. **curvatos** (*ps*): contrast the *plenum orbem*.

　　58. **tertium...ortum**: for the grouping see on P. 15.

　　III. 1. **semel** (*s*) i.e. 'if once only (thou hast seen).' Compare *Odes* I. 24. 16. It is tempting to read *simul* (a variant at *Epist.* I. 7. 96) i.e. ἅμα φυόμενον, 'at the moment of birth.'

　　2. **placido** (*p*) i.e. 'with smiles (in your eye)'; see on P. 27.

　　4. **pugilem** i.e. 'as a boxer'; the word is predicative by position. The antitheses are clearly heard by reason of the position of *victorem* (l. 6), *ducem* (l. 7), *Capitolio* (l. 9).

　　5, 6. **Achaico** (*s*): the implied antithesis is *Romanus currus* of the triumphal procession referred to in the word *Capitolio* l. 9. But see P. 21.

　　victorem has stress (see on *Odes* 4. 9. 26) and equals 'will lead to *victory.*'

　　6, 7. **Deliis...ducem**: for the grouping see on P. 9. The 'Delian leaves' are probably palms (see Gow, and contrast *Odes* 3. 30. 15).

　　8. **regum** (*ps*) i.e. 'kings (and their pride)'; see on P. 38 and P. 43.

　　tumidas (*ps*): see P. 21.

　　contuderit may quite well be future perfect indicative (like *videris* l. 2) in view of *ducet* (l. 5) and *ostendet* (l. 9).

　　9. **Capitolio** coming last has interest; see on *Achaico* l. 5 above. Compare, however, on *Odes* I. 3. 16.

　　10. **quae Tibur aquae fertile**: for the separation of *quae* from *aquae*

et spissae nemorum comae
    fingent Aeolio carmine nobilem.
Romae, principis urbium,
    dignatur suboles inter amabilis
vatum ponere me choros,   15
    et iam dente minus mordeor invido.
o testudinis aureae
    dulcem quae strepitum, Pieri, temperas,
o mutis quoque piscibus
    donatura cycni, si libeat, sonum,   20
totum muneris hoc tui est,
    quod monstror digito praetereuntium
Romanae fidicen lyrae:
    quod spiro et placeo, si placeo, tuum est.

compare *Odes* 2. 7. 25 *quem Venus arbitrum*, and see note on *Odes* I. 27. 11.
If we regard *quae* as an adjective, we may compare the groupings noted at
P. 17.
    12. **Aeolio** (*p*): contrast *Romae* of l. 13. Compare too *Odes* 3. 30. 13.
nobilem is proleptic by position.
    13. **Romae** (*ps*) i.e. 'Rome (and her sons)'; see on P. 38. Its position
makes it virtual subject, as if we had *Romani*, or *Romana suboles*.
    14, 15. **inter amabilis...choros**: for the grouping, with *ponere me* intrusive,
see P. 46 *b*.
    16. **invido** (*s*) i.e. '(the tooth) of envy'; see on P. 27.
    17, 18. **o testudinis...temperas**: a Roman would read these lines thus:
'o shell of gold, whose notes to sweetness, thou Pierian, dost order.' It is
possible that Horace would feel *testudinis aureae* to be a genitive of exclamation, as in Greek. One might compare Catullus 9. 5 *o mihi nuntii beati*;
Propertius 4 (5). 7. 21 *foederis heu taciti*; Lucan 2. 45 *o miserae sortis*.
Ultimately the genitive of our passage depends on *strepitum* (see P. 43).
    dulcem (*ps*) is perhaps proleptic; see on P. 30.
    quae: the position is very awkward, but *quae* next to *aureae* would make
things worse. I wish there were evidence for *cui* (*testudini*) or *qua* (*testudine*)
as the original reading.
    19. **mutis** (*ps*) i.e. 'dumb though they be.'
    20. **cycni** (*ps*) i.e. 'even of the swan.'
    21. **totum** (*s*) equals an adverb 'wholly'; see on P. 31.
    tui (*s*) i.e. *tui, non alieni*.
    23. **Romanae** (*ps*): a Greek instrument (*lyrae*) is played by a *Roman* (so
Wickham). Compare *Odes* I. 32. 3.
    Romanae fidicen lyrae: for the grouping see on P. 20 *a*. These words
form an emphatic addendum (see on P. 53).

IV.

Qualem ministrum fulminis alitem,
cui rex deorum regnum in avis vagas
   permisit expertus fidelem
     Iuppiter in Ganymede flavo,

olim iuventas et patrius vigor   5
nido laborum propulit inscium,
   vernique iam nimbis remotis
     insolitos docuere nisus

venti paventem, mox in ovilia
demisit hostem vividus impetus,   10
   nunc in reluctantis dracones
     egit amor dapis atque pugnae;

qualemve laetis caprea pascuis
intenta fulvae matris ab ubere
   iam lacte depulsum leonem   15
     dente novo peritura vidit:

IV. This Ode is also good in parts like too many laureate efforts.

3, 4. **expertus...flavo** is a causal addendum; see on P. 53.

Iuppiter in Ganymede: the persons concerned are grouped together, but, this time, at the end. See on *Odes* I. 2. 17.

5. **olim** coming early is answered, it would seem, by *iam* (l. 7), *mox* (l. 9), and *nunc* (l. 11).

patrius (*p*) i.e. 'the race (and its vigour),' as if we had *patrum* preposited. Page well compares ll. 30, 31 below, where see my note on *patrum*. On the other hand *iuventas* is not a suitable word applied to a nestling, and Scaliger's objections will be partly met by taking *iuventas* and *vigor* as belonging to the parent bird; in that case *patrius* lies in ἀπὸ κοινοῦ position with both nouns (see on P. 33).

6. **laborum** (*ps*): for a preposited objective genitive see on P. 39. The separation from *inscium* is, perhaps, for the sake of improving the sound (see on P. 19, especially *ad fin.*).

7. **verni** (*ps*) merely equals *vere* 'in spring' (see on P. 31); or the subject lurks in *verni*, as if we had *ver...docuit* (see on *Odes* I. 15. 33).

8. **insolitos** (*ps*) echoes *inscium* of l. 6. See too P. 21.

9, 10. **paventem,** placed last, prepares us for the antithesis *hostem* (l. 10), and the idea of eagerness in *vividus* (*p*).

11. **reluctantis** (*p*): contrast 'the unresisting weakness' (Wickham) of the sheep.

13, 14. **laetis caprea pascuis | intenta:** for the grouping see on P. 17. But

videre Raeti bella sub Alpibus
Drusum gerentem Vindelici (quibus
   mos unde deductus per omne
    tempus Amazonia securi   20

dextras obarmet, quaerere distuli,
nec scire fas est omnia), sed diu
   lateque victrices catervae
    consiliis iuvenis revictae

sensere, quid mens rite, quid indoles   25
nutrita faustis sub penetralibus
   posset, quid Augusti paternus
    in pueros animus Nerones.

laetis caprea pascuis may be read first as 'the hind in lush pasture'; for the order see on *Odes* 4. 8. 33, and 3. 2. 32.

    intenta probably has stress (see on *Odes* 4. 9. 26); the hind is *busy eating* and suddenly looks up to see—death!

    14, 15. **fulvae** (*p*): the order has no point. Indeed it is hopeless to discover the true construction of these lines. See the manifold variety of the commentators.

    matris ab ubere: the order is paralleled by *Odes* 4. 6. 20; see too note on 3. 27. 12.

    iam lacte depulsum: this preposited group emphasizes the hungry condition of the young lion; he wants his mother and what she can give him (hence, perhaps, *matris* is preposited); but new instincts suggest that the *caprea* may form a satisfactory substitute.

    16. **novo:** (1) 'never used before,' from the lion's point of view (see on *Odes* 1. 31. 2); (2) 'dread,' 'awful,' from the hind's point of view (see the note on *novus* at *Odes* 1. 2. 6). Here, perhaps, the adjective has stress by being postposited.

    17, 18. **Raeti:** the separation of *Raeti* from *Vindelici* is meaningless and almost without parallel in the Odes and Epodes (see on *Odes* 4. 1. 10, 11). Is it possible that the Romans fancifully associated the root of *vindex* with *Vindelici*? If this were the case, the adjective thus separated would have ironical point. Others read *Raetis* (*ps*) i.e. 'in Raetia'; see on *Odes* 1. 31. 9. The subject too may be found in *Raetis* i.e. 'the Raeti' (see on *Odes* 1. 15. 33).

    18–22. **quibus...omnia:** this ridiculous parenthesis calls for little comment. If Horace wrote it, he shows to what depths a poet laureate can descend.

    20. **Amazonia** (*p*): our attention is drawn, by the order, to this epithet, but why we cannot tell. The scholiasts are, I suspect, just guessing.

    22–24. **diu | lateque victrices:** this group, being emphatic, is rightly preposited. The group *consiliis iuvenis revictae* forms a second epithet, and we have the type of *Odes* 1. 1. 2 *dulce decus meum* (see on P. 34).

fortes creantur fortibus et bonis;
est in iuvencis, est in equis patrum   30
  virtus, neque imbellem feroces
    progenerant aquilae columbam:
doctrina sed vim promovet insitam,
rectique cultus pectora roborant;
  utcumque defecere mores,   35
    indecorant bene nata culpae.

quid debeas, o Roma, Neronibus,
testis Metaurum flumen et Hasdrubal
  devictus et pulcher fugatis
    ille dies Latio tenebris,   40
qui primus alma risit adorea,
dirus per urbes Afer ut Italas
  ceu flamma per taedas vel Eurus
    per Siculas equitavit undas.

25. **sensere, quid**: there is no real pause after *sensere* and, therefore, no stress (see on *Odes* 4. 9. 26).

26. **faustis** (*ps*) i.e. 'blessed by heaven'; the word is religious, as Wickham points out, like *penetralibus*. The effect of the stress is as if one should say 'brought up in a *Christian* home.'

27. **posset** perhaps has emphasis; see on *Odes* 4. 9. 26.

27, 28. **Augusti**: the genitive placed early is logical subject, as if we had *Augustus paterno...animo* (see P. 38). The lines speak about the relations of Augustus with the Nerones; Augustus very properly comes first and the Nerones last. But both *Augusti* and *Nerones* may stand outside *paternus in pueros animus* on the principle mentioned at P. 48. We need not, therefore, regard *Nerones* as an emphatic addendum (P. 53).

30. **patrum** (*p*): one may almost say that this is logical subject (see on P. 38); in any case Horace is harping on the value of heredity. Compare the preposited *patrius* of l. 5 above.

31. **virtus** has stress (see on *Odes* 4. 9. 26); it prepares us for *doctrina* of l. 33.

31, 32. **imbellem...columbam**: for the grouping see on P. 8.

33. **doctrina** has stress because it precedes *sed*; contrast *virtus* l. 31. **insitam** (*s*) i.e. provided it is there to be drawn out. See too P. 21.

34. **recti** (*p*): contrast *pravi*.

35. **mores**: for its position see on *Odes* 1. 3. 16.

38. **Metaurum** (*p*) is said to be a quasi-adjective. Its position is natural enough; we remember 'Boyne,' 'Modder,' 'Marne,' and 'river' is of secondary importance.

39, 40. **pulcher fugatis...dies...tenebris**: for the grouping see on P. 9.

post hoc secundis usque laboribus   45
Romana pubes crevit, et impio
　　vastata Poenorum tumultu
　　　fana deos habuere rectos,

dixitque tandem perfidus Hannibal:
'cervi, luporum praeda rapacium,   50
　　sectamur ultro, quos opimus
　　　fallere et effugere est triumphus.

gens, quae cremato fortis ab Ilio
iactata Tuscis aequoribus sacra
　　natosque maturosque patres   55
　　　pertulit Ausonias ad urbes,

Latio may be dative of advantage with the whole group of words, or ablative with *fugatis*.

41–44. These lines are unsatisfactory. The order is continually strained. There are two ἅπαξ λεγόμενα, as far as Horace is concerned, viz. *adorea* and *ceu*. The *ut* of l. 42 is rare in meaning and ugly in position (but compare *ubi* of *Odes* 4. 5. 6).

41. **alma** (*ps*) is, perhaps, felt first with *risit*, as if 'which first with kindly smile of victory.' The adjective suits *dies* (compare *Odes* 4. 7. 7) as well as *adorea*. See too P. 21.

42. **dirus per urbes Afer**: the group must first be read as it stands i.e. 'The African dreaded throughout the cities.' But as *Afer* is substantival, the grouping may be that of P. 17. Perhaps the words *dirus per urbes Afer* precede *ut* to bring them near *adorea* i.e. 'victory and over dread Hannibal.' The antithetical juxtaposition of *Afer* and *Italas* is just.

44. **Siculas** (*ps*): see on P. 21.

45. **secundis usque laboribus**: for the position of the adverb compare Livy I. 21. 6 *duo deinceps reges* and *passim*.

46. **Romana** (*p*): contrast *Poena*.

46–48. **impio | vastata...tumultu | fana**: for the grouping see on P. 9.

impio...Poenorum tumultu: see on P. 46. But *impio* may be felt adverbially with *vastata*; see on P. 31, and compare *Odes* 3. 6. 7, and *Epod.* 16. 9 *impia perdemus*.

rectos goes with *habuere* i.e. 'have the gods upright on their pedestals.'

49. **tandem** (*pp*) is emphatic.

perfidus (*p*): the stock epithet (like the ritual epithet; see on *Odes* 1. 7. 5) is preposited. In English we insert the article and use a capital letter, making the epithet postposited e.g. Hannibal the Perfidious, Charles the Great etc.

50. **luporum** is well placed close to *cervi*. See also on P. 20 *a*.

51, 52. **ultro** (*pp*) has stress i.e. (in colloquial English) 'we have the impudence to attack....'

opimus (*ps*): to escape such a foe is a triumph and that the *highest*.

duris ut ilex tonsa bipennibus
nigrae feraci frondis in Algido,
   per damna, per caedes, ab ipso
      ducit opes animumque ferro.   60

non hydra secto corpore firmior
vinci dolentem crevit in Herculem,
   monstrumve submisere Colchi
      maius Echioniaeve Thebae.

merses profundo: pulchrior *exsilit*;   65
luctere: multa proruet integrum
   cum laude victorem geretque
      proelia coniugibus loquenda.

53. **cremato** (*ps*) **fortis** i.e. 'brave in spite of the burning (of Ilium)'; see on P. 26.

54. **iactata...sacra:** the familiar grouping of P. 10 suggests that *iactata* agrees with *sacra*; if it agrees with *gens*, *Tuscis* is preposited in contrast to *Ilio* (l. 53), and we may compare *Ausonias* (*p*) of l. 56. Possibly *iactata* is heard first with *gens,* then with *sacra.*

aequoribus: see on *Odes* I. 14. 9.

55. **maturos** (*p*) i.e. in spite of their age they were taken. In ancient warfare old men received scant attention when a retreat began.

56. **Ausonias** (*ps*) i.e. (carried them through) right to *Italy.* Compare on *Odes* I. 31. 9.

57. **duris...bipennibus:** for the grouping see on P. 15. The position of *ut* may be due to metrical convenience; but the *cruelty* to the oak (*duris ilex*) only makes it grow the more (see on P. 27). For the position of *ut* in comparison see on *Odes* I. 15. 29, and for words like *durus* preposited or separated see *Odes* 2. 14. 23.

58. **nigrae feraci frondis in Algido:** for the grouping see on P. 9. The order says 'mid darkness in plenty, leafage on Algidus.'

59, 60. **ab ipso:** the far separation results in great emphasis for *ferro.* We wait for the noun, expecting anything but *ferro.*

61. **non** = 'it is not the case that...'; see on *Odes* 2. 9. 13.

hydra secto corpore firmior: the grouping may be that of P. 18. But *secto* (*p*)...*firmior* may mean 'stronger with the cutting (of its body)'; see on P. 26. In fact *firmior* does double duty i.e. 'The Hydra, more strong with..., not more strongly grew....' See on *Odes* I. 23. 12.

62. **vinci dolentem** (*ps*): see on P. 21.

64. **maius** (*pps*) is predicative i.e. 'that was greater'; see too on *Odes* 4. 9. 26.

Echioniae (*p*): perhaps the position is on the analogy of preposited patronymic genitives; see P. 41, and on *Odes* I. 15. 22.

66, 67. **multa...victorem:** for the grouping see on P. 9.

Carthagini iam non ego nuntios
mittam superbos: occidit, occidit   70
   spes omnis et fortuna nostri
     nominis Hasdrubale interempto.'
nil Claudiae non perficient manus,
quas et benigno numine Iuppiter
   defendit et curae sagaces   75
     expediunt per acuta belli.

V.

Divis orte bonis, optume Romulae
custos gentis, abes iam nimium diu;
   maturum reditum pollicitus patrum
     sancto concilio, redi.

68. **coniugibus**: the commentators say 'wives' or 'widows.' But may not the picture be of husband and wife, at table or over the fire, talking about past campaigns (see Ovid *Her.* I. 30)? Just as *reges* can mean 'king and queen,' so *coniuges* can mean 'man and wife.'

69. **iam non** (*s*): the adverbial combination is emphatic.

ego is emphatic because inserted i.e. οὐκ ἔγωγε, whatever others may do.

70. **superbos** (*s*) i.e. *his* messengers can only be *tristes, trepidi.* See too P. 21.

71. **omnis** (*pp*) has emphasis. It is also in ἀπὸ κοινοῦ position with *spes* and *fortuna*.

nostri (*p*): contrast *Romani*.

72. **Hasdrubale interempto**: see on *Odes* 3. 1. 34. The clause is an emphatic addendum (see on P. 53), and stresses the extent of the disaster.

73. **Claudiae** (*ps*): the adjective amounts to 'the Claudii'; see on *Odes* I. 15. 33. For *manus* see *Odes* I. 3. 16.

74. **benigno** (*p*) i.e. 'by the kindness (of his will)'; see on P. 27.

75, 76. **defendit** may have some stress (see on *Odes* 4. 9. 26) in contrast to *expediunt*: Jupiter defends, skilful diligence extricates from peril. The sentiment is 'Thank God and the British Navy.'

V. 1, 2. **bonis** (*s*): contrast *iratis* or the like. Compare *Odes* I. I. I *atavis edite regibus*. For an intervening vocative see on *Odes* I. 5. 3. See too P. 24.

optume...gentis: for the grouping see P. 9.

iam nimium diu (*pp*): the adverbs are emphatic.

3, 4. **maturum** (*p*): contrast *tardum, serum*.

patrum (*p*) i.e. 'the fathers (in august council),' as if we had *patribus* (see on P. 38); hence the normal order *sancto patrum concilio* is abandoned (see on P. 43). The preposited *sanctus* is common with *senatus* e.g. Vergil *Aen.* I. 496.

> lucem redde tuae, dux bone, patriae: 5
> instar veris enim vultus ubi tuus
> affulsit populo, gratior it dies
>   et soles melius nitent.
>
> ut mater iuvenem, quem Notus invido
> flatu Carpathii trans maris aequora   10
> cunctantem spatio longius annuo
>   dulci distinet a domo,
>
> votis ominibusque et precibus vocat,
> curvo nec faciem litore dimovet:
> sic desideriis icta fidelibus   15
>   quaerit patria Caesarem.

5. **tuae** (*ps*) i.e. 'thy beloved'; see on *Odes* I. 26. 8, and also on *Odes* I. 5. 3.

dux bone: see on P. 36 *ad fin*. But *tuae dux bone patriae* might be classed under P. 15.

6. **ubi:** for its position compare *ut* of *Odes* 4. 4. 42; perhaps *tuus* gains some stress by separation.

7. **populo:** see on *Odes* I. 3. 16.

gratior is predicative with *it*.

9. **mater iuvenem:** note the case relations grouped together early (see on *Odes* I. 2. 17); the topic is 'mother and son.' See on l. 16 below.

invido (*p*): see on *Odes* 2. 14. 23; but the epithet may be felt equally with *Notus* (see on P. 52). The *Notus* would drive him north to the perilous seas of Crete and the Aegean, if, as Wickham says, 'he may be supposed to be in Egypt or Syria.'

10. **Carpathii** (*ps*): the position emphasizes the danger of this sea on the east of Crete. Compare on *Odes* I. I. 14.

maris (*p*): see on P. 42.

11. **spatio longius annuo:** this group is in ἀπὸ κοινοῦ position with *cunctantem* and *distinet*. If *spatio...annuo* be comparative ablative, compare for the order *Odes* 2. 20. 13 *Daedaleo ocior Icaro*, and see P. 24. But is it not possible to take *spatio...annuo* as ablative of measure of difference? If so, *annuo* has stress by separation and the sense is 'too long by the space of a *year*.' We may imagine him to have left in April, and now he cannot return till the following April. He ought to have been at home at the end of October. To his mother his absence is too long in any case; now it is too long by twelve months.

12. **dulci** (*ps*) i.e. 'the sweets (of home)'; see on P. 27 and P. 21.

14. **curvo** (*ps*) i.e. 'the curve (of the shore)'; see on P. 27. The picture of the *bay* and harbour is made vivid. Compare *curvo* (*p*) *litore porrecta* at *Epod*. 10. 21.

15. **desideriis icta fidelibus:** for the grouping see on P. 24.

tutus bos etenim rura perambulat,
nutrit rura Ceres almaque Faustitas,
pacatum volitant per mare navitae.
culpari metuit fides,   20

nullis polluitur casta domus stupris,
mos et lex maculosum edomuit nefas,
laudantur simili prole puerperae,
culpam poena premit comes.

quis Parthum paveat, quis gelidum Scythen,   25
quis Germania quos horrida parturit
fetus, incolumi Caesare? quis ferae
bellum curet Hiberiae?

condit quisque diem collibus in suis
et vitem viduas ducit ad arbores;   30
hinc ad vina redit laetus et alteris
te mensis adhibet deum;

16. **patria Caesarem:** note the order parallel to *mater iuvenem* of l. 9.

17. **tutus** (*p*) equals *tuto* (*s*); see on P. 31.

18. **alma** is in ἀπὸ κοινοῦ position with *Ceres* and *Faustitas*. See on P. 33.

19. **pacatum** (*ps*) i.e. 'because safe'; it serves to give the ground for the frequentative *volitant*. See too P. 21.

21. **nullis...casta domus stupris:** for the grouping see on P. 10. The adjective *nullis* also equals a strong negative, as so often in Cicero.

22. **maculosum** (*ps*) i.e. 'the stain (of sin)'; see on P. 27 and P. 21.

23. **simili** (*p*) i.e. 'for likeness (in offspring)'; see on P. 27 (especially *ad init.*).

24. **comes** is an emphatic addendum (see on P. 53); it sounds like a postposited adverb e.g. *extemplo, simul.*

25. **gelidum** (*p*) i.e. 'the chill (of the Scythian and his country)'; see on P. 27. In a Scythian campaign deaths from cold would be more frequent than deaths at the hands of the enemy.

26. **Germania:** a Roman who knew Greek would read this as if *Germaniam*; for the preceding *Scythen* is tantamount to *Scythiam.*

27, 28. **fetus** has stress (see on *Odes* 4. 9. 26). The word is invidious and suggests swarms of creatures rather than of men; so frequently is it used of beasts, fishes, birds etc. Compare *C.S.* 31.

incolumi Caesare is a corrective addendum (see on P. 53) i.e. 'provided Caesar be safe.' See on *Odes* 4. 4. 72.

ferae (*ps*) | **bellum...Hiberiae:** for the grouping see on P. 20 *a*. A Roman might feel the adjective with both *bellum* and *Hiberiae* (see on P. 52).

29. **suis** (*s*) has emphasis.

30. **viduas** (*ps*): the position has point. Peace has made possible again

te multa prece, te prosequitur mero
defuso pateris, et Laribus tuum
miscet numen, uti Graecia Castoris   35
et magni memor Herculis.

'longas o utinam, dux bone, ferias
praestes Hesperiae!' dicimus integro
sicci mane die, dicimus uvidi,
cum sol Oceano subest.   40

VI.

Dive, quem proles Niobea magnae
vindicem linguae Tityosque raptor
sensit et Troiae prope victor altae
Phthius Achilles,

the cultivation of the vine; trees (notably elms) on which the vine was supported
have been *viduae* too long. See also P. 21.

31. **alteris** (*ps*): the stress probably draws attention to the fact that the
farmer could now afford two courses. Libations were poured before the
mensae secundae.

32. **te...deum** i.e. 'thee as a god.'

34. **defuso pateris:** for the position of *pateris* see on P. 47.

tuum (*ps*) echoes *te...te* of l. 33. See too P. 21.

36. **magni** (*s*) has emphasis. See also P. 20 β.

37. **longas** (*s*) is far separated for emphasis.

dux bone: see on l. 5 above.

38. **Hesperiae:** for its position see *Odes* 1. 3. 16.

38, 39. **integro | sicci mane die:** the words *mane die* form a compound
meaning 'morning'; compare *Sat.* 2. 3. 290 *illo mane die* i.e. 'upon that
morn.' Here *integro* is preposited and separated because it gives the reason
for the *siccitas*. See also on P. 24.

VI. 1. **magnae | vindicem linguae:** for the grouping see on P. 20 a.
Probably there is stress on *magnae* (a *boastful* tongue is the point); compare
Odes 4. 5. 36 *magni memor Herculis*.

3. **sensit** has some stress (see on *Odes* 4. 9. 26) i.e. 'found to his cost'
(Gow); but see also on *Odes* 3. 17. 15.

Troiae...victor altae: for the grouping see on P. 20 a. There is stress on
Troiae.

altae (*s*) i.e. 'for all its high towers'; compare *Dardanas* l. 7 below.

4. **Phthius** (*p*): perhaps in artificial contrast to *Troiae*. But see *Odes*
1. 15. 22 *Pylium*.

5. **tibi** is brought outside *miles* and *impar* to emphasize the antithetical
ceteris.

6. **filius quamvis Thetidis:** the interposition of *quamvis* gives stress to

ceteris maior, tibi miles impar,   5
filius quamvis Thetidis marinae
Dardanas turris quateret tremenda
    cuspide pugnax.

ille, mordaci velut icta ferro
pinus aut impulsa cupressus Euro,   10
procidit late posuitque collum in
    pulvere Teucro.

ille non inclusus equo Minervae
sacra mentito male feriatos
Troas et laetam Priami choreis   15
    falleret aulam,

sed palam captis gravis, heu nefas heu,
nescios fari pueros Achivis
ureret flammis, etiam latentem
    matris in alvo,   20

both *filius* and *Thetidis*; he is son (not a distant descendant) and of a goddess. Compare on *Odes* 1. 8. 13, 14.

    7. **Dardanas** (*p*): their height and strength were famous; hence the order. Compare on *altae* (*s*) l. 3 above.

    tremenda (*p*): the word is a picturesque *ingenti* and therefore preposited. But see note on *Epod*. 6. 9. Perhaps the walls are imagined as shaking with terror of his spear; if so, see on P. 27.

    9. **mordaci** (*ps*) i.e. 'by the tooth (of the axe)'; see on P. 27, and also on P. 24.

    10. **Euro** stands outside *impulsa* and *pinus*; it may have stress in artificial contrast to *ferro*. See note on *Odes* 3. 17. 11.

    11. **late** (*pp*) has emphasis i.e. μέγας μεγαλωστί (see Page *ad loc.*).

    collum in: see on *Odes* 1. 35. 39.

    13, 14. **equo Minervae | sacra**: the genitive *Minervae* is ἀπὸ κοινοῦ with *equo* and *sacra*. The horse was the invention of Minerva (see Vergil *Aen.* 2. 17, and Euripides *Tro.* 10), and the pretended rites were in her honour.

    male feriatos (*p*) is quasi-proleptic i.e. would not have deceived them *into ill-timed revelry*. See on P. 30.

    15, 16. **laetam...aulam**: for the grouping with intrusive *falleret* see on P. 46 *a*. *Priami* comes early in contrast to *Troas*, the whole body of citizens.

    falleret is a conative impossible. Just as *fallebat* can mean 'he tried to deceive,' so *falleret* can mean 'he would not have been trying to deceive.' The imperfect subjunctive of an impossible hypothetical may have any sense of the imperfect. See Duff's note on Juvenal 4. 85.

    18, 19. **Achivis | ureret flammis**: see on P. 21.

ni tuis victus Venerisque gratae
vocibus divum pater adnuisset
rebus Aeneae potiore ductos
    alite muros.

doctor argutae fidicen Thaliae,   25
Phoebe, qui Xantho lavis amne crinis,
Dauniae defende decus Camenae,
    levis Agyieu.

spiritum Phoebus mihi, Phoebus artem
carminis nomenque dedit poetae.   30
virginum primae puerique claris
    patribus orti,

Deliae tutela deae, fugacis
lyncas et cervos cohibentis arcu,
Lesbium servate pedem meique   35
    pollicis ictum,

ureret, literally translated, equals 'would have been burning.' It represents a frequentative indicative 'he used to burn.' See on *falleret* l. 16.

20. **matris in alvo:** the whole is set before the part (as in Greek); compare *Odes* 4. 4. 14 *matris ab ubere,* and see note on 3. 27. 12.

21. **ni tuis victus** = 'unless thou hadst conquered'; the true subject lies in *tuis* (see *Odes* I. 15. 33). Moreover the preposited *tuis* prepares us for *Veneris* (*p*).

22. **divum** (*p*): the order emphasizes Jove's importance; *a fortiori* he is *hominum pater.*

23, 24. **potiore...muros:** for the grouping see on P. 9.

25. **doctor argutae fidicen Thaliae:** like *spectator, bellator, victor, auctor* etc., *doctor* may here be a quasi-adjective with *fidicen* i.e. 'master harpist'; the grouping is therefore that of P. 9.

26. **Xantho** is placed early to prepare us for the antithesis *Dauniae.*

27. **Dauniae** (*ps*): contrast the Muse of Greece and Asia Minor implied in *Xantho.*

28. **levis** (*p*): for preposited ritual epithets see on *Odes* I. 7. 5, and for preposited adjective with vocative see P. 36.

30. **poetae** (*s*) i.e. 'of a true *poet.*'

31. **virginum** (*p*): contrast *pueri.*
claris (*p*) echoes *primae.*

33. **Deliae tutela deae:** for the grouping see on P. 20 *a.*
fugacis (*p*) i.e. 'the flight (of lynxes)'; see on P. 27.

34. **arcu** possibly has stress (see on P. 53); contrast Orpheus and others who *cohibebant voce.*

rite Latonae puerum canentes,
rite crescentem face Noctilucam,
prosperam frugum celeremque pronos
    volvere menses.   40

nupta iam dices: 'ego dis amicum,
saeculo festas referente luces,
reddidi carmen docilis modorum
    vatis Horati.'

VII.

Diffugere nives, redeunt iam gramina campis
    arboribusque comae;
mutat terra vices et decrescentia ripas
    flumina praetereunt;
Gratia cum Nymphis geminisque sororibus audet   5
    ducere nuda choros.
immortalia ne speres, monet annus et almum
    quae rapit hora diem.

35, 36. **Lesbium** (*ps*) i.e. Greek metre but Latin words; but see too P. 21. **mei** (*p*): contrast Sappho's.

pollicis (*p*) i.e. 'my thumb (as it beats)'; see on P. 38.

37. **Latonae** (*p*): see on P. 41. Compare *Odes* I. 21. 2.

39. **pronos** (*ps*) is happily placed next to *celerem*; perhaps *pronos* is proleptic (see P. 30). See too P. 21.

41. **dis amicum** (*ps*) is predicative with *reddidi* i.e. 'I rendered the song acceptable' (see on P. 30).

42. **saeculo...luces:** for the grouping see on P. 14.

43. **carmen:** for its position see *Odes* I. 3. 16.

43, 44. **docilis...Horati** is a causal addendum (see P. 53) i.e. 'because I learned the music of the bard Horace.'

VII. 1, 2. **gramina campis | arboribusque comae:** note the chiasmus.

3. **decrescentia** (*ps*) i.e. 'because growing less.'

ripas: for its position see P. 50 *b*.

5. **geminis** (*p*) i.e. 'pair (of sisters)'; see on P. 27.

6. **nuda** goes with *ducere* i.e. 'she dares to lead in nakedness,' because the warmer weather is coming.

7, 8. **immortalia** precedes *ne* and has stress; to hope *modica* is sane enough.

almum | quae rapit hora diem: the words *quae rapit* are the equivalent of an adjective (as if *almi raax hora diei*), and the grouping is that of P. 10.

frigora mitescunt Zephyris, ver proterit aestas
  interitura, simul   10
pomifer autumnus fruges effuderit, et mox
  bruma recurrit iners.
damna tamen celeres reparant caelestia lunae:
  nos, ubi decidimus,
quo pius Aeneas, quo Tullus dives et Ancus,   15
  pulvis et umbra sumus.
quis scit an adiciant hodiernae crastina summae
  tempora di superi?
cuncta manus avidas fugient heredis, amico
  quae dederis animo.   20
cum semel occideris et de te splendida Minos
  fecerit arbitria,
non, Torquate, genus, non te facundia, non te
  restituet pietas:

9. **Zephyris:** for its position see on *Odes* 1. 3. 16.

10. **interitura** has stress (see on *Odes* 4. 9. 26) i.e. 'only to die.' See *Odes* 1. 28. 6.

11. **pomifer** i.e. 'the apple-bearing (of Autumn)'; see on P. 27.

12. **iners** goes with *recurrit* i.e. speeds back only to bring torpidity; compare *pigris* (*ps*) at *Odes* 1. 22. 17. The picture is, perhaps, of a runner falling inert from exhaustion.

13. **damna...lunae:** for the grouping see on P. 13.

14. **nos** is emphatic because inserted i.e. 'but we,' contrast *lunae*.

15. **quo pius** (*p*): *pius* seems to be a better reading than *pater*. The preposited *pius* has point, like the *dives* (*p*) of many MSS, i.e. 'whither Aeneas *for all his piety and patriotism*, and Tullus *despite his wealth*...' (compare *pudicum* of l. 25 below). If we read *Tullus dives, dives* may be ἀπὸ κοινοῦ with *Tullus* and *Ancus* (see too Juvenal 5. 57).

17, 18. **hodiernae...tempora:** for the grouping see on P. 9.

19, 20. **heredis** is out of place for emphasis (see on P. 44) i.e. everything will escape from the greedy hands of your *heir*; *he* will squander it in spite of all your saving.

amico (*ps*) should have emphasis. Why can it not mean 'in spite of your *kindliest intentions* in leaving your estate to him'? But see the editors.

animo: for its position see *Odes* 1. 3. 16.

21. **de te** is put early on purpose; it is the *argumentum ad hominem*. For the same reason *te* comes early twice in l. 23.

splendida (*ps*): the adjective colours both *Minos* and *arbitria* (see on P. 52); Minos in state will give stately decisions.

22. **arbitria:** for its position see *Odes* 1. 3. 16.

infernis neque enim tenebris Diana pudicum   25
    liberat Hippolytum,
nec Lethaea valet Theseus abrumpere caro
    vincula Pirithoo.

VIII.

Donarem pateras grataque commodus,
Censorine, meïs aera sodalibus.
donarem tripodas, praemia fortium
Graiorum, neque tu pessuma munerum
ferres, divite me scilicet artium,   5
quas aut Parrhasius protulit aut Scopas,
hic saxo, liquidis ille coloribus
sollers nunc hominem ponere, nunc deum.
sed non haec mihi vis, non tibi talium
res est aut animus deliciarum egens.   10

23. **te...te:** see on l. 21 above, and also on P. 51.

25. **infernis** (*ps*): 'of hell' is the point.

pudicum (*ps*): 'for all his purity.' Compare *pius* (*p*) and *dives* (*p*?) of l. 15. See too P. 21.

27, 28. **Lethaea...caro | vincula Pirithoo:** for the stress on *Lethaea* by separation compare *infernis* (*ps*) in l. 25, and for the grouping see P. 9.

VIII. 1. **pateras grataque commodus:** a Roman would read thus: 'cups and things pleasing because I am anxious to please (*commodus ὤν*)'; then in the next line *grata* is defined by *aera* i.e. 'even bronzes.' For the sentiment of *grata commodus* compare Ovid *Her.* 17. 71 *acceptissima semper | munera sunt, auctor quae pretiosa facit.* It is the opposite of 'Rich gifts wax poor when givers prove unkind.'

2. **meïs** (*ps*) i.e. 'my loved (comrades)'; see on *Odes* 1. 26. 8.

3. **fortium** (*p*) i.e. '(rewards) of bravery'; see on P. 27. The large number of rhymes in this doubtful Ode is surprising; note—*um* ll. 3, 4, 5, 8, 9, 25, 26, and—*ae* ll. 15, 16, 17.

4. **Graiorum** should have stress (see on *Odes* 4. 9. 26); perhaps the word 'Greeks' suggests Greek workmanship, and therefore objects of great artistic value.

5. **ferres** should have stress (see on *Odes* 4. 9. 26); its sense is 'carry off freely as your spoil.'

divite me scilicet i.e. 'if I, of all people in the world, were rich in...'; *scilicet* seems to be little more than δή, and to signify 'what a notion!'

7. **liquidis** (*ps*) is brought close to its antithesis *saxo*.

9, 10. **non haec** is predicative i.e. 'not in this direction lies my *vis*.'

talium res...deliciarum egens: for the grouping see on P. 17.

gaudes carminibus: carmina possumus
donare et pretium dicere muneri.
non incisa notis marmora publicis,
[per quae spiritus et vita redit bonis
post mortem ducibus, non celeres fugae   15
reiectaeque retrorsum Hannibalis minae,
non incendia Carthaginis impiae
eius, qui domita nomen ab Africa
lucratus rediit, clarius indicant
laudes, quam Calabrae Pierides; neque   20
si chartae sileant, quod bene feceris,
mercedem tuleris. quid foret Iliae
Mavortisque puer, si taciturnitas
obstaret meritis invida Romuli?
ereptum Stygiis fluctibus Aeacum   25
virtus et favor et lingua potentium
vatum divitibus consecrat insulis.]

11. **carminibus: carmina:** the words with point are set together.

13. **non** = 'it is not the case that...'; see on *Odes* 2. 9. 13.

incisa...publicis: for the grouping see on P. 17.

14. **bonis | post mortem ducibus:** in prose this could only mean 'generals who are good after death'; in poetry the pause at the end of the line saves us from this painful necessity (see P. 50 *b*). But few editors accept all the lines from 14 to 27.

15. **celeres** (*p*) i.e. 'the speed (of flight)'; see on P. 27.

18. **domita** (*ps*) i.e. 'the conquest (of Africa)'; see on P. 26.

20. **laudes:** there is no real pause after this word, but see on *Odes* 4. 9. 26.
Calabrae (*p*): the order enforces the antithesis of Latin *Calabrae* and Greek *Pierides*; it also reminds us that from the far away parts of Italy came a great poet.

22, 23. **Iliae | Mavortisque puer:** for the position of the genitives see on P. 41.

23, 24. **taciturnitas | ...meritis invida Romuli:** if we regard *Romuli* as the equivalent of *Romulis* (adjective), then the grouping is that of P. 16. But *invida Romuli* may be viewed as a causal addendum (see on P. 53) with *Romuli* an objective genitive. Probably *Romuli* is felt with both *meritis* and *invida*.

25. **Stygiis** (*p*) has stress i.e. 'from Hell itself.'

25, 26. **Aeacum | virtus...consecrat:** for the order see on P. 51.
potentium (*p*): the potency of the bard to bring eternal fame is the point.

27. **divitibus** (*ps*) has stress i.e. '(the islands) of the *Blest*'; compare *Epod.* 16. 42 *divites* (*ps*) *et insulas*. See too P. 21.

dignum laude virum Musa vetat mori.
caelo Musa beat: sic Iovis interest
optatis epulis impiger Hercules,   30
clarum Tyndaridae sidus ab infimis
quassas eripiunt aequoribus rates,
ornatus viridi tempora pampino
Liber vota bonos ducit ad exitus.

IX.

Ne forte credas interitura, quae
longe sonantem natus ad Aufidum
non ante vulgatas per artis
verba loquor socianda chordis.

non, si priores Maeonius tenet   5
sedes Homerus, Pindaricae latent
Ceaeque et Alcaei minaces
Stesichorique graves Camenae,

28. **dignum laude virum:** the phrase is placed early for emphasis i.e. 'It
s the man who deserves fame that the Muse....'

mori comes last with stress and anticipates *caelo*. Horace could have
scanned with *mori vetat*.

29. **caelo** comes early in contrast to *mori*.

Iovis (*ps*) ought to have emphasis, especially since its normal position is
between *optatis* and *epulis* (see on P. 43). Compare *Odes* 1. 28. 9 *et Iovis
arcanis*, and see on 4. 9. 6–8.

30. **impiger** (*p*) i.e. 'because he had shown himself strenuous.'

31, 32. **clarum Tyndaridae sidus:** for the position of *Tyndaridae* see on
Odes 3. 24. 42, and for the Tyndaridae *Odes* 1. 3. 2.

ab infimis...rates: for the grouping see on P. 7.

33. **viridi tempora pampino:** the temples are surrounded, in sense and
in order, by the greenery of the vine; compare *Odes* 3. 25. 20 *viridi tempora
pampino*, 4. 1. 32 *novis tempora floribus*. Add 1. 20. 1, 2 *modicis Sabinum |
cantharis*, 4. 4. 13 *laetis caprea pascuis*, 4. 12. 24 *plena dives ut in domo*,
Vergil *Aen.* 1. 52 *vasto rex Aeolus antro*; and compare on *Odes* 1. 1. 21,
1. 16. 11, 1. 16. 26, 27, 1. 37. 31, 32, 3. 2. 32, 3. 17. 10, and *Epod.* 5. 19.

34. **bonos** (*ps*) has emphasis; compare Livy *Pref.* 13 *cum bonis potius
ominibus...inciperemus.* See too P. 21.

IX. 2. **longe sonantem** (*ps*): for the order see on *Odes* 3. 30. 10.

3. **non ante vulgatas** (*ps*): the emphasis reminds Lollius that the *artis*
of the lyric bard were not generally known (*vulgatas*) until Horace unlocked
the secrets of Greek poetry.

4. **socianda chordis:** an emphatic addendum (see on P. 53) i.e. '(words)
to be sung to music.'

nec, siquid olim lusit Anacreon,
delevit aetas; spirat adhuc amor   10
    vivuntque commissi calores
        Aeoliae fidibus puellae.

non sola comptos arsit adulteri
crines et aurum vestibus illitum
    mirata regalisque cultus   15
        et comites Helene Lacaena,

primusve Teucer tela Cydonio
derexit arcu; non semel Ilios
    vexata; non pugnavit ingens
        Idomeneus Sthenelusve solus   20

5, 6. **non**='it is not the case that...'; see on *Odes* 2. 9. 13.

priores...Homerus: for the grouping see on P. 7.

6–8. **Pindaricae** (*ps*): contrast *Homerus*. The same contrast accounts for *Ceae* (*ps*), and for the position of the genitives *Alcaei* and *Stesichori* (see on P. 43). The normal order would, of course, be *minaces Alcaei* (*Camenae*) and *graves Stesichori Camenae*. The abnormal order stresses the antithetical genitives, and also the antithetical adjectives.

9. **Anacreon** comes last in contrast to the poets named above.

10. **adhuc** (*pp*) has stress.

11, 12. **vivunt** is placed early to echo *spirat adhuc*.

commissi (*p*): i.e. because entrusted, in trust to.

commissi calores...fidibus: for the position of *fidibus* see on P. 47.

Aeoliae fidibus puellae: for the grouping see on P. 20 a.

13, 14. **non sola**: note the emphasis; so *primus* (l. 17), *non semel* (l. 18), *solus* (l. 20), *primus* (l. 24).

comptos...crines: for the grouping, with intrusive *arsit*, see on P. 46 a. The order surely demands that *crines* be governed first by *arsit* and then by *mirata*.

15. **regalis** (*p*) i.e. 'the royalty (of his bearing and retinue)'; see on P. 27.

17. **Cydonio** (*ps*) i.e. 'Cretan.' The word implies, perhaps, the best possible bow, as we might speak of a Toledo dagger (see on *Odes* 1. 16. 9). Compare too P. 21.

18. **non semel**: doubtless *Ilios* may stand for any city, but it must be remembered that Troy, according to the myth, was twice destroyed (see *Aen.* 2. 642).

19. **vexata** should have stress; see on l. 26 below.

ingens: the position of this word with its air of mystery (see on *Odes* 1. 7. 32) makes vivid the picture of combats between the giant warriors of old.

21, 22. **ferox** (*p*)...**acer** (*p*): the fire of Hector and the boldness of Deiphobus are contrasted artificially.

gravis (*ps*) has stress. See too P. 21.

dicenda Musis proelia; non ferox
Hector vel acer Deiphobus gravis
    excepit ictus pro pudicis
        coniugibus puerisque primus.

vixere fortes ante Agamemnona   25
multi; sed omnes illacrimabiles
    urgentur ignotique longa
        nocte, carent quia vate sacro.

23, 24. **pro pudicis...primus**: an emphatic addendum (see P. 53).

pro pudicis (*p*) i.e. 'to save the purity (of wives)'; see on P. 27.

primus comes last to echo the *primus* of l. 17.

26. **multi** is emphatic for two reasons (1) because it is an addendum (see P. 53); (2) because it stands alone at the commencement of the line. This latter ground for emphasis is seen more or less convincingly in the following passages: *Odes* I. 1. 18, I. 1. 21 (?), I. 2. 30, I. 2. 49, I. 3. 12, I. 3. 16, I. 3. 23, I. 5. 11, I. 5. 12, I. 6. 2 (?), I. 7. 3 (?), I. 7. 4 (?), I. 7. 17, I. 8. 10, 11 (cp. *Sat.* I. 2. 114), I. 8. 15, I. 9. 2, I. 9. 11, I. 9. 15, I. 9. 18, I. 10. 18, I. 11. 6, I. 11. 8, I. 12. 14 (?), I. 12. 22 (?), I. 12. 23, I. 12. 27, I. 13. 11, I. 14. 2, I. 14. 3, I. 14. 9 (?), I. 14. 15, I. 15. 10, I. 15. 11, I. 15. 19, I. 15. 22, I. 15. 24 (?), I. 15. 25, I. 15. 27, I. 16. 18 (?), I. 16. 20, I. 17. 24, I. 18. 9, I. 20. 2, I. 24. 6, I. 25. 6 (?), I. 26. 6, I. 27. 14 (?), I. 28. 4, I. 28. 11, I. 29. 2, I. 31. 2, I. 31. 6, I. 31. 15, I. 33. 15, I. 34. 7, I. 34. 12, I. 35. 34, I. 35. 35, I. 35. 36 (?), I. 37. 12, I. 37. 16, I. 37. 20 (?), 2. 2. 10, 2. 2. 21, 2. 3. 4 (?), 2. 3. 11 (?), 2. 5. 2 (?), 2. 5. 9, 2. 6. 11 (?), 2. 8. 5, 2. 9. 4, 2. 9. 15, 2. 10. 6, 2. 10. 10 (?), 2. 10. 15 (?), 2. 10. 17, 2. 11. 4 (?), 2. 11. 10, 2. 11. 11, 2. 11. 22 (?), 2. 11. 23, 2. 12. 14, 2. 12. 26 (?), 2. 13. 8, 2. 13. 10, 2. 13. 18, 2. 13. 19, 2. 13. 35 (?), 2. 14. 11, 2. 14. 22, 2. 16. 18, 2. 17. 8, 2. 17. 18, 2. 18. 32, 2. 19. 7, 2. 19. 31 (?), 2. 20. 3, 2. 20. 4, 2. 20. 10, 2. 20. 11, 3. 1. 13 (?), 3. 2. 6, 3. 2. 26 (?), 3. 3. 35 (?), 3. 3. 43 (?), 3. 4. 6, 3. 4. 13, 3. 4. 46, 3. 4. 59 (?), 3. 4. 67, 3. 4. 70 (?), 3. 4. 79, 3. 5. 15 (?), 3. 5. 27, 3. 6. 11, 3. 7. 5, 3. 9. 6 (?), 3. 10. 7, 3. 10. 16, 3. 10. 17, 3. 11. 23, 3. 11. 51 (?), 3. 13. 4, 5 (?), 3. 14. 10, 3. 16. 7, 3. 16. 30, 3. 17. 3 (?), 3. 17. 10 (?), 3. 17. 12 (?), 3. 17. 15 (?), 3. 19. 11, 3. 19. 15, 3. 19. 22, 3. 20. 10 (?), 3. 21. 6, 3. 21. 10, 3. 23. 12 (?), 3. 24. 7, 3. 24. 11 (?), 3. 24. 20, 3. 24. 22, 3. 24. 50 (?), 3. 25. 2, 3. 25. 11 (?), 3. 26. 6, 3. 27. 2 (?), 3. 29. 26 (?), 3. 29. 54 (?), 3. 29. 59, 4. 1. 10 (?), 4. 1. 40, 4. 2. 14 (?), 4. 2. 22, 4. 2. 30, 4. 2. 34, 4. 2. 47, 4. 2. 55, 4. 3. 6, 4. 4. 27 (?), 4. 4. 31, 4. 4. 64, 4. 4. 75 (?), 4. 5. 27, 4. 6. 3 (?), 4. 7. 10, 4. 8. 4 (?), 4. 8. 5 (?), 4. 8. 20 (?), 4. 9. 19 (?), 4. 9. 28, 4. 9. 34, 4. 9. 43, 4. 11. 5, 4. 11. 14, 4. 11. 26, 4. 11. 34, 4. 13. 10, 4. 13. 11, 4. 14. 5, 4. 14. 43, 4. 15. 8 (?), *C. S.* 11 (?), 58 (?), 59 (?), 71 (?), *Epod.* 1. 32, 2. 55, 9. 18 (?), 13. 16, 17. 57.

27. **urgentur** is in ἀπὸ κοινοῦ position with *illacrimabiles* and *ignoti*.

longa: the pause at the end of the line makes the sentence drag out like the monotony of eternal night.

28. **nocte**: the stress on this word (see on l. 26) is most effective.

carent has emphasis by its position; see on *Odes* 4. 2. 26.

paulum sepultae distat inertiae
celata virtus. non ego te meis   30
    chartis inornatum silebo
       totve tuos patiar labores

impune, Lolli, carpere lividas
obliviones. est animus tibi
    rerumque prudens et secundis   35
       temporibus dubiisque rectus,

vindex avarae fraudis et abstinens
ducentis ad se cuncta pecuniae
    consulque non unius anni,
       sed quotiens bonus atque fidus   40

iudex honestum praetulit utili,
reiecit alto dona nocentium
    vultu, per obstantis catervas
       explicuit sua victor arma.

29. **paulum** (*s*) has stress.

sepultae distat inertiae: a Roman would read thus: 'Little *in the grave* doth differ from cowardice....' For the position of *sepultae* see P. 21 and P. 26.

30. **celata** (*p*) i.e. 'the concealment (of *virtus*)'; see on P. 26. The full sense is '*virtus*, if kept in the dark, differs little from cowardice, when coward and hero lie forgotten in the tomb.'

non ego te meis: note how pronouns and case-relations are grouped together (see on *Odes* 1. 2. 17); *meis* is preposited to echo *ego*, which is emphatic because inserted; compare *Odes* 4. 12. 22.

32. **tuos** (*ps*) is in artificial contrast to *meis* l. 30. See too P. 21.

33, 34. **impune** (*s*) has stress.

lividas (*p*) | **obliviones** i.e. 'the envy (envious tooth) of forgetfulness'; see on P. 27.

obliviones: for the stress of its position see l. 26 above; for the weight of the word see on *Odes* 3. 17. 3.

35, 36. **rerum:** for the position of the genitive see on P. 39.

secundis (*p*): contrast *dubiis*.

37. **avarae** i.e. 'the greed (of *fraus*)'; see on P. 27.

40, 41. **bonus atque fidus** sc. ὤν i.e. 'being good and faithful....'

honestum...utili: compare Tennyson *Ulysses* l. 39 '...through soft degrees| Subdue them to the useful and the good.'

42. **alto** (*ps*) equals an adverb 'loftily'; see P. 31.

43. **vultu** has stress (see l. 26 above); the sense is 'he rejects the offers with a *look*' i.e. words are unnecessary.

obstantis (*p*) i.e. 'the obstacle (formed by crowds)'; see P. 26, and compare *Odes* 3. 5. 51.

non possidentem multa vocaveris   45
recte beatum; rectius occupat
　　nomen beati, qui deorum
　　　muneribus sapienter uti

duramque callet pauperiem pati
peiusque leto flagitium timet,   50
　　non ille pro caris amicis
　　　aut patria timidus perire.

X.

O crudelis adhuc et Veneris muneribus potens,
insperata tuae cum veniet pluma superbiae
et, quae nunc umeris involitant, deciderint comae,
nunc et qui color est puniceae flore prior rosae,
mutatus, Ligurine, in faciem verterit hispidam,   5
dices 'heu,' quotiens te speculo videris alterum,
'quae mens est hodie, cur eadem non puero fuit,
vel cur his animis incolumes non redeunt genae?'

44. **sua victor arma**: the order is that of the normal *sua victoris arma*; but *sua* (*ps*) emphasizes the fact that he needs no extraneous aid.

45, 46. **non** = 'it is not the case that...'; see on *Odes* 2. 9. 13.
recte is felt, probably, with both *vocaveris* and *beatum*.

47. **deorum** (*p*): contrast *dona nocentium* of l. 42 above. The gifts of men are sought by the average man: the ideal man is satisfied with the gifts of God and uses these wisely.

49. **duram** (*ps*) i.e. 'the hardships (of poverty)'; see on P. 27, and on P. 21, P. 23. See further the note on *Odes* 2. 14. 23. The words *duram pauperiem* may be read first with *callet* (=learns the lesson of) and then with *pati*.

51. **pro caris** (*p*) i.e. 'for the love (of friends)'; see on P. 27, and compare *pro pudicis* l. 23 above.

X. 1. **adhuc** placed after *crudelis* has stress i.e. 'still,' 'in spite of everything.' It may also be, by position, ἀπὸ κοινοῦ with *potens*.

Veneris (*p*) i.e. the attractions of Ligurinus are sensual, not attractions of mind and soul.

2. **insperata...superbiae**: for the grouping see on P. 7.

3. **comae**: for its position see on *Odes* 1. 3. 16.

4. **puniceae flore...rosae**: for the grouping see on P. 20 a.

5, 6. **hispidam** (*s*): see on P. 21. The position has point: the change is from soft cheeks to bristliness; so *alterum* (*s*) has stress i.e. 'you see yourself—another man.'

7. **hodie** (*pp*): contrast *puero*.

8. **incolumes** goes with *non redeunt* i.e. 'come not back unmarred.' See too P. 21.

XI.

Est mihi nonum superantis annum
plenus Albani cadus; est in horto,
Phylli, nectendis apium coronis;
    est hederae vis

multa, qua crinis religata fulges;   5
ridet argento domus; ara castis
vincta verbenis avet immolato
    spargier agno;

cuncta festinat manus, hùc et illuc
cursitant mixtae pueris puellae;   10
sordidum flammae trepidant rotantes
    vertice fumum.

ut tamen noris, quibus advoceris
gaudiis: Idus tibi sunt agendae,
qui dies mensem Veneris marinae   15
    findit Aprilem,

iure sollemnis mihi sanctiorque
paene natali proprio, quod ex hac
luce Maecenas meus affluentis
    ordinat annos.   20

XI. 1. **nonum superantis annum**: see on P. 24. The separated *nonum* emphasizes the excellence of the wine. The group *nonum superantis annum* forms a compound adjective; hence the grouping from *nonum* to *cadus* is that of P. 9.

3. **nectendis** (*ps*) i.e. 'for the weaving (of garlands)'; see on P. 26.

4. **hederae** (*p*) i.e. 'there is ivy (in plenty)'; see on P. 38, and P. 35.

5. **multa** (*pp*) has emphasis; see also on *Odes* 4. 9. 26.

6, 7. **ara...verbenis**: for the grouping see on P. 14.

7, 8. **immolato** (*ps*) i.e. 'with the sacrifice (of a lamb)'; see P. 26 and 21. Compare *Odes* 1. 19. 16.

9. **cuncta** (*s*) i.e. 'the whole without exception'; see too P. 21.

11, 12. **sordidum flammae...fumum**: for the grouping see P. 15.

13, 14. **quibus...gaudiis**: for the separation see on *Odes* 1. 27. 11, 12, and compare *Odes* 4. 12. 21.

gaudiis has stress; see on *Odes* 4. 9. 26.

15, 16. **mensem...Aprilem**: for the grouping see on P. 46 *a*.

17. **iure** goes with the whole sentence; see on *Odes* 2. 9. 13.

19, 20. **affluentis** (*ps*) i.e. 'the increase (of years)'; see on P. 26 and P. 21.

Telephum, quem tu petis, occupavit
non tuae sortis iuvenem puella
dives et lasciva tenetque grata
  compede vinctum.

terret ambustus Phaethon avaras   25
spes, et exemplum grave praebet ales
Pegasus terrenum équitem gravatus
  Bellerophontem,

semper ut te digna sequare et ultra
quam licet sperare nefas putando   30
disparem vites. age iam, meorum
  finis amorum

(non enim posthac alia calebo
femina), condisce modos, amanda
voce quos reddas: minuentur atrae   35
  carmine curae.

21. **Telephum:** the order tells the new topic at once i.e. 'as for Telephus.'

22. **tuae** (*p*) has stress i.e. 'not of *your* (sort).'

23. **grata** (*p*): the order heightens the oxymoron: a fetter that *pleases*. See on *Epod.* 5. 82.

25. **ambustus** (*p*) i.e. 'the burning up (of Phaethon)'; see on P. 26.

avaras (*p*) i.e. 'the covetousness (of hopes)'; see on P. 27.

26. **spes:** a monosyllable in such a position must have intentional stress; see on *Odes* 4. 9. 26, and compare in l. 30 below *ultra | quam licet sperare nefas putando.*

26, 27. **ales** (*p*): in contrast to *terrenum* (*p*). The creature of air resents the creature of earth.

29. **semper** has stress (1) because it is separated from *sequare*; (2) because it precedes *ut*.

31, 32. **meorum | finis amorum:** for the grouping see P. 20 *a*. It is possible that *meorum* (*ps*) may mean 'my darling (loves)'; see on *Odes* 1. 26. 8.

33. **alia** (*ps*): see on P. 21.

34. **femina** must have emphasis (1) by separation, (2) by position (see on *Odes* 4. 9. 26). One antithesis is, I fear, that of *Odes* 4. 1. 29.

amanda (*p*) i.e. 'that *deserves* love.'

35. **voce** has stress because it precedes *quos reddas*; the stress prepares us for *carmine* of l. 36.

atrae (*ps*) i.e. 'the blackness (of cares)'; see on P. 27, and compare on *Odes* 2. 14. 23. The pause at *atrae* saves us from grouping *atrae carmine curae* together (see on P. 50 *b*).

XII.

Iam veris comites, quae mare temperant,
impellunt animae lintea Thraciae;
iam nec prata rigent, nec fluvii strepunt
　　hiberna nive turgidi.

nidum ponit, Ityn flebiliter gemens,　　　　　　　5
infelix avis et Cecropiae domus
aeternum opprobrium, quod male͜barbaras
　　regum est ulta libidines.

dicunt in tenero gramine pinguium
custodes ovium carmina fistula　　　　　　　　10
delectantque deum, cui pecus et nigri
　　colles Arcadiae placent.

adduxere sitim tempora, Vergili;
sed pressum Calibus ducere Liberum
si gestis, iuvenum nobilium cliens,　　　　　　15
　　nardo vina merebere.

XII. 1. **veris** is preposited because it indicates the topic of the stanza. Compare too *hiberna* (*p*) of l. 4.

2. **Thraciae** (*s*) i.e. 'from Thrace' i.e. (see Gow) 'from the West.' See on *Odes* 1. 31. 9.

4. **hiberna nive turgidi**: the group is a causal addendum (see P. 53). **hiberna** (*p*): contrast *veris* (*p*) of l. 1.

6. **infelix** (*p*) echoes *flebiliter*. **Cecropiae domus**: these words precede *aeternum opprobrium* with point. The crime was almost as much a disgrace to Procne's side of the family as to Thracian Tereus. See too P. 43.

7, 8. **aeternum** (*p*) has stress i.e. 'for ever and for ever.' Compare on *Odes* 2. 1. 15. **male** might be read first with *barbaras*, and then later, emphasized by separation, with *est ulta*. **barbaras...libidines**: for the grouping and intrusive verb see on P. 46 *a*.

9, 10. **tenero** (*p*)...**pinguium** (*ps*): the preposited adjectives heighten the picture of soft grass and fat sheep. **pinguium | custodes ovium**: for the grouping see on P. 20 *a*.

11, 12. **nigri | colles Arcadiae**: for the order see on P. 35. The stress on *nigri* (*p*) may signify 'the shadow (of trees on the hills)'; see on P. 27. There is a reading *nigrae colles Arcadiae* (see P. 20 *a*); this *nigrae* would assuredly be 'corrected' to agree with *colles*.

14. **pressum...Liberum**: for the order with intrusive *ducere* see on P. 46 *a*. But *pressum Calibus* deserves stress. The wine was a famous one, and the sense is 'if it is champagne you are wanting.'

nardi parvus onyx eliciet cadum,
qui nunc Sulpiciis accubat horreis,
spes donare novas largus amaraque
    curarum eluere efficax.   20

ad quae si properas gaudia, cum tua
velox merce veni: non ego te meis
immunem meditor tinguere poculis,
    plena dives ut in domo.

verum pone moras et studium lucri,   25
nigrorumque memor, dum licet, ignium
misce stultitiam consiliis brevem:
    dulce est desipere in loco.

XIII.

Audivere, Lyce, di mea vota, di
audivere, Lyce: fis anus, et tamen
    vis formosa videri,
        ludisque et bibis impudens

15. **iuvenum nobilium** (*p*): the stress lies on the young nobility with its luxury and extravagance.

17. **nardi** is placed outside *parvus onyx* (see on P. 43) to pick up *nardo* of the preceding line. Horace harps on the word: nard, nard is wanted, if you want a dinner.

cadum: for its position see on *Odes* 1. 3. 16.

18. **Sulpiciis** (*ps*): see on P. 21, and P. 37. Horace also suggests that he does not keep such fine stuff *in suis horreis*.

19. **spes donare novas:** see on P. 21.

novas i.e. 'never existing before.' The adjective is usually preposited; here therefore, being postposited and separated, it has some emphasis; see on *Odes* 1. 2. 6.

21. **gaudia:** for its position compare on *Odes* 4. 11. 14.

tua (*ps*) i.e. come with *your* side of the bargain; contrast *meis* (*ps*) of the next line.

22, 23. **non ego te meis:** compare on *Odes* 4. 9. 30, and on *Odes* 1. 2. 17.

immunem (*s*) has the stress of warning i.e. 'if you come giftless.'

24. **plena dives ut in domo:** for the rich man set, in sense and position, within his well-stored home, see on *Odes* 4. 8. 33 and 3. 2. 32. For the position of *ut* see on *Odes* 1. 15. 29. The juxtaposition of *plena* and *dives* is picturesque: I am no bloated millionaire in my home.

26. **nigrorum** (*ps*) i.e. the blackness, literal and tropical (of funeral torches and fires); see on P. 27, and *Epod.* 5. 82.

27. **brevem** (*s*) i.e. 'though brief,' 'however brief.' See too P. 50 *c*.

28. **in loco** (*pp*) has stress and equals ἐν καιρῷ γε. See also P. 53.

et cantu tremulo pota Cupidinem   5
lentum sollicitas. ille virentis et
    doctae psallere Chiae
      pulchris excubat in genis.

importunus enim transvolat aridas
quercus et refugit te quia luridi   10
    dentes te quia rugae
      turpant et capitis nives.

nec Coae referunt iam tibi purpurae
nec clari lapides tempora, quae semel
    notis condita fastis   15
      inclusit volucris dies.

XIII. 1. **mea** (*p*): whatever they have done in the case of other people.

6, 7. **virentis...Chiae:** this genitive group comes early as if it were the object of some verb for which the reader waits (see on P. 38). One may read it thus: 'He (loves) fresh beauty, skill on the lyre; he loves Chia and keeps watch on her fair cheeks.'

virentis (*p*) i.e. 'the freshness, fresh beauty (of Chia)'; see on P. 27.

8. **pulchris** (*ps*): see on P. 21. The adjective is causal i.e. 'because they are fair.'

9. **aridas** (*p*) i.e. 'the dryness (of oaks)'; see on P. 27.

10. **quercus** should have stress (see on *Odes* 4. 9. 26). The word comes as a paraprosdokian; we are half expecting *anus*; we find a gnarled oak, the symbol of longevity.

te has emphasis because it follows *refugit*; it is also object of *turpant*.

luridi (*p*) i.e. 'the dirtiness (of teeth)'; see on P. 27.

11. **dentes:** if a comma is put after this word (instead of after *te*) there is offensive stress (see on *Odes* 4. 9. 26). The dirty teeth stick out, as it were.

te, emphatic because preceding *quia*, unpleasantly echoes *te* of l. 10. See too P. 51.

12. **capitis** (*p*): as if we had *in capite*. Horace travels up the face; first those awful teeth, then the wrinkled face and brow, and then the *head* and white hair.

13. **Coae** (*ps*) i.e. not even *Coan* purple (the very best) and its transparent material.

iam (*pp*) i.e. it is too late, too late!

14. **clari** (*p*) i.e. 'the flash (of stones)'; see on P. 27. The reading *cari* will be concessive 'though costly.'

semel (*s*) i.e. 'once for all,' said with stress.

15. **notis** (*ps*): every one knows your age. See P. 24.

quo fugit venus, heu, quove color? decens
quo motus? quid habes illius, illius,
   quae spirabat amores,
      quae me surpuerat mihi,   20

felix post Cinaram notaque *dotium*
gratarum facies? sed Cinarae brevis
   annos fata dederunt,
      servatura diu parem

cornicis vetulae temporibus Lycen,   25
possent ut iuvenes visere fervidi
   multo non sine risu
      dilapsam in cineres facem.

XIV.

Quae cura patrum quaeve Quiritium
plenis honorum muneribus tuas,
   Auguste, virtutes in aevum
      per titulos memoresque fastus

16. **volucris** (*p*) i.e. 'the swift flight (of time)'; see on P. 27.

17, 18. **decens** is probably felt with both *color* and *motus*; if it goes with the latter only, then, being preposited, it means 'the grace (of movement)'; see on P. 27.

21, 22. **nota...facies:** *dotium* is Palmer's emendation of *et artium*, in which the *et* seems to mean 'also.' The question whether *felix* agrees with *Lyce* or *facies* is beyond settlement. If we read *facie* (*facies* may be due to dittography) one awkwardness disappears.

   brevis (*p*): contrast *diu* (*pp*) of l. 24.

24. **servatura** is concessive, 'though they were going to preserve.'

25. **cornicis** (*p*) i.e. 'like the crow (with his long life)'; see on P. 38.

26. **possent ut:** perhaps the position of *possent* sounds like 'only to enable young men....' But see on *Odes* I. 37. 20. Horace could have written *ut possent* and made the line scan.

   fervidi (*s*): contrast 'the cold, burnt-out torch' (Wickham).

27. **multo** (*s*) has emphasis and equals *plurimo*.

XIV. This is another laureate Ode. There is no caesura at l. 17 (compare *Odes* I. 37. 14—another laureate performance); and in l. 41 no one can honestly pause after *non*.

2. **tuas** (*ps*) i.e. *thy* praises, whatever may be said of others. For the intervening vocative see on *Odes* I. 5. 3.

4. **memores** goes with both *titulos* and *fastus*; see on P. 33.

aeternet, o qua sol habitabilis   5
illustrat oras, maxime principum?
    quem legis expertes Latinae
        Vindelici didicere nuper,

quid Marte posses, milite nam tuo
Drusus Genaunos, implacidum genus,   10
    Breunosque velocis et arces
        Alpibus impositas tremendis

deiecit acer plus vice simplici.
maior Neronum mox grave proelium
    commisit immanisque Raetos   15
        auspiciis pepulit secundis,

spectandus in certamine Martio,
devota morti pectora liberae
    quantis fatigaret ruinis,
        indomitas prope qualis undas   20

5. **aeternet** has stress (see on *Odes* 4. 9. 26) and draws attention to the
pleonasm of *in aevum aeternare*.

habitabilis (*ps*) i.e. wherever there are *inhabitants*, Augustus is known.
See too P. 21.

7. **legis expertes Latinae**: for the grouping see on P. 24 *ad fin.* But as
expertes=inscii, we may regard *legis* as objective genitive (see P. 39 and
compare *Odes* 3. 11. 11); in that case *Latinae* (*s*) has stress in contrast to
barbarae.

8. **nuper** (*pp*) i.e. '*only* of late.'

9. **milite nam**: for *nam*, second, see on *Epod.* 14. 6.

10, 11. **implacidum genus**, | **Breunosque velocis**: note the chiasmus.

11, 12. **tremendis**: for its position see on P. 48. Compare too the grouping
of P. 16 *a*, and see on *Epod.* 6. 9.

13. **acer** and **plus vice simplici** are emphatic addenda. See on P. 53.

14. **grave** (*p*): contrast *leve proelium.*

15. **commisit** is tied closely with the subsequent words by *que*; contrast
on *Odes* 4. 9. 26.

15, 16. **immanis** (*p*) echoes *grave* (*p*) of l. 14, and anticipates the contrast *secundis* (*s*); a *formidable* enemy is *successfully* dealt with. But see
also on *Odes* 2. 14. 23.

secundis (*s*): contrast *infaustis*; see too on P. 21.

18. **devota...liberae**: for the grouping see on P. 48, and P. 17. Compare
l. 12 above. The line is object of *fatigaret* and precedes *quantis* in order to
enhance, by stress, the victory of Tiberius over a courageous foe.

19. **quantis**: for its separation from *ruinis* see on *Odes* 1. 27. 11.

exercet Auster Pleiadum choro
scindente nubes, impiger hostium
    vexare turmas et frementem
      mittere equum medios per ignes.

sic tauriformis volvitur Aufidus,   25
qui regna Dauni praefluit Apuli,
    cum saevit horrendamque cultis,
      diluviem meditatur agris,

ut barbarorum Claudius agmina
ferrata vasto diruit impetu,   30
    primosque et extremos metendo
      stravit humum, sine clade victor,

te copias, te consilium et tuos
praebente divos. nam tibi, quo die
    portus Alexandrea supplex   35
      et vacuam patefecit aulam,

20. **indomitas** (*ps*) has emphasis.

prope: 'objection has been justly taken to *prope* as prosaic' (Gow). Shelley is no less guilty when he writes 'I love waves, and winds, and storms | Everything almost | Which is Nature's'; and 'Bird thou never wert, | That from heaven, or near it....'

21, 22. **Pleiadum** (*p*) **choro:** the Pleiades are more important than the descriptive *choro*; see on P. 38. For *Pleiadum choro scindente* see on P. 35.

nubes: for its position see on P. 47, and compare *Odes* 3. 14. 15 (a laureate effort).

22, 23. **hostium** (*ps*)...**turmas** i.e. 'the enemy in squadrons'; see on P. 38.

23, 24. **frementem** goes with *mittere* i.e. 'send snorting'; see too P. 21.

medios (*ps*) i.e. 'right through.'

25. **tauriformis** (*ps*): see P. 21. It is practically an adverbial phrase; see on P. 31.

26. **Apuli** (*s*): as if we had 'in Apulia'; see on *Odes* 1. 31. 9, and on P. 21.

27, 28. **horrendam...agris:** for the grouping see on P. 9.

29, 30. **barbarorum** (*ps*)...**agmina** i.e. 'barbarians in their hordes'; see on P. 38.

barbarorum...agmina | ferrata: for the grouping see on P. 35.

vasto (*ps*) has stress; see on P. 21.

32. **sine clade victor:** an emphatic addendum (see P. 53).

33. **tuos** (*ps*) i.e. 'gods that were thine'; the battles were fought *tuis* (*p*), *non eorum auspiciis*. See too P. 21.

fortuna lustro prospera tertio
belli secundos reddidit exitus,
    laudemque et optatum peractis
        imperiis decus arrogavit.   40

te Cantaber non ante domabilis
Medusque et Indus, te profugus Scythes
    miratur, o tutela praesens
        Italiae dominaeque Romae.

te fontium qui celat origines   45
Nilusque et Hister, te rapidus Tigris,
    te beluosus qui remotis
        obstrepit Oceanus Britannis,

36. **vacuam** goes with *patefecit* i.e. 'left empty and open.' See too P. 30 and P. 21.

37. **fortuna...tertio**: for the grouping see on P. 16 *a*.

38. **belli** seems to be in ἀπὸ κοινοῦ position with *fortuna, lustro,* and *exitus.* If it goes with *exitus* only, the order is abnormal (see on P. 43).

secundos goes with *reddidit* i.e. 'rendered prosperous'; see on P. 30 and P. 21.

39, 40. **optatum peractis | imperiis decus**: the grouping may be that of P. 10, in which case editors are justified in taking *peractis imperiis* as dative with *arrogavit* (see on *C. S.* 27, 28). But what prevents us from taking *peractis imperiis* with the words between which they lie? Thus *optatum... decus* may mean 'the glory longed for when campaigns are ended.' This glory fortune has claimed for her favourite i.e. *tibi* (l. 34), which goes with both *reddidit* and *arrogavit.*

42. **profugus** (*ps*): contrast *non ante domabilis* of l. 41. Compare *Odes* I. 35. 9 *te Dacus asper, te profugi Scythae,* where *profugi* (*p*) is contrasted with *asper.*

43, 44. **miratur** should be emphatic (see on *Odes* 4. 9. 26); it amounts to *veneratur.*

tutela praesens | Italiae: for the grouping see on P. 44.

44. **dominae** may be ἀπὸ κοινοῦ with *Italiae* and *Romae*; see on P. 33.

45-48. **fontium** (*ps*): the important word is *fontium,* and is felt as object (see on P. 38). The characteristics of the rivers, ocean, and peoples are stressed; the Nile is interesting for its source (*fontium* precedes the relative), the Tigris for its speed (*rapidus,* preposited), the ocean for its monsters (*beluosus,* preposited and separated), the Britons for their distance from Rome (*remotis* preposited and separated).

47, 48. **beluosus...Britannis**: for the grouping see on P. 7.

49. **non paventis funera Galliae...tellus**: the preposited genitive phrase s practically subject; see on P. 38. Bentley reads *paventes.*

te non paventis funera Galliae
duraeque tellus audit Hiberiae,   50
    te caede gaudentes Sygambri
    compositis venerantur armis.

XV.

Phoebus volentem proelia me loqui
victas et urbes increpuit lyra,
    ne parva Tyrrhenum per aequor
    vela darem. tua, Caesar, aetas

fruges et agris rettulit uberes   5
et signa nostro restituit Iovi
    derepta Parthorum superbis
    postibus et vacuum duellis

50. **durae** (*ps*) i.e. 'for all its hardiness and endurance'; but see also P. 20 *a*.

51. **caede gaudentes** is a quasi-compound αἱματοχαρής, αἱματοχαρμής (see on *Odes* 3. 1. 24). It is preposited because concessive, 'though delighting in blood.'

52. **compositis** (*ps*) i.e. 'by the laying to rest laying down (of arms)'; see on P. 26, and P. 21.

XV. 1. **proelia me**: the normal order would be *me proelia*; both words therefore have stress, and their juxtaposition is significant (see on *Odes* 1. 2. 17) i.e. 'battles! me!' as if Phoebus said '*quid tibi cum proeliis?*'

2. **victas** (*ps*) i.e. 'the sacking (of cities)'; see on P. 26.

lyra goes, of course, with *increpuit*. See on *Odes* 1. 3. 16.

3, 4. **parva...vela**: for the grouping see on P. 10.

tua (*ps*) i.e. 'it is thy lifetime that has....' For the intervening vocative (*Caesar*) see *Odes* 1. 5. 3.

5. **et** is out of place *metri gratia*, unless we read *agros*.

uberes goes with *rettulit* i.e. 'has brought back in richness'; compare *Odes* 4. 14. 38.

6. **nostro** (*ps*): perhaps as Wickham says 'opposed to the foreign gods, in whose temples they have been hanging hitherto.' The possessive might mean 'our beloved' (see on *Odes* 1. 26. 8). Compare too P. 21.

7, 8. **Parthorum** (*ps*): 'snatched from the Parthians' is the effect; 'Parthians' is more important than what follows; hence the order, for which see P. 38, and P. 43. Compare on *Odes* 4. 14. 21.

8. **postibus**: the position seems to have no point (see on *Odes* 4. 9. 26). The pause, however, is very slight.

8, 9. **vacuum duellis | Ianum Quirini**: the words *Ianum Quirini* form a quasi-compound; but in any case the second complement may stand outside *vacuum* and *Ianum* (see on P. 48).

Ianum Quirini clausit et ordinem
rectum evaganti frena licentiae   10
    iniecit emovitque culpas
       et veteres revocavit artes,

per quas Latinum nomen et Italae
crevere vires famaque et imperi
    porrecta maiestas ad ortus   15
       solis ab Hesperio cubili.

custode rerum Caesare non furor
civilis aut vis exiget otium,
    non ira, quae procudit enses
       et miseras inimicat urbes.   20

non qui profundum Danuvium bibunt
edicta rumpent Iulia, non Getae,
    non Seres infidive Persae,
       non Tanain prope flumen orti.

9, 10. **ordinem | rectum evaganti**: this group is preposited and separated because the sense is causal. The word *licentia* has originally no bad connotation; it is the noun of *licet* and means properly 'freedom to do what is open to one'; but freedom too often degenerates into licence, and hence comes its bad meaning. The sense therefore is 'he checked with reins *licentia*, because it went beyond due limits.'

12. **veteres** may be in ἀπὸ κοινοῦ position with *culpas* and *artes*; see on P. 33. If it goes with *artes* only, compare P. 21.

13. **Latinum** (*p*): in artificial contrast to *Italae*.

13, 14. **Italae | crevere vires**: see on P. 21.

14, 15. **imperi** is in ἀπὸ κοινοῦ position with *fama* and *maiestas*; hence it stands outside *porrecta* and *maiestas* (see on P. 43). Somewhat similar is the position of *Iovis* at *C. S.* 32.

16. **Hesperio** (*p*): contrast *ortus solis*.

18. **civilis** perhaps qualifies both *furor* and *vis*.
otium: for its position see on *Odes* I. 3. 16; so *enses* l. 19.

20. **miseras** (*ps*) i.e. 'to their misery'; see on P. 30, and also on P. 21.

21. **profundum** (*p*) is picturesque for *magnum* and is therefore preposited, like all adjectives of number and quantity.

22. **Iulia** (*s*) i.e. whatever other statutes they may break. See too P. 21.

23. **infidi** (*p*) i.e. despite their faithlessness in general. Compare too P. 33.

24. **Tanain prope flumen**: compare on *Odes* 4. 1. 19.

25. **profestis** (*p*): contrast *sacris*.

26. **iocosi munera Liberi**: for the grouping see on P. 20 *a*.

nosque et profestis lucibus et sacris   25
  inter iocosi munera Liberi,
    cum prole matronisque nostris
      rite deos prius adprecati,

virtute functos more patrum duces
Lydis remixto carmine tibiis   30
    Troiamque et Anchisen et almae
      progeniem Veneris canemus.

28. **rite** (*s*) perhaps has stress; but Horace may have wished to keep two adverbs apart.

29. **virtute functos more patrum duces:** certain editors say that *more patrum* goes with *canemus*. If this is true, then *any* order will do for poetry, and no deductions from order are possible. What is wrong with 'leaders who have done their duty as their fathers did before them'? We have two complements, *virtute* and *more patrum*; the former stands outside *functos* and *duces* (see on P. 48).

30. **Lydis...tibiis:** for the grouping see on P. 10.

31, 32. **almae | progeniem Veneris:** for the grouping see on P. 20 β.

CARMEN SAECULARE

Phoebe silvarumque potens Diana,
lucidum caeli decus, o colendi
semper et culti, date quae precamur
    tempore sacro,

quo Sibyllini monuere versus   5
virgines lectas puerosque castos
dis, quibus septem placuere colles,
    dicere carmen.

alme Sol, curru nitido diem qui
promis et celas, aliusque et idem   10
nasceris, possis nihil urbe Roma
    visere maius!

rite maturos aperire partus
lenis, Ilithyia, tuere matres,
sive tu Lucina probas vocari   15
    seu Genitalis:

   1. **silvarum** (*p*): see on P. 39, and compare *Odes* 1. 6. 10 *lyrae Musa potens*.

   3. **semper** lies in ἀπὸ κοινοῦ position with *colendi* and *culti*.

   5. **Sibyllini** (*ps*): see on P. 21.

   7. **septem** (*s*): see on P. 21.

   8. **carmen:** for its position see *Odes* 1. 3. 16.

   9, 10. **alme** (*p*): see on P. 36.

   qui | promis et celas: the relative clause is placed in the position of the equivalent *promens et celans*.

   11. **nasceris:** the position seems to have no point (see on *Odes* 4. 9. 26).

   12. **maius** has stress because placed last and separated from *nihil*.

   13. **rite:** for its position see on *Odes* 2. 9. 13.

   maturos (*ps*) i.e. 'only when ready for birth.' See too P. 21.

   17. **patrum** (*ps*): there is a stress of innuendo on 'fathers'; the patricians had not been true to their name : childlessness among them had been notorious.

diva, producas subolem patrumque
prosperes decreta super iugandis
feminis prolisque novae feraci
    lege marita,   20

certus undenos deciens per annos
orbis ut cantus referatque ludos,
ter die claro totiensque grata
    nocte frequentis.

vosque veraces cecinisse, Parcae,   25
quod semel † dictum stabilis per aevum
Terminus servet, bona iam peractis
    iungite fata.

fertilis frugum pecorisque tellus
spicea donet Cererem corona;   30
nutriant fetus et aquae salubres
    et Iovis aurae.

condito mitis placidusque telo
supplices audi pueros, Apollo;
siderum regina bicornis, audi,   35
    Luna, puellas.

18. **iugandis** (*p*) i.e. 'the marriage (of women)'; see on P. 26.

19, 20. **prolis** (*p*): see on P. 39 for the objective genitive placed in front.
novae (*pp*) probably has stress, since it is usually preposited.
feraci | lege marita: for the adjectives on either side of the noun see on
P. 34.

  21, 22. **certus...orbis** i.e. 'an unbroken cycle.' The phrase precedes *ut*
because it contains the idea connecting this stanza with the previous one:
Rome must have children to preserve the cycle unbroken.

  undenos deciens per annos: note the adverb (*deciens*) between adjective
and noun, as so often in Livy.

  referatque: see on *Odes* I. 30. 6.

  23. **die claro** (i.e. hot)...**grata** (i.e. cool) **nocte**: note the chiasmus.

  27, 28. **bona iam peractis | iungite fata**: if we feel *fatis* with *peractis*, the
grouping is that of P. 10. The construction here is easier than at *Odes*
4. 14. 39, 40. To make the passages parallel we should have *fatis* inserted
after *peractis*, and *fata* preceding *iungite*. But a Roman could probably read
the words thus: 'good things to past things join as our fate.'

  30. **spicea** (*ps*) i.e. 'with wheat-ears (for crown)'; see on P. 27 (*ad init.*).

  32. **Iovis** is by position ἀπὸ κοινοῦ with *aquae* and *aurae*. See on *Odes*
4. 15. 14, 15.

Roma si vestrum est opus Iliaeque
litus Etruscum tenuere turmae,
iussa pars mutare lares et urbem
    sospite cursu,   40

cui per ardentem sine fraude Troiam
castus Aeneas patriae superstes
liberum munivit iter, daturus
    plura relictis:

di, probos mores docili iuventae,   45
di, senectuti placidae quietem,
Romulae genti date remque prolemque
    et decus omne;

quaeque vos bobus veneratur albis
clarus Anchisae Venerisque sanguis,   50
impetret, bellante prior, iacentem
    lenis in hostem.

33. **condito mitis...telo**: see on *Odes* 1. 10. 14.

34. **supplices** (*ps*) i.e. 'the prayers (of boys)'; see on P. 27, and P. 21.
pueros comes last in contrast to *puellas* of l. 36.

35. **siderum regina bicornis**: see on P. 35. The preposited *siderum* enforces the contrast *Apollo*, the god of day.

37. **Roma** precedes *si* in contrast to *Ilium* contained in *Iliae* (*ps*).
vestrum (*ps*) has emphasis i.e. '*your* work.'

38. **turmae**: for its position see on *Odes* 1. 3. 16.

39. **iussa** (*p*) i.e. *non sine divom numine*; not *ultro*.

40. **sospite** (*p*) has stress; they were *safe* because 'under divine safeguard' (Wickham).

41. **sine fraude** must go with *ardentem* and *Troiam* i.e. 'burning without hurt (to Aeneas).' See *Odes* 2. 19. 20.

42. **castus** (*p*) has stress because Aeneas is thus 'under the protection of the goddess of chastity' (Wickham). The Dido episode comes later!

43, 44. **liberum** is predicative with *munivit*, for this verb is little more than *fecit* or *reddidit*. See too P. 21.
daturus plura relictis: an emphatic addendum (see on P. 53).

45. **probos** (*p*) i.e. 'probity (of character)'; contrast *malos*. See on P. 27.
docili (*p*): contrast *indocili*; 'give teachableness to the young' is part of the prayer. See P. 27.

47. **Romulae** (*p*) i.e. 'of Romulus'; he is now one of themselves; they should support a member of the Union.

48. **omne** (*pp*) has emphasis i.e. 'every possible,' 'all manner of.'

iam mari terraque manus potentis
Medus Albanasque timet securis,
iam Scythae responsa petunt, superbi   55
    nuper, et Indi.

iam Fides et Pax et Honor Pudorque
priscus et neglecta redire Virtus
audet, apparetque beata pleno
    Copia cornu.   60

augur et fulgente decorus arcu
Phoebus acceptusque novem Camenis,
qui salutari levat arte fessos
    corporis artus,

si Palatinas videt aequus aras,   65
remque Romanam Latiumque felix
alterum in lustrum meliusque semper
    prorogat aevum.

quaeque Aventinum tenet Algidumque
quindecim Diana preces virorum   70
curat et votis puerorum amicas
    applicat auris.

49. **albis** (*s*): the position perhaps stresses their choiceness ; but see too P. 21.

51. **iacentem** (*ps*): contrast *bellante*.

54. **Albanas** (*ps*): this antiquarian reference emphasizes the long life of Rome's greatness. See too P. 21.

56. **nuper** (*pp*) i.e. 'but yesterday.'

58. **priscus** perhaps has the stress of regret (see on *Odes* 4. 9. 26), like *neglecta* (*ps*).

58–60. **redire Virtus | audet, apparetque...Copia:** note the chiasmus ; *audet* may have stress (see on *Odes* 4. 9. 26).

beata...cornu: for the grouping see on P. 9.

61, 62. **fulgente...Phoebus:** for the grouping see on P. 9. See also P. 24 (*ad init.*).

63. **salutari** (*ps*): the epithet stresses his aspect as *healer* in contrast to *archer*. See too P. 21.

65. **Palatinas** (*ps*) i.e. 'on the Palatine'; see note on *Odes* 1. 31. 9.

aequus goes closely with *videt* i.e. 'beholds with favour.'

67. **alterum** (*ps*) i.e. 'to a *second* period.'

melius (*ps*) is proleptic ; see on P. 30.

69. **tenet** lies in ἀπὸ κοινοῦ position between *Aventinum* and *Algidum*.

haec Iovem sentire deosque cunctos
spem bonam certamque domum reporto,
doctus et Phoebi chorus et Dianae   75
          dicere laudes.

70. **quindecim** (*s*): see on *Odes* 4. 1. 10, 11.

71. **curat:** there should be stress; see on *Odes* 4. 9. 26.

amicas (*ps*) i.e. 'ears that are *friendly.*' Compare Livy 34. 5. 13 *superbas* (*ps*), *me dius fidius, aures habemus*, and *malas* at *Epod.* 3. 6, 7. See too P. 21.

73. **cunctos** (*pp*) has stress.

75, 76. **Phoebi** is set in front of *chorus* in artificial contrast to *Dianae.* The genitives go with both *chorus* and *laudes.*

EPODES

I.

Ibis Liburnis inter alta navium,
    amice, propugnacula,
paratus omne Caesaris periculum
    subire, Maecenas, tuo.
quid nos, quibus te vita si superstite   5
    iucunda, si contra, gravis?
utrumne iussi persequemur otium,
    non dulce, ni tecum simul,
an hunc laborem, mente laturi, decet
    qua ferre non mollis viros?   10
feremus, et te vel per Alpium iuga
    inhospitalem et Caucasum,
vel Occidentis usque ad ultimum sinum
    forti sequemur pectore.

I. 5, 6. **quibus te vita si superstite|iucunda**: this piece of obscure brevity (if the reading be correct) stands for *quibus vita, si te superstite vivitur, iucunda est.*

    te vita...superstite iucunda may, perhaps, be grouped under P. 16 a.

    7. **otium**: for its position see on *Odes* 1. 3. 16.

    8. **tecum simul**: compare Cicero *Pro Arch.* 11. 28 *vobiscum simul.*

    9, 10. **decet qua**: for the order see on *Odes* 4. 2. 26. Perhaps *decet* has stress.

    non mollis (*p*): the litotes makes *non mollis* emphatic; see on P. 29.

    11, 12. **Alpium** (*p*): see on P. 42. Horace may wish to stress the dangers of the *Alps.*

    inhospitalem (*p*) i.e. 'the perils (of the Caucasus)'; see on P. 27. Compare too *Odes* 1. 22. 6, and the note on *Odes* 2. 14. 23.

    13. **Occidentis** is a pendent genitive (see on P. 40) i.e. 'or as for the West—to the very end of it.'

    ultimum (*p*): superlative adjectives, especially of place, naturally tend to come first; compare *in summo monte, sub imo colle, ab extrema parte* etc.

    14. **forti** (*ps*) i.e. 'with courage (of heart)'; see on P. 27 and P. 21.

roges, tuum laborem quid iuvem meo,　　　　　　15
　　imbellis ac firmus parum?
comes minore sum futurus in metu,
　　qui maior absentis habet:
ut assidens implumibus pullis avis
　　serpentium allapsus timet　　　　　　　　　20
magis relictis, non, ut adsit, auxili
　　latura plus praesentibus.
libenter hoc et omne militabitur
　　bellum in tuae spem gratiae,
non ut iuvencis illigata pluribus　　　　　　　25
　　aratra nitantur meis,
pecusve Calabris ante sidus fervidum
　　Lucana mutet pascuis,

15. **tuum** (*p*) **laborem**: contrast *meo* alone at the end of the line. If we read *labore*, then *meo* has stress by separation in contrast to *tuum* alone at the beginning of the clause.

16. **parum** (*pp*) is emphatic.

17. **minore** (*s*): the position prepares us for *maior* of the next line.

19. **assidens...avis**: for the grouping compare on P. 10.

implumibus (*p*) i.e. 'because featherless.'

20. **serpentium** (*p*) i.e. 'snakes (and their approach)'; see on P. 38.

21, 22. **magis relictis** is an addendum (see on P. 53) i.e. 'but more when she has left them'; the position of the words prepares us for the antithesis *praesentibus*.

auxili (*ps*): see on P. 38, and especially on *Odes* 1. 2. 1. Prose would have *plus latura auxili* ordinarily.

plus (*pps*) has stress.

23. **libenter** first and separated from *militabitur* has stress; compare *satis superque* l. 31 below.

omne (*s*) has emphasis. See also P. 21.

24. **tuae spem gratiae**: for the grouping see on P. 20 *a*.

25. **pluribus** (*pps*) has emphasis, for comparatives are usually preposited (see P. 28), and so are adjectives of quantity. But see too P. 24.

26. **meis** (*s*) has great stress, the oxen are *mine*, not the property of a landlord or the result of borrowing. Compare *proprio, patrios* at *Odes* 1. 1. 9, 1. 1. 11, and *suis* at *Epod*. 2. 3. There is a reading *mea*, for which see on P. 21.

27. **Calabris** (*ps*) prepares us for the antithesis *Lucana*. It probably is read as 'in Calabria' (see on *Odes* 1. 31. 9).

28. **pascuis**: there is a variant *pascua* (see on P. 21) which would give stress to *Lucana* in contrast to *Calabris*.

29. **superni villa candens Tusculi**: for the grouping see on P. 15. Surely

nec ut superni villa candens Tusculi
    Circaea tangat moenia.   30
satis superque me benignitas tua
    ditavit: haud paravero,
quod aut avarus ut Chremes terra premam,
    discinctus aut perdam ut nepos.

II.

'Beatus ille, qui procul negotiis,
    ut prisca gens mortalium,
paterna rura bobus exercet suis,
    solutus omni faenore,
neque excitatur classico miles truci,   5
    nec horret iratum mare,

superni...Tusculi must go with *villa* first, though later with *moenia* also.
For the quasi-locative genitive *superni...Tusculi* compare Livy 1. 31. 3
vocem...ex summi cacuminis luco.

30. **Circaea** (*ps*): see on P. 21.

31. **satis superque**: for the emphasis by separation compare on *libenter*
l. 23.

me precedes the abstract subject; see on P. 51.

32. **ditavit** has stress (see on *Odes* 4. 9. 26): Maecenas has not merely
helped Horace; he has made him a rich man, rich, that is, in the eyes of
Horace.

33, 34. **avarus** sc. ὤν agreeing with *ego* understood; the same is true of
discinctus; both epithets are felt again with *Chremes* and *nepos* respectively.
Compare Ovid *Her.* 12. 26 *quam pater est illi, tam mihi dives erat,* for *quam
pater dives est illi, tam mihi pater dives erat.* See too on *Epod.* 5. 27, and
6. 16.

34. **discinctus** precedes *aut* to enforce the antithesis *avarus*.

II. 2. **prisca gens mortalium**: for the grouping see on P. 35, but *gens
mortalium* is a mere compound for *homines* (compare *ramis arborum* in l. 56),
and *prisca* then has some stress, 'the good old' (see on *Odes* 3. 9. 17) in
contrast to *haec nova gens.*

3. **paterna** (*p*): he is no newcomer, no returned soldier put on the land;
these fields belonged to his fathers.

suis (*s*): see on *Epod.* 1. 26, and *Odes* 1. 1. 9, 1. 1. 11. Compare too on
P. 21.

4. **solutus...faenore** is a causal addendum explaining *suis* of l. 3. See on
P. 53.

5. **truci**: perhaps the separated adjective is read as if *ad truculentiam*
with *excitatur*; in any case it colours *miles* as well as *classico* (see on P. 52).

6. **iratum** (*p*) i.e. 'the anger (of the sea)'; see on P. 27.

> forumque vitat et superba civium
> potentiorum limina.
> ergo aut adulta vitium propagine
> altas maritat populos,   10
> aut in reducta valle mugientium
> prospectat errantis greges,
> inutilisve falce ramos amputans
> feliciores inserit,
> aut pressa puris mella condit amphoris,   15
> aut tondet infirmas ovis;
> vel cum decorum mitibus pomis caput
> Autumnus agris extulit,
> ut gaudet insitiva decerpens pira,
> certantem et uvam purpurae,   20
> qua muneretur te, Priape, et te, pater
> Silvane, tutor finium.
> libet iacere modo sub antiqua ilice,
> modo in tenaci gramine:

10. **altas** (*ps*) has point; the vines, as Wickham says, 'are now grown large enough to clamber a tree which would have been too tall for them before.' See too P. 21.

11, 12. **reducta** (*p*) i.e. 'in the depths (of the valley)'; see on P. 26.

mugientium (*ps*): the order is as if we had *mugitus prospectat* (*exaudit*) *errantium gregum*. It is the *mugitus* that makes him look. He looks and descries the wanderers. Thus both *mugientium* and *errantis* are the important parts of the picture, and normal order (*errantis mugientium greges*) is forsaken. For *mugientium* (*ps*) see on P. 38, and, for the grouping, P. 43.

13. **inutilis** (*ps*) i.e. 'because useless'; contrast too *feliciores*. The result is an awkward position of *falce*; see on P. 50 *d*.

15. **pressa...amphoris**: for the grouping see on P. 9.

16. **infirmas** (*p*) **ovis** almost equals *infirmitatem ovium* (see on P. 27), just as *tarditatem Lepidi* means 'the slow Lepidus'; but *infirmas* is also causal: only because sheep are unresisting can they be shorn. Compare *Epist.* I. 16. 14 *infirmo capiti...utilis* i.e. 'useful for weakness in the head.'

17. **decorum mitibus pomis caput**: for the grouping see on P. 10. But *mitibus* (*p*) may be intentional; contrast 'unripe.' The order is then normal (see on *Odes* I. 7. 29).

19. **insitiva** (*ps*): the owner feels an additional pleasure in pears which he has *artificially* produced. See also P. 21.

20. **purpurae** probably has stress by its position outside *certantem* and *uvam*; but see P. 47 and P. 49. Compare too on l. 60 below.

23. **antiqua** (*p*): age implies shade and charm.

labuntur altis interim ripis aquae,   25
    queruntur in silvis aves,
fontesque lymphis obstrepunt manantibus,
    somnos quod invitet levis.
at cum tonantis annus hibernus Iovis
    imbres nivesque comparat,   30
aut trudit acris hinc et hinc multa cane
    apros in obstantis plagas,
aut amite levi rara tendit retia
    turdis edacibus dolos,

    24. **tenaci** (*p*) i.e. 'the thickness, deep-rootedness (of the grass)'; see on P. 27.

    25. **altis interim ripis** (v. l. *rivis*): the context seems decisively in favour of *ripis*. We are talking of summer (contrast l. 29) and therefore the stream is low and the banks are deep. The adverb ought to go, by position, with *altis* and *ripis* i.e. 'between banks that are for a while steep,' i.e. during the summer months. Horace has *interim* elsewhere once only viz. *Odes* 3. 20. 9, where it bears its ordinary sense *interea*. Quintilian is quoted as using *interim* = 'for a while,' and we may be permitted to assume this meaning here. For the position of the adverb compare Livy 1. 19. 4, 1. 21. 6 and *passim*. If *interim* is taken with *labuntur* i.e. 'while one sleeps,' the order is very abnormal (see P. 50 *e*).

    27. **fontes** (Markland *frondes*): whichever we read, the stress on *manantibus* remains i.e. 'the fountains murmur with *flowing* (not *ruentibus*) waters,' or 'the leaves rustle in chorus with the *flowing* waters.' If the waters did more than *manare*, the leaves would not be heard, and one could hardly sleep.

    28. **levis** (*s*): contrast *gravis* (heavy and unhealthy). Compare *Odes* 2. 16. 15.

    29. **tonantis...Iovis:** for the grouping see on P. 15.

    31. **acris** is proleptic with *trudit* i.e. 'drives into wildness'; like our colloquial 'drives him wild.' See on P. 30.

    32. **obstantis** (*p*) i.e. 'into the obstacle (formed by nets).' See on *Odes* 3. 5. 51 and P. 26.

    33. **amite:** as we do not know the quantity of the *a*, we do not know, with certainty, the quantity of the *e* in *levi*.

    rara (*ps*): see on P. 21. The meaning of *rara* is doubtful. Wickham says 'wide-meshed,' a sense which would suit a net for catching boars and deer, but hardly a net for catching thrushes. Perhaps the word means no more than 'full of holes' (compare Ovid *Met*. 12. 437 *rari sub pondere cribri*), and has grown into a stock epithet of nets. See Conington on *Aen*. 4. 131. One would expect *rara* to mean 'fine-meshed' in contrast to the *densae plagae* for catching deer (see *Odes* 3. 5. 31, 32).

pavidumque leporem et advenam laqueo gruem   35
    iucunda captat praemia.
quis non malarum, quas amor curas habet,
    haec inter obliviscitur?
quodsi pudica mulier in partem iuvet
    domum atque dulcis liberos,   40
Sabina qualis aut perusta solibus
    pernicis uxor Apuli,
sacrum vetustis extruat lignis focum
    lassi sub adventum viri,
claudensque textis cratibus laetum pecus   45
    distenta siccet ubera,
et horna dulci vina promens dolio
    dapes inemptas apparet:
non me Lucrina iuverint conchylia
    magisve rhombus aut scari,·   50

35. **pavidum** (*p*) i.e. in spite of its powers of flight which are inspired by fear.

advenam: lit. 'and a stranger in his net—even a crane—he takes....' The order makes *gruem* interesting ; for according to Pliny (10. 23. 31 § 61) the *grues* are *aestatis advenae*. The hunter would not expect to find a *grus* in the winter.

36. **iucunda** (*ps*) goes closely with *captat*, as if we had *iucunde* ; see on P. 31, and P. 21.

37. **quas amor curas**: see on *Odes* I. 27. 11.

38. **haec inter**: the order gives *haec* some stress ; compare l. 61 below.

39. **pudica** (*p*): the suggested antithesis is the *amor* of l. 37, 'with its follies and fancies' (Wickham).

40. **domum atque dulcis liberos**: the words form one idea, 'Home.' **dulcis** colours both nouns; see on P. 33.

41. **Sabina** precedes *qualis* in artificial contrast to *Apuli* of l. 42.

42. **pernicis uxor Apuli**: for the grouping see on P. 20 β. The adjective *pernicis* has point; contrast the *supinus* idler of the city, and compare the *lassi* (*ps*) *viri* of l. 44.

43. **sacrum...focum**: for the grouping see on P. 8.

44. **lassi sub adventum viri**: see on P. 20 a, and compare l. 42.

45. **textis** i.e. 'a prison (of hurdles)'; see on P. 26.

laetum (*p*): the epithet has point; the beasts are glad to be in such a prison, because they wish to be milked and to rest without fear of wolves.

46. **distenta** (*ps*) is causal. See too P. 21.

47. **horna...dolio**: for the grouping see on P. 9.

49. **me** comes early with emphasis ; contrast the luxurious man-about-town.

siquos Eois intonata fluctibus
    hiems ad hoc vertat mare.
non Afra avis descendat in ventrem meum,
    non attagen Ionicus
iucundior, quam lecta de pinguissimis   55
    oliva ramis arborum,
aut herba lapathi prata amantis et gravi
    malvae salubres corpori,
vel agna festis caesa Terminalibus,
    vel haedus ereptus lupo.   60
has inter epulas ut iuvat pastas ovis
    videre properantis domum,
videre fessos vomerem inversum boves
    collo trahentis languido,
positosque vernas, ditis examen domus,   65
    circum renidentis Lares.'

Lucrina (*ps*): these oysters were the most celebrated. See too P. 21.

51, 52. Eois...hiems: for the grouping see on P. 9.

ad hoc vertat mare: see on P. 21.

53. Afra (*p*): this is the normal position in referring to the guinea-fowl ; it is *par excellence* the *African* bird. Compare Juvenal *Sat.* 11. 142, and our 'turkey.'

55, 56. iucundior is equal to an adverb ; see on P. 31. For the stress compare on *Odes* 4. 9. 26.

lecta...ramis: for the grouping see on P. 9.

ramis arborum is practically one word, like our 'tree-trunks.' Compare on l. 2 above.

57, 58. gravi...corpori: for the grouping see on P. 15.

59. agna...Terminalibus: for the grouping see on P. 14.

60. lupo: for its position outside *haedus* and *ereptus* see on P. 47.

61. has (*s*) has stress i.e. 'mid feasts like *these*.' Compare *haec inter* l. 38 above.

pastas (*p*) is causal. Their well-fed condition is the cause of the owner's pleasure, and of the haste of the sheep.

63. fessos...boves: for the grouping see on P. 15. The juxtaposition of *fessos* and *vomerem* is happy, as if we had *fessos vomere*.

64. languido (*s*) echoes *fessos* above. See too P. 24.

65. positos (*p*) i.e. 'the settling (of the slaves)'; see on P. 26.

ditis (*ps*): contrast *pauperis*; but see also on P. 20 β.

66. renidentis (*p*) i.e. 'the glow (of the fire on the images)'; see on P. 27.

haec ubi locutus faenerator Alfius,
    iam iam futurus rusticus,
omnem redegit Idibus pecuniam,
    quaerit Kalendis ponere.   70

III.

Parentis olim siquis impia manu
    senile guttur fregerit,
edit cicutis alium nocentius.
    o dura messorum ilia!
quid hoc veneni saevit in praecordiis?   5
    num viperinus his cruor
incoctus herbis me fefellit, an malas
    Canidia tractavit dapes?
ut Argonautas praeter omnis candidum
    Medea mirata est ducem,   10
ignota tauris illigaturum iuga
    perunxit hoc Iasonem,
hoc delibutis ulta donis paelicem
    serpente fugit alite.

69. **omnem** (*s*) has emphasis i.e. 'every single farthing of....'

III. 1, 2. **Parentis** (*ps*)...**impia** (*p*)...**senile** (*p*): the horror of the crime is brought out by the order; it is a crime against a *father* (see too P. 43), the hand therefore is *impia* (see too on *Odes* 2. 14. 23), the victim is old and cannot protect himself.

olim, by its emphatic position, almost equals *umquam*; the horror is nearly unthinkable.

3. **cicutis** is emphatic; it should lie between *alium* and *nocentius*. See on P. 49.

6, 7. **viperinus his cruor | incoctus herbis:** as *incoctus* is merely an elongation of the preposition *in*, the grouping is that noted at P. 9.

malas (*ps*) i.e. '(a feast) that is poisonous'; compare *C. S.* 71, and note on *Odes* 2. 14. 23.

9. **omnis** (*pps*) has stress.

candidum (*ps*) i.e. 'the fair complexion (of their leader)'; see on P. 27, and compare *Odes* 2. 4. 3 *niveo*.

11. **ignota...iuga:** for the grouping, with *illigaturum* intrusive see on P. 46. The participle *illigaturum* is causal; hence its separation from *Iasonem*. No doubt *tauris* is dative with both *ignota* and *illigaturum*.

13. **hoc** goes closely with *delibutis* (*ps*) i.e. 'thus anointed were the gifts with which....' Compare *Epod.* 5. 74 *multa fleturum*.

nec tantus umquam siderum insedit vapor   15
  siticulosae Apuliae,
nec munus umeris efficacis Herculis
  inarsit aestuosius.
at si quid umquam tale concupiveris,
  iocose Maecenas, precor   20
manum puella savio opponat tuo,
  extrema et in sponda cubet.

IV.

Lupis et agnis quanta sortito obtigit,
  tecum mihi discordia est,
Hibericis peruste funibus latus
  et crura dura compede.
licet superbus ambules pecunia,   5
  fortuna non mutat genus.
videsne, sacram metiente te viam
  cum bis trium ulnarum toga,

delibutis ulta donis: see on P. 24.

14. **alite** (*s*): see on P. 21. The effect is to heighten the miracle of this *serpens*.

15. **tantus...siderum insedit vapor:** for the grouping, with *insedit* intrusive see P. 46 *a*.

umquam is close to *tantus*, since it qualifies it. Compare *quid umquam* l. 19 below.

16. **siticulosae** (*p*) is proleptic; see on P. 30.

17. **efficacis** (*p*): see on *Odes* 1. 7. 5; but the implication is 'in spite of his great achievements.'

19. **umquam:** compare *tantus umquam* l. 15 above.

20. **iocose** (*p*): see on P. 36.

21. **tuo** (*s*): perhaps the force is 'even your'; but see too P. 21.

22. **extrema** (*ps*) i.e. 'at the very end (of the *sponda*).' See on P. 27.

IV. 3, 4. **Hibericis** (*ps*): see P. 24. Perhaps there is stress on the adjective implying a Spanish *provenance* for the person attacked.

funibus latus | et crura...compede: note the chiastic arrangement.

4. **dura** (*p*) i.e. 'the galling (of the chain)'; see on P. 27, and compare the note at *Odes* 2. 14. 23.

5. **pecunia** comes last with stress; contrast *nobilitate*.

6. **genus,** perhaps, has emphasis by position; but see on *Odes* 1. 3. 16.

7. **sacram metiente te viam:** for the grouping see on P. 10. But there is point in emphasizing *sacram*, for the man is a pollution to its sanctity. See also on *Odes* 4. 1. 10, 11.

ut ora vertat huc et huc euntium
    liberrima indignatio?   10
'sectus flagellis hic triumviralibus
    praeconis ad fastidium
arat Falerni mille fundi iugera
    et Appiam mannis terit
sedilibusque magnus in primis eques   15
    Othone contempto sedet.
quid attinet tot ora navium gravi
    rostrata duci pondere
contra latrones atque servilem manum,
    hoc, hoc tribuno militum?'   20

V.

'At o deorum quicquid in caelo regit
    terras et humanum genus,

8. **trium ulnarum:** for the position of the genitive see on P. 42.

9, 10. **huc et huc** may be ἀπὸ κοινοῦ with *vertat* and *euntium*; but it is more natural to take *huc et huc* with *euntium*. The group *huc et huc euntium* is then ἀπὸ κοινοῦ with *ora* and *liberrima indignatio*; hence it may stand outside these last two words (see on P. 43, and P. 49 with note there inserted on *Odes* 1. 2. 23).

11. **triumviralibus** (*s*): the stress reminds us that he was flogged as a *slave* by the *triumviri capitales*.

praeconis (*ps*) i.e. till even the *praeco* was tired of it; much more the flagellator. The *praeco* was said to go on proclaiming the culprit's offences.

13. **Falerni...iugera:** for the grouping see on P. 9.

15. **sedilibus...eques:** for the grouping see on P. 14.

17, 18. **ora...gravi | rostrata...pondere:** for the grouping see on P. 14. But *gravi* colours both *navium* and *pondere* (see on P. 52).

tot ora navium...rostrata: for the order see on P. 48.

19. **servilem** (*p*) echoes *latrones*, and has the same effect as *servorum* (*p*) *manum*, where the genitive comes first because it is the more important word (see on P. 38).

20. **hoc, hoc...militum** is a scornful and emphatic addendum; see on P. 53.

V. 1. **deorum** is preposited, as if we had *o di qui...regitis*. See also P. 38. Wickham quotes *Sat.* 1. 6. 1. Horace rushes *in medias res*. See Dr Johnson on 'Ruin seize thee, ruthless king!' (Croker's Boswell, p. 137).

2. **humanum** (*p*): as if Horace had written *terras hominesque*; see on *servilem Epod.* 4. 19.

quid iste fert tumultus, et quid omnium
    vultus in unum me truces?
per liberos te, si vocata partubus   5
    Lucina veris adfuit,
per hoc inane purpurae decus precor,
    per improbaturum haec Iovem,
quid ut noverca me intueris aut uti
    petita ferro belua?'   10
ut haec trementi questus ore constitit
    insignibus raptis puer,
impube corpus, quale posset impia
    mollire Thracum pectora,
Canidia, brevibus implicata viperis   15
    crinis et incomptum caput,
iubet sepulcris caprificos erutas,
    iubet cupressos funebris
et uncta turpis ova ranae sanguine
    plumamque nocturnae strigis   20
herbasque, quas Iolcos atque Hiberia
    mittit venenorum ferax,

3. **iste fert tumultus**: see on P. 21.

omnium (*p*) anticipates *unum* of l. 4.

5, 6. **per liberos te**: see on *Odes* 1. 8. 1, 2. Here the order is normal.

vocata partubus | Lucina veris: the grouping may be that of P. 17. But *vocata partubus Lucina* can be taken together, and then *veris* may go closely with *adfuit* i.e. 'true, genuine (in your case).' With *vocata* the case of *partubus* might be dative or ablative.

11. **trementi** (*ps*) i.e. 'with trembling (of the voice)'; see on P. 27.

13, 14. **impube** (*p*): the position heightens the pathos.

impia...pectora: for the grouping with *mollire* intrusive see on P. 46 *a*.

15. **brevibus implicata viperis**: see on P. 24, and compare Ovid *Her.* 2. 119 *brevibus torquata colubris*.

16. **incomptum** is in ἀπὸ κοινοῦ position with *crinis* and *caput*; see on P. 33.

17. **sepulcris** would normally lie between *caprificos* and *erutas*; its position adds to the horror. See on P. 49.

19, 20. **et uncta...strigis**: see the discussion of these lines at P. 5.

nocturnae (*p*): the stress on 'night' heightens the horror. Compare l. 92 below, and see note on *Odes* 2. 13. 7.

22. **venenorum** (*p*): see on P. 39.

et ossa ab ore rapta ieiunae canis
  flammis aduri Colchicis.
at expedita Sagana per totam domum   25
  spargens Avernalis aquas
horret capillis ut marinus asperis
  echinus aut currens aper.
abacta nulla Veia conscientia
  ligonibus duris humum   30
exhauriebat ingemens laboribus,
  quo posset infossus puer
longo die bis terque mutatae dapis
  inemori spectaculo,
cum promineret ore, quantum extant aqua   35
  suspensa mento corpora:

23. **ieiunae canis**: for the position of these words see on P. 48.

ieiunae (*p*): the starving condition of the bitch emphasizes the disgusting nature of the *ossa*.

24. **Colchicis** (*s*): heard last, this word sums up the awful picture i.e. 'in flames of witchcraft.' Compare *Marsis* (*ps*) at l. 76 below. See too P. 21.

25. **expedita** (*p*) equals an adverb e.g. *celeriter*; see on P. 31.

26. **Avernalis** (*p*): more sorcery. Compare the effect of *sepulcris* l. 17, *nocturnae* l. 20, and *Colchicis* l. 24.

27. **capillis** is read with *horret*; then, after *echinus*, the words *capillis horret* are heard again and the grouping is that of P. 14. Compare on *Epod.* I. 33, 34.

28. **currens** (*p*): Bentley, after Heinsius, reads *Laurens* on the ground that a boar's bristles do not rise when he is running. But Horace, like Ovid *Hal.* 60, may have believed that a boar, when flying from the dogs, behaves like a porcupine. In any case the epithet is not pointless, for *currens* echoes *expedita* of l. 25; the boar runs, and so does Sagana.

29. **abacta...conscientia**: for the grouping see on P. 9.

32. **quo posset infossus** (*p*)**...inemori**: the effect of *infossus* preposited is as if we had *quo posset infodi puer et...inemori*. Compare *cum semel fixae* of l. 39 below, and see *Epod.* 10. 5, 10. 6, 10. 13, 11. 13, 17. 5. Add *Odes* 3. 3. 7, and 3. 6. 40.

33, 34. **bis terque**: the words lie in ἀπὸ κοινοῦ position with *die* and *mutatae*.

mutatae (*p*) i.e. 'a change (of feast)'; see on P. 26.

dapis (*ps*): the position adds to the cruelty by a kind of oxymoron. There is a fresh (*mutatae*) 'spread' (*dapis*) every few hours, but it kills (*inemori*) instead of sustaining him, because he only sees it (*spectaculo*).

37. **exsucta** (*ps*), **exsecta**, **exesa** etc., and **aridum** (*p*): both epithets are important, for the philtre requires dried up organs.

exsucta uti medulla et aridum iecur
    amoris esset poculum,
interminato cum semel fixae cibo
    intabuissent pupulae.   40
non defuisse masculae libidinis
    Ariminensem Foliam
et otiosa credidit Neapolis
    et omne vicinum oppidum,
quae sidera excantata voce Thessala   45
    lunamque caelo deripit.
hic irresectum saeva dente livido
    Canidia rodens pollicem
quid dixit aut quid tacuit? 'o rebus meis
    non infideles arbitrae,   50

---

38. **amoris** (*ps*): i.e. 'a *love*-potion'; compare *Epod.* 17. 80 *desideri temperare poculum*.

39, 40. **interminato...fixae cibo...pupulae:** for the grouping see on P. 9.

interminato is concessive i.e. 'although forbidden to him with threats'; the sense justifies its emphatic position before *cum semel*. The poor boy is here thought of as dead. Then at last his eyes are fixed on the food and threats are hurled at him no longer.

cum semel fixae...intabuissent = *cum semel fixae essent et intabuissent*; see on *quo posset infossus* l. 32 above.

pupulae: for its position see on *Odes* I. 3. 16.

41. **masculae** (*p*) i.e. not *femineae* merely.

libidinis (*p*): the genitive is quasi-subject i.e. the passion of Folia was not wanting. See on l. 71, and P. 38, P. 43.

42. **Ariminensem** (*p*): the order emphasizes the distance she had come, right from Ariminum, to attend these ceremonies in western Italy.

43. **otiosa** (*ps*) i.e. 'the idleness, idlers (of Naples)'; see on P. 27 and P. 21.

44. **vicinum** (*p*): places near Naples would be infected with the same passion for gossip.

45. **voce Thessala** goes with both *excantata* and *deripit*; hence the order (see at P. 49 on *Odes* I. 2. 23).

47. **irresectum** (*ps*) i.e. 'with nail grown long'; the stress adds to the horror. Compare l. 55.

saeva (*ps*) equals an adverb 'savagely'; see on P. 31, and *Odes* 2. 14. 23.

49. **rebus meis:** for the abnormal order see on P. 49, and compare *Epod.* 16. 6.

50. **non infideles** (*p*): for the position see on P. 29 and P. 36.

Nox et Diana, quae silentium regis,
    arcana cum fiunt sacra,
nunc, nunc adeste, nunc in hostilis domos
    iram atque numen vertite.
formidulosis cum latent silvis ferae   55
    dulci sopore languidae,
senem, quod omnes rideant, adulterum
    latrent Suburanae canes,
nardo perunctum, quale non perfectius
    meae laborarint manus.   60
quid accidit? cur dira barbarae minus
    venena Medeae valent,
quibus superbam fugit ulta paelicem,
    magni Creontis filiam,
cum palla, tabo munus imbutum, novam   65
    incendio nuptam abstulit?

52. **arcana** (ps): *secret* rites require the patronage of Night. Compare l. 55 below for the grouping.

53. **hostilis** (p): see on P. 37, and note at *Odes* 2. 12. 22.

55, 56. **formidulosis** (ps): the stress again adds to the horror (compare ll. 47, and 52). For the grouping compare *arcana cum fiunt sacra* at l. 52 above.

ferae...languidae: for the grouping see on P. 18. In any case *dulci sopore* would lie between *ferae* and *languidae*. Perhaps *ferae* and *dulci* are purposely set together for the sake of the antithesis.

57. **senem** is separated from *adulterum* to bring out the point—the comicality of an old man playing Don Juan.

58, 59. **Suburanae** (p): the dogs of a *low* quarter bark at and betray a 'swell' who is *nardo perunctus*. The words *nardo perunctum* come as a surprise, as an emphatic addendum; see on P. 53.

60. **meae** (p) i.e. αἴ γε ἐμαί, whatever other hands have done. See too P. 21.

61, 62. **dira barbarae...venena Medeae:** for the grouping see on P. 9. **minus** has emphasis by separation from *valent*.

63. **superbam** (p) i.e. 'the haughtiness (of her rival)'; see on P. 27. There is a variant reading *superba*.

64. **Creontis** (p): see on P. 41.

65, 66. **tabo** would normally lie between *munus* and *imbutum*; the words *palla tabo* make us expect *imbuta*, but the intervening *munus* changes *imbuta* to *imbutum* (see on P. 49).

novam here approaches the sense of *recentem* (see on *Odes* 1. 31. 2, 3). Juvenal *Sat.* 2. 120 also has *nova nupta*. After all, a recently wedded bride has also 'never existed before' (*nova*), so far as regards her husband. The

atqui nec herba nec latens in asperis
    radix fefellit me locis:
indormit unctis omnium cubilibus
    oblivione paelicum.   70
a a, solutus ambulat veneficae
    scientioris carmine.
non usitatis, Vare, potionibus,
    o multa fleturum caput,
ad me recurres, nec vocata mens tua   75
    Marsis redibit vocibus;
maius parabo, maius infundam tibi
    fastidienti poculum,

pause at the end of the line makes it unnecessary to group *novam incendio nuptam* together (see on P. 50 *b*).

There is a *varia lectio* viz. *nova*, and one is tempted to wonder whether Horace wrote *novo* (dread, horrible), felt with both *tabo* and *incendio*. The latter word seems to require some epithet, and the separation of *novam* from *nuptam* has little point, unless it is intended to heighten the pathos, or to emphasize the meanness of taking another wife.

67, 68. **latens in asperis | radix...locis:** for the grouping see on P. 9. The phrase *latens in asperis* is concessive i.e. 'though hidden and hard to reach.'

69, 70. **unctis...paelicum:** the phrase *unctis omnium cubilibus oblivione* i.e. 'on couches anointed with forgetfulness of all' is normal enough in its order (see on P. 48). The third complement *paelicum* may also stand outside *unctis* and *cubilibus*, but possibly it carries some stress of bitterness.

71. **veneficae** (*p*) i.e. by the charm of a *fellow-professional* and one more skilled. The genitive is of greater importance than the noun on which it depends; see on P. 38.

73. **non usitatis** (*ps*): see on P. 29, and compare *Odes* 2. 20. 1. For the intervening vocative see on *Odes* 1. 5. 3.

74. **multa** goes closely with *fleturum* (πολυδάκρυτον); compare *Epod.* 3. 13 *hoc delibutis.*

fleturum (*p*): see on P. 36.

75. **vocata mens tua:** for the grouping see on P. 34.

76. **Marsis** (*ps*): the Marsians were famous for sorcery; even their enchantments will not avail in this case. Compare *Colchicis* (*s*) l. 24 above, and *Epod.* 17. 28, 29, 17. 35, 17. 60. Add *Odes* 1. 27. 21 *Thessalis magus venenis.* See also P. 21.

The words *Marsis vocibus* are heard with both *vocata* and *redibit*, for *redibit* is equivalent to *referetur* (sc. *ad te* or *ad me*). Compare Cicero *Rosc. Amer.* 44. 128, and Ovid *Her.* 20. 172 where *redit=redditur.*

77. **maius parabo:** doubtless, as Wickham says, this first *maius* is quite vague (sc. *quiddam*), but so is the second *maius* until the word *poculum* is heard. Possibly one may feel *poculum* as object of *fastidienti* also.

priusque caelum sidet inferius mari,
    tellure porrecta super,   80
quam non amore sic meo flagres uti
    bitumen atris ignibus.'
sub haec puer iam non, ut ante, mollibus
    lenire verbis impias,
sed dubius, unde rumperet silentium,   85
    misit Thyesteas preces:
'venena magnum fas nefasque non valent
    convertere humanam vicem.
diris agam vos; dira detestatio
    nulla expiatur victima.   90
quin, ubi perire iussus exspiravero,
    nocturnus occurram furor,

79. **prius:** the anticipatory position (with *quam* following in l. 81) is common in all Latin.

80. **super** has emphasis because it lies outside *tellure* and *porrecta*. Compare *Odes* 3. 4. 26, and P. 49.

81. **sic** is anticipatory of *uti*; compare *prius* of l. 79.
meo (*s*) has stress i.e. 'love of *me*.'

82. **atris** (*p*): the position heightens the oxymoron; compare *Odes* 1. 33. 2, 1. 33. 14, 1. 34. 2, 2. 12. 26, 2. 14. 24, 3. 4. 5, 6, 3. 5. 48, 3. 21. 13, 14, 3. 24. 12, 4. 2. 12, 4. 11. 23, 4. 12. 26. A pitch torch, of course, gives out thick smoke.

83. **mollibus** (*ps*) has stress; contrast the dread *preces* of l. 86 below. See too P. 21.

84. **lenire:** the only instance of an historic infinitive in the *Odes*, *Epodes* and *C. S.* But see *Sat.* 1. 5. 31, and 1. 9. 66.

86. **Thyesteas** (*p*) i.e. 'of a Thyestes.' For the generic adjective in front see on P. 37.

87, 88. **venena...convertere humanam vicem:** for this notorious crux see Wickham's note.
humanam (*p*): contrast *divinum* implied in *fas*. This order of *humanam* and the fact that *humanam vicem* is in the position of an emphatic addendum (see P. 53) support the rendering 'sorceries cannot overset the mighty laws of right and wrong—these are not like *human* things.'

89. **vos** has stress because it comes last i.e. 'curses are the only things to move *you*!'
dira (*p*) echoes *diris*.

90. **nulla** (*s*) is an emphatic *non*, as so often in Cicero. See too P. 21.

92. **nocturnus** (*ps*) equals *noctu*; see on P. 31, and compare *Odes* 4. 1. 37. The position also heightens the horror; see on l. 20 above. Compare too P. 21.

petamque vultus umbra curvis unguibus.
quae vis deorum est manium,
et inquietis assidens praecordiis   95
pavore somnos auferam.
vos turba vicatim hinc et hinc saxis petens
contundet obscenas anus;
post insepulta membra different lupi
et Esquilinae alites,   100
neque hoc parentes, heu mihi superstites,
effugerit spectaculum.'

VI.

Quid immerentis hospites vexas canis
ignavus adversum lupos?
quin huc inanis, si potes, vertis minas
et me remorsurum petis?
nam qualis aut Molossus aut fulvus Lacon,   5
amica vis pastoribus,

93. **umbra** and **curvis unguibus** are unpleasant addenda (see on P. 53).
curvis (*p*): the stress on 'curved' adds to the abomination; the spirit has become a sort of Harpy.
94. **deorum** (*s*) seems to be quasi-adjectival, as if we had *divi manes* (Lucretius 6. 759) i.e. such is the might of the Manes, who have *divine* powers.
95. **inquietis** (*ps*) is proleptic i.e. 'so that they are restless'; see on P. 30, and also on P. 24 and 25.
98. **obscenas** (*p*): see on *Odes* 2. 14. 23. The two words *obscenas anus* are causal addenda (see P. 53).
99. **insepulta** (*p*) is causal.
100. **Esquilinae** (*p*) is quasi-generic i.e. 'carrion (birds)'; see on P. 37.
101. **hoc** is emphatic by far separation. They shall not miss *this* sight, if they do miss what is going on now.
VI. 1. **immerentis** (*p*) is concessive i.e. 'though they do not deserve it.' Compare *immerentis* (*ps*) of *Epod.* 7. 19. The whole point of the Epode lies in *immerentis*: the innocent should not be attacked by the writer of lampoons.
2. **ignavus** i.e. 'though a coward (against wolves).'
3. **inanis** (*ps*) is proleptic i.e. 'so that they fall powerless'; see on P. 30.
minas for its position see on *Odes* 1. 3. 16.
5. **fulvus** appears to be ἀπὸ κοινοῦ with *Molossus* and *Lacon*; see on P. 33.
6. **amica vis pastoribus**: for the order see on P. 47.

agam per altas aure sublata nives,
    quaecumque praecedet fera.
tu, cum timenda voce complesti nemus,
    proiectum odoraris cibum.   10
cave, cave: namque in malos asperrimus
    parata tollo cornua,
qualis Lycambae spretus infido gener
    aut acer hostis Bupalo.
an, siquis atro dente me petiverit,   15
    inultus ut flebo puer?

VII.

Quo, quo scelesti ruitis aut cur dexteris
    aptantur enses conditi?

7. **per altas aure sublata nives:** the grouping may be that of P. 15; but the position of *aure sublata* between *altas* and *nives* suggests that the whole group is connected in sense; the snow is deep and, we may assume, still falling; hence the dog must use ears rather than eyes.

8. **quaecumque...fera:** for the separation see on *Odes* 1. 27. 11, 12.

9. **timenda** (*p*) i.e. 'with the terror (of your voice)'; see on P. 27. Compare the position of *tremendus* at *Odes* 1. 16. 11, 4. 2. 15, 4. 6. 7, 4. 14. 12.

nemus: for its position see on *Odes* 1. 3. 16.

10. **proiectum** (*ps*): see on P. 21. The sense is 'I go straight for my quarry, but you—you make a great noise and then sniff the first piece of meat thrown out.' Others say that *cibum* is the bait thrown by the thief; but Horace is thinking rather of a fox or wolf that has to be driven off.

12. **parata** (*ps*) has emphasis i.e. 'all ready'; see too P. 21.

13. **Lycambae...gener:** we may regard the grouping as that of P. 14. But the words *Lycambae spretus infido* may be classed under P. 24, 25, and *gener* may be taken as in apposition with the subject contained in *spretus* i.e. the man despised as son-in-law.

14. **Bupalo** stands outside *acer* and *hostis* in artificial antithesis to *Lycambae*; see on P. 47, and compare *Epod.* 17. 3.

15. **atro** (*p*) i.e. 'with the venom (of his tooth)'; see on P. 27, and note at *Odes* 2. 14. 23.

16. **inultus ut flebo puer:** the commentators say 'The order is *inultus flebo ut puer.*' It is sufficient to reply that the order isn't. This much may be urged in defence of Horace's order: (1) that the person or thing or idea compared may precede *ut* (see on *Odes* 1. 15. 29, and note an extreme case in *Sat.* 1. 3. 89 *historias, captivus ut, audit*); but these passages merely show how *inultus ut* may mean 'as if unavenged' (contrast *Epod.* 17. 56) or 'as if unable to avenge oneself,' like *contemptus*=contemptible; (2) that *inultus* belongs equally to the subject of *flebo* and to *puer*. Such an ἀπὸ κοινοῦ use is

parumne campis atque Neptuno super
    fusum est Latini sanguinis?
non ut superbas invidae Carthaginis   5
    Romanus arces ureret,
intactus aut Britannus ut descenderet
    sacra catenatus via,
sed ut secundum vota Parthorum sua
    urbs haec periret dextera.   10
neque hic lupis mos nec fuit leonibus,
    numquam nisi in dispar feris.
furorne caecus an rapit vis acrior
    an culpa? responsum date!
tacent, et ora pallor albus inficit,   15
    mentesque perculsae stupent.
sic est: acerba fata Romanos agunt
    scelusque fraternae necis,
ut immerentis fluxit in terram Remi
    sacer nepotibus cruor.   20

common, if not universal, in sentences of comparison (see on *Epod.* 1. 34). Thus Horace is saying 'as unavenged shall I weep, (like) an unavenged boy?'

VII. 3, 4. **parum...sanguinis:** for the separation of these words see on *Odes* 1. 2. 1.

Latini (*p*): the stress implies civil war, as the following lines show.

5, 6. **superbas invidae Carthaginis...arces:** for the grouping see on P. 10. **Romanus** is set next to *Carthaginis* in artificial antithesis.

7. **intactus** (*ps*) has emphasis i.e. *non ante devictus*. **Britannus** precedes *ut* in contrast to *Carthaginis*.

8. **sacra catenatus via:** see on P. 24, 25. The words *sacra...via* are felt with *descenderet* and also, as they ought to be, with *catenatus*. Compare on *Odes* 1. 17. 24, 25.

9, 10. **sua** (*ps*) i.e. 'by its own hand.' Wickham quotes *Epod.* 16. 2. **haec** (*pp*) is emphatic i.e. 'this city of *ours*, not Carthage.'

11. **hic** is subject ('this has been the custom of wolves'), as the order shows.

12. **numquam...feris:** the line is an emphatic addendum, see on P. 53.

17. **acerba** (*p*) has stress i.e. 'it is an implacable fate that....'

18. **fraternae** (*p*): the position echoes *Latini* (*p*) of l. 4. As a brother fell then, so brothers are falling now.

19. **immerentis** (*ps*) almost equals an adverb (see on P. 31); compare on *Epod.* 6. 1.

Remi may perhaps go with both *terram* and *cruor*; if with the latter only, see on P. 48.

VIII.

Rogare longo putidam te saeculo
   viris quid enervet meas,
cum sit tibi dens ater et rugis vetus
   frontem senectus exaret,
hietque turpis inter aridas natis   5
   podex velut crudae bovis?
sed incitat me pectus et mammae putres,
   equina quales ubera,
venterque mollis et femur tumentibus
   exile suris additum.   10
esto beata, funus atque imagines
   ducant triumphales tuum,
nec sit marita, quae rotundioribus
   onusta bacis ambulet.
quid quod libelli Stoici inter sericos   15
   iacere pulvillos amant?
illitterati num minus nervi rigent,
   minusve languet fascinum?
quod ut superbo provoces ab inguine,
   ore allaborandum est tibi.   20

VIII. 1. **longo...saeculo:** for the grouping see on P. 10.

2. **meas** (*s*): contrast *te* of l. 1.

3. **vetus** (*ps*) equals an adverb e.g. *iam diu*; see on P. 31.

5, 6. **turpis...podex:** for the grouping see on P. 10.

crudae (*p*): the beast, because *cruda, non potest facile exonerare ventrem.*

8. **equina** (*ps*): the thing likened comes early (compare on *Odes* 1. 15. 29, 30), and moreover *equina* is a generic adjective (see on P. 37). See also the note on *Odes* 3. 14. 1.

9, 10. **femur tumentibus | exile suris:** the antithetical words are stressed by their order; *tumentibus* is preposited and separated, and *exile* is separated. For the grouping see on P. 14.

11, 12. **atque:** for its abnormal position see *Epod.* 17. 4, and *Sat.* 1. 5. 4. There is no parallel in the Odes.

funus...tuum: for the grouping see on P. 16 β.

13, 14. **rotundioribus | onusta bacis:** for the grouping see on P. 24, and for the preposited comparative see on P. 28.

15. **sericos** (*ps*): contrast the austere *Stoici*; see also P. 21.

17. **illitterati** (*ps*) is causal, hence its position.

19. **superbo provoces ab inguine:** for the order see on P. 21.

IX.

Quando repostum Caecubum ad festas dapes
    victore laetus Caesare
tecum sub alta (sic Iovi gratum) domo,
    beate Maecenas, bibam,
sonante mixtum tibiis carmen lyra,   5
    hac Dorium, illis barbarum?
ut nuper, actus cum freto Neptunius
    dux fugit ustis navibus,
minatus urbi vincla, quae detraxerat
    servis amicus perfidis.   10
Romanus eheu (posteri negabitis)
    emancipatus feminae
fert vallum et arma miles et spadonibus
    servire rugosis potest,

IX. 1. **ad festas dapes:** for the position of these words see on P. 47.

festas (*p*): contrast *profestas*. The point is a day of *festival*.

2. **victore** (*p*) **laetus** i.e. 'rejoicing in the victory (of Caesar)'; see on P. 27, and also on P. 24.

3. **alta** (*bs*) i.e. 'the tower (of thy home)'; see on P. 27.

4. **beate** (*p*): see on P. 36.

5. **sonante...lyra:** see on *Odes* 3. 1. 34.

mixtum tibiis carmen is normal (see on *Odes* 1. 7. 29), and, being a complement, lies between *sonante* and *lyra*.

7, 8. **actus cum freto...fugit:** the position of *actus* before *cum* allows us, perhaps, to feel *freto* with both *actus* and *fugit*.

Neptunius may be a noun, like *Saturnius* (Ovid *Met.* 8. 703) for Jove. If it is a preposited adjective, the stress signifies 'though son of Neptune he was driven from the sea.'

ustis navibus is an emphatic addendum; see P. 53, and compare too on *Odes* 3. 1. 34.

9. **minatus** equals *idque quamquam minatus erat*.

10. **servis** goes first with *detraxerat*, then with *amicus*.

amicus perfidis may be read as an emphatic addendum (see on P. 53) i.e. 'the friend of traitors.'

11–13. **Romanus...miles:** both words have great stress by separation i.e. Romans! and soldiers!

12. **feminae** goes with both *emancipatus* and *fert* i.e. 'handed over to a woman they carry for a woman.'

14. **rugosis** (*s*) i.e. 'wrinkled, feeble, unmanned'; hence the greater dishonour to Roman soldiers who obeyed them. See too P. 21.

interque signa turpe militaria   15
    sol aspicit conopium.
† at hoc frementis verterunt bis mille equos
    Galli canentes Caesarem,
hostiliumque navium portu latent
    puppes sinistrorsum citae.   20
io triumphe, tu moraris aureos
    currus et intactas boves?
io triumphe, nec Iugurthino parem
    bello reportasti ducem,
neque † Africani cui super Carthaginem   25
    virtus sepulcrum condidit.
terra marique victus hostis punico
    lugubre mutavit sagum.
aut ille centum nobilem Cretam urbibus,
    ventis iturus non suis,   30
exercitatas aut petit Syrtis Noto,
    aut fertur incerto mari.

15, 16. **militaria** (*s*) has stress. If, however, *turpe* may be taken with *conopium*, we have the grouping of P. 14.

conopium coming last has the emphasis of disdain.

17. **frementis** with *equos* i.e. 'neighing for the fight.' With other readings *frementes* belongs to *Galli* e.g. *ad hunc* 'chafing at him (Antony),' *ad hoc* sc. *conopium*, *ad haec* (the sight of Romans serving under eunuchs), *at huc* (to our side), etc. See the commentators.

18. **Galli:** a comma after this word would give it some stress (see on *Odes* 4. 9. 26) i.e. Gauls deserted to us, if Romans would not.

19. **hostilium** (*p*): see P. 37, and note on *Odes* 2. 12. 22.

hostiliumque navium (*ps*) is the real subject; see on P. 38. For the epithet *hostilium navium* in front of *puppes*, and *sinistrorsum citae* behind see on P. 34.

21, 22. **tu** is emphatic because inserted.

aureos (*p*)...**intactas** (*p*): both epithets have stress because they are essential to the picture of a triumph.

23, 24. **Iugurthino...ducem:** for the grouping see on P. 9.

25. **Africani:** Madvig's *Africani* gives an order which can scarcely be paralleled.

28. **lugubre** (*ps*) is brought close to *punico* for the sake of the artificial antithesis; but see also P. 21.

29. **centum...urbibus:** for the grouping see on P. 10, and compare *Odes* 3. 27. 33.

capaciores affer huc, puer, scyphos
   et Chia vina aut Lesbia,
vel quod fluentem nauseam coerceat   35
   metire nobis Caecubum.
curam metumque Caesaris rerum iuvat
   dulci Lyaeo solvere.

X.

Mala soluta navis exit alite,
   ferens olentem Mevium:
ut horridis utrumque verberes latus,
   Auster, memento fluctibus;
niger rudentis Eurus inverso mari   5
   fractosque remos differat;

30. **non suis** (*s*) equals *adversis*; see on P. 29, and also on P. 24.

31. **exercitatas** (*ps*) i.e. 'the turmoil (of the Syrtis)'; see on P. 26.
Noto must be felt in part with *petit* i.e. by means of Notus, by tacking in face of Notus. If *Noto* went only with *exercitatas*, why did not Horace write the obvious *aut Noto Syrtis petit*? See too on *Odes* I. 14. 10.

32. **incerto** (*p*) i.e. 'by the fickleness (of the sea)'; see on P. 27.

33. **capaciores** (*ps*) i.e. 'that hold *more*'; see on P. 28.

34. **vina** lies in ἀπὸ κοινοῦ position between *Chia* and *Lesbia*.

35. **fluentem** (*p*) i.e. 'the flow (of nausea)'; see on P. 27.

37. **Caesaris** may be felt first as objective genitive with *metum*, then as possessive genitive with *rerum*.

38. **dulci** (*p*) i.e. 'the sweetness (of wine)'; see on P. 27, and compare *Odes* 3. 12. 2, 3. 13. 2, etc.

X. 1. **Mala...alite:** for the grouping see on P. 10.

2. **olentem** (*p*) i.e. 'the smell (of Maevius)'; see on P. 27.

3, 4. **horridis utrumque verberes latus...fluctibus:** for the grouping see on P. 8. The juxtaposition of *horridis utrumque* (horrors on both sides) is happy.

5, 6. **niger** (*ps*) seems to equal an adverbial phrase e.g. 'in the blackness'; see on P. 31. The adjective may colour *rudentis* as well as *Eurus*; see on P. 52.

niger rudentis: the elements of the picture are set early (see on *Odes* I. 2. 17) i.e. 'blackness and rattling ropes'—both the results of Eurus. The meaning of *niger* is 'bringing storm-clouds'; contrast *albus*, *Odes* I. 7. 15, 3. 27. 19.

inverso (*p*) is kept close to its subject *Eurus*, as if we had *invertat mare et...differat*. See on *Epod.* 5. 32 and compare *fractos* (*p*) i.e. *invertat et frangat et differat*. See too *usto* l. 13 below.

insurgat Aquilo, quantus altis montibus
frangit trementis ilices;
nec sidus atra nocte amicum appareat,
qua tristis Orion cadit;   10
quietiore nec feratur aequore,
quam Graia victorum manus,
cum Pallas usto vertit iram ab Ilio
in impiam Aiacis ratem.
o quantus instat navitis sudor tuis   15
tibique pallor luteus
et illa non virilis heiulatio,
preces et aversum ad Iovem,
Ionius udo cum, remugiens sinus
Noto carinam ruperit.   20
opima quodsi praeda curvo litore
porrecta mergos iuveris,
libidinosus immolabitur caper
et agna Tempestatibus.

7. **altis** (*p*) i.e. 'on the tops, heights (of the mountains)'; see on P. 27.

8. **trementis** (*p*) perhaps means 'though they bow before him.'

9. **sidus atra nocte amicum**: for the grouping see on P. 18.

atra (*p*) **nocte** i.e. 'in the darkness of the night'; see on P. 27.

amicum goes closely with *appareat*, as if we had *amico more*. The collocations in this line are happy: not a star in the darkness, in the night not a friend.

10. **tristis** (*p*): for the position see on *Odes* 2. 14. 23. But the adjective may be predicative i.e. 'sets lowering.' See on *Odes* 3. 27. 18, and *Epod.* 15. 8. Here the reference might be to Orion's evening setting, which occurs simultaneously with the sun's about the end of May.

11. **quietiore** (*ps*): see on P. 28.

13. **usto** is brought close to Pallas, as if it were a perfect participle active in agreement with *Pallas*. Compare *Eurus inverso* of l. 5.

15. **quantus instat navitis sudor tuis**: for the grouping see on P. 17.

17. **non virilis** (*p*): see on P. 29.

18. **et** is trajected for metrical reasons; compare *Epod.* 11. 8.

aversum (*p*) has emphasis i.e. 'a Jove who will not hear'; compare *Odes* 3. 23. 19.

19, 20. **Ionius udo cum remugiens sinus | Noto**: for the grouping see on P. 7.

21. **opima** (*ps*) i.e. a rich, fat booty, not *macra, tenuis*.

curvo (*p*) i.e. 'on the bend (of the shore)'; see on P. 27. Bodies would be washed up in some cove; compare *Odes* 4. 5. 14.

XI.

Petti, nihil me sicut antea iuvat
    scribere versiculos amore percussum gravi,
amore, qui me praeter omnis expetit
    mollibus in pueris aut in puellis urere.
hic tertius December, ex quo destiti   5
    Inachia furere, silvis honorem decutit.
heu me, per urbem (nam pudet tanti mali)
    fabula quanta fui! conviviorum et paenitet,
in quis amantem languor et silentium
    arguit et latere petitus imo spiritus!   10
'contrane lucrum nil valere candidum
    pauperis ingenium?' querebar adplorans tibi,
simul calentis inverecundus deus
    fervidiore mero arcana promorat loco.
'quodsi meis inaestuet praecordiis   15
    libera bilis, ut haec ingrata ventis dividat

23. **libidinosus** (*ps*) i.e. still full of passion and therefore young. See too P. 21.

XI. 2. **amore percussum gravi** is an emphatic causal addendum; see on P. 53.

gravi (*s*) has some stress; but see P. 24.

4. **mollibus** (*ps*): the epithet is important because it implies effeminacy. Compare *Odes* I. 4. 19 *tenerum* (*p*) *Lycidan*.

7. **me** is ultimately the object of *pudet*; but *heu me* may first be read as if *heu mihi*, and, despite the modern comma, *me per urbem* can be heard together i.e. 'I am the object of scandal throughout the city.'

8. **quanta** (*pp*) has stress.

et is trajected; compare *Epod.* 10. 18.

9. **amantem languor**: see on P. 51.

10. **latere...spiritus**: for the grouping see on P. 14.

13. **calentis** (*ps*): the position is as if we had *calenti* (*mihi*), and gives the effect of *simul calueram et...deus...promorat* (see on *Epod.* 5. 32). So Greek brings forward the genitive, as if, like the ethical dative, it belonged to the whole sentence. See *C. R.* vol. XXVIII. p. 227. Compare too on P. 40.

inverecundus (*p*) stands, with point, next to *calentis*. Bacchus ceases to be *verecundus* (see *Odes* I. 27. 3) when the drinker *calet*.

14. **fervidiore** (*p*): see on P. 28.

loco: for its position see on *Odes* I. 3. 16.

15. **meis** (*ps*) equals an ethical dative *mihi*; see on *Odes* I. 13. 3, and compare *Odes* I. 15. 33. See also on P. 21.

16. **libera** (*p*) is proleptic i.e. 'till it boils over'; see on P. 30.

fomenta vulnus nil malum levantia,
  desinet imparibus certare summotus pudor. '
ubi haec severus te palam laudaveram,
  iussus abire domum ferebar incerto pede   20
ad non amicos heu mihi postis et heu
  limina dura, quibus lumbos et infregi latus.
nunc gloriantis quamlibet mulierculam
  vincere mollitia amor Lycisci me tenet;
unde expedire non amicorum queant   25
  libera consilia nec contumeliae graves,
sed alius ardor aut puellae candidae
  aut teretis pueri longam renodantis comam.

16, 17. **haec ingrata** may be a loose neuter plural 'these wretched things';
the words *fomenta vulnus nil malum levantia* then form an emphatic
addendum (see on P. 53), more closely defining *haec ingrata* i.e. 'wretched
things which are like dressings that sting without relieving the wound.' See
Gow *ad loc.*

17. **nil** (*s*) and **malum** (*s*) have stress: the dressings do *no* good because
the wound is *severe*.

18. **desinet** is more vivid than *desinat*; the protasis is a remote possibility,
the result is certain. Compare *Odes* 3. 3. 8 *illabatur...ferient.*

summotus: may the metaphor be from a person 'moved on' by the lictors,
with whom he has ceased to struggle, submitting to *force majeure*? He will
not fight the 'low' (*imparibus*) policemen. Horace seems to imply that it is
a struggle between honour (*pudor*) and monied vulgarity (*imparibus*). But
see Wickham and Gow.

19. **te palam**: these words are in ἀπὸ κοινοῦ position with *severus* and
laudaveram.

20, 21. **domum** is first felt with both *abire* and *ferebar*; then comes
incerto (*p*) *pede*, and we are not surprised to find that *domum* has changed
to the dwelling of his love. For this inevitable change the stress on *incerto* (*p*)
has prepared us. Horace here makes very clever use of order.

non amicos (*ps*): see on P. 29.

22. **lumbos et infregi latus**: for the position of *infregi* see on *Odes* 1.
30. 6.

23, 24. **gloriantis...amor Lycisci**: for the grouping see on P. 20 β.

25. **amicorum** (*ps*) is the real subject; see on P. 38.

26. **libera...graves**: note the chiastic order of the adjectives.

27, 28. **candidae | aut teretis**: again note the chiastic order of the adjec-
tives.

28. **pueri longam renodantis comam**: the grouping may be that of P. 14.
But *teretis pueri...renodantis* may be classed under P. 34, and *longam renodantis comam* under P. 21.

XII.

Quid tibi vis, mulier nigris dignissima barris?
    munera quid mihi quidve tabellas
mittis nec firmo iuveni neque naris obesae?
    namque sagacius unus odoror,
polypus an gravis hirsutis cubet hircus in alis,   5
    quam canis acer ubi lateat sus.
qui sudor vietis et quam malus undique membris
    crescit odor, cum pene soluto
indomitam properat rabiem sedare; neque illi
    iam manet umida creta colorque   10
stercore fucatus crocodili, iamque subando
    tenta cubilia tectaque rumpit!
vel mea cum saevis agitat fastidia verbis:
    'Inachia langues minus ac me;
Inachiam ter nocte potes, mihi semper ad unum   15
    mollis opus. pereat male, quae te

XII. 1. **nigris dignissima barris:** see on P. 24.

3. **nec...obesae:** these words form a causal addendum (see on P. 53) i.e. 'seeing that I am neither young, lusty, nor without nice feelings.'

firmo (*p*): the point lies in the adjective.

4. **sagacius** (*s*): the comparative adverb naturally has stress; compare on P. 28.

5. **gravis...alis:** for the grouping see on P. 7.

7, 8. **vietis** (*ps*): the position emphasizes her age, and also makes *vietis membris* ἀπὸ κοινοῦ with both *sudor crescit* and *odor crescit*.

quam malus is separated, like *quantus* or *qualis*, from the noun; see on *Odes* I. 27. 11, 12.

undique is so placed as to qualify *malus*, *membris*, and *crescit*.

9. **indomitam** (*ps*) has emphasis.

10, 11. **umida** (*p*) i.e. 'because it is wet.'

crocodili: for the second complement outside see on P. 48.

12. **tenta** (*p*) is causal.

13. **mea...verbis:** for the grouping see on P. 7.

14. **minus** (*pp*) has stress.

ac equals *quam*; compare *Epod.* 15. 5, and, perhaps, *Odes* I. 25. 18. The use is frequent in the *Satires* e.g. I. 1. 46, 1. 2. 22, 1. 5. 5, 1. 6. 130, 1. 10. 34, 2. 7. 96, etc. Add Vergil *Aen.* 3. 561.

15. **unum** (*s*): contrast *ter*.

16. **male** (*pp*) has stress.

16, 17. **quae te | Lesbia (mihi) quaerenti:** note the early grouping of case

Lesbia quaerenti taurum monstravit inertem,
   cum mihi Cous adesset Amyntas,
cuius in indomito constantior inguine nervus
   quam nova collibus arbor inhaeret.   20
muricibus Tyriis iteratae vellera lanae
   cui properabantur? tibi nempe,
ne foret aequalis inter conviva, magis quem
   diligeret mulier sua quam te.
o ego non felix, quam tu fugis ut pavet acris   25
   agna lupos capreaeque leones!'

XIII.

Horrida tempestas caelum contraxit, et imbres
   nivesque deducunt Iovem; nunc mare, nunc siluae
Threicio Aquilone sonant; rapiamus, amici,
   occasionem de die, dumque virent genua

relations (see on *Odes* I. 2. 17), and the scornful insertion of Lesbia's name (a nice disciple of Sappho!).

taurum lies in ἀπὸ κοινοῦ position with *quaerenti* and *monstravit*.

inertem comes last with contemptuous emphasis i.e. 'only to find you a useless creature.'

18. **Cous** (*ps*): Cos was the island of voluptuousness and immorality. See too P. 21.

19. **indomito...nervus**: for the grouping see on P. 9.

20. **collibus** may first be taken with *nova* i.e. 'new to the hills' (compare Livy I. 10. 5 *quercum pastoribus sacram*), and then with *inhaeret*. Compare on P. 50 *a*.

21. **muricibus Tyriis iteratae**: these words form a compound (compare *Epod.* 16. 6 and note on *Odes* 3. 1. 24) which is emphasized by being preposited. But see also P. 20 *a*.

23. **magis** is emphatic because it precedes *quem* and is separated from *diligeret*.

25. **o ego non felix**: the order is on the analogy of *me miserum*; contrast P. 29.

acris (*ps*) i.e. 'the cruelty (of wolves)'; see on P. 27, and *Odes* 2. 14. 23.

XIII. 1. **Horrida** (*p*): see on *Odes* 2. 14. 23; but *tempestas* is a colourless word and the epithet is therefore of greater importance than the noun.

2. **Iovem**: see, for its position, *Odes* I. 3. 16.

3. **Threicio** (*p*): the order emphasizes the bitter cold of it. Compare, perhaps, *Odes* I. 25. 11 *Thracio...vento*.

amici i.e. 'as friends.' Bentley reads *amice*, a postposited adverb with stress.

et decet, obducta solvatur fronte senectus.   5
   tu vina Torquato move consule pressa meo,
cetera mitte loqui: deus haec fortasse benigna
   reducet in sedem vice. nunc et Achaemenio
perfundi nardo iuvat et fide Cyllenea
   levare diris pectora sollicitudinibus,   10
nobilis ut grandi cecinit Centaurus alumno:
   'invicte mortalis dea nate puer Thetide,
te manet Assaraci tellus, quam frigida ravi
   findunt Scamandri flumina, lubricus et Simois,
unde tibi reditum certo subtemine Parcae   15
   rupere, nec mater domum caerula te revehet.
illic omne malum vino cantuque levato,
   deformis aegrimoniae dulcibus alloquiis.'

4. **de die** is put late with emphasis i.e. 'ere evening comes' (Wickham).

5. **obducta** (*ps*) i.e. 'from the frown (on its brow)'; see on P. 26, and also on P. 21.

6. **vina Torquato move consule pressa**: for the grouping compare on P. 16 β.

meo (*s*) i.e. 'my very own, my loved,' because I was born in his consulship. See on *Odes* 1. 26. 8.

7, 8. **benigna** (*ps*) equals an adverb; see on P. 31.

sedem seems to mean 'quiet fixity'; its position next to *vice* (change) is not unhappy.

Achaemenio (*ps*): the stress reminds us of its costliness; but see also P. 21. Compare *Odes* 3. 1. 44.

10. **diris** (*ps*) i.e. 'from the dread (of cares)'; see on P. 27, and also on *Odes* 2. 14. 23.

11. **nobilis...alumno**: for the grouping see on P. 7.

12. **invicte mortalis dea nate puer Thetide**: perhaps it is best to put a comma after *mortalis*, and to regard *invicte* and *dea nate* as preposited adjectives with vocatives (see on P. 36); then *Thetide* comes last as if we had *divinae puer Thetidis* (see on P. 20 β).

13. **te manet...tellus**: see on P. 51.

Assaraci (*p*): the more important word comes first (see on P. 38); not Greece but *Troy* awaits him.

13, 14. **frigida...flumina**: for the grouping see on P. 8. The MSS have *parvi*, of which there are many emendations e.g. *ravi, proni, puri, tardi, flavi*, etc.

lubricus (*p*) i.e. 'smoothly flowing,' in contrast to Scamander, which cuts its way through; see on *Odes* 1. 31. 7.

15. **certo** (*p*) has stress: the fates are inexorable (compare *Odes* 1. 15. 35).

16. **rupere** is stressed; see on *Odes* 4. 9. 26.

XIV.

Mollis inertia cur tantam diffuderit imis
　　oblivionem sensibus,
pocula Lethaeos ut si ducentia somnos
　　arente fauce traxerim,
candide Maecenas, occidis saepe rogando:　　　　5
　　deus, deus nam me vetat
inceptos, olim promissum carmen, iambos
　　ad umbilicum adducere.
non aliter Samio dicunt arsisse Bathyllo
　　Anacreonta Teium,　　　　　　　　　　10
qui persaepe cava testudine flevit amorem
　　non elaboratum ad pedem.
ureris ipse miser: quodsi non pulchrior ignis
　　accendit obsessam Ilion,

caerula (*s*): perhaps concessive, 'though a sea nymph' i.e. 'though a demi-goddess'; but the adjective may be felt with *domum* also (see on P. 52).

18. **deformis** (*p*): see on *Odes* 2. 14. 23; but there is the antithesis of *dulcibus*, which is itself preposited by way of contrast. The position of *deformis aegrimoniae* (see on P. 43) suggests that the two words may be heard ἀπὸ κοινοῦ with *omne malum* and *dulcibus alloquiis*; compare on *Epod.* 4. 9.

XIV. 1, 2. **Mollis** (*p*) i.e. 'the softness (of indolence)'; see on P. 27.
tantam...sensibus: for the grouping see on P. 9.
3. **pocula Lethaeos...ducentia somnos**: for the grouping see on P. 14.
4. **arente fauce**: a causal ablative absolute, 'because my throat was dry.'
5. **candide** (*p*): see on P. 36.
6. **nam** is second and even third in Horace, especially when the preceding words are emphatic; see on *Odes* 1. 18. 3, and compare 4. 14. 9, *Epod.* 17. 45, *Sat.* 2. 3. 20, 2. 3. 41, 2. 3. 302, 2. 6. 78, *Epist.* 2. 1. 186.
7. **inceptos** (*ps*)...**promissum** (*p*): both participles have stress i.e. begun but never ended, promised long ago but never carried out.

olim would normally lie between *promissum* and *carmen*, but a Roman would probably hear it with *inceptos* as well as *promissum*. See P. 49, especially on *Odes* 1. 2. 23 there quoted.

9, 10. **Samio** (*ps*)...**Bathyllo | Anacreonta Teium**: note the artificial chiasmus. The effect of *Samio* (*ps*) is 'in Samos'; see on *Odes* 1. 31. 9.
11. **persaepe** goes with the whole sentence; see on *Odes* 2. 9. 13.
cava (*p*) **testudine** i.e. 'with the hollowness (=sounding-board) of his shell'; see on P. 27.
12. **non elaboratum** (*ps*): see on P. 29. The whole line is an addendum; see on P. 53.

gaude sorte tua: me libertina nec uno   15
   contenta Phryne macerat.

XV.

Nox erat et caelo fulgebat luna sereno
   inter minora sidera,
cum tu, magnorum numen laesura deorum,
   in verba iurabas mea,
artius atque hedera procera adstringitur ilex   5
   lentis adhaerens brachiis,
dum pecori lupus et nautis infestus Orion
   turbaret hibernum mare,
intonsosque agitaret Apollinis aura capillos,
   fore hunc amorem mutuum.   10
o dolitura mea multum virtute Neaera!
   nam siquid in Flacco viri est,

13. **pulchrior** (*p*): see on P. 28.

14. **obsessam** (*p*) i.e. 'even when besieged': the beauty of Helen fired to enthusiasm even a besieged city.

15, 16. **me** comes early in contrast to *tua*.

libertina (*p*) **nec uno | contenta** (*p*): both epithets have stress: she is of low class and faithless at that.

XV. 1. **sereno** (*s*) i.e. 'because clear'; it explains *fulgebat*, which, preceding *luna*, has slight stress.

2. **inter minora sidera**: the words form an emphatic addendum (see on P. 53); the moon puts out the lesser lights.

minora (*p*): see on P. 28.

3. **magnorum numen...deorum**: for the grouping see on P. 20 a.

4. **mea** (*s*) i.e. 'mine, and mine only'; see on P. 21.

5. **atque** equals *quam*; see on *Epod.* 12. 14.

procera (*ps*) means either 'for all its height,' or 'up all its height.' See too P. 21.

6. **lentis** (*ps*) equals *lente* with *adhaerens*; see on P. 31, and also on P. 24.

7. **infestus** belongs to both *lupus* and *Orion*, and, till the end of the line, we mentally supply *esset*, but Horace suddenly writes *turbaret*, and *lupus* is left without a verb.

8. **hibernum** (*p*) may be proleptic i.e. 'churned into storm' (see on P. 30), or Orion's morning setting in November and evening rising in December may be referred to, and hence the stress on *hibernum*.

9. **intonsosque agitaret Apollinis aura capillos**: for the normal *intonsos Apollinis capillos* with two intrusive words see on P. 46 b. Had not *intonsos* preceded, the position of *aura* would be intolerable.

non feret assiduas potiori te dare noctes,
 et quaeret iratus parem,
nec semel offensi cedet constantia formae,   15
 si certus intrarit dolor.
et tu, quicumque es felicior atque meo nunc
 superbus incedis malo,
sis pecore et multa dives tellure licebit
 tibique Pactolus fluat,   20
nec te Pythagorae fallant arcana renati
 formaque vincas Nirea,
heu heu, translatos alio maerebis amores:
 ast ego vicissim risero.

XVI.

Altera iam teritur bellis civilibus aetas,
 suis et ipsa Roma viribus ruit.

11. **dolitura mea...virtute Neaera**: for the grouping see on P. 10. **multum** (*pps*) has emphasis; compare *Epod.* 17. 20.

12. **viri** echoes *virtute* of l. 11. For its position see on *Odes* I. 2. 1.

13. **assiduas** (*ps*) equals an adverb emphasized by separation from *dare* (see on P. 31); but there may be stress on *assiduas* to prepare us for *semel* of l. 15 below.

14. **parem** comes last with some point i.e. 'a true mate' (Page and Gow).

15. **offensi**: the MSS have *semel offensae* (*ps*) which seems to be concessive i.e. 'though it had offended, become hateful, but once.' Gow supports *offensi* (*ps*) = the determination of me once angered will not give way.

16. **certus** (*ps*) i.e. 'if it is an unquestioned wrong whose pain has entered my soul'; see too P. 21.

17, 18. **meo** (*ps*): the stress implies that some day the *malum* will be *tuum*.

malo: for its position see on *Odes* I. 3. 16.

19. **multa** goes, by position, with *pecore* as well as with *tellure*; see on P. 33.

multa dives tellure: see on *Odes* 4. 8. 33.

21. **te...fallant arcana**: for the place of *te* see on P. 51.

Pythagorae (*ps*) i.e. 'Pythagoras (and his esoteric doctrines)'; see on P. 38. But for *Pythagorae arcana renati* with the intrusive *fallant* see P. 20 β.

22. **Nirea** comes last with stress.

23. **translatos** (*ps*) **alio** (*pp*): the words are causal i.e. 'because they have been transferred *elsewhere*.' See also P. 21.

XVI. 1. **Altera** (*s*) almost equals *iterum*; see on P. 31.

2. **suis** (*ps*): compare *Epod.* 7. 9, 10, and Livy Pref. § 4 *ut* (*res*) *iam magnitudine laboret sua.*

quam neque finitimi valuerunt perdere Marsi,
minacis aut Etrusca Porsenae manus,
aemula nec virtus Capuae nec Spartacus acer   5
novisque rebus infidelis Allobrox,
nec fera caerulea domuit Germania pube
parentibusque abominatus Hannibal:
impia perdemus devoti sanguinis aetas,
ferisque rursus occupabitur solum.   10
barbarus heu cineres insistet victor et urbem
eques sonante verberabit ungula,
quaeque carent ventis et solibus ossa Quirini,
nefas videre! dissipabit insolens.
forte quid expediat communiter aut melior pars   15
malis carere quaeritis laboribus?

3. **finitimi** (*ps*) i.e. 'though at our doors.'

4. **minacis...manus**: for the grouping see on P. 9.

5. **Capuae** stands outside *aemula* and *virtus* in artificial antithesis to Spartacus and the rest. See too on P. 35.

6. **novis rebus infidelis**: the group forms a compound adjective (see on *Odes* 3. 1. 24) and there is thus a chiasmus with *Spartacus acer*. See too P. 49, and compare *Epod.* 5. 49.

7. **fera...pube**: for the grouping see on P. 7.

8. **parentibusque abominatus**: the stress is on *parentibus* i.e. parents, not soldiers, loathe him; this may excuse the order (see on P. 49).

9. **impia...devoti sanguinis aetas**: for the grouping see on P. 10.

impia (*ps*) is almost adverbial with *perdemus*; see on P. 31, and compare *impio* (*ps*) at *Odes* 4. 4. 46.

devoti (*p*) echoes *impia*.

10. **solum**: for its position see on *Odes* 1. 3. 16.

11. **barbarus** may be regarded as a noun.

victor goes closely with *insistet* i.e. as victor, in the hour of victory.

12. **sonante** (*ps*): see P. 21.

14. **insolens** equals an adverb with *dissipabit*; see on P. 31.

15. **quid expediat**: the ambiguity of *expediat* (which ought to mean 'what is the use of?') inclines one to support Rutgers' *quod expediat*. But see the editors.

communiter seems to equal (*vos*) *universi*. If Gow is right in taking *communiter* mainly with *expediat*, then the postposited adverb has stress i.e. 'you ask what is to the *common* interest.'

melior (*p*): see on P. 28. In any case it is equivalent to an adjective of quantity.

16. **malis** (*ps*) i.e. 'the curse (of troubles)'; see on P. 27, and *Odes* 2. 14. 23.

nulla sit hac potior sententia: Phocaeorum
  velut profugit exsecrata civitas
agros atque Lares patrios habitandaque fana
  apris reliquit et rapacibus lupis,   20
ire, pedes quocumque ferent, quocumque per undas
  Notus vocabit aut protervus Africus.
sic placet, an melius quis habet suadere? secunda
  ratem occupare quid moramur alite?
sed iuremus in haec: 'simul imis saxa renarint   25
  vadis levata, ne redire sit nefas;
neu conversa domum pigeat dare lintea, quando
  Padus Matina laverit cacumina,
in mare seu celsus procurrerit Appenninus,
  novaque monstra iunxerit libidine   30
mirus amor, iuvet ut tigris subsidere cervis,
  adulteretur et columba miluo,

17. **nulla** (*ps*) equals μηδὲ μία, μηδαμῶς. Compare *Odes* 2. 2. 1.

Phocaeorum: the position tickets, as it were, the whole stanza; the topic is the Phocaeans and their departure. The genitive is logical subject constructed ultimately with *civitas*. See on P. 38.

18. **exsecrata** goes with *profugit* i.e. 'under an oath of imprecation' (Wickham).

19, 20. **habitandaque fana | apris**: the order gives stress to both *habitanda* and *apris*; for we build *fana* to worship in, not to live in; and if they are to be habitations, they should not house wild beasts (see on P. 49). Moreover *apris* goes with *reliquit* also; see on *Odes* 1. 2. 23.

rapacibus may colour *apris* as well as *lupis*; see on P. 33.

21. **pedes** precedes *quocumque* to prepare us for the antithesis *naves* implied in *per undas*; compare *Odes* 3. 11. 49.

22. **protervus** (*p*) i.e. 'the caprice (of Africus)'; see on P. 27, and 33.

23. **melius** (*s*) has emphasis, καὶ βέλτιόν τι.

secunda (*ps*) is very emphatic i.e. 'when omens are *favourable*'; contrast *inominata* l. 38 below.

25, 26. **imis...levata**: for the grouping see on P. 17.

27. **conversa domum** (*ps*) echoes *redire* of l. 26 and with stress.

28. **Matina** (*ps*) is purposely set next to *Padus*, i.e. from north to south; but see too P. 21.

29. **celsus** (*ps*) i.e. 'the heights (of the Appenninus)'; see on P. 27, and also P. 21.

30. **nŏvā** (*s*) is very emphatic and means 'strange,' 'unheard of'; compare on *Odes* 1. 2. 6. In spite of the quantity, *nova* may colour *monstra* also (see on P. 52).

credula nec ravos timeant armenta leones,
    ametque salsa levis hircus aequora.'
haec et quae poterunt reditus abscindere dulcis   35
    eamus omnis exsecrata civitas,
aut pars indocili melior grege; mollis et exspes
    inominata perprimat cubilia.
vos, quibus est virtus, muliebrem tollite luctum,
    Etrusca praeter et volate litora.   40
nos manet Oceanus circumvagus: arva, beata
    petamus arva, divites et insulas,
reddit ubi Cererem tellus inarata quotannis,
    et imputata floret usque vinea,
germinat et numquam fallentis termes olivae,   45
    suamque pulla ficus ornat arborem,

31. **mirus** (*p*) echoes *nova* of l. 30.

iuvet ut: the position of *iuvet* may make it emphatic i.e. 'so that they positively like to....' But see on *Odes* I. 37. 20.

32. **adulteretur** has some stress by preceding *et*; there is actual consummation of wedlock.

33. **credula...leones**: for the grouping see on P. 7.

34. **salsa...aequora**: for the grouping see on P. 10. The normal *hircus* is *hirsutus, hirtus, hispidus, horridus*, etc.; hence *lēvis* is naturally preposited.

35. **reditus abscindere dulcis**: see on P. 21.

36. **exsecrata** belongs to both *omnis* and *civitas* i.e. 'let us go all under oath as a state....'

37. **indocili** (*ps*) i.e. 'superior to the stupidity (of the mob)'; see on P. 27. But the grouping is also that of P. 14.

38. **inominata** (*ps*) has stress; contrast *secunda* (*ps*) of l. 23. See also P. 21.

39. **vos** is emphatic because inserted.

muliebrem (*ps*): see on P. 37 and P. 21. Moreover the juxtaposition of *virtus* and *muliebrem* is good. Compare *Epod* 15. 11, 12.

40. **Etrusca** (*ps*) **praeter**: the words have stress by separation and because they precede *et*, i.e. beyond the *Etrurian* sea, Westward Ho!, beyond the pillars of Hercules to the Islands of the Blest.

41, 42. **beata** (*ps*) is emphatic; compare *divites* (*ps*).

43. **reddit** has stress because it precedes *ubi* i.e. 'gives duly and in full' =ἀποδίδωσιν.

quotannis (*s*) has emphasis i.e. 'and that too every year'; it colours *reddit* and *inarata*.

44. **imputata** (*ps*) is concessive, 'though unpruned.'

usque (*pp*) i.e. 'and that continually.'

45. **germinat** has some stress because it precedes *et* i.e. 'actually shoots.'

mella cava manant ex ilice, montibus altis
    levis crepante lympha desilit pede.
illic iniussae veniunt ad mulctra capellae,
    refertque tenta grex amicus ubera;   50
nec vespertinus circumgemit ursus ovile,
    neque intumescit alta viperis humus.
pluraque felices mirabimur, ut neque largis
    aquosus Eurus arva radat imbribus,
pinguia nec siccis urantur semina glaebis,   55
    utrumque rege temperante caelitum.
non huc Argoo contendit remige pinus,
    neque impudica Colchis intulit pedem;
non huc Sidonii torserunt cornua nautae,
    laboriosa nec cohors Ulixei;   60

fallentis termes olivae: see on P. 20 β.

46. **suamque...arborem**: for the grouping see P. 10.

47. **cava** (*ps*) i.e. 'from the hollow (in an oak)'; see on P. 27, and P. 21.

48. **levis...pede**: for the grouping see P. 9. Notice the pretty alliteration of *levis, lympha, crepante, pede*.

levis (*ps*) equals *leviter*, and qualifies both *crepante* and *desilit*; see on P. 31.

49. **iniussae** goes with *veniunt* and equals *iniussu*; see on P. 31.

50. **tenta...ubera**: for the grouping see on P. 15.

51. **vespertinus** (*ps*) equals an adverbial phrase e.g. *vespere*; see on P. 31, and compare *nocturnus*, *Epod*. 5. 92.

52. **alta** goes closely with *intumescit* and is equivalent to *alte*; see on P. 31.

53, 54. **largis | aquosus Eurus...imbribus**: for the grouping see on P. 10.

55. **pinguia...glaebis**: for the grouping see on P. 7.

56. **caelitum** (*s*) has point: the king of heavenly beings will, naturally, control the heavens.

57. **Argoo** (*ps*) equals 'The Argo (with its rowers)'; see on *Odes* 1. 33. 16. See too P. 21.

58. **impudica** (*p*): see on *Odes* 2. 14. 23. She was a foul sorceress.

pedem: for its position see on *Odes* 1. 3. 16.

59. **Sidonii** (*ps*) equals 'from Sidon,' and is purposely kept near to *huc*; see on *Odes* 1. 31. 9.

60. **laboriosa** (*ps*) may equal 'the labours (of the crew)'; see on P. 27.

laboriosa...cohors Ulixei: for the grouping see on P. 35; but *Ulixei* may stand outside to round off the list of adventurers; contrast Phoenicians, Medea, Argonauts.

[nulla nocent pecori contagia, nullius astri
    gregem aestuosa torret impotentia.]
Iuppiter illa piae secrevit litora genti,
    ut inquinavit aere tempus aureum;
aere, dehinc ferro duravit saecula, quorum   65
    piis secunda vate me datur fuga.

XVII.

Iam iam efficaci do manus scientiae,
supplex et oro regna per Proserpinae,
per et Dianae non movenda numina,
per atque libros carminum valentium
refixa caelo devocare sidera,   5
Canidia, parce vocibus tandem sacris
citumque retro solve, solve turbinem.

61, 62. **nulla** (*ps*) is again a strong negative, as often in Cicero. Compare *Epod.* 17. 24.

nullius astri (*ps*) is the logical subject; see on P. 38.

aestuosa (*ps*) i.e. 'the burning (of its rage)'; see on P. 27, and P. 21,

63. **illa...genti**: for the grouping see on P. 7. See too on l. 66.

65. **saecula**: for its position see on *Odes* 1. 3. 16.

quorum goes with *fuga* i.e. 'escape from which'; but the order is strange indeed. One might parenthesize *ut inquinavit...saecula*, and accept Bentley's *quo nunc*, referring *quo* to *litora*.

66. **piis** is heard with *secunda*, and later with *datur*. The separation of *piis secunda* from *fuga* echoes the *piae* of l. 63.

secunda vate me...fuga i.e. 'a flight favourable because I am the sooth-sayer.' For the intrusive *datur* see on P. 46 *a*.

XVII. 1, 2. **efficaci** (*ps*) i.e. 'the effectiveness (of your knowledge)'; see on P. 27.

supplex may well belong to both *do manus* and *oro*. The comma can be omitted after *scientiae*.

3. **per et Dianae**: *Dianae* stands outside *non movenda* and *numina* for the sake of artificial contrast to *Proserpinae*; compare *Epod.* 6. 14, and see on P. 43. The genitive *Dianae* amounts to an accusative with *per* (see on P. 38). Compare also on *Odes* 1. 8. 1.

4. **atque**: for its position see on *Epod.* 8. 11.

5. **refixa** (*ps*)**...sidera** i.e. *refigere caelo et devocare sidera*, 'to unfasten from the sky and call down from it the stars'; see on *Epod.* 5. 32.

caelo is in ἀπὸ κοινοῦ position with *refixa* and *devocare*.

6. **tandem** may be felt as if in a bracket='I pray,' or as emphatic by separation from *parce* in its ordinary sense 'at length.' Compare on *Odes* 2. 9. 18 *desine mollium tandem querellarum*, and see on P. 50 *c*.

movit nepotem Telephus Nereium,
in quem superbus ordinarat agmina
Mysorum et in quem tela acuta torserat.　　　　　10
unxere matres Iliae addictum feris
alitibus atque canibus homicidam Hectorem,
postquam relictis moenibus rex procidit
heu pervicacis ad pedes Achillei.
saetosa duris exuere pellibus　　　　　　　　　　15
laboriosi remiges Ulixei
volente Circa membra: tunc mens et sonus
relapsus atque notus in vultus honor.
dedi satis superque poenarum tibi,
amata nautis multum et institoribus.　　　　　　20
fugit iuventas, et verecundus color
reliquit ossa pelle amicta lurida,
tuis capillus albus est odoribus;
nullum a labore me reclinat otium,

7. **citum** (*ps*) equals *cito*; see on P. 31.

8. **Nereium** (*s*): the adjective is far more important than *nepotem*.

10. **Mysorum** is probably heard with both *agmina* and *tela*.

11, 12. **addictum feris** (*ps*) i.e. 'though the due victim of the beasts.'

feris (*p*) i.e. 'the fierceness (of bird and beast)'; see on P. 27. But the word may, conceivably, be a noun, with *alitibus* and *canibus* in apposition.

alitibus...Hectorem: the metre, with its resolved feet, is surprising. Nothing would be lost, and something gained, by its omission; *addictum feris* needs no more explanation than *rex* in l. 13.

homicidam may be regarded as a noun, with *Hectorem* in apposition.

14. **heu pervicacis** (*ps*) i.e. 'for all his obstinacy.' But see too P. 20 β. 'The exclamation emphasizes the epithet' (Wickham).

15–17. **saetosa duris exuere pellibus...membra**: for the grouping see on P. 8.

15. **duris...pellibus**: these words are heard partly with *saetosa*, partly with *exuere*; for the latter see P. 21.

16. **laboriosi remiges Ulixei**: for the grouping see on P. 20 a.

18. **notus in vultus honor**: the order is as if we had *notus vultuum honor*; but the form of expression is due to *relapsus*.

20. **multum** is emphatic by separation from *amata*, and lies in ἀπὸ κοινοῦ position with both *nautis* and *institoribus*; compare *Epod.* 15. 11.

21. **verecundus** (*p*) i.e. 'modesty (of colour)'; see on P. 27.

22. **ossa pelle amicta lurida**: for the grouping see on P. 16 a.

23. **tuis** (*ps*) i.e. 'it is through your unguents that....'

urget diem nox et dies noctem, neque est   25
levare tenta spiritu praecordia.
ergo negatum vincor ut credam miser,
Sabella pectus increpare carmina
caputque Marsa dissilire nenia.
quid amplius vis? o mare et terra, ardeo,   30
quantum neque atro delibutus Hercules
Nessi cruore nec Sicana fervida
virens in Aetna flamma: tu, donec cinis
iniuriosis aridus ventis ferar,
cales venenis officina Colchicis.   35
quae finis aut quod me manet stipendium?
effare! iussas cum fide poenas luam,
paratus expiare, seu poposceris

24. **nullum** (*ps*) is an emphatic negative; compare *Epod.* 16. 61, 62 and
passim.

25. **diem nox et dies noctem**: note the chiastic order.

26. **spiritu** is heard, by position, with *tenta...praecordia* i.e. 'strained with
sighing' (Page). It is possible to feel it with *levare* also i.e. 'relieve by sighing'
(Gow).

27. **negatum**, separated from *credam*, has emphasis i.e. 'though it was
denied before.'

miser, like τάλας, equals 'alas !'

28, 29. **Sabella** (*ps*)...**Marsa** (*ps*): both adjectives have stress and importance because Sabines and Marsians were famous for sorcery and witchcraft.
Compare on *Epod.* 5. 76, and see ll. 35 and 60 below.

Marsa (*ps*): see also P. 21.

31, 32. **atro delibutus Hercules...cruore**: for the grouping see on P. 10.
atro...Nessi cruore: for the grouping with two intrusive words (*delibutus
Hercules*) see on P. 45 *b*, and compare *Epod.* 15. 9.

32, 33. **Sicană fervidā...in Aetnā flammă**: for the grouping see on P. 11.
virens in Aetna flamma is, of course, normal; see on *Odes* 1. 7. 29.

33, 34. **cinis...ventis**: for the grouping see P. 14.

35. **venenis** is heard first with *cales*, then with *officina Colchicis*.
Colchicis (*s*) probably has stress to increase the horror of the poisons;
compare ll. 28, 29 above.

venenis officina Colchicis i.e. 'a laboratory of Colchian poisons'; for the
grouping see on *Odes* 3. 2. 32.

36. **quod...stipendium**: for the separation see on *Odes* 1. 27. 11.

37. **iussas cum fide poenas**: the order almost requires that these words
should mean 'penalties ordered with a pledge' i.e. a pledge given under
penalties; but *cum fide* may be heard again with *luam*, in the sense of 'faithfully'; see on P. 50 *a*, and compare l. 63 below.

centum iuvencos, sive mendaci lyra
voles sonari: 'tu pudica, tu proba   40
perambulabis astra sidus aureum.'
infamis Helenae Castor offensus vicem
fraterque magni Castoris, victi prece
adempta vati reddidere lumina:
et tu (potes nam) solve me dementia,   45
o nec paternis obsoleta sordibus,
nec in sepulcris pauperum prudens anus
novendialis dissipare pulveres!
tibi hospitale pectus et purae manus,
tuusque venter Pactumeius, et tuo   50
cruore rubros obstetrix pannos lavit,
utcumque fortis exsilis puerpera.
'quid obseratis auribus fundis preces?
non saxa nudis surdiora navitis

39. **mendaci** (*p*): contrast *veridica*.

42. **infamis** (*p*) i.e. 'the defamation (of Helen)'; see on P. 27, but also on *Odes* 2. 14. 23.

Helenae (*ps*): the order is due to the desire to group together the persons concerned in the story. The topic is 'Helen and Castor.' See on *Odes* 1. 2. 17.

44. **adempta...lumina:** for the grouping with *reddidere* intrusive see on P. 46 *a*. The effect is to make *vati* ἀπὸ κοινοῦ with *adempta* and *reddidere*.

45. **potes nam:** for the position of *nam* see on *Epod.* 14. 6.

46. **paternis** (*ps*) i.e. quite apart from *tuis* (*p*) *sordibus*. See too P. 24.

47. **prudens** (*p*): see on P. 36. The adjective is explained by *pauperum*: she is cunning enough to choose the unguarded graves of the poor.

48. **novendialis** (*ps*): see P. 21. Wickham explains by 'fresh buried'; for a witch was supposed to gather the bones when warm. Gow says 'nine days old' i.e. abandoned by the mourners so that the grave could be rifled with safety.

49. **hospitale...purae:** both epithets are predicative i.e. your heart is kindly, your hands are pure.

50, 51. **tuus** (*p*) i.e. *non alienus*; so *tuo* (*p*).

tuo | cruore rubros (*ps*): the words are emphatic i.e. 'red with *your* blood are the cloths that the midwife....'

52. **fortis** goes closely with *exsilis* i.e. 'when you jump out of bed strong....' See too P. 21.

puerpera (sc. οὖσα) is concessive 'though a new mother.'

53. **obseratis** (*p*): contrast *patulis*. Compare *Epist.* 1. 18. 70, 2. 2. 105. **preces:** for its position see on *Odes* 1. 3. 16.

54. **non** goes with the whole sentence; see on *Odes* 2. 9. 13.

Neptunus alto tundit hibernus salo.   55
inultus ut tu riseris Cotyttia
vulgata, sacrum liberi Cupidinis,
et Esquilini pontifex venefici
impune ut urbem nomine impleris meo?
quid proderit ditasse Paelignas anus,   60
velociusve miscuisse toxicum?
sed tardiora fata te votis manent:
ingrata misero vita ducenda est in hoc,
novis ut usque suppetas doloribus.
optat quietem Pelopis infidi pater   65
egens benignae Tantalus semper dapis,

saxa nudis surdiora navitis: for the grouping see P. 14.

55. Neptunus...salo: for the grouping see P. 13.

56. inultus has stress because it precedes *ut*; compare *impune* l. 59 below. See too *Epod.* 6. 16.

57. vulgata has some added interest by position (see on *Odes* 4. 9. 26); it is causal i.e. 'because you have divulged them.'

liberi (*p*): contrast *modesti*.

58. Esquilini pontifex venefici: for the grouping see on P. 20 *a*.

59. meo (*s*) i.e. '*my* name'; but see P. 21.

60. proderit: if this is read, Canidia professes that Horace intends learning about potions in order to kill himself; if we read *proderat*, then Canidia is represented as asking 'what was the use of learning about speedy poisons, if I let you go?'

Paelignas (*p*): the district was famous for witches; compare ll. 28, 29 above and see *Epod.* 5. 76.

61. velocius (*ps*): see on P. 28 and P. 21.

62. sed: a variant is *si*, which would require a question mark after *manent* and a comma after *toxicum* l. 61.

tardiora (*p*): see on P. 28; the comparative has stress in contrast to *velocius* of l. 61.

votis: if the ablative is one of comparison, the word ought to lie between *tardiora* and *fata* (see P. 49); it seems, however, possible to take *votis* as causal ablative with *te...manent* i.e. 'a slow death awaits you because of your imprecations against me.'

63. misero goes first with *ingrata*, then with *ducenda*; compare l. 37 above, and see P. 50 *a*.

64. novis (*s*) i.e. 'unheard of,' 'horrible'; see on *Odes* 1. 2. 6, and 2. 14. 23.

65. Pelopis (*p*): the son's faithlessness is important as implying a similar or worse characteristic in the father. As Wickham says, 'Tantalus' character is to be gathered from that of his son.' But see on *Odes* 1. 28. 7, and P. 41.

66. egens benignae Tantalus...dapis: for the grouping see on P. 9.

optat Prometheus obligatus aliti,
optat supremo collocare Sisyphus
in monte saxum: sed vetant leges Iovis.
voles modo altis desilire turribus,   70
modo ense pectus Norico recludere,
frustraque vincla gutturi nectes tuo
fastidiosa tristis aegrimonia.
vectabor umeris tunc ego inimicis eques,
meaeque terra cedet insolentiae.   75
an quae movere cereas imagines,
ut ipse nosti curiosus, et polo
deripere lunam vocibus possim meis,
possim crematos excitare mortuos
desiderique temperare poculum,   80
plorem artis in te nil agentis exitus?'

semper (*pps*) has emphasis.

67. **aliti:** for its position see on P. 47.

68. **supremo** (*ps*) has great stress; his one desire is to place the stone *on the very top*, so that it may at last stand still.

70. **altis** (*p*) i.e. 'the top (of a tower)'; see on P. 27 and P. 21.

71. **Norico** (*s*): the word implies the sharpest steel; see on *Odes* 1. 16. 9.

72. **frustra** (*s*) has emphasis.

tuo (*s*): see on P. 21.

73. **fastidiosa** (*ps*) i.e. 'the weariness (of pain),' as if we had *fastidio aegrimoniae*; see on P. 27, and P. 24.

74. **umeris...ego inimicis eques:** as *eques* is quasi-adjectival, the grouping is that of P. 16 (*ad fin.*).

tunc (*pps*) has emphasis; compare *semper* l. 66 above.

75. **meae** (*ps*) is emphatic i.e. 'to *my* arrogance'; if to that of no one else.

76. **cereas** (*p*) i.e. 'though only of wax.'

77. **curiosus** sc. ὤν i.e. 'because you pry.'

78. **meis** (*s*): see on P. 21.

79. **crematos** (*ps*) i.e. 'even when they have been burnt'; for *mortuos* is equivalent to a noun.

80. **desideri** (*ps*) i.e. 'a *love*-potion'; compare *amoris* (*ps*) *esset poculum* at *Epod.* 5. 38.

81. **artis...nil agentis:** the genitive is the more important object of *plorem*; see on P. 38. A Roman would read the line thus: 'Am I to lament a craft that against you is unavailing—after all?'

For EU product safety concerns, contact us at Calle de José Abascal, 56–1°, 28003 Madrid, Spain or eugpsr@cambridge.org.

www.ingramcontent.com/pod-product-compliance
Ingram Content Group UK Ltd.
Pitfield, Milton Keynes, MK11 3LW, UK
UKHW042154130625
459647UK00011B/1325